Sound Choices

Sound Choices

Guiding Your Child's Musical Experiences

WILMA MACHOVER

MARIENNE USZLER

New York Oxford

OXFORD UNIVERSITY PRESS

1996

OXFORD UNIVERSITY PRESS

Oxford   New York
Athens   Auckland   Bangkok   Bombay
Calcutta   Cape Town   Dar es Salaam   Delhi
Florence   Hong Kong   Istanbul   Karachi
Kuala Lumpur   Madras   Madrid   Melbourne
Mexico City   Nairobi   Paris   Singapore
Taipei   Tokyo   Toronto

and associated companies in
Berlin   Ibadan

Copyright © 1996 by Oxford University Press, Inc.

Published by Oxford University Press, Inc.,
198 Madison Avenue, New York, New York 10016

Oxford is a registered trademark of Oxford University Press

Library of Congress Cataloging-in-Publication Data
Machover, Wilma
Sound choices : guiding your child's musical experience /
Wilma Machover and Marienne Uszler
p.   cm.   Includes bibliographical references and index.
ISBN 0-19-509207-4 (cloth)   ISBN 0-19-509208-2 (pbk.)
1. Instrumental music—Instruction and study—Juvenile.   2. Education—Parental participation.   3. Music in the home.   I. Uszler.   II. Title.
MT741.U89   1996
780'.7—dc20   95-35429

Photographs by
Lee R. Aks for Philharmonia Virtuosi, page 162;
Elizabeth Ann Arey, page 48;
Chris Christodolou, page 276;
Rosmarie Hausherr, pages xiv, 179, 308, 313;
Roberta Hershenson, pages 125, 234;
John R. Kennedy, pages ii, xi, 2, 59, 72;
Paul Siemion, pages xiii (bottom), 15, 220, 271;
Ira N. Toff, pages xii (top), 161.
Photographs courtesy of Hoff-Barthelson Music School, pages xii (bottom), xiii (top), 1, 40, 80, 101, 112, 204, 253, 272, 338.

Examples of studio policies used especially in Chapter Six: from *The MTNA Book of Policies, Letters and Forms,* © 1989 by Music Teachers National Association. Excerpted materials used by permission.

Excerpt on practicing, page 137, from *Practicing for Artistic Success,* by Burton Kaplan.

9 8 7 6 5 4 3 2 1

Printed in the United States of America
on acid-free paper

Acknowledgments

Sound Choices is a response to requests. Most of these requests came from parents, directed to us throughout many years of teaching. These parents, of course, were not asking for a book. They were searching for answers to particular questions. Most of these questions were similar, although driven by concerns reflecting the needs of specific people in specific circumstances. Every music teacher hears and answers these same questions, and does so repeatedly as he or she interacts with the parents of their students or responds to queries from neighbors, friends, and even strangers.

Trying to answer such questions in one-on-one situations, most teachers don't have the time to discuss the pros and cons of different solutions. Nor do they have ready access to names, organizations, figures, and enrichment resources to give parents, which would in turn, assist parents to become better informed and able—to some degree, at least—to help themselves. As teachers, we too often wish we could hand over a neat package of what we know and where to find it. That desire fueled our determination to produce this guide. The immediate "push," however, came directly from our editor Maribeth Anderson Payne. Not only (as editor-in-chief) did she see the clear need for such a book, but (as a parent) she was asking these very questions with reference to her own children. That created a particular kind of urgency, and the project was begun.

As we sketched outlines, amassed information, and considered viewpoints, we drew heavily on the expertise and generosity of a large number of people who offered everything from hints to careful scrutiny of substantial parts of the manuscript. Numerous instrumental and vocal teachers from the Hoff-Barthelson Music School, the University of Southern California School of Music, and the Colburn School of Performing Arts critiqued and made suggestions for the information in Chapter Five. The Music Teachers National Association shared statistics and examples from several of their official publications. Several music educators, music dealers, and manufacturing specialists provided information for Chapter Seven. A number of parents also read chapters and gave helpful feedback.

Special thanks must be given to Scott McBride Smith who read a

ACKNOWLEDGMENTS

number of chapters in draft stages and suggested many useful changes and additions: to Alice Darrows, Jane Hughes, Wanda Lathom, and Marvin Mayes—all experts in music therapy and/or special education—who generously guided and critiqued the information in Chapter Nine; to Peter Webster who has served as sounding board and wise counselor on many occasions; to Toby Mayman and Joseph Thayer of the Colburn School of Performing Arts who allowed us to search their files for photographs; to Tom Chapin for his gracious and friendly foreword; to Mary Helton, director of the Hoff-Barthelson Music School, for her enthusiastic support and for permission to select photographs from the school's archive; and to Ruth Alperson, an expert in early childhood music education, for her suggestions for Chapter One. We are grateful as well to all those who have refined and shaped the book in its production stages: to the reviewers who challenged our thoughts or recommended modifications; to our careful copy editor; to Leslie Phillips who worked graciously and painstakingly to guide the book into print; and—once more—to Maribeth Anderson Payne who "tried out" our advice and worked to make sure that "sound choices" were made on our behalf.

Much of our support and inspiration has come from our families. We thank Tod, Julie, and Linda Machover who had been early catalysts for searching out "sound choices," and now bring their adult insight to this project: Tod Machover by his generous sharing of concepts and resources in music technology, providing data for Chapter Four and "General Resources;" Julie Machover Anderson by her wise musician/parent critique of the manuscript; Linda Machover Samuels by her invaluable organizational suggestions and introduction to Tom Chapin; June Kinoshita for her wise critique; and the next generation, Allison, Cassie, Ryan, Allegra, and Hana, whose joyous response to the world of music gave impetus to many current ideas; Mary Gassen and J. Michael Uszler whose loving interest gave support and encouragement; and Lorraine Uszler who, although no longer here to read the book, would have been the first to celebrate its existence.

Words cannot express our deep gratitude to Carl Machover who has given both of us invaluable assistance, wise perspective, patient indulgence, and loving support in his warm, witty, inimitable style.

Finally, we salute each other. Our collaboration has been a pleasure and privilege, a rare kind of chamber music through which we are both immeasurably enriched.

White Plains, New York   W. M.
San Juan Capistrano, California   M. U.

Foreword

From my earliest memory, music was a constant in my life. My father was a jazz drummer. Music was his job, and he loved it. My mother played the piano, not frequently and not particularly well. What she really loved was opera. Every Saturday afternoon she had the Metropolitan Opera radio broadcast wafting through the house.

As a teenager, my oldest brother James (he sometimes calls himself the "non-musical Chapin") was a faithful listener to pop radio. Because of him we all knew every song on top 40 radio in the late 50s and early 60s.

My father's mother, Abby Forbes Chapin, insisted that her grandchildren take music lessons, and she paid for them. She was an educator and wanted us to know "the language of music."

In 1953 when I was 8, we moved to Brooklyn Heights in New York City. Shortly thereafter my brother Steve and I joined the Grace Episcopal Church Choir of Boys and Men. We learned to sing harmony and to sight-read music. And we experienced the discipline and delight of making music with other people.

In the summer of 1958, my brothers, Harry and Steve, and I heard a record—"The Weavers at Carnegie Hall"—that pointed the way toward the rest of our musical lives. All summer we listened to the voices of Pete Seeger, Ronnie Gilbert, Fred Hellerman, and Lee Hayes. We marveled at the strength and simplicity of the guitar and banjo arrangements. And we loved the sense of commitment and community these great songs and singers evoked.

At the end of that summer, my brother Harry said, "We could do that!" And so we did. Harry got a five-string banjo and the Pete Seeger book and began to play. I scraped together twenty-five dollars for my first guitar. With Steve on bass, we became "The Chapin Brothers."

Flash forward thirty-five years. Now I'm a professional musician who makes a living doing what he loves. I'm a writer and singer of songs for old and young. I still travel the road that The Weavers introduced me to so long ago. I look back and feel blessed to have grown up in such a creative atmosphere.

But I am also a father trying to nurture his own children. Like you, I'm very involved and concerned with how to help my kids know and appreciate "the language of music." In this TV world of sound bites and electronic noise, it seems increasingly difficult to create a fertile musical environment for our kids. Parents who want to do so could use a little help and some practical advice.

Well, here is our guide. I have found *Sound Choices* to be a wonderful and invaluable book. It is chock full of useful information, yet easy and fun to read. Like my grandmother, the authors are educators who believe that playing music is not only fun, but also a means of self-expression and self-development. They provide signposts and suggestions, make maps, plot routes, and share experiences. They introduce us to a wealth of resources that can empower us to help ourselves.

Best of all, the authors outline the joyful ways in which we as parents can join our children in making that magic we call music.

Hudson Valley, New York   Tom Chapin
1995

Contents

Why Music?

Why Music?

Children must receive music instruction as naturally as food, with as much pleasure as they derive from a ball game, and this must happen from the beginning of their lives.

—Leonard Bernstein

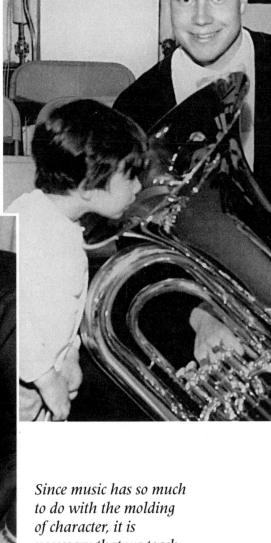

Since music has so much to do with the molding of character, it is necessary that we teach it to our children.

—Aristotle

*What I might have become if I
didn't play an instrument—
I never stopped to think about that.
Judging from the neighborhood
I lived in, if it hadn't been for the
clarinet, I might just as easily
have been a gangster.*
                    —Benny Goodman

*Music is everything. Music is the
oldest entity. The scope of music is
immense and infinite. Without
music I feel blind, atrophied,
incomplete,* inexistent....
                    —Duke Ellington

Why Music?

Music is not a recreation for the elite, but a source of spiritual strength which all cultured people should endeavor to turn into public property.
—Zoltán Kodály

Introduction

Music in the family

This book focuses on choices that relate to making music part of your child's life. That implies far more than providing an instrument and lessons. The most lasting and important musical experiences your child will have will happen in your home, as part of your family life. These are the experiences that will truly color and support your child's involvement with music. They are experiences that you can arrange and in which you can participate.

Sound Choices is written to support and encourage you in this exciting venture. The book offers information, suggests parent-child activities, provides reading and listening lists, and recommends videos, CD-ROMs, games, and catalogs that may help you get started or move in new directions.

Parents often ask questions such as:

How can I tell if my child should take music lessons?

What's the best age to begin?

What instrument should my child play?

How do I find a good teacher?

Will I need to help my child practice?

What do music lessons cost?

There are no quick answers to these questions. They are linked to your child's development, so finding answers and working out solutions will take time—not just the time needed to read this book, but the time that must elapse as your child grows and changes.

Your opinions and attitudes about music make a difference. They will determine and affect the musical experiences you arrange for your child. They will also influence how you make music with your child—whether or not you sing, play an instrument, or read music. The music programs you attend together, the family listening and reading habits, and the use of other resources will shape the musical environment your child will enjoy.

Make time for music

You want your child to have every opportunity to explore a rich and broad world. It is tempting to regard the many available educational and enrichment programs as a kind of cafeteria from which you can select a little here, a little there, to see what pleases and interests your child. It is true that some children can absorb and thrive on a great deal of stimulation, but even the most avid and curious child needs time to play and dream.

In guiding your child's choice of activities, it is important to understand that learning about music or learning to play an instrument does not happen without commitment and involvement on the part of both parent and child. It is not like going to camp or taking swimming lessons. Development depends on continuity and dedication. This does not mean that a musical program for your child should be rigorous or tedious. It means, rather, that musical growth occurs as a result of sustained exposure and experience. It is cumulative effort that leads to success, not intermittent moments of enthusiasm or occasional bursts of energy.

Another caveat is in order as you consider whether, or to what degree, your child should become involved with music. Enjoying and knowing about music, even learning to play an instrument or to sing, is not the same thing as becoming an outstanding performer, much less a prodigy. Your child may learn a great deal by listening to and experimenting with musical sound even though such learning may not ultimately emerge as masterful playing or singing. You cannot always measure a child's passion for music in the number of pieces played or books completed. Your "sound choice" is to be supportive, interested, and participatory—not critical, indifferent, or absent. Join your child. Explore and enjoy music together.

How the book is organized

PART ONE The first section of the book looks at specific age groups, from preschool through teenage years.

- If your child is very young, your challenge is to respond to basic needs as they occur. Chapter One suggests ways to create a musical environment in the home, provides a sampling of parent-child activities, and surveys prominent preschool music programs.
- If your child is six or a bit older, you are helping him make adjustments to formal education. Chapter Two compares differences between children who have had preschool music instruction and those who begin music study at this time. Because you will need to guide your child's practice at this stage, we suggest ways to help your child listen and think while practicing, and we examine some common practice problems.

- If your child is nine and venturing into a larger world outside the home, your charge is to aid her in becoming a self-governing person and an independent learner. Chapter Three shows you how to back off from guiding the practice period, and looks at some pitfalls that are likely to occur at this juncture. Because your child's world is expanding, we suggest ways you can help your child share music with a broader community.

- The greatest challenge comes as your child enters adolescence. Questions are no longer simple, and it becomes clear that you must share the process of making choices with your child. Chapter Four discusses what to do when academic pressures and the attractions of social life threaten to supersede music study. Your teenager may be preparing for college, perhaps even considering a career in music. We outline ways in which your child's musical accomplishments may enhance the college application and give a brief overview of what it means to prepare for a college audition as a music major.

At each stage, it is important to have a qualified and suitable teacher for your child. In each chapter in this section, therefore, we list characteristics that will help you identify an appropriate teacher for the age group.

PART TWO The second section focuses on practical issues and choices that are made less regularly.

- Chapter Five suggests ways to help your child choose an instrument. We survey instruments by families and categories in terms of their physical features, how and where they are played, when is a good time to begin on each, and what makes each instrument special. Your child's voice is the instrument, and we offer some cautions if you are considering having your child take singing lessons. We provide a brief survey of electronic instruments and outline issues you may want to consider if your child expresses interest in playing an electronic instrument.

- Chapter Six encourages you to examine your reasons for wanting your child to study music, and it suggests that these priorities affect the kind of teacher you seek. The survey of music learning environments—from lessons in your own home to study in a conservatory preparatory division—gives you an idea of the instructional settings available. We provide a directory of sources for finding a teacher, provide scripts for the first phone and in-person interview, and outline what to note when observing a teacher in action. Because the match between your child and the teacher is individual and sensitive, these are all important considerations.

- The costs involved in music study are examined in Chapter Seven. Lesson fees vary widely, and we acquaint you with factors that affect cost. Samples of policy statements from music studios in different parts of the country give you some idea of what to expect. You will need to consider costs relating to the purchase or rental and maintenance of an instrument. Parents often ask, "How good does the first instrument have to be?" We offer opinions and comparative price lists.

PART THREE The third section deals with matters that may not affect each parent or family.

- Perhaps you wonder whether your child has unusual musical talent. Chapter Eight investigates theories of musical giftedness and sketches a profile of the musically talented child. We discuss issues that relate to how a musically talented child develops as a person and what it means to parent such an individual.
- If you have a child with special needs, you may not realize how music might contribute to your child's happiness and growth. Although Chapter Nine can make only general recommendations and suggestions, we want you to know how a child with physical or cognitive limitations, a partially sighted or blind child, a child with a hearing loss, or a child with a learning disability may make and enjoy music. We also provide lists of resources, books, and organizations that offer specialized and informed guidance in these areas.

PART FOUR This section entitled "General Resources" is a real treasure trove. Many talented and creative people have provided materials that will enhance your own life as well as that of your child. We want you to know these exist, and we encourage you to sample the riches.

How to use this book

We have designed this book for easy use. Chapters are organized to help you find information quickly. Each chapter opens with a list of what you will find in it and ends with a recap of the contents in a section called "highlights." By scanning either of these, you should be able to tell which chapters may meet your needs or interests. Lists and charts are found throughout so that if something catches your eye, search the area around the list or chart for a more extended treatment of the ideas or issues.

The margin icons are a further aid:

 An important or good idea is introduced in the text opposite.

 Multiple choices are given in the text opposite.

 See "Chapter Resources" at the end of the chapter you are reading.

 See the chapter numbered inside the icon for further information on topics related to the text opposite.

 See "General Resources," the last section of the book.

 The ideas mentioned in the text opposite involve money.

It is likely that you will use chapters that meet your immediate needs or answer puzzling questions. We hope, however, that you browse a bit and scan pages or chapters that do not seem to fit your current situation. If your child is a preschooler, look ahead and find out what to anticipate in the next few years. If your child is eight, and struggling with practice, read about practicing at other ages to gain a clear view of the entire process. If you feel your child is gifted, look also in sections that refer to your child's age group for clues about a variety of developmental traits that give you a broader picture of your child. You and your child might use parts of the book together, perhaps to discuss the points of view suggested at the ends of several chapters.

We have chosen to deal with gender references by changing freely from masculine to feminine forms. It makes it easier to blur stereotypical gender associations with specific people or roles—teachers are not always female, trumpet players male, and so on.

The choice is yours

Throughout the years that we have been teaching children and adults, from beginners to professionals, we have interacted with countless parents and families. It is from them, and with them, that we discovered what we share in this book. We know we don't have all the answers, nor are we able to offer a complete warehouse of failure-proof solutions. We try to point in the right direction, however, knowing that you will weigh our opinions against your own, as you should.

Our ultimate aim is to provide you with ideas that may set you thinking in new ways, to offer leads and encouragement as you seek your own solutions, and to put you in touch with many rich resources that can assist and inspire you to make "sound choices."

White Plains, New York   W. M.
San Juan Capistrano, California   M. U.
September 1995

Sound Choices

PART ONE

CHOICES AT CERTAIN AGES

Early Childhood

What you will find in this chapter

- The child from birth to eighteen months
- Creating a music environment in the home
- The child from eighteen months to three years
- The child from three to six
- What parents can do
- Judging readiness for more structured music experiences
- Characteristics of early childhood music programs
- A brief history
    Dalcroze, Orff, Kodály, Suzuki,
    Yamaha Music Eduction System,
    Kindermusik®, Music Together®
- Researching a good program
- Teacher credentials
- Questions for the teacher
- Early childhood music charts
- Practice, preschoolers, early schoolers, and parents
- Highlights
- Chapter resources

WHETHER you are the parent of an infant, toddler, or pre-schooler, some of the most natural and intuitive choices you will make are probably those related to music. The songs of your own childhood still ring in your ears. Your child is the beneficiary of your fondest memories as you create a musical environment in your home. This chapter explores the experiences that can be woven into the fabric of even the busiest of lives. Also discussed are some of the many instructional programs developed to enrich the early childhood music experience outside the home.

The hope is to expand your child's musical horizons and to help nurture the multiple miracles of early childhood growth. Parents can be partners in this dramatic blossoming. By being alert to your child's emerging interests and strengths, you can help shape this development. Day-to-day opportunities to create "sound choices" are yours for the imagining. In the best of all scenarios, you will create an environment that includes not only the sounds of your childhood and past heritage, but as wide an array of musical styles as possible.

Children must receive music instruction as naturally as food, with as much pleasure as they derive from a ball game, and this must happen from the beginning of their lives.—Leonard Bernstein

The child from birth to eighteen months

Let's examine the very early years. What musical response can you expect from your infant?

The child from birth to eighteen months

- hears moderately well, even as newborn.
- can discriminate sounds and seek the source in infancy.
- has growing curiosity about the visual and aural world.
- has limited fine motor control.
- shows full body response to music.
- by five to eight months, recognizes often heard songs.
- has growing motor control (sit, crawl, walk, run).
- has growing ability to imitate motions and sounds.
- identifies with and needs nurturing adults.
- is generally involved only in parallel play with peers.
- has some pitch-matching and imitation ability.

Creating a music environment in the home

As you imagine all the experiences you hope to bring to your infant, you'll remember a song your parents or grandparents sang to you or tunes from your growing-up years that spring quite easily to mind. You may hum or murmur improvised sounds that soothe or excite your infant. You begin to notice the growing response to your voice, the look of sheer delight at some sounds, the startled reaction to sounds that are too sudden or noisy.

Between five and eight months of age, babies can be expected to respond to music quite gleefully, with somewhat uncoordinated rhythmic movement of the whole body, and may soon try to join in singing games. One study suggests that before the age of one year, children can learn to distinguish individual songs that have been repeated frequently over a period of months. In fact, it is possible to cultivate a musical environment even before birth. Experiments with expectant mothers at the Eastman School of Music in Rochester, New York, indicate that when sounds are played at proper decibels while the baby is in utero, the baby's response to music at birth and in early development stages is notably keener.

How can you begin to shape this early musical environment? Your own library of tapes and CDs may include country and western, jazz, blues, folk and ethnic music. You may be a classical music buff. Now you can add beautiful recordings of lullabies and folk tunes. The more sounds, the merrier. In a sense, you are the taste maker in sound just as you are in food exploration. The more varied your tastes, the richer your child's musical heritage.

One of the most creative baby gifts we have heard of was a selection of CDs and tapes for baby that included the following:

You know that the beginning is the most important part of any work, especially in the case of a young and tender thing; for that is the time at which the character is being formed.—Plato

- *Lullabies Around the World*
- *Disney on Parade*
- Mozart's *String Quartets*
- Bach's *Brandenburg Concertos*
- *Best of the Beatles*
- *Brubeck and Sons*
- *Folk Songs by Woody Guthrie*
- *Peter, Paul and Mommy Sing*
- Stravinsky's *The Rite of Spring*

Something old, something new, something just for baby, and something blues! The lucky recipient of this gift was bathed in a wide variety of musical sounds for several years. One day, when she was four, her mother put on a recording in the morning as the family was getting dressed. The preschooler came out of her room in quite a dreamy state, saying "Oh, Mommy, what is that? It's the most beautiful thing I've ever heard." "That's Mozart," her mother replied. "Oh, could you please take me to meet him? I want to tell him how much I love it."

That same little girl has been known to respond equally enthusiastically to folk, jazz, and contemporary music. Certainly a varied starter kit of musical wonders can help develop an open ear and a broad taste palette.

If you want to try before you buy, check the adult's and children's sections of your local library and borrow CDs, audiotapes, or videotapes until you find the selection that pleases you.

The child from eighteen months to three years

As your child grows to the toddler stage, increased skills in many areas open even more musical possibilities.

The child from eighteen months to three years
- has keen hearing and curiosity.
- is physically more mobile.
- is developing competence in the use of language.
- generally has a short attention span.
- prefers active to passive play.
- learns best through a combination of mind and body experiences.
- enjoys singing and creating songs.
- prefers one-on-one to group experiences.
- is able to learn and perform quite complex imitative actions.
- is more able to move away from parents.
- shows motor development without stimulus from parents.
- is more overtly loving, humorous, cooperative.
- can control balance, posture, and fine motor skills.
- has neurologically sophisticated abilities in many areas.
- is beginning to problem-solve and control own behavior.

Piaget, the Swiss educator who influenced much of our knowledge of the way children learn, tells us, "Children learn best from active exploration." The structured music programs explored later in this chapter make use of this instinct for active exploration. You can encourage the same at home. The combination of at-home and outside enrichment extends the range of musical possibilities. Most important, though, is the attitude you cultivate that says: "We can play with sound just as we play with clay or paint or sand." "We can sing, dance, and invent with sound just as we invent with words or blocks." "Tell me a story. Draw me a picture. Dance me a dance. Sing me a song." Let your curiosity and inventiveness soar. Your child will follow your lead.

We do not need to be music experts who always talk about "rules." Children are full of music. We simply need to help them unlock this wealth of music inside themselves.
—Peter Magadini

The child from three to six

By the time your child enters the preschool years, the list of acquired skills is truly awesome. There is increased complexity of emotional response combined with intellectual and physical growth.

The child from three to six

- needs opportunities for free play and experimentation.
- needs experiences that give a sense of accomplishment.
- is capable of using symbols to represent objects.
- is able to concentrate on one thing at a time.
- is learning to follow directions and to get along with others.
- is extremely active with good large motor control.
- enjoys activity for its own sake.
- needs frequent rest periods.
- seldom recognizes the need to slow down.
- has large muscles more developed than small muscles.
- still needs to develop eye/hand coordination.
- is flexible socially.
- expresses emotions freely.
- has frequent outbursts of anger.
- is jealous when having to share adult attention.

What parents can do

Whether you and your child are gently discovering together during the first year and a half, tentatively venturing forth as your child grows toward three, or taking more daring steps as you prepare your child for the larger world, there is much for you to do yourself to make music a part of everyday life. At each of these stages, just as

Education should try to preserve the most remarkable features of the young: its adventurousness, its generativity, its resourcefulness, and its flashes of flexibility and creativity.—Howard Gardner

you are your child's guide in exploring, naming, describing, touching, and observing, you can sharpen awareness as you both explore the world of sound. Even if you have opted for an away-from-home music experience described later in the chapter, there are still day-to-day projects that you can share to supplement and enhance the more organized activities.

Whatever your child's age, it helps to have a mental checklist of some of the basic elements of sound that you can use as building blocks for this exploration.

Basic elements		
High/low	Long/short	Fast/slow
Up/down	Sound/silence	Loud/soft

More sophisticated elements like timbre (the sound quality of a particular instrument or object) and texture (how many sounds are heard at one time from thin to thick) can be incorporated when the basic elements are understood. There are many opportunities to use these elements in the course of a day. Other ideas will occur to you once you get started.

On the next few pages you will find projects and activities that you and your child can share—a "starter kit" of ideas. Readiness varies. You are the best judge of when to try a particular project.

Sound toys. Be sure that the music toys you buy (or receive) for your infant or young child are truly musical. Select beautiful-sounding ethnic drums, bells, and chimes—music toys made with thought to safety *and* sound. No matter how well approved the toys are for safety, be sure the sound is appealing, not brash or tinny.

Simple sounds. Even at the earliest stages, try experiments with sounds around you. How many different sounds can you make with your tongue, teeth, voice, or hands? How does the container of baby powder sound when it is tapped? How does the door sound when it is knocked or tapped or rubbed? Be as curious with your child about the sounds of everyday objects as you are about the sight of them.

Playing with the elements. Just as you name objects, body parts, colors, and shapes, use your mental sound checklist and use the elements of sound as you go about your daily routines. "I swing you slowly—and now we go fast." "I whisper softly—I call you very loud."

By learning—music learning specifically—I mean getting acquainted with the tools with which sounds can be joined in a chain, to form a shape or design of one's own, or into shapes or designs that developed over the centuries. This learning . . . can begin in early chilhood when everything is a new experience, when everything seen or done is full of surprises and excitement and pleasure.—Helen Lanfer

Up/down. Sing an up-curving melody, saying "Up, Up, Up" as you swing high, "Down, Down, Down" as you land. Sing pitches up or down the scale as you walk the stairs.

Fast/slow. Swing or rock your child at different speeds. Describe them as you do them; "So-o-o slow" or "Fast, fast, fast." Try this poem as you move together:

Steamboat, steamboat, go so slow.
Steamboat, steamboat, get some gas.
Steamboat, steamboat, go so fast.

Slow dance/ fast dance. Carefully select several of your favorite CDs or audiotapes, basing your choice on the contrast between fast and slow music. For the earliest stages, dance with your child in your arms. When your child is ready to dance on his own, get out some colored scarves and, together, make the scarves "dance" to the music. This is a fun activity for friends and family.

Loud/soft. Vary the volume of your speech when you talk to your child. Try using stuffed animals of various sizes as puppets, matching voice to size.

Secret sounds. Ask your child to sing or tell you a secret (using her "near" voice) or to call out an important announcement (using her "far" voice) so that you can hear it all the way in the next room. Play hide-and-seek with your near or far voice as a clue. Wherever you are hiding, sing or call. Your child will find you "by ear."

1 2 3 4 5. Try counting or singing to five or ten, getting louder with each number. Move closer to each other as you get louder. (When you meet, it's a good time to hug.) Gradually get softer as you count backward. (5 4 3 2 1).

High/low. Sound comes in sizes too. Try the story of *Goldilocks and the Three Bears* and exaggerate the high, medium, and low qualities of Baby Bear, Mama Bear, and Papa Bear. Or, using stuffed animals or puppets, choose animals whose voices are obviously high or low (kitten and lion). If you have a keyboard, let it help you "speak." Eventually your child will be able to find the high kitten and low lion.

Sound guessing games. Make your own set of sound boxes from small, opaque, plastic (or other child- proof material) containers. Place a different "sound" object in each container: bells, beans, rice, buttons, paper clips, salt, whatever. Have fun with your choices. When your baby is just six to eight months old, you can begin guessing games, describing the sounds as crisp, musical, swishing, strong, gentle, and so on. Try high/low, fast/slow, loud/soft experiments. As your child grows, use the elements of sound in more challenging guessing games.

Kitchen sounds. Pots, pot covers, spoons, strainers, and a variety of other kitchen tools are also marvelous for discovering sound possibilities. Try: one tap, then two taps; loud sound, then soft sound; and fast sounds, then slow sounds. Sometimes try to imitate your child's sound. Eventually she will imitate yours.

Screened Sound. Collect a number of familiar objects. Behind a door, around the corner in the next room, or behind an improvised screen, make a sound with each object. Your child will enjoy guessing the sound, or having you guess. Jingle keys, tap pencils, crumple or tear paper, ring bells, and so on. This makes a good family activity.

Sing as you go. Make up your own simple songs as you dress or bathe your child or as you walk or march or run together. You may have a range of only one note, but the fact that you sometimes chant or rap or sing about a familiar activity as you are doing it, leads to early childhood creativity. Soon your child will begin to chant or rap or sing, perhaps his name or yours or the cat's. Homemade songs can become part of your child's memory bank. Try putting some of these first sound experiments on tape. You'll be glad you did.

Mirror sound. Imitate your child's sound, whether it is a cooing sound, a sung pitch, or the first attempts at speech. The fact that the child is the leader in this encourages further experimenting on the child's part. You will be tuning in to the child's vocal range, rather than expecting the child to take your much broader range.

Fast line/slow line. When your child is drawing, have her sometimes make very fast strokes, sometimes slow ones. She can try drawing the sound of a train leaving the station, going slow, faster, faster, and vice versa. Try playing her fast and slow lines on a drum or other soundmaker and ask her to dance to them.

Morse code. Invite your child to draw some messages using long and short dashes. (——— ——— — — ———) Point to them on the page and say "long, long, short, short, long." Then, with your child, try the message on the drum or other potentially interesting sound producer in the room (door, wall, floor, or pot). Using colored paper, make a collection of these messages to play with from time to time.

Long/short. Using kitchen tools or drums, have a conversation with long and short sounds. Tap "long-long" on a pot lid or other object that makes a sustained sound. At first your child may not repeat what you do. It doesn't matter. In fact, let your child sometimes send the "message" first as you imitate him. Eventually he will be able to duplicate your sound or his own. Gradually make the message longer:

"Long-long-short-short-long"
or
"Short-short-short-long"

Sound/silence. With a drum, hand clap, or other percussion sound, make a steady, walking beat. Ask your child to walk to the beat and let his ears tell him to stop when the sound stops. "Freezing" at the silence is fun. Sometimes decide together that when you "freeze," you will try to look your funniest—or cutest or most graceful or beautiful. (This is a form of the game of "Statues.") Give your child a chance to be the sound-maker. She may like to see how good you are at stopping when the sound stops.

Listening party. Make listening to music a family activity. Let the lights be low or try listening with eyes closed. Get very comfortable. Let each family member select a favorite piece of music. Keep the listening short. Encourage quiet. Snacks go well with these sessions, but not when your eyes are closed!

The Listening House. Put a blanket or sheet over the kitchen or dining-room table to turn it into a "listening house." Collect a group of familiar objects. Your child and a friend will enjoy climbing into the "house" to guess the sounds they hear you make. The Listening House makes a good spot to have a snack and listen to a few CDs.

Sound treasure hunt. When a child has passed the "into-the-mouth-with-everything" stage, take an exploratory walk around the block with bag or basket in hand and look for objects of nature or other objects that might make interesting sounds. Stones, leaves, sticks, acorns, a piece of paper—all have possibilities. Curiosity is courted and observation is expanded. At home, experiment with the sounds of each found object. How does one sound alone? How does it sound in combination with others? Can you guess which sound it is? Play a tape or CD and use your newfound instruments as accompaniment. When you are finished with sound experiments, use the materials for a collage.

Make an instrument. Making musical instruments is an excellent rainy-day project, which works as well as baking cookies or drawing or painting.

Play me a picture. You'll need a large roll of brown wrapping paper, some felt-tipped markers, and a selection of varied music. For example: "Aviary" from *Carnival of the Animals* (Saint-Säens), "Scooting" from *Six Ings* (Cowell), or "Lullaby" from *The Firebird Suite* (Stravinsky). Spread the paper in a long enough strip so that a few family members or friends can join in the drawing party. Let the mood and sweep of the music dictate the way the markers are moved.

Draw or dance me a song. As an extension of the previous activity, for five- and six- year-olds, read the story of some favorite program music—*Peter and the Wolf* (Prokofiev), *The Nutcracker* (Tchaikovsky), or *The Sorcerer's Apprentice* (Dukas). When the story and music are familiar, draw a frame-by-frame picture of the music with your child, or dance the story together.

Musical puppet show. Using music that tells a story (program music), you can make a project with your child and friends. *The Firebird Suite* (Stravinsky) makes a good model. Make puppets of the characters. Draw scenery. Play the music as you animate the puppets to "tell" the story. Rehearse often. Videotape the results.

Sound conversation. Start a "conversation" using hand sounds or any percussion sound. Have your child answer with a different sound. Make it a family affair and pass the sounds around the table after dinner. As the family gets better at it, try playing the game of "Add-a-sound"—each person copies the last sound, then adds a sound, until the sound chain is as long as possible.

Gift of sound. Give music as a gift to someone you love. So often we encourage children to draw a picture for Grandma or make a birthday card for Daddy. Using a tape recorder or camcorder, plan a musical gift that includes favorite songs that your child sings or plays—the more the merrier. Any number of family members and friends should be able to play.

Concert time. By the time your child is three or four years old, you should be able to attend a short children's concert together. A good children's concert lasts for an hour or less. It should have age- appropriate repertoire, and much to see as well as to hear. Generally, concert brochures state the recommended ages for attendance. An example of an outstanding series for children is mounted each year in Westchester County, New York, by Richard Kapp, conductor of the Philharmonia Virtuosi. Called *Cushion Concerts,* a typical season includes an appealing variety of programs, such as *Playing Percussion, Hansel and Gretel, The Mime Field,* and *Old Fashioned Marionette Theater.* Parents and children bring cushions and sit on the floor, assuring the informal ambiance of the programs.

Music in the schools. Bring your child, especially as he approaches age six, to concerts in the local elementary, junior high school, senior high school, or community music school. Young people making music become excellent role models, especially as you and your child begin to think about which instrument to choose.

A sound record. If your child does begin the study of an instrument, keep a "sound" record. Every time a piece is completed, record it on audio- or videotape. You will have an aural history of your child's musical development, worth its weight in gold.

Parents, I invite you to review the history of your own art life. If you feel nostalgia or regret at what has been "lost," I think that those feelings are your own creativity just looking for a place to happen. Your creativity is still there.—Sally Warner

Judging readiness for more structured music experiences

At some point, you may decide that it is time for your child to have a more structured music experience under the guidance of an early childhood music specialist. Whether that experience is with a group, in private, or a combination of the two is your choice.

How will you know when your child is ready for more structured music experiences? Whichever level of early childhood music you examine, the most important thing to keep in mind is that once you seek a more structured program, you should select professionals who have been specifically trained in early childhood music.

The director or teacher of such a program should be able to help you

14

*We believe that music
ability is as much a basic
life skill as walking or talking, and that all children can
achieve competence in music
provided their early music
environment is sufficiently
rich.—Kenneth Guilmartin*

assess your child's readiness for this more organized activity, taking into consideration attention span, large and small muscle coordination, and learning maturity. Some programs commence in infancy and include a rather wide range of ages in each group. Some are based on the concept that the age span from youngest to oldest child in a group is kept to a minimum. These programs generally have overlapping age groupings (twos and threes, threes and fours, fours and fives) that allow the variety of choice in grouping, placing children of similar ability together. Of course, age is not the only factor in good grouping. Personality, family interaction, and other developmental patterns all need to be considered.

Why begin this early training? First of all, children at this age are eager. They are patient with repetition, have strong rhythm skills, listen with a keen ear, and are not inhibited by performing for others. Those who begin the study of an instrument at an early age develop practice habits before life in the bigger world becomes complicated.

In many of these programs, an adult caregiver is expected not only to attend, but also to participate actively in classes or lessons. For working parents, this is often not so easy. If you can manage to participate, the benefits for both you and your child are not only in the shared experience, but in the increased musical vocabulary to which you now have access. The world of music will have opened a bit more for both of you. The description of these early music programs includes information on the degree of parent participation. Be assured that your presence and support will affect the quality and depth of your child's response.

What can you expect of a good early childhood music program?

Characteristics of early childhood music programs

The early childhood music program
- is most often a group experience.
- often requires some parent or other caregiver involvement.
- provides opportunities for listening.
- includes movement and rhythm activities.
- allows for experiments with a variety of sounds.
- includes singing activities.
- may provide an introduction to music symbols.
- encourages creative response.
- has progressive short- and long-term musical goals.

A brief history

What are some of the programs developed to address the needs of the young child? Much of the early experimentation began outside of the United States in the late 1800s and the first half of this century. The ideas of innovators Émile Jaques-Dalcroze, Carl Orff, Zoltán Kodály (pronounced COULD eye), and Shinichi Suzuki have influenced much of today's early childhood music curriculum.

Émile Jaques-Dalcroze, a professor of music in Geneva, Switzerland, devised an approach that sought to awaken and develop the listening and creative abilities of his students. Exercises involved a whole-body response to music, using the body's natural movements and rhythm in order to stimulate awareness of the sound. Gradually, the term eurhythmics (good rhythm) was applied to the Dalcroze method in particular,

DALCROZE

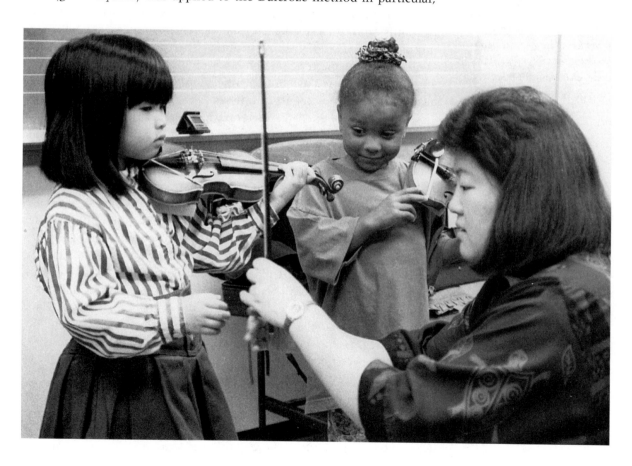

but also, in a more general sense, to any system teaching rhythm through movement.

Dalcroze encouraged this rhythmic movement along with ear training and improvisation. The linking of these elements with imagination, a keen listening sense, and immediacy of response to musical stimuli are cornerstones of this program, laying the foundation for thorough musicianship.

ORFF

There is every indication that movement is integral to a child's musical experiences . . . . The physical self is vital to music learning; the body is an important pedagogical tool. As music flows in time, children are triggered into movement, the key to successful music education.
—*Patricia Shehan*

In 1924, Carl Orff, a highly successful German composer, began to adapt some of Dalcroze's ideas on movement and music for young adults. The school in which he did his experiments was destroyed during World War II, along with most of the instruments he had developed for the program. After the war, he was persuaded by radio officials in Bavaria to use his ideas to teach music to young children over the air-waves. His basic assumption was that the unmusical child is rare or nonexistent. All children, he believed, can develop some perception of rhythm, pitch, and musical form. The characteristic xylophones and metallophones of his method were designed to encourage students to improvise without their having to master the technique required to play more sophisticated instruments. Folk music, movement, singing, and speaking all play important roles in Orff Schulwerk. There are four stages to the program: imitation of pitched and nonpitched sounds, exploration of sound possibilities, literacy (competency in reading and writing music), and improvisation, the ultimate stage at which creative response is cultivated.

KODÁLY

Composer Zoltán Kodály devoted much of his life to the establishment of a music education system for the children of his native Hungary. His goal was to integrate the musical training of all children with their growing literacy in other subjects. This training was planned from the age of three years, when children entered nursery school, and continued throughout their entire education. Based on the learning abilities of the child, the program uses the voice as the primary instrument. Hand signals accompany the singing of different pitches. The system has underscored parent and teacher awareness of the readiness of preschool children to become music-literate.

SUZUKI

Shinichi Suzuki, the Japanese music educator, based his concept of music learning on the same premise as the child's learning of his native language, or "mother tongue." With children as young as two years of age, he began a program whereby children first heard, then repeated by rote as they learned a specific instrument. At first, the program used the violin only, and developed gradually to include the viola, cello, harp, and guitar, as well as the piano and flute. The string instruments are sized from one-sixteenth to full size to accommodate the physical needs of the student.

The parent is usually an integral part of student learning. Some public and parochial schools provide Suzuki training in groups, in which case, no parent attendance is required. In those programs in which parent participation is expected, parents attend lessons with the child and, in addition, learn to play the instrument along with the child. The parent is then able to help the child practice correctly at home. Some group Suzuki lessons include movement and rhythm games. The program is focused on the learning of the instrument and the development of musical ability.

Beginners learn so slowly. Same as mother-tongue. The baby does not say 'Mama' and then immediately speak many different words. The child must repeat and repeat if he is to learn. Knowledge is not skill. Knowledge plus 10,000 times is skill.
—Shinichi Suzuki

YAMAHA

The Yamaha Music Education System, which was developed in the 1950s to teach music to young children, has since modified its program. Its philosophy regards the study of music as training in comprehensive musicianship rather than as instruction in performing on a particular instrument; keyboard training, however, is used to develop musicianship. Students are expected to have a keyboard at home. The six- year curriculum includes movement, singing, ear training, keyboard ensemble, reading and writing, with strong emphasis on creative work. Instruction is for groups of up to ten children at the first two levels of training. By the third level, students have both group and private lessons. Parents participate in classes and supervise home practice. The goal of the program is to develop intelligent listeners who can describe and discuss music they hear, make, and create.

KINDERMUSIK ®

Kindermusik traces its origins to West Germany in the 1960s. It is a group introduction to music for children four to seven years old. The curriculum is structured, yet flexible. It builds sequentially from speaking, singing, and moving to writing and reading music. Whether the child is listening, moving, vocalizing, playing an instrment, creating, or reading music, the focus is on the process, not on performance.

It wasn't until the 1970s that the idea of teaching music to groups of preschool children was widely recognized in this country. The Head Start program gave impetus to programs for children three years old and older, but programs for children under that age were almost nonexistent. Although nursery schools and day-care centers taught songs and movement, the issue of how to help children express *their* music, to develop *their* awareness of sound, had hardly been explored.

By the 1980s, there was a continuing focus on the development of an early childhood curriculum. Edwin E. Gordon did significant work in studying the sequence in which children develop musically. This sequential learning has been a model for many early childhood music programs. His goal of helping the child develop inner hearing has been widely studied and incorporated into newly emerging programs.

Early childhood special interest groups were formed at this time to share information. In 1984, there was a Music and Early Childhood Conference held at Brigham Young University, cosponsored by the Music Educators National Conference and the Association for Childhood Education International. Collaborative projects between musicians and early childhood specialists were launched and, by 1991, a research journal, *Early Music Childhood,* began publication. One early childhood specialist, Donna Brink Fox, of the Eastman School of Music in Rochester, New York, points out that "These babies taught me that parents held the key to early musical behavior."

The early childhood music programs just described recognized that children do best when there is a balance between structure and freedom, that there needs to be a sufficient amount of time for the child to observe before doing, and that a frame of mind for exploring the world of sound is best nurtured in the home as well as in group activities. The focus is not on the product or performance, but on the process.

MUSIC TOGETHER ®

In 1985, Kenneth K. Guilmartin founded the Center for Music and Young Children. Guilmartin, licensed as a teacher of Dalcroze, saw the need for a program that projected not only to parents, both of whom often work full time, but to the newly emerging number of primary caregivers who increasingly are not the parents. In 1981, he was joined by Lili Levinowitz in establishing the Center's Lab School at Princeton, N.J. There they work with over 300 babies and young children in mixed-age classes in a program called Music Together. The goal of the program is to give basic competence in music to children through their own playful process. By gradually learning to sing in tune and to keep a beat in an informal, nondemanding environment, children are being prepared for more formal instruction later on if they wish.

The Music Together catalog of materials includes tapes, songbooks, and information on classroom techniques for use not only by trained instructors, but by teachers and families not directly involved in the program. We can expect more such programs that combine early childhood music programs with contemporary early childhood development concepts.

Children in the 1990s are reaping the rewards of this century's experimentation. Some colleges and universities offer special courses for music teachers so that they can learn these historic techniques. New teaching materials for the very young have been developed. The best of the music-readiness and instrumental training methods are age-appropriate and designed to teach a broad range of music skills. Songs in varied moods are selected with the interests of children in mind. Books are often colorfully illustrated. Humor is an important ingredient. Games and puzzles are used to train the eye and ear. Writing or drawing activities reinforce music concepts. Music software has been designed for the very young, opening even more possibilities for sound exploration.

In the best of public school music education, private studio, and community music school programs, children benefit from these music-readiness programs, instrumental training, or a combination of the two. Dalcroze, Orff, Kodály, Suzuki, Yamaha, or adaptations are increasingly incorporated into the curriculum.

Researching a good program

Researching an early childhood music program is similar to investigating a nursery school or day care program. How do you decide whether you and your child are more suited to a group experience or to performance training? In addition to visiting lessons in different programs, you will have to decide how much time you are willing to set aside and what the end results will be for your child. The program should have a clearly defined philosophy. It should not be just a genial playtime, but a path to real learning as well as joy.

A good preschool music program
- encourages good listening skills.
- builds rhythmic understanding.
- increases attention span.
- aids motor coordination.
- helps aspects of later reading (left to right, similar/different).
- uses full body and multisensory experiences.
- provides social interaction.

Teacher credentials

What are the credentials of an early childhood music specialist? At the most advanced levels of early childhood certification, the teacher will have a degree in music or music education. Credits toward certification are most often earned by courses in child development, performance, theory, music history, music pedagogy, movement, vocal development, and ensemble techniques. Each of the major systems of early music education described in this chapter has somewhat different, but detailed, requirements for licensing and certification. In general, there are levels of training from novice to master teacher. Each system requires a certain number of contact hours of training per level.

Create an environment in your studio of calm, peace, support, and unconditional acceptance, a haven and refuge where your students can let go and totally be themselves. Encourage them in their total acceptance of themselves as they see themselves mirrored in you.
—Sharon Jones

A good early childhood music teacher

- is well trained.
- preferably has a degree in music or music education.
- loves children.
- loves music.
- has enthusiasm and warmth.
- has self-discipline.
- is a good storyteller.
- has a sense of the dramatic.
- is able to change pace quickly.
- has the ability to praise.
- is good at group management.
- has performance skill (in instrument-specific programs).
- has ability to sing, dance, and improvise (in movement programs).

Ruth Alperson, an expert in Dalcroze eurhythmics, says, "You can tell if the teacher is good if you find you are 'moving' to the music when you observe the teacher at work. You may find yourself tapping your foot or hand. There should be lots of music and sound activity during the class, not a lot of talk. With a good teacher, you will be more interested in watching the children than the teacher, and you should be smiling a lot."

Questions for the teacher

Arrange to visit several classes to observe some of these skills in action.

> ### *Questions for the teacher*
> - Are there readinesses expected before the child begins?
> - Are there trial lessons?
> - Must I buy an instrument?
> - Will my child learn to play a specific instrument?
> - Is there attention to playing technique?
> - Are there audio or video resources with the materials?
> - What comes after this training?

Early childhood music charts

The following charts describe some major early childhood music programs.

DALCROZE
Dalcroze Society of America
c/o Anne Farber
161 West 86th Street
New York, NY 10024
800-471-0012

DESCRIPTION The Émile Jaques-Dalcroze system is based on inclusion of rhythmic movement (eurhythmics) with ear training and improvisation. The elements of music are experienced through whole-body response. Training prepares students for later instrumental or movement studies. The system is valued as applied not only to early childhood music training, but to musicianship training for all ages and levels.

TEACHER TRAINING Bachelor's degree, preferably in music or equivalent. 60 hours of training before entering program. On entering, 180 hours of training, generally at college or university.
Levels of training:
Level 1: Certificate by examination.
Level 2: Licensing by examination after 180 hours training.
Level 3: Master teacher diploma at Dalcroze Institute, Geneva.
Note: To check teacher credentials, contact the Dalcroze Society, giving the name of the teacher's primary Dalcroze instructor and the year of certification.

PUPIL AGE Two years and up.

PARENT PARTICIPATION Parents participate in many programs for children through the age of four. Ideally they engage in all activities with their children. No formal practice is required. By the age of four and up, parent participation is at the discretion of the teacher.

KINDERMUSIK®
Music Resources International
Box 26575
Greensboro, NC 27415
800-628-5687

DESCRIPTION An early childhood development program taught through music. Structured, flexible curriculum based on developmentally appropriate placement. Builds sequentially from speaking, singing, and moving to writing and reading music. Basic rhythm instruments and glockenspiel are used as learning tools. Some concepts of Dalcroze, Orff, and Kodály are part of the program.

TEACHER TRAINING While Kindermusik teachers do not have to be certified or be licensed to teach, board certification is a form of recognition of professional development. There are three levels of certification. Educators may apply for the highest level for which they meet the requirements.
Level 1: Standard certification. For the newest teacher. Two-day workshop, one year of teaching experience for two different semesters.
Level 2: Professional certification. For more experienced teachers. All of the above, plus four years of teaching experience.
Level 3: Master teacher. For the most experienced, highly qualified teachers. Training equivalent to Levels 1 and 2, plus bachelor's degree, submitted personal portfolio, and at least eight years of teaching the full curriculum.
At each level, three to five continuing education units are required per year.

PUPIL AGE *Beginnings:* Eighteen months to three years. *Growing:* Three and a half to five years. *The Young Child:* Four to seven years.

PARENT PARTICIPATION *Beginnings:* With parents. *Growing:* 30-minute class, no parent; 15 minutes with parent. *The Young Child:* 60–75 minute class, no parent; 10 minutes with parent.

KODÁLY
Organization of American Kodály Educators
Glenys Wignes, Director
1457 S. 23rd Street
Fargo, ND 58108
701-235-0366

DESCRIPTION   Built on the work of Zoltán Kodály, this is a structured format of music education shaped to the learning abilities of the child. Program is based on the voice as the primary instrument. Hand signals are coordinated with vocal pitches. Uses tapping, walking, large motor response before introducing refinements.

TEACHER TRAINING   Most teachers enter the program with a music education degree. Teacher certification after one year of study plus two or three summer courses at college or university. Training includes studies in pedagogy, movement, recorder, and dulcimer as well as Kodály vocal and gesture techniques.

PUPIL AGE   *Level 1*: K–Grade 1. *Level 2:* Grades 2–4. *Level 3:* Grades 5–6 .

PARENT PARTICIPATION   None.

MUSIC TOGETHER®
Center for Music and Young Children
217 Nassau Street
Princeton, NJ 08542
800-728-2692

DESCRIPTION   In the Music Together program, students are encouraged to hear, think, sing, and move freely to music. The program focuses on training a variety of types of caregivers to become competent guides for basic music skills. With developmentally appropriate music and movement activities, children are helped to cultivate competency in singing in tune and keeping a beat by the use of music games, singing, and simple rhythm instruments. Available materials: tapes, songbooks, simple instruments. Parent education publications include *Music and Your Child: A Guide for Parents and Caregivers.*

TEACHER TRAINING   Music educators, preschool, kindergarten, and first grade teachers, Suzuki teachers, day care providers, music therapists, performers, dance and movement teachers, and interested parents may attend teacher training workshops, scheduled at sites throughout the country.

PUPIL AGE   From birth to five years.

PARENT PARTICIPATION   Either a parent or other caregiver, as described above under *Teacher Training,* is integral to the program.

ORFF SCHULWERK
American Orff Schulwerk Association
Box 391089,
Cleveland, OH 44139
216-543-5366

DESCRIPTION   Based on the work of Carl Orff, this is a way to teach and learn music using songs, chants, poems, and games. The use of special Orff instruments (pitched percussion, wood xylophone, and metallophone) is integral to the program.

TEACHER TRAINING   Three levels: 60 contact hours per level.
Level 1: Two-week introductory course for all interested teachers.
Level 2: For classroom and instrumental music teachers.
Level 3: Preparation to teach Orff techniques to teachers. Teachers must successfully apprentice-teach in order to be on the approved list of Orff teachers.

PUPIL AGE   Prenatal and up.

PARENT PARTICIPATION   To ages four or five years.

SUZUKI
Suzuki Association of the Americas
Box 17310
Boulder, CO 80308
303-444-0948

DESCRIPTION   Based on the concepts of Shinichi Suzuki that children learn music as they learn language by repetition and imitation. Child plays scaled-down instrument, listens to recordings of own music as well as music of outstanding quality, and learns to read notes after experiencing the music-making process. Instruction in violin, viola, cello, harp, guitar, piano, and flute. Some Suzuki teachers use group activities and games to teach prereading and reading concepts.

TEACHER TRAINING   Three methods of training, all with certified teacher trainers at Suzuki teacher institutes throughout the United States. Most Suzuki teachers have a degree in music. Each teacher must send a performance tape for entry into the training program.
1. Short-term teaching: two five-day courses for Suzuki Book 1. There is one five-day course for each of the other books in the series (as many as ten or eleven books, depending on the instrument).
2. Apprentice program: teacher works privately with certified teacher trainer, advancing through each book level. Level of book becomes certification level.
3. Advanced level: teacher trainer. College or university training with a degree in music.

PUPIL AGE   Two years and up.

PARENT PARTICIPATION   Parent attends lessons and group activities (typically one group and one private lesson per week), and guides home practice until student is ready for independent study. Suzuki programs in public schools may not require parent attendance.

YAMAHA
Yamaha International Music in Education
6600 Orangethorpe Avenue
Buena Park, CA 90622
800-722-8856

DESCRIPTION A comprehensive program that teaches a child total musicianship through weekly group lessons. Students experience and perform a wide variety of musical styles. Curriculum offers keyboard repertoire, keyboard ensemble, expressive singing, rhythm training, movement, reading, writing, improvisation, and composition.

TEACHER TRAINING Yamaha instructors undergo a series of rigorous examinations in music fundamentals and keyboard performance (repertoire, sight reading, and improvisation). Initial certification is granted after a week-long seminar, with further training provided on a regular basis to maintain certification. Additional examinations and training are required to teach the advanced curriculum. Most Yamaha instructors have a music degree.

PUPIL AGE *Level 1:* Four to five years. *Level 2:* Six to seven years. *Level 3:* Eight to nine years.

PARENT PARTICIPATION *Level 1:* Parent participates in a 60-minute class weekly; guides home practice. *Level 2:* Parent participates, but less than at previous level. *Level 3:* Little or no parent participation, but it is suggested that parents supervise home practice.

Practice, preschoolers, early schoolers, and parents

If your child is involved in learning a specific instrument, you will be learning how to practice together. It is important to recognize that practicing is a learned skill, so it shouldn't surprise you if your child needs your help. After all, young children are not expected to do independent study in any other area of their lives. You and the teacher will need to be partners as you help your child learn this invaluable skill.

Here are a few guidelines that may be helpful as you and your child learn to practice together.

Same time. Same station. Every day. Help your child to weave practice into a pleasant daily routine. Even on hectic days, five minutes is better than nothing. Suzuki himself has said, "You practice on the days you eat." Let your child know that you expect daily practice.

Plan ahead. Your child needs you to help her plan her time. Plan one task at a time. Vary the tasks. Make an attractive chart. Decorate it with stickers or use colorful markers as you complete each task.

Do Not Disturb! Your child needs your help to keep the practice time free of interruptions from siblings, TV, or other distractions.

Practicing should be a pleasurable and happy experience for the child. All human beings do their best when they are doing things they like most. Consequently if children enjoy practice, they will learn better.

—Carole Bigler and Valerie Lloyd-Watts

Be there. Your child needs your companionship while she practices. She is too young to "go it alone."

Sing praises. Your child needs frequent and honest praise. Praise effort. Praise good posture. Praise knowing the right finger or note. Praise getting to the instrument without being reminded.

Hear ye! Be an attentive, appreciative listener.

The gift of music. Use audio- or videotapes to monitor progress. Make a tape as a gift for someone special.

What a treat! Try small candies, raisins, or carrot pennies as a treat after each successful repetition of a song or part. An unsuccessful try means Mom or Dad gets the treat.

A perfect audience. Line up your child's favorite toys as an audience for your child.

What a child does need is the opportunity to practice a skill once it has emerged. Here the influence of parents can be highly significant. Take your cue from your child. Don't try to mold him into the person you want him to be or the person you wish you had been.

—Richard Landsdown and Marjorie Walker

"Ace" it. Using a deck of cards, have the child pick a card and repeat a passage or technique as many times as the card indicates.

Parents as partners. If you can play a musical instrument, accompany your child when appropriate. Family music making is a special delight.

Practice is its own reward, but. . . . Let your child earn special privileges by consistent, quality practice. A day or even a few hours of shared time with you is a meaningful reward.

One is fun. Two is better. Arrange for your child to play a duet with a friend.

The riches of role-reversal. Ask your child to be the teacher, to demonstrate and teach you a particular song or skill.

Practice should be fun. There are many games and teaching aids to help you. The above are all positive suggestions for helping your young child to practice. The Suzuki Association of the Americas' minijournal, Summer 1993, adds to many specific helpful practice projects a list of the following non-effective strategies.

Practice dont's for parents
- Don't yell or threaten.
- Don't ask a child to practice when a friend is visiting, or when something exciting is taking place at home.
- Don't practice when both you and your child are tired and irritable.
- Don't make the home practicing session too long or difficult.
- Don't use criticism without adding praise.
- Don't compare musical skill with that of a sibling.
- Don't say "Later," because later never comes.

As you and your child "play" with sound, making it an integral part of your environment at home and away, the rewards are inestimable. At its best, sharing music experiences with your young child does require a commitment of time. However, finding the time means that you will be giving your child the gift of music—a lifetime pleasure.

HIGHLIGHTS

☆ The rate of growth is dramatic in these early years.

☆ Early experiences stem from your memories of childhood and your present curiosity. You are your child's first guide to the world of sound.

☆ From birth to eighteen months, the challenge is to create a musical environment in the home.

☆ From eighteen months to three years, your child may be ready for parent/child group activities outside the home.

☆ By the ages of three to six years, in addition to enrichment activities at home, your child may be ready for music-readiness classes or instrument-specific lessons. Some instrument-specific programs begin at age two.

☆ What you can do to enrich your child's music environment:

> Help your child be curious about sound.
>
> Find opportunities to play with sound as you would with any other enrichment tools.

☆ There are books, tapes, CDs, and other resources to help you.

☆ Some considerations in gauging your child's readiness for a group music experience:

> Attention span.
>
> Large and small muscle coordination.
>
> Social and learning maturity.
>
> Personality.
>
> Family interaction.

☆ You will need a trained professional to help you decide the best time to begin.

☆ There are reasons for early music training. Your young child:

> Is eager and patient.
>
> Has a keen ear and strong sense of rhythm.
>
> Is uninhibited.
>
> Has time.
>
> Enjoys other children.

☆ A good early childhood music program:

> Is most often a group experience.
>
> Generally requires parent involvement.
>
> Provides opportunities for listening.
>
> Includes rhythm and movement activities.
>
> Allows for experimenting with a variety of sounds and instruments.
>
> Includes singing activities.
>
> Encourages creative response.
>
> Has long- and short-term musical goals in a sensible progression.

☆ Early childhood music programs have a history from the late 1800s; pioneers included Émile Jaques-Dalcroze, Zoltán Kodály, and Carl Orff.

**CHOICES AT
CERTAIN AGES**

☆ Dalcroze focused on creative whole-body response to rhythm (eurhythmics).

☆ Orff developed special instruments that were easy for the young child to play and beautiful to listen to.

☆ Kodály based his work on vocal skills as well as movement.

☆ Suzuki pioneered the teaching of children as young as two years to play the violin as naturally as they speak their mother tongue.

☆ Yamaha Music Education System uses keyboards as a means of teaching comprehensive musicianship, and combines concepts from the Suzuki and music-and-movement systems.

☆ Kindermusik ® has adapted features from the music and movement systems, adding new materials to the earlier concepts.

☆ Music Together®, one of the newer programs, is based on the earlier research. It considers caregivers as well as parents as links to the child's musical development.

☆ More adaptations of these early music programs can be expected.

☆ Some of these programs require varying degrees of parent participation.

☆ When you consider these programs, decide:

How much time you have to devote to these activities.

Whether your child will do best in a weekly music and movement class or learning a particular instrument.

☆ The early childhood music specialist is:

Well-trained, loves children, loves music, has a flair for the dramatic, is well organized, and has good group skills.

☆ Questions to ask the teacher:

Are there readinesses expected before the child begins lessons?

Are there trial lessons or classes?

Must I buy an instrument?

Will my child play a specific instrument?

What comes after this training?

☆ If you and your child have chosen to learn an instrument, you will be learning how to practice together. Some guidelines for practicing:

Have a daily routine, if possible, at the same time each day.

Expect that your child will need your help and companionship.

Be sure that practice is undisturbed.

Give frequent honest praise.

Be an appreciative listener.

☆ There are many tools to help make practice fun (see Part IV: "General Resources").

CHAPTER RESOURCES

The resources listed below are appropriate for the age group discussed in this chapter. Age recommendtions are listed only if an item has more narrow appeal. Some items have wide appeal and are listed in the chapter resources of more than one chapter.

Take special note of Part IV, "General Resources," for a listing of books, recordings, movies, games, teaching aids, CD-ROMs, and catalogs.

BOOKS FOR YOU

Andress, Barbara (ed.). PREKINDERGARTEN MUSIC EDUCATION. Reston, 1902 Association Dr., Reston, VA 22091: Music Educators National Conference,1989.

A collection of articles on early childhood music and movement written by several experts in the field. It includes essays on the characteristics of the young child, and many specific music and movement activities. For teachers, but useful to parents of young children.

Armstrong, Thomas. AWAKENING YOUR CHILD'S NATURAL GENIUS: ENHANCING CURIOSITY, CREATIVITY, AND LEARNING ABILITY. Los Angeles: Tarcher, 1991.

A natural outgrowth of the author's *In Their Own Way*, here Armstrong examines specific learning styles in greater depth. Among these are chapters on math, art, music, and science. Giftedness, computer learning, special education, Montessori, Waldorf, and superlearning are also discussed and, often, criticized. The text is broken up by the insertion of lists, headings, and rich and diverse quotations. A wonderful book.

Bigler, Carole L. and Valerie Lloyd-Watts. MORE THAN MUSIC: A HANDBOOK FOR TEACHERS, PARENTS, AND STUDENTS. Athens, OH: Ability Development, 1979.

Although written for those involved in Suzuki piano training, all parents will find the introductory chapters helpful. Especially useful are the chapters entitled "The Role of the Parents in the Education of Their Children," "The Role of Parents and Relatives at Lessons and at Home," and "Parental Aids: Motivating Students." Specific guidelines for assisting with practice are stated clearly.

Chroninger, Ruby. TEACH YOUR KIDS ABOUT MUSIC. New York: Walker, 1994.

A unique activity handbook using children's literature to stimulate creative activities related to the elements of sound. There is an annotated bibliography of general literature, music literature, and a discography. Useful for parents and teachers.

Elkind, David. MISEDUCATION: PRESCHOOLERS AT RISK. New York: Knopf, 1993.

Elkind shows us the very real difference between the mind of a preschool child (how it works) and that of a school-age child. He makes clear how much young children can and do learn when they are presented with developmentally appropriate parenting practices and education. And, in turn, he shows how early miseducation can cause permanent damage to a child's self-esteem by blocking natural gifts and potential talent.

Farnan, Laurie and Faith Johnson. EVERYONE CAN MOVE: MUSIC AND ACTIVITIES THAT PROMOTE MOVEMENT AND MOTOR DEVELOPMENT. New Berlin, WI: Jenson, 1988.

A cassette of all the music in the book is available from MMB Music. Original songs for group participation designed to be repetitive and specific. Each chapter begins with brief commentary on the type of movement involved. The music is in vocal/accompaniment style, and could be performed on a keyboard, guitar, autoharp, or similar instrument. The cassette provides all the music for those who can't play or read music. Could be used as family activities.

Findlay, Elsa. RHYTHM AND MOVEMENT APPLICATIONS OF DALCROZE EURHYTHMICS. Evanston, IL: Summy Birchard/Warner, 1971.

A book for teachers, but gives some indication of Dalcroze exercises that parents might use.

Gardner, Howard. THE UNSCHOOLED MIND: HOW CHILDREN THINK AND HOW SCHOOLS SHOULD TEACH. New York: Basic Books, 1991.

Gardner asks how we can help students move beyond rote learning to achieve genuine understanding. He makes a strong case for restructuring schools, using the latest research on learning as a guide. Here are new ideas about education—from the world of the young child as "natural learner" to the adolescent's search for meaning. A serious, provocative book.

Healy, Jane M. ENDANGERED MINDS: WHY OUR CHILDREN DON'T THINK. New York: Simon & Schuster, 1990.

The message here is that electronic media, unstable family patterns, fast-paced lifestyles, and other reflections of current society change not only how a child thinks, but also affect his actual brain structure. Healy presents research in the neuropsychology of learning and attacks popular opinions—for example, that watching *Sesame Street* aids your child's learning or that day care programs give a child a head start in school. Not Sunday afternoon reading fare, but written in friendly language, with many helpful anecdotes.

McDonald, Dorothy and Gene M. Simons. MUSICAL GROWTH AND DEVELOPMENT: BIRTH THROUGH SIX. New York: Schirmer Books, 1989.

This is a music education textbook, but it contains information that parents might find useful. It does a wonderful job of briefly explaining popular preschool programs, such as Dalcroze, Orff, Suzuki, and Kodály. You might wish to look it up in your library. If you can read music yourself, the "Materials for Instruction" provide many songs and games you could use at home with your toddler or preschooler. There is also an extensive chapter, by Kate Gfeller, on working with the handicapped child.

Saunders, Jacqulyn with Pamela Espeland. BRINGING OUT THE BEST: A RESOURCE GUIDE FOR PARENTS OF YOUNG GIFTED CHILDREN. Minneapolis: Free Spirit, 1991.

The authors deal with recognizing giftedness in preschool children, although examples and anecdotes throughout extend the age level. This is very much a hands-on book, with lists, cartoons, and photos that lighten up the text. Each chapter concludes with suggested down-to-earth activities. The reading and source lists are wonderful. The section on music (within "Creativity Activities") is brief but accurate. Of special interest are "Making the Most of Your Home Computer" and "Choosing a Preschool."

BOOKS FOR YOU WITH YOUR CHILD

Aronoff, Frances. MOVE WITH THE MUSIC. Pittsburgh: Music Innovations, 1982. 800-677-8863.

An excellent collection of short folk songs with sample lessons on how to teach them. Meant for teachers, but also helpful for parents.

Bennett, Jill. NOISY POEMS. New York: Oxford University Press, 1994.

A picture book of twelve solidly noisy poems by James Reeves, David McCord, Elisabeth Coatsworth, and Jack Prelutsky will surely provoke a robust response. Excellent material for inspiring movement and original music.

Cohn, Amy L. FROM SEA TO SHINING SEA: A TREASURY OF AMERICAN FOLKLORE AND FOLK SONGS. New York: Scholastic, 1993.

This treasury of folk songs and stories covers the entire history of America from the time before the early settlers to the present. There are generous color illustrations and easy piano scores for the songs. A family browser.

Danes, Emma. THE USBOURNE FIRST BOOK OF MUSIC. London: Usbourne Publishing, 1993.

A colorful introduction to music for young children, with simple activities to encourage active involvement in all aspects of music from listening to sounds and making simple instruments to dancing, performing, and composing.

Drew, Helen. MY FIRST MUSIC BOOK. New York: Dorling Kindersley, 1992.

A colorful guide to making and playing simple musical instruments at home. Instructions on making simple shakers, a pencil xylophone, a noisy drum, and more. Easy-to-follow directions, clear step-by-step photographs throughout.

Dunn, Sonja. BUTTERSCOTCH DREAMS. Portsmouth, NH: Heinemann, 1987.

This collection of chants comes alive, given rhythmical reading. As texts for creating original songs, they are best presented to children four to ten years old.

Feierabend, John. MUSIC FOR LITTLE PEOPLE. New York: Boosey & Hawkes, 1989.

Feierabend, John. MUSIC FOR VERY LITTLE PEOPLE. New York: Boosey & Hawkes, 1986.

Both of these delightful books have word games, music scored for voice only, accompanying cassette tapes, and charmingly illustrated text describing motions for finger plays and other activities. Two to seven years old.

Fellner, Betty, et al. SOUND ALL AROUND. Philadelphia: The Philadelphia Orchestra Association, 1992. (1420 Locust St., Philadelphia, PA 19102. 215-893-1900).

This collective effort by a group of music educators and educational personnel of the Philadelpia Orchestra is an activity book dealing with many parameters of sound, including fast/slow, loud/soft, high/low. There are pictures to draw or color, sounds to explore, suggested listening, and activities called "Beyond the Page" that illustrate each concept.

Fox, Dan and Claude Marks. GO IN AND OUT THE WINDOW. New York: Henry Holt, 1987.

This collection of songs of childhood is varied in moods and ideas. Each song is illustrated with paintings from The Metropolitan Museum of Art collection. Piano accompaniments require an ability to play melodies with simple chords. Ideal for family sings and for showing the correlation between art and music.

Hausherr, Rosmarie. WHAT INSTRUMENT IS THIS? New York: Scholastic, 1992.

The great charm of this book is the photography (half in color, half in black-and-white). The color photographs are unique in showing small children of all races playing and reacting to instruments. The black-and-white photographs are shots from real life of varying instrumentalists such as folk singers, country fiddlers, and concert and rock performers. The text is minimal, each instrument being introduced by a question (What instrument looks like a shiny boa constrictor with a wide-open mouth?). The answer and brief overview is on the next page. This is a book to savor for its beauty and quality rather than for its informational content.

Hayes, Phyllis. MUSICAL INSTRUMENTS YOU CAN MAKE. New York: Franklin Watts, 1981.

An activity book with simple, effective ideas. For each item there is a recipe: what you need, and how to do it. A brief introduction to each "instrument" provides a perspective and some background information. Useful to parents with children four to six years old.

Hughes, Langston. THE SWEET AND SOUR ANIMAL BOOK. New York: Oxford University Press, 1994.

The publication of a lost manuscript by Hughes is an important event in American literature. With fanciful three-dimensional animals built especially for the book by young students from the Harlem School of the Arts, an introduction by Ben Vereen, and an afterword for older children and adults by Hughes scholar George Cunningham, this has potential to become a classic. Three and older.

Koch, Kenneth and Kate Farrell. TALKING TO THE SUN. New York: Henry Holt, 1985.

An illustrated anthology of poems selected for young people and illustrated with art treasures from The Metropolitan Museum of Art. Presents an opportunity to correlate art, music, and literature. This exquisite book makes a wonderful gift.

Krull, Kathleen. GONNA SING MY HEAD OFF. New York: Knopf, 1992.

Folk songs for children, collected from all regions of the United States, are beautifully illustrated by Allen Garns with an introduction by Arlo Guthrie. Piano accompaniments require ability to play melodies with simple chords.

Magadini, Peter. MUSIC WE CAN SEE AND HEAR. Oakville, Ontario, Canada: Frederic Harris, 1982.

Presents musical ideas that any adult can teach to a child. There is a series of lessons that includes instrument-making and composing, and encourages exploration of sounds and rhythms in a most imaginative manner.

Onassis, Jacqueline (ed.) *THE FIREBIRD* **AND OTHER RUSSIAN FAIRY TALES.** New York: Viking, 1978.

Lavishly illustrated by Boris Zvorykin, this collection of fairy tales, especially *The Firebird,* is an excellent catalyst for a project on Stravinsky's work of the same name. A work like this helps to make the connection between literature, music, and dance.

Parkinson, Marie G. MOMMY, CAN WE PRACTICE NOW? Athens, OH: Ability Development, 1981.

Practical games and suggestions for helping young children to practice, written by a parent helping her own children to practice using the Suzuki method. The games, charts, and activities are equally applicable to any parent-child team working to make practice a productive and enjoyable experience.

Schenk, Beatrice de Regniers et al. SING A SONG OF POPCORN. New York: Scholastic, 1988.

This collection of poems vibrates with diversity in its wide range of moods and subjects—for example, humor, spookiness, weather, animals, and people. They are perfect for inspiring musical responses. Nine of the world's best children's illustrators have each taken a chapter and brought it to life in vibrant color. An absolute treasure.

Williams, Sarah. ROUND AND ROUND THE GARDEN. New York: Oxford University Press, 1994.

Williams, Sarah. PUDDING AND PIE. New York: Oxford University Press, 1994.

Two collections of knee-bouncing rhymes, clapping songs, lullabies, and nursery rhymes with colorful illustrations and accompanying cassettes.

BOOKS FOR YOUR CHILD

Greves, Margaret. *THE MAGIC FLUTE:* **THE STORY OF MOZART'S OPERA.** New York: Henry Holt, 1989.

This picture-book account of Mozart's opera, stunningly illustrated by Francesca Crespi, is intended for the very young. The simple retelling of the story and the jewel-like illustrations bring this great work to life.

Kuskin, Karla. THE PHILHARMONIC GETS DRESSED. New York: Harper & Row, 1982.

A delightful and unusual view of orchestra members preparing for performance. The illustrations and simple text follow various musicians from their homes to the concert hall. This is a picture book the entire family will enjoy.

Martin, Bill, Jr. THE MAESTRO PLAYS. New York: Henry Holt, 1994.

This picture book for preschoolers combines the writing virtuosity and humor of Martin with the brilliant illustrations of Vladimir Radunsky. The text is an invitation for the child to play with and move to the pulsating, adverb-rich words. Who can resist this "Maestro" and his merry musicians?

Rachlin, Ann and Susan Hellard. FAMOUS CHILDREN: BACH. HANDEL. HAYDN. MOZART. London: Victor Gollancz, 1992.

Delightful personal biographies of Bach, Handel, Haydn, and Mozart, each a separate volume, relate incidents from the childhood of these composers. Well illustrated. Younger children will enjoy hearing the stories. At a comfortable reading level for elementary school children.

Rubin, Mark and Alan Daniel. THE ORCHESTRA. Buffalo: Firefly Books, 1992.

This picture book is an illustrated introduction to music and to the orchestra. In simple language, the families of instruments are described and charmingly illustrated.

Storr, Catherine and Dianne Jackson. *HANSEL AND GRETEL. THE NUTCRACKER. PETER AND THE WOLF. SWAN LAKE.* London: Faber Music, 1991.

These beautifully illustrated books give a simple synopsis of each work. For parents who play the piano, there are short musical excerpts of major themes to help acquaint the child with the score. Even without the music, the books are an appealing introduction to these classic works.

Willard, Nancy. *THE SORCERER'S APPRENTICE.* New York: Scholastic, 1993.

This cautionary tale, about a powerful sorcerer and the servant who misuses his master's magic, was popularized in the late 1700s. Paul Dukas based an orchestral work on the tale. Walt Disney later used it in *Fantasia*. Poet Nancy Willard adds her own magic to the retelling, aided by the beautiful illustrations of Leo and Diane Dillon.

Willson, Robina. MOZART'S STORY. London: A & C Black, 1991.

This short biography is written in a pleasant, intimate style. There are attractive color drawings and reproductions of paintings of the period, including portraits of Mozart.

VIDEOS

DALCROZE EURHYTHMICS WITH ROBERT ABRAMSON. GIA Productions, 7404 S. Mason Avenue, Chicago, IL 60638. 708-496-3800.

This is a vivid glimpse into the world of Dalcroze eurhythmics as taught to a group of adults by master teacher Robert Abramson. For parents and teachers.

EARLY MUSIC EDUCATION WITH SUZUKI. Films for the Humanities. 800-257-5126.

The film follows a three-year-old boy and his mother as they begin Suzuki training in violin, and shows classes, lessons, scenes at home (with sibling interruptions), and a festival at which Suzuki himself interacts with a group of over a hundred Suzuki violin students.

THE SNOWMAN. Raymond Briggs. SVS: Snowman Enterprises. Available from educational retailers.

An Academy Award nominee, this delightful animation weaves a spell of magic as a young boy's snowman comes to life and escorts him on a fantasy dream visit to the North Pole. There is very little narrative, allowing the captivating music and beautifully drawn images to create a calm enchantment.

TUBBY THE TUBA. Paul Tripp and George Kleinsinger. Live Entertainment. Van Nuys, CA. Available from educational retailers.

The enchanting tale of the winsome little tuba who tires of only being able to sing "oompah," *Tubby the Tuba* is a delightful musical fantasy. In the process of searching for his own identity and voice, he encounters the instruments of the orchestra. The animation is graced by the voices of Dick Van Dyke, Pearl Bailey, Cyril Ritchard, and other notables.

CD-ROMs

Call the telephone number of each company to ask for a catalog. Check system requirements before ordering. Ask for a try-before-you-buy arrangement.

MUSICAL INSTRUMENTS. Microsoft Home. 800-426-9400

This provides wonderful access to information about more than 200 instruments. There are four ways to navigate: "Families of instruments," "A–Z of instruments," "Instruments of the world," "Musical ensembles." You can see how the instruments work, hear musical examples, and "play" limited pitches on each instrument. There is reference to jazz, rock, classical, and other ensembles. For Macintosh and Windows.

THE MUSICAL WORLD OF PROFESSOR PICCOLO: THE FUN WAY TO LEARN ALL ABOUT MUSIC. Opcode Systems. 415-856-3333

Includes reading music, fun musical games, music history, music notation, and musical instruments data. It is a self-paced interactive course in music theory and musical styles, with excellent graphics. Good for some four- and five-year-olds, but best for elementary school age. Macintosh and Windows.

SILLY NOISY HOUSE. The Voyager Company. 800-446-2001

Almost every object sounds off with sound effects, tongue twisters, rhymes, and songs. A good introduction to the computer and to "sound play" for the preschool set. Macintosh.

The Child from Six to Nine

What you will find in this chapter

- A traditional time to begin
- Begin in summer
- Lessons may help a shy child
- The six-year-old who is not a beginner
    Music and movement. Preschool study on an instrument.
- Learning to read
- Early burnout
- Opening up
- Learning to practice
    Practice conditions. Make a schedule.
    Your role during the practice time. Practice problems.
- Music technology as a new dimension
- The right teacher
- Guiding discovery
- Your child's personal learning style
- Patience
- Discipline
- What parents can do
- Three points of view
- Highlights
- Chapter resources

THE YEARS from age six to nine are often the time during which parents enroll children in music study. The child now has some sense of independence, is ready to accept others beyond parents and family as authority figures, has a longer concentration span, knows numbers and letters, and has had some reading experience.

The child from six to nine
- likes to talk.
- is eager to learn.
- is literal about rules and procedures.
- is beginning to be sensitive to others.
- has not yet attained complete bone growth.
- may have difficulty in focusing on small print.
- has more control over large muscles than small.
- is beginning to choose friends and enjoy team activities.
- is acquiring a group role (such as leader, loner, cooperator).
- is very active, loves noise and excitement, but still needs rest.

A traditional time to begin

When your child enters the first grade, he must adjust to a more formal school situation, even though he may have spent several years in day care or nursery school. This adjustment usually means a longer school day, more time spent sitting quietly for instruction, homework, and a more organized home schedule. Your child may now be spending the entire day away from home, and may find that demands of school life must be taken more seriously.

For some children, starting music lessons when entering first grade may be difficult, especially if the child is highly active, does not deal easily with longer separation from home, cannot cope with fulfilling expectations of several authority figures, or has language or reading problems. To this child, music lessons may seem to steal from the dwindling amount of playtime resulting from a full school day.

Begin in summer

Consider having your child begin music study in summer, before she must adjust to a new school day. Time for music lessons and practice will be easier to find in the summer. A routine to deal with these commitments can be established prior to the onset of coping with the schedule your child will face in the fall. Music teachers often offer special summer activities, such as introductory sessions and supervised practice, that are not always included in the September–June instruction cycle. The teacher's schedule, too, is often more flexible during the summer, and getting a head start in a teacher's studio may ease the way into the fall schedule for both you and the teacher.

Neighborhood and community schools, churches, temples, and recreation centers may also offer special summer sessions for beginners. This is often a good way to "break the ice." The activities are apt to be group oriented, and your child begins music study with a sense of community. Many times these classes and programs include field trips, some game playing, and a general sense of exploration. If your child is not sure whether music lessons are really what he wants, this may be the way to test the waters. If you are uncertain about which instrument is right for your child, look for a class or program that might use a variety of instruments. There your child will have a chance to sample several instruments, and may discover a personal preference for playing a certain type of instrument. Often, schools and centers also will have summer concerts during which your child may hear others performing on different instruments. Hearing other children perform has a further advantage. It shows your child what is possible, and is more believable because other children (not a teacher) are making music.

Lessons may help a shy child

It is possible, however, that your child may enjoy beginning music study at the same time as entering first grade because the lesson provides attention that your child misses in the school environment. A child may feel lost in the bigger group, especially if day care or nursery school provided the child with a small peer group. If the music lesson puts your child in contact with a supportive teacher who sees your child as an individual, this relationship offsets the "loss of self" felt in the class atmosphere. The lesson becomes a just-for-me event. It eases anxiety and reinforces self-worth.

The six-year-old who is not a beginner

Music lessons may not be new to a six-year-old. A child who began music study as a preschooler has some advantages over one who begins

The child is now a learner among as many as thirty-five. No longer is [he] alone and under the care of a parent who is thrilled and eager to entertain any whimsical curiosity that might be displayed.
—*Raymond Wlodkowski and Judith Jaynes*

grade school and music lessons simultaneously. Exposure to music at a time when sensory information is alertly received and processed is a valuable head start. Some properties of musical sound (such as high/low, fast/slow, loud/soft) have become part of the child's experience and vocabulary. Even if only in a very general way, music literacy has begun.

Music and movement

If your child was in a music and movement class (such as Dalcroze, Orff, or Kindermusik®), he learned to combine listening with singing and coordinated movement, and knows, to some degree, that symbols can represent sounds. Playing a particular instrument is not the main goal of these methods, although various percussion, wind, and keyboard instruments are played in order to explore how music is made. At-home practicing did not play a crucial role in your child's success or advancement, even though home activities were encouraged.

Your child equated music with group activity. Both children and parents participated jointly, and activities were quite varied. A change to individual lessons, even if your child desires it and is ready for this transition, is a shift to an instructional mode that places more direct attention on your child. What she may miss most is the energy release provided by the movement activities because tasks within the lesson are less varied in the sense that they do not often allow for alternation between whole-body action and small-gesture control. Focusing on playing an instrument requires more centered attention on acquiring physical habits.

With this acquired concentration come new expectations (both on your part and the part of the teacher) related to practice. Your child discovers that he is asked to do specific assignments, and that progress will not be made until at-home tasks are mastered. However, your child may not yet be ready to take on independent study. School homework, also a new task, rarely takes more than ten to fifteen minutes at this stage; music practice may require double that. You must expect to support your child's efforts in this regard with guidance and encouragement. This is not the time to say, "Learn to do it by yourself."

Playing a particular instrument also requires attention to technique. The idea, as well as the reality, of acquiring a technique to play an instrument is something that your child must accept. This doesn't happen automatically, and may even be resisted. Your child can't yet think in terms of long-range goals, and she may be unaccustomed to sticking to a task, once it has ceased being fun. Let her see *you* in the process of

It is difficult to imagine teaching young children about music without using movement as an instructional tool. Music is movement.
—Dorothy McDonald and Gene Simons

acquiring a new skill, so that she can draw parallels to her own practice sessions.

While techniques vary according to the instrument, you should know some basic aspects of technique, and what it takes to attain them.

Some basic techniques

- Posture of the entire body
- Positions of shoulders, arms, and hands
- Position and/or flexible use of the wrist
- Finger and knuckle shape and firmness
- Finger/breathing drills related to producing tone
- Gestures that make louder and softer sounds
- Gestures that make longer and shorter sounds

Some basic means to acquire technique

- Think about posture when beginning to play.
- Check on posture while continuing to play.
- Learn the feel of natural relaxation and effort.
- Look at shoulder, arm, hand, and finger positions.
- Listen for differences in tone production.
- Repeated practice of short, specific drills.
- Learn to relax completely between short tasks.

Acquiring a technique can take a lifetime, but beginnings are very important. If initial physical habits are incorrect, advancement will be problematic—changing a habit is more difficult and time consuming than acquiring a habit in the first place. It is also possible that, because of bad physical habits, injury and pain could result somewhere down the line. Don't fool yourself into thinking that careful attention to basic technique at the beginning of music study is a waste of time or something that only the teacher cares about, or that your child can acquire and perfect technique at a later time.

Preschool study on an instrument

If your child had Suzuki or preschool lessons on a specific instrument, he may face different challenges during these years. He has learned to relate qualities like high/low and loud/soft to how these are produced on the instrument. This kind of instruction usually relies on rote learning. The teacher demonstrates; the child observes, listens, and imitates, with the teacher guiding this process minutely and precisely. Your child enjoyed this and has come to expect that instruction takes place that way. To a degree, it is a system that is ideal for music study because attention to sound (rather than to visual data) is the hallmark of music-making. The rote, or imitation, model has been a mainstay of music training in all cultures and across many centuries for that reason.

Learning to read

At this age, however, the child must learn to read music, a skill necessary for independent learning. The child goes through a similar stage in language development—speech must be translated into the written word. In somewhat the same manner, musical sounds must be equated with visual symbols. Learning to play music and learning to read music are separate skills. For some children, there may be resistance to making the transition from learning by imitation to learning to read. A quality Suzuki program will ease the transition, but the challenge involved in doing so may arise at this age. The point is noted here only because it underscores the matter under discussion—a child who begins instrumental music study as a preschooler goes through such a transitional phase.

Early burnout

Some primary children who have been playing an instrument for several years experience a kind of burnout. For the seven-year-old who has been playing since the age of three, lessons may have become predictable, especially if there is little variety in the lesson activities or in the pieces themselves. This child experiences now what more often challenges the older child—the stakes are higher and the payoff less appealing. Some aspects of the lesson may need to change in order to refuel an interest in music study. While this situation is sometimes "cured" by changing teachers, that may not be the real, or the best, solution. Both you and the teacher need to get at the root of the problem before deciding what to do. Surface readings of what your child says or does may not uncover the reality.

If your child insists, "I hate practicing!" he may be stating the truth. But it is also possible that what he actually "hates" is the music assigned, the fact that practicing interferes with playing on the soccer team, or that his big sister is always held up as a perfect model. In most cases, your child is unaware of these underlying causes, so you must help him sort out actual feelings from ready-made arguments and assumptions.

A child may mask other feelings with a façade of boredom when outside pressure and premature expectations are placed on him by parent or teacher.

—Mildred Portney Chase

Questions that can help sort out feelings
- "Would you play your favorite piece for me?"
- "What do you like most about your music teacher?"
- "Would you like me to sit near you while you practice?"
- "What if you took lessons on a different day than Jill?"
- "Have you ever thought about playing the guitar?"

Opening up

Questions like these serve a single purpose—they open up conversation that may, in fact, lead to something else. Your child may dislike the music she's playing, but doesn't mention this because she feels she has no options. By asking to hear a favorite piece, you may uncover that she likes none of her pieces, or really does enjoy a certain kind of music. Although matters pertaining to choice of pieces will need to be referred to the teacher, your child knows that you are trying to see her side and that you would help her discuss this with the teacher.

By asking a somewhat oblique question about the teacher, you let your child know that it is all right to discuss the teacher and the dynamics of what goes on in the lesson. Especially if you do not sit in on the lesson, you may be unaware that the teacher is too demanding (or not demanding enough) or that the teacher may be sarcastic or threatening. Keep in mind that what your child reports is how it looks through his eyes, not necessarily how it is. Until such feelings are brought into the open, however, no one knows that there are mixed signals.

Similar points could be made with other questions. It is what they lead to that may matter most. The suggested questions contain no magic. You may come up with questions more suitable to your situation. When your child responds to questions of this kind, he begins to learn that his opinions and feelings matter, and that he has the power to take a more active role in things that affect him. He also discovers that individual opinions and feelings must be considered in relation to other factors. Good questions are powerful. Too often, parents (and teachers) *assume* they know what is going on in a child's mind. Asking a good question—and truly listening to the answer—may be revealing, sometimes even reassuring. You may find that your child is more perceptive than you imagined!

Reflective listening, whereby you reflect back to the child the feelings he seems to you to be expressing, can often be a useful approach. . . . In the gently encouraging atmosphere created, underlying problems may gradually surface.

—Richard Landsdown and Marjorie Walker

Learning to practice

One of the big misconceptions among parents (and even some teachers) is that students will automatically know how to practice. Practice is actually independent study, a skill that evolves gradually. Public school education takes this into account. Students in the first and second grade usually get short, specific assignments. Progressively they are given more challenging unsupervised tasks until, by the fifth or sixth grade, students may be assigned more lengthy drill work, research projects, and independent reading. In the best of schools, independent study assignments are outlined and guided.

Children from six to nine years old who are in the first years of music study need the same careful guidance. At first, practice instructions must be specific. Expectations increase gradually, and practice skills are constantly expanded and perfected throughout the course of a student's musical life. This training is the province of the teacher, but parents who are realistic about the ever-growing nature of this skill will be more supportive if they remember that excellent practice skills are not acquired in a year or two.

Practice conditions

It is your responsibility to create and ensure proper practice conditions in the home. Ideally, the practice space should be a quiet spot as far away from the television as possible. In the case of piano practice, this can be a problem, since pianos are often in the most family-active room. If there is a choice, the practice space should have a door that can be closed during practice time to aid privacy and concentration. You provide further help by screening phone calls and keeping siblings and pets under control during practice time. "Do not disturb" should be the order of the day.

Your child may need you to guide what to do during practice. Encourage your child to help decide in what order to follow the assignment, whether he has covered all parts of it, and whether he has made sufficient progress each day. Checking off each part of the assignment in a notebook is a graphic way of keeping track.

Making a colorful practice chart is helpful to you and fun for your child. For instance, if the assignment is to play part of a piece five times slowly and softly, five times powerfully, and five times with firm fingers, these instructions go on the chart and are checked off when finished. Marking the completion of each task gives a true sense of accomplishment and helps organize practice sessions. If your child likes stickers, use these as tasks are fulfilled.

Make a schedule

At any age, music students will admit that the hardest part of practicing is getting started. Once the momentum is going, practice can be a source of tremendous gratification. Effective scheduling sets practice at the same time each weekday. On weekends, practice in the early part of the day ensures that it gets done. You can help your child make a realistic schedule, having it reflect the pattern of family life.

If your child finds it hard to organize time, help her make a color chart of a typical week. Along the left margin of a white sheet of paper,

Children, especially those who are not reflective by nature, may need lots of reminders from adults to stop and think, to contemplate the possible consequences of a decision or an action and to plan successful strategies.
—Richard Landsdown and Marjorie Walker

A practice schedule can become self-regulating. . . . This may sound too easy to be true, but giving children a choice and expecting them to live up to this choice works remarkably well.

—*Dorothy Rich*

list the time vertically in 15-minute segments. List the days horizontally, along the top. Color in the events of your week, for example:

Blue   When you get up, eat, go to school, return, and go to bed.
Green   Your school time.
Orange   Your after-school activities.
Purple   Your music lesson and practice times.
Red   Your *free* time.
Black   Your television time.

Color in this chart as you go through the week, experimenting with different times for practice until you and your child find the best time (when he is most alert and productive). Know that weekends are different and plan accordingly.

It is useful for your child to see that there really *is* free time, that he has more time than imagined, and that (with planning) he can be productive. If you wish, reward effort by giving a gift of music, perhaps a cassette, a CD, or some sheet music. One of the most appreciated gifts is the gift of time. When a certain number of weeks of effective practice has taken place, that effort might be rewarded with a "special day" (quality time shared doing a favorite activity with the child).

Your role during the practice time

Your child may need your companionship as much as your specific help. Practice can be lonely. Your presence in the room (you might read or listen quietly) may be all the assistance your child needs. You must assess your child's ability to study independently. Active guidance may be absolutely necessary in the beginning; but the ultimate goal of effective practice is that your child listens so well that judgment about what is satisfactory comes not from you, but from her. Use a tape recorder, a video recorder, or perhaps a digital keyboard with recording capability to help your child gain perspective in listening to her own performance. Make a recording at the beginning and end of a week's practice (every day is too often). Your role in guiding practice during these years is to help your child develop good listening habits without making her feel that the real judgment is being made by your appraising ears. You can speed this self-evaluation by asking your child a number of questions during a practice session, or when listening to a recorded performance.

*Questions to help your child
listen and think while practicing*

- "Did you count? Was your counting steady?"
- "Did you play all the right notes?"
- "Did you check your fingering?"
- "Did you bring out the loud/soft qualities?"
- "Did you capture the mood of the piece?"
- "Did you play without stops and starts?"

These are sample questions. Some pieces and exercises will require different questions, just as some questions may lead to others. For example, you might follow up with questions such as "How do you know the notes were correct?" or "Can you tell why you stopped in the places that you did?" The important point is that questions like these help because they are specific. They direct your child's attention to just one item at a time, or challenge her to improve a single skill. These are reasonable goals for a child at this age. Although many skills must eventually merge in order to play pieces satisfactorily, a young child is usually unable to keep several things in mind simultaneously, especially if the skills or concepts are new. Avoid questions that are too general.

Questions to avoid

- "How did you feel about that performance?"
  (The answer could be anything.)
- "Do you think that was good?"
  (What was good?)
- "Would you like to play that again?"
  (Why should I play it again?)
- "Are you really listening to what you play?"
  (What does really listening mean?)
- "Why aren't you concentrating?"
  (What does concentrating mean?)

Encourage your child by letting him know that you are listening, not as a critic, but as someone who appreciates his effort. Support your child's own effort to evaluate what he does. Help your child to evaluate himself by directing his attention with remarks such as, "Do you think you are playing as smoothly as you can?" or "I'm going to be very still so that I can enjoy hearing you play softly." or "How careful you must be in order to make each staccato note really short." Encourage your child to end the practice session by performing something that he does

Evaluative praise is often experienced as a threat. It brings discomfort, not delight; fear, not joy. Children resent the intent and defy the manipulation.—Haim Ginott

well, however short or "old" the example might be. Successful performing is the best reminder that making music is enjoyable, and that he is making progress. Praise effort, even if you can't always praise results. "That was a well-organized session!" or "I noticed that you were really concentrating." The book by Bigler and Lloyd-Watts, *More Than Music,* offers parents many helpful suggestions on how to guide practice.

A good teacher will suggest practice procedures with you and help you become an effective partner in guiding your child's practice. In a notebook, the teacher probably lists specific tasks and steps to achieve the next week's goals. That is a starting point from which you can help your child make daily goals.

Students at beginning levels need to know that there are many layers of learning involved when working on a piece. The teacher is likely to focus on these separate layers during the lesson by calling attention to:

- tapping, swinging, or saying rhythms alone.
- conducting or singing.
- doing fingering on a table or in the air.
- naming notes, intervals, chords, or patterns.
- becoming aware of loud/soft levels.
- becoming aware of short/long/longer sounds.
- gaining comfort, grace, and skill at the instrument.
- creating expressive moods.

If you are present at the lesson, you learn from the teacher how to work on individual skills. Teachers vary in the types of practice advice they suggest, but there are some common expectations of students at this age. It may help you to know these.

> ### Some common expectations
> Should be secure in 1 week: notes, rhythm, and fingering
> Should be secure in 2 weeks: motions, touches, and dynamics
> Should be secure in 3 to 6 weeks: memory
> If these goals are unrealistic, the piece is too hard.

Practice problems

No matter how creative and active you are in participating in your child's practice, problems may arise. The most colorful schedule may be ignored. Lessons that were so exciting in the beginning become a chore instead. It is more fun, and easier, to watch TV. As a parent, you don't want to engage in a battle over music lessons. What do you do?

For one thing, speak to the teacher about this situation. Do so in private, not within your child's hearing. You may sometimes observe the downward curve in enthusiasm or effort before the teacher does. The teacher will appreciate any clues you offer. Perhaps the teacher is going too fast; your child needs to reinforce old concepts and firm up skills before moving ahead. Your child may need a shorter assignment for a while, or different material. The converse may be true; your child may need something more challenging and be allowed to move at a faster pace. There may be growth or situational stresses that show themselves in all, or other, areas of your child's life, not just in practice. Family or school crises, as well as normal developmental shifts, may be reflected in the practice pattern.

If, after talking with the teacher, a curricular adjustment is made and you *still* encounter resistance, you may have to struggle with when to insist, when to encourage, and when to step back.

Parents and teachers have a responsibility to contact each other when help is needed in the domain of learning. This works best when the attitude is one of gumption, the feeling is one of trust, and the action taken is one of cooperation.
—Raymond Wlodkowski and Judith Jaynes

Some strategies of last resort

- Agree on a magic word (perhaps "abracadabra"). If your child hasn't practiced by an agreed-upon time, just say the magic word. It is a reminder, with the nagging edge removed.
- Decide on a special privilege (a movie, a special time together, a dinner of the child's favorite foods) that he can earn for practicing OMO (on my own), without needing to be reminded. Negotiate how long OMO practice must continue. If your child sees it through, provide a great treat!

At its best, practice is a creative endeavor. You will learn about practicing as your child does. No one can be offered, up front, all the secrets, tricks, and devices that most musicians acquire only after years of experience—through trial and error and perseverance. One thing, however, is certain and vital. Your active, imaginative, and supportive participation in these formative years will provide your child not only with reinforcement along the way, but also with a model of how to go about personal problem solving—thus, empowering your child to face life with self-assurance!

Music technology as a new dimension

Using many forms of technology is becoming increasingly important for the child who studies music. Most children at this age level are familiar with computer learning in school. Adding technology to the home is a powerful step toward enriching and accelerating learning, and it is a step that is becoming increasingly easier to take.

The child who has access to a digital keyboard or sequencer at a young age can begin to think of sound in new ways. The ear is opened to a variety of timbres with which to experiment. These include the sounds of many existing instruments as well as sounds that have been sampled from the environment. Children who manipulate this rich array of sounds during their early years become as creative with sound as they are with crayons and paints or words and storytelling. We know of children ages four through seven years old who comfortably turn on a digital keyboard, create and record original sounds, and fashion layers of intriguing design with ease and great pleasure.

There is also an increasing number of CD-ROMs that can help young children explore extended realms of sound. The potential for new ways of learning is further enhanced by using videotape. If children observe themselves as they practice and perform, such feedback encourages them to think visually as well as aurally.

In a 1994 technology survey conducted by the Music Teachers National Association, over 400 teachers who use technology in their teaching commented on the positive benefits:

- "Students have more creative practice techniques because of tapes we make with the computer."
- "Exciting for teacher and students, especially in composition. Theory is more fun."
- "Students think about pieces in more in-depth manner, both from the creative and theoretical points of view."
- "Technology has given incentive to students who might otherwise have quit. Competes favorably with other student activities."

Finding a teacher who uses technology may not be easy, but the trend continues to grow. If you think that your child would benefit from this kind of training, check with the Music Educators National Conference, the Music Teachers National Association, and the Association for Technology in Music Instruction. (See the directory of sources in chapter six for contact information.) Ask for a list of music teachers in your area who use technology.

The right teacher

What kind of teacher works best with children between ages six and nine? These are some characteristics.

> ### *The primary teaching specialist*
> - likes working with the highly active child.
> - adjusts to serve individual learning styles.
> - is friendly and encouraging, yet not casual or lenient.
> - is calm and accepting, yet keeps the learning situation active.
> - knows how to direct physical energies rather than curtail them.
> - knows the child's physical limitations during this growth period.
> - knows how to stimulate exploration and guide creative activities.

Many teachers, especially those who teach piano, have a large number of students who are six to nine years old, making it seem as if these teachers are uniquely qualified to teach students at this age level just from sheer experience alone. While there is no doubt that experience is a factor in deciding who is an excellent primary teacher, it is not the sole factor. Some teachers have reputations as being successful or the best in the neighborhood. Word of mouth is useful, but can be misleading if satisfied parents and students are attracted by a teacher's cheerfulness or easygoing manner rather than by what kind of performing and learning the teacher stimulates and guides.

Because the child at this age is still very active, the teacher must be able to live comfortably with a good bit of noise and high spirits. A six-year-old can certainly be constrained to remain quietly controlled for extended periods, but it is better to direct a child's energies to productive ends than to curtail movement by coercion. A controlled child fidgets physically and wanders off mentally. The teacher's ability to channel energies to effective outcomes is one of the hallmarks of the good primary teacher.

Guiding discovery

An effective primary teacher stimulates the child to explore, choose, invent, and initiate. This is the surest way to foster the growth of self-reliance and self-esteem. At this age, your child is still an explorer. Her

The key to planning experiences for young children is to make available a wide variety of mind-engaging experiences and allow the child some freedom in following her own internal promptings.

—Jane Healy

exploring is not as physical as when she was a preschooler, but she continues to "test the waters." While not giving up hands-on exploration of how things work, she begins to reflect on what is experienced—why another child (or adult) acts in certain ways, why obeying rules makes things smoother, why preparing for an event (whether picnics or tests) leads to good results.

The teacher whose principal concern is to impart information and generate activities that lead to "products"—such as naming all the notes on the staff, practicing scales, or playing in a recital—is the teacher likely to shortchange a child at this age by placing greater emphasis (and, therefore, value) on conformity rather than discovery. It is often during these years that a child's capacity to imagine and create is sidetracked, if not derailed, by undue attention to learning facts and playing pieces.

Your child's personal learning style

At this age, your child is just beginning to sort out a personal learning style. He begins to sense the ways that learning takes place and becomes aware of which feels best for him. You also detect facets of your child's learning style at this time. Is yours an intuitive child, one who reaches ends quickly and is impatient if asked to examine means to those ends? Does your child mull things over, cautiously searching for the safe route? Is yours an ebullient child, one who responds with initial enthusiasm, but lacks staying power? Do you have a probing child who is never content until all possibilities have been tested? Are you raising a determined child, one who is not satisfied until all the puzzle pieces are in place?

Because a child's personality may evolve in so many different ways, and in view of the fact that "the way" for your child is not yet clear at this time, allowances must be made—by you and the teacher—for the cultivation of individual styles of learning and exploration.

The effective primary teacher is able to say the same thing in many ways, to present the same concept in numerous guises, and to guide the same drill from diverse starting points. A teacher who uses the same method for each student, whose students always play the same pieces, or whose teaching style never varies may block the evolution of an individual at any level. But especially in these years, when your child is searching for how to succeed as a learner, it is vital that he know there are options and acceptable differences.

A few words are in order concerning two traits that parents often

The teacher listens even to the unspoken word of the student, learning how best to share knowledge in a way to fit the student's individual nature.

—Mildred Portney Chase

rank as desirable teacher attributes—patience and discipline. The first is overrated; the second is misunderstood.

Patience

Patience often has passive connotations. A good teacher is never an outstandingly patient person, if by "patience," one means leniency. A teacher must remain calm and tolerant of your child's capacity to succeed at each moment, but this does not mean ready acceptance of things as they are. There should always be a quality of intensity to the teacher-student relationship so that the student remains alert, not out of fear or confusion, but as someone who acts responsibly. Too many things are casual these days. Learning should not be one of them.

Discipline

The misunderstanding regarding discipline is epidemic. Parents often state that they want a no-nonsense teacher, one who is strict and firm. This implies that discipline can be "applied," and that the teacher is expected to do the job. No teacher wants to control by coercion. Discipline that is not self-discipline is resented (even by the young) and rejected (out of rebellion or relief) when the discipliner is absent.

As a parent, you expect the teacher to lead your child to value self-discipline, to suggest means to develop it, and to encourage growth in that direction. This is also your job, however, so helping your child gain self-discipline as part of music study must take place in the home as well as in the studio. Parents are often frustrated over how to go about this.

First of all, how to promote self-discipline as part of practice is something that a good music teacher will communicate to you. If the teacher doesn't, or if what to do and say at home is not clear to you, ask him for suggestions. "How can I help Nikki use her practice time wisely?" "What should I say if I see Jon is not listening to what he's doing?" "Should I be more insistent, or is this the time to step back a little and give Cheryl some space to try things on her own?"

A teacher will usually welcome such discussion. The conversation, however, should not take place in front of your child, nor should you expect the teacher to deal with this issue during someone else's lesson time. Ask when to phone, or set up an appointment. If a teacher is unwilling to work with you along these lines, or if the advice goes against your policies (the teacher may advocate punishment or deprivation, for instance), this may be the time to consider changing teachers.

Teaching children to be responsible involves finding ways to help children feel competent, to know what's right and to do what's right. If children need to wake up on time, you show them how to use an alarm clock and expect them to use it.

—Dorothy Rich

Keep in mind that self-discipline and working alone are traits that take time to emerge. Your child can reach these goals only gradually and needs your support in order to do so. Children vary widely in how quickly they respond or in which guise they are likely to accept direction. This is where you test your own insights about your child's learning style, or come to grips with your own need for patience and sensitivity.

What parents can do

Although much of what this chapter contains refers to formal music study and your role in that process, there are many informal ways that you can stimulate interest in music or foster respect for listening to and thinking about music. Keep in mind that activities in which you and your child are involved together cement and expand your child's affection for music in its many forms, styles, and sounds.

Family listening time. Arrange a family listening time, with each person choosing his favorite music. Relax and enjoy what each family member selects.

Family music time. Create a family music time during which family members play for each other or together and combine their assorted skills in playing, singing, or dancing. The type of music may vary, depending on family interests, the season, the current mood, and the like.

Outings. Plan a special outing to a ballet, concert, folk music festival, or a local production of a musical.

  Resources. Use a resource like Barlow's *Happy Listening Guide* to give focus to a listening experience.

Storytelling. Read a music story to, or with, your child. This may be a story about composers or a classic music story (such as *The Magic Flute* or *Hansel and Gretel*).

Videos. Enjoy a video together. *Beethoven Lives Upstairs* or *Tubby the Tuba* are good examples.

Game playing. Join your child in playing a music game. (See "General Resources" for leads and suggestions.)

Software. If you have a home computer, explore some of the software suggested in "General Resources."

Revive old skills. Revive your own music skills. You may even decide to take lessons yourself!

Three points of view

In each learning situation your child, your child's teacher, and you have unique frames of reference. The points of view that follow may not reflect each child, parent, or teacher with dead-on accuracy, but reviewing them may help you formulate your own attitudes and opinions.

> ### Your child's point of view
> - "I like to do something, not just listen to the teacher talk."
> - "Rhythm is fun, especially when it's fast and loud."
> - "I like to fool around and explore."
> - "I'd like to be helped with my practice."
> - "It's nice to play for others; my parents and teacher like it."
> - "I get mixed up if the teacher says one thing and Mom says another."
> - "I like pieces I can play almost right away, without too much practice."

> ### Your point of view
> - "I'd like my child to have every opportunity; music is just one of these."
> - "I hope that my child will enjoy music-making, perhaps for a lifetime."
> - "I don't know much about music. How can I help my child?"
> - "I hope that practicing will not become 'an issue.'"
> - "I hope music gives my child poise, discipline, and an antidote to TV."
> - "I'm proud when my child plays for others, especially music that I like."
> - "Long- and short-term goals of music study are somewhat vague to me."

The teacher's point of view

- "Studying music should be enjoyable, but not necessarily fun."
- "Many things contribute to music learning; playing pieces is just one."
- "Practice must be consistent and focused in order to make progress."
- "Listening to music, talking about it, and going to concerts are important."
- "Music is worthy in itself. Learning poise and discipline is an adjunct."
- "Performing is a means of sharing, but it is also a learning experience."
- "Learning will take time and effort; there are long-term goals."

Compare these views. There are similarities, but also differences.

Each person wants music study to be pleasurable.

- Your child enjoys playing, responding to rhythms, and exploring new sound effects.
- You hope your child will be successful and happy making music.
- The teacher hopes that the excitement and beauty of music will be enjoyed.

Each person has concerns about practice.

- Your child is looking for direction, support, and encouragement.
- You are unsure of your role regarding practice. You hope it will not become a problem.
- The teacher expects practice, knowing that not much will be gained without it.

Each person has opinions about playing in public.

- Your child enjoys the applause and attention, and sees this as a way of pleasing you.
- You want others to see how well your child is doing, even if the results are not perfect.
- The teacher regards performance as important and as an expression of learning.

Each person has an attitude about "pieces."

- Your child enjoys making sound. What she plays is often of less consequence to her.
- If your child plays familiar pieces, you take that as an indication of success.
- The teacher values playing pieces as only one of your child's important experiences.

Each person reacts differently to extramusical benefits.

- Your child is not looking for anything beyond learning to play.
- You may regard music study as a means to help your child acquire other good habits.
- The teacher values the study of music per se. Any resulting benefits are good, but auxiliary.

Each person has a different concept regarding goals.

- Your child cannot think and plan much beyond the immediate.
- You recognize long-term goals of music study, but in your mind these are quite general.
- The teacher knows what's ahead and has sights set on future, as well as present, goals.

It is not necessary, or even possible, to change differing viewpoints so that there is agreement. What matters is that, as a parent, you are aware of these differences and do what you can to smooth out problems if they arise. (They may not arise.) Your child is not capable of seeing a broad picture, but can be helped to stretch a little in order to learn that others may see things differently. The teacher, while certainly aware of different points of view, is the person with the clearest ideas about your child's musical development and will naturally resist attitudes or behaviors that are contrary to musical refinement. That puts you in the middle. Perhaps just realizing what differences may exist in the child-parent-teacher triangle will help you keep the balance, if and when the going gets a little rocky.

A thumbnail summary of the chapter may help you fix the highlights in your mind. Use what makes sense in your situation. You may have questions or concerns that were not addressed in this chapter. Reference to other chapters or additional reading sources may supply what you seek. There are no quick and ready answers for everything, and it is often in the process of searching that we learn to refine, and perhaps even change, the original question.

HIGHLIGHTS

☆ These are traditional years for beginning music study.

☆ If your child is beginning music study now:

Be aware that starting first grade and music lessons at the same time might be difficult.

Consider options such as beginning in summer or with group-oriented activities.

It is also possible that your child may need the special attention a music lesson offers.

There are ways to help your child select which instrument to play.

☆ If your child is continuing music study begun earlier:

Music and movement classes provided a broad focus and a variety of activities.

Your child must acquire some basic playing techniques and practice habits.

Instruction on a specific instrument may have placed great reliance on rote learning.

Your child must make a transition from rote learning to learning to read music.

☆ If your child suffers from early burnout:

Lessons and practice may have become predictable or overly challenging.

Your child may dislike or resent only certain aspects of music instruction.

You need to sort out what is the true cause of your child's boredom or discomfort.

It is helpful to ask questions that may stimulate further discussion.

☆ With regard to practicing:

Practicing is independent study. That takes time to develop, and requires guidance.

You control the practice conditions in the home. "Do not disturb" is the basic idea.

You can help your child make a realistic (and colorful) schedule.

☆ Your role during the practice time:

Your child may need your companionship as much as your guidance.

There are questions you can ask to help your child listen and think while practicing.

Beware of asking questions that are too general or unfocused.

Avoid making evaluative comments yourself; guide your child to assess her own results.

☆ Some things you should know about practicing:

There are many layers to music learning. Individual skills are worked on separately.

There are some common practice expectations for children at this age level.

Speak with the teacher if you notice a downward curve in your child's interest or progress.

Practice is a creative endeavor. Excellent practice habits are developed over a lifetime.

☆ A good teacher for this age group has several attributes:

Likes working with an active child, and is friendly and encouraging.

Knows how to stimulate and guide your child to explore, choose, and invent.

Can respond flexibly to children with different learning styles.

Knows how to channel your child's physical energies in productive ways.

☆ Patience and discipline may be misunderstood:

Patience must not be confused with leniency.

An effective teacher is tolerant, but stimulating and compelling.

Discipline cannot be "applied."

Both you and the teacher must help your child acquire self-discipline.

CHAPTER RESOURCES

The resources listed below are appropriate for the age group discussed in this chapter. Age recommendations are listed only if an item has more narrow appeal. Some items have wide appeal and are listed in the chapter resources of more than one chapter.

Take special note of Part IV, "General Resources," for a listing of books, recordings, movies, games, teaching aids, CD-ROMs, and catalogs.

BOOKS FOR YOU

Armstrong, Thomas. AWAKENING YOUR CHILD'S NATURAL GENIUS: ENHANCING CURIOSITY, CREATIVITY, AND LEARNING ABILITY. Los Angeles: Tarcher, 1991.

A natural outgrowth of the author's *In Their Own Way*, here Armstrong examines specific learning styles in greater depth. Among these are chapters on math, art, music, and science. Giftedness, computer learning, special eduation, Montessori, Waldorf, and superlearning are also discussed and, often, criticized. The text is broken up by the insertion of lists, headings, and rich and diverse quotations.

Bigler, Carole L. and Valerie Lloyd-Watts. MORE THAN MUSIC: A HANDBOOK FOR TEACHERS, PARENTS, AND STUDENTS. Athens, OH: Ability Development, 1979.

Although written for those involved in Suzuki piano training, all parents will find the introductory chapters helpful. Especially useful are the chapters entitled "The Role of the Parents in the Education of Their Children," "The Role of Parents and Relatives at Lessons and at Home," and "Parental Aids: Motivating Students." Specific guidelines for assisting with practice are stated clearly.

Canter, Lee and Lee Hausner. HOMEWORK WITHOUT TEARS. New York: Harper & Row, 1987.

This parent's guide for motivating children to do homework and to succeed in school has a good-humored approach. Chapter 10, "Solving the Seven Most Common Homework Problems," will ring a responsive chord for parents struggling to guide their children in music practice. Includes helpful long- and short-range planning charts.

Chroninger, Ruby. TEACH YOUR KIDS ABOUT MUSIC. New York: Walker, 1994.

A unique activity handbook using children's literature to stimulate creative activities related to the elements of sound. There is an annotated bibliography of general literature, music literature, and a discography. Useful for parents and teachers.

Gardner, Howard. FRAMES OF MIND. New York: Basic Books, 1985.

This book has already become a classic since Gardner's theory of multiple intelligences, introduced in this work, has attracted many followers. Musical intelligence is discussed more from the standpoint of the composer of music than the performer. Gardner speaks of how one perceives music in relation to the functions of the brain, and he also addresses unusual talents, such as that of the idiot savant. While the reading style is friendly, the general tone of the book is serious.

Gardner, Howard. THE UNSCHOOLED MIND: HOW CHILDREN THINK AND HOW SCHOOLS SHOULD TEACH. New York: Basic Books, 1991.

Gardner asks how we can help students move beyond rote learning to achieve genuine understanding. He makes a strong case for restructuring schools, using the latest research on learning as a guide. Here are new ideas about education—from the world of the young child as "natural learner" to the adolescent's search for meaning. A serious, provocative book.

Healy, Jane M. ENDANGERED MINDS: WHY OUR CHILDREN DON'T THINK. New York: Simon & Schuster, 1990.

The message here is that electronic media, unstable family patterns, fast-paced lifestyles, and other reflections of current society change not only how a child thinks, but also affect his actual brain structure. Healy presents research in the neuropsychology of learning and attacks popular opinions—for example, that watching *Sesame Street* aids your child's learning or that day care programs give a child a head start in school. Not Sunday afternoon reading fare, but written in friendly language, with many helpful anecdotes.

Satir, Virginia. THE NEW PEOPLEMAKING. Mountain View, CA: Science and Behavior Books, 1988.

Written by a pioneer in family therapy, this book explores all facets of family living and interaction, from self-worth to the family of the future. The writing style is direct, humorous, and right on target. Each chapter is full of useful advice that is sometimes framed in diagrams, conversations, or anecdotes.

Wlodkowski, Raymond J. and Judith Jaynes. EAGER TO LEARN: HELPING CHILDREN BECOME MOTIVATED AND LOVE LEARNING. San Francisco: Jossey-Bass, 1990.

The authors speak directly to parents about understanding and supporting a child's desire to learn. The writing style is practical, listing specific steps that parents can take. Discussions are often handled in a question-and-answer format. Especially useful are the chapters entitled "Building a Positive Parent-Teacher Relationship," and "Encouraging Effort and Perseverance," as well as the resource section that includes such information as how to prepare for a parent-teacher conference. There are also two videos, called "Motivation to Learn," associated with this book. (See videos listed below.)

BOOKS FOR YOU WITH YOUR CHILD

Barlow, Amy. HAPPY LISTENING GUIDE. Secaucus, NJ: Summy-Birchard, n.d.

A booklet that gives helpful hints on improving music listening. Could be used by parents and students during live or recorded performances. There are sample listening charts, checklists of "what to listen and watch for" during performances, pages to note favorites, and an autograph page. For parents with children six and older.

Bennett, Jill. NOISY POEMS. New York: Oxford University Press, 1994.

This picture book of twelve solidly noisy poems by James Reeves, David McCord, Elisabeth Coatsworth, and Jack Prelutsky will surely provoke a robust response. Excellent material for inspiring movement and original music. For the young child.

Chang, Nai Y. AN ILLUSTRATED TREASURY OF SONGS: NATIONAL GALLERY OF ART, WASHINGTON. New York: Rizzoli, 1994.

This beautiful volume presents traditional American songs, ballads, folk songs, and nursery rhymes by coupling each song (vocal line, words, simple piano accompaniment) with masterpiece paintings from the collection of the National Gallery of Art. The reproductions usually occupy an entire page. A family browser.

Cohn, Amy L. FROM SEA TO SHINING SEA: A TREASURY OF AMERICAN FOLKLORE AND FOLK SONGS. New York: Scholastic, 1993.

This treasury of folk songs and stories covers the entire history of America from the time before the early settlers to the present. There are generous color illustrations and easy piano scores for the songs. A family browser.

Dunn, Sonja. BUTTERSCOTCH DREAMS. Portsmouth, NH: Heinemann, 1987.

This collection of chants comes alive, given rhythmical reading. As texts for creating original songs, they are best presented to children four to ten years old.

Hausherr, Rosmarie. WHAT INSTRUMENT IS THIS? New York: Scholastic, 1992.

The great charm of this book is the photography (half in color, half in black-and-white). The color photographs are unique in showing small children of all races playing and reacting to instruments. The black-and-white photographs are shots from real life of varying instrumentalists such as folk singers, country fiddlers, and concert and rock performers. The text is minimal, each instrument being introduced by a question (What instrument looks like a shiny boa constrictor with a wide-open mouth?). The answer and brief overview is on the next page. This is a book to savor for its beauty and quality rather than for its informational content. Read with younger children. Can be read alone by children eight and older.

Koch, Kenneth and Kate Farrell. TALKING TO THE SUN. New York: Henry Holt, 1985.

An illustrated anthology of poems selected for young people and illustrated with art treasures from the Metropolitan Museum of Art. Presents an opportunity to correlate art, music, and literature. This exquisite book makes a wonderful gift. All ages.

Krull, Kathleen. GONNA SING MY HEAD OFF. New York: Knopf, 1992.

Folk songs for children, collected from all regions of the United States, are beautifully illustrated by Allen Garns with an introduction by Arlo Guthrie. Piano accompaniments require ability to play melodies with simple chords. All ages.

Magadini, Peter. MUSIC WE CAN SEE AND HEAR. Oakville, Ontario, Canada: Frederick Harris, 1982.

Presents musical ideas that any adult can teach to a child. There is a series of lessons that includes instrument-making and composing and encourages exploration of sounds and rhythms in a most imaginative manner. For parents with children four to nine years old.

Schenk, Beatrice de Regniers et al. SING A SONG OF POPCORN. New York: Scholastic, 1988.

This collection of poems vibrates with diversity in its wide range of moods and subjects—for example, humor, spookiness, weather, animals, and people. They are perfect for inspiring musical responses. Nine of the world's best children's illustrators have each taken a chapter and brought it to life in vibrant color. An absolute treasure. All ages.

Turner, Jessica and Ronny Schiff. LET'S MAKE MUSIC: AN INTERACTIVE MUSICAL TRIP AROUND THE WORLD. Milwaukee, WI: Hal Leonard, 1995. Book and CD.

This book of multicultural songs and activities illustrates how to make simple ethnic instruments from recycled materials to accompany the music. One song uses American Sign Language (shown in photographs). For each song there is a vocal line, words, and guitar symbols. Occasional use of words and phrases from other languages extends the vocabulary. Six and older.

BOOKS FOR YOUR CHILD

Arnold, Caroline. MUSIC LESSONS FOR ALEX. New York: Clarion Books, 1985.

The charm of this book lies in its photographs by Richard Hewett. This is the story of Alex, a little girl who decides to take violin lessons. The text covers the first year of her study, including how her instrument is purchased, and how she practices and rehearses, and concludes with her first recital. The photographs are of many people beside Alex, and depict with realism and poetry the world of the young violinist. Larger size print. Eight and older.

Downing, Julie. MOZART TONIGHT. New York: Bradbury Press, 1991.

Mozart tells his story in the first person from his early years when he and his father traveled from city to city to later years when he and his wife, Constanze, lived in Vienna. Glowing illustrations enhance this attractive picture book. Six to nine years old.

Goffstein, M. B. A LITTLE SCHUBERT. Boston: David R. Godine, 1984.

A whimsical story with pictures—short, sweet, and charming. A delightful gift for Schubert lovers. Eight and older.

Greves, Margaret. *THE MAGIC FLUTE*: THE STORY OF MOZART'S OPERA. New York: Henry Holt, 1989.

This picture-book account of Mozart's opera, stunningly illustrated by Francesca Crespi, is intended for the very young. The simple retelling of the story and the jewel-like illustrations bring this great work to life. Four to eight years old.

Lewis, Richard. MIRACLES. New York: Simon & Schuster, 1966.

A classic of its kind, these poems by children of the English-speaking world provide excellent material for setting words to music. Because they spring from the imaginations of young children, they are especially appealing for creative work. Six and older.

McLeish, Kenneth and Valerie McLeish. THE OXFORD FIRST COMPANION TO MUSIC. New York: Oxford University Press, 1982.

Specially designed for young children, this book uses large type, has hundreds of illustrations, and covers all kinds of music including Oriental, African, pop, and jazz music. Six and older.

Onassis, Jacqueline (ed.) *THE FIREBIRD* AND OTHER RUSSIAN FAIRY TALES. New York: Viking, 1978.

Lavishly illustrated by Boris Zvorykin, this collection of fairy tales, especially *The Firebird*, is an excellent catalyst for a project on Stravinsky's work of the same name. A work like this helps to make the connection between literature, music, and dance. Eight and older.

Rachlin, Ann and Susan Hellard. FAMOUS CHILDREN: BACH. HANDEL. HAYDN. MOZART. London: Victor Gollancz, 1992.

Delightful personal biographies, each a separate volume, relate incidents from the childhoods of these composers. Well illustrated. Younger children will enjoy hearing the stories. At a comfortable reading level for elementary school children. Four to eight years old.

Storr, Catherine and Dianne Jackson. *HANSEL AND GRETEL. THE NUTCRACKER. PETER AND THE WOLF. SWAN LAKE.* London: Faber Music, 1991.

These beautifully illustrated picture books give a simple synopsis of each work. For parents who play the piano, there are short musical excerpts of major themes to help acquaint the child with the score. Even without the music, the books are an appealing introduction to these classic works. Older students might enjoy playing the piano parts. Four to ten years old.

Willson, Robina. MOZART'S STORY. London: A & C Black, 1991.

This short biography is written in a pleasant, intimate style. There are attractive color drawings and reproductions of paintings of the period, including portraits of Mozart. Six to ten years old.

VIDEOS

AGAINST THE ODDS: LUDWIG VAN BEETHOVEN. Films for the Humanities. 800-257-5126.

The focus in this short biographical film is on Beethoven's ability to compose in spite of his increasing hearing loss. Extremely well produced. Though expensive, it gets its message across remarkably effectively. Eight and older.

BEETHOVEN LIVES UPSTAIRS. The Children's Group. 800-456-2334.

A dramatization centering around Christophe, a ten-year-old in nineteenth-century Vienna, whose mother rents the rooms "upstairs" to Beethoven. The boy learns to accept Beethoven's odd habits as well as his music. There is no condescension in this presentation. It offers a superior evocation of the era as well as Beethoven's music. Eight and older.

EARLY MUSIC EDUCATION WITH SUZUKI. Films for the Humanities. 800-257-5126.

The film follows a three-year-old boy and his mother as they begin Suzuki training in violin, and shows classes, lessons, scenes at home (with sibling interruptions), and a festival at which Suzuki himself interacts with a group of over a hundred violin students. Will be informative to those with an interest in Suzuki training. Six and older, especially Suzuki students and parents.

LEONARD BERNSTEIN'S YOUNG PEOPLE'S CONCERTS SERIES WITH THE NEW YORK PHILHARMONIC. Music in Motion. 800-445-0649.

Ten videos of twenty-five digitally remastered programs originally broadcast from

1958 to 1970. Topics include What Does Music Mean? What Is Classical Music? What Is Sonata Form? What Makes Music Symphonic? There is a book of Bernstein's lectures taken from these videos. A remarkable series from a great communicator.

MOTIVATION TO LEARN: HOW PARENTS AND TEACHERS CAN HELP. GUIDELINES FOR PARENT-TEACHER CONFERENCES. ASCD (Association for Supervision and Curriculum Development). 703-549-9110.

These videotapes have been prepared in conjunction with the book *Eager To Learn*, by Wlodkowski and Jaynes. Tape One is for parents and teachers. In the first segment, we see an unmotivated boy (of middle-school age) at various times in his day. A parent-teacher conference involving this boy makes up the second segment. Interdependent roles of parent and teacher are discussed. Tape Two is primarily for teachers and contains edited parent-teacher conferences dealing with student motivational problems. Although these videos are designed with workshop presentation in mind, parents would find them useful as examples of real-life coping strategies.

TRYIN' TO GET HOME: A HISTORY OF AFRICAN-AMERICAN SONG. Heebie Jeebie Music. 510-548-4613.

Written and performed by Kerrigan Black, this is a stirring performance and a musical record of an important part of American musical heritage.

TUBBY THE TUBA. Paul Tripp and George Kleinsinger. Live Entertainment: Van Nuys, CA. Available from educational retailers.

The enchanting tale of the winsome little tuba who tires of only being able to sing "oompah," *Tubby the Tuba* is a delightful musical fantasy. In the process of searching for his own identity and voice, he encounters the instruments of the orchestra. The animation is graced by the voices of Dick Van Dyke, Pearl Bailey, Cyril Ritchard, and other notables.

WE REINVENT THE CIRCUS. NOUVELLE EXPERIENCE. SALTIMBANCO. Cirque du Soleil. 800-727-2233.

This combination of acrobatics, costumes, music, and effects is truly a spectacle. The circus is taken to new heights of creativity and fantasy, and the Montreal-based ensemble provides excitement way beyond the entertainment level. Music, performed live, plays a major role in these productions.

CD-ROMs

Call the telephone number of each company to ask for a catalog. Check system requirements before ordering. Ask for a try-before-you-buy arrangement.

MUSICAL INSTRUMENTS. Microsoft Home. 800-426-9400.

This provides wonderful access to information about more than 200 instruments. There are four ways to navigate: "Families of instruments," "A–Z of instruments," "Instruments of the world," "Musical ensembles." You can see how the instruments work, hear musical examples, and "play" limited pitches on each instrument. There is reference to jazz, rock, classical, and other ensembles. For Macintosh and Windows. All ages.

THE MUSICAL WORLD OF PROFESSOR PICCOLO: THE FUN WAY TO LEARN ALL ABOUT MUSIC. Opcode Systems. 415-856-3333.

Includes reading, fun musical games, music history, music notation, and musical instruments data. It is a self-paced interactive course in music theory and musical styles, with excellent graphics. Good for some four- and five-year-olds, but best for elementary school age. Macintosh and Windows.

CHAPTER THREE

The Child from Nine to Twelve

What you will find in this chapter

THE YEARS from nine to twelve are make-or-break years with regard to music study. Some children find these years just the right time to begin. This is especially true for those who want to play band or orchestra instruments such as the trumpet, flute, saxophone, or clarinet (some of the most popular choices). The child now has the physical readiness to hold and play these instruments that was not possible when he was younger. If your child doesn't begin to study during these years, it is much less likely to happen when he is a teenager.

Make-or-break years

The child from nine to twelve

- is experiencing physical growth and change.
- has greater control of fine motor coordination.
- enjoys making small goals, creating checklists, and keeping score.
- has a more fully defined learning style.
- often gravitates toward the same-sex group.
- begins responding to peer group influence.
- enjoys clubs, cliques, and similar social groups.
- is aware of a broader world and an individual place in it.
- is growing to understand both freedom and responsibility.
- responds to authority, but is more conscious of its limitations.

For children who began music study earlier, these are make-or-break years in another sense. The child who has played for a few years may start to lose interest because taking lessons no longer seems special, because hobbies and other school activities may offer exciting new challenges, or because music studies were chosen by parents and the child is now more forceful about following personal inclinations. These are the years in which a child is likely to quit unless something happens to expand and support the child's interest in music study.

Beginning music study at this age

A child who begins music study during these years may be attracted to the sound, look, and feel of a particular instrument. He may also be attracted to an instrument because someone he admires plays it, because there may already be an instrument in the home, or (more rarely) because you suggest it.

If your child wants to play an instrument but is not sure which, there are several ways you can help (and probably learn something yourself in the process). Take your child to a concert or music program so that she has the opportunity to hear and see a number of instruments at once, and can form some impression of the various instrumental "roles" within a large performing group. Be on the lookout for young people's concerts in your area. Many professional and semiprofessional groups sponsor these, and the programs are designed to captivate the young audience. Approach the music teacher in your local junior high or high school and ask if you and your child can attend a rehearsal. Buy or rent a videotape on which the orchestral instruments are demonstrated. Visit your local music store to see and handle instruments there.

There is another reason that a child often chooses to study a band or orchestra instrument at this time. Bands and orchestras are social, as well as musical, groups. Becoming part of the group is an important link in a child's outreach to an identity beyond the family. Rehearsing—the "practicing" part of such study—is also done with the group. Often, too, the music played (especially in bands) appeals to children at this age, partly because it often *is* entertaining or light music, and also partly because the group often performs as part of a larger event such as a parade, an all-school musical, or a football game.

Reasons for beginning music study at this time may also arise from a change in external circumstances—Grandma's piano arrives at your house, a new music teacher comes to your child's school, or friends who take lessons coax your child into joining them. Sometimes a child discovers a latent musical talent and wants to study because recognition of this talent by others is a strong motivator. Your child may discover her "voice" as she sings in a group working on a school play. Others remark on how good she is and how beautiful she sounds. Or one of your son's friends has a drum set; as your son fools around with it, he finds that he has a knack for drumming, and his friends are impressed by his abilities.

I was always told that I had a beautiful soprano voice. I prayed that my voice would never change because there was such a level of self-esteem garnered by people always talking about how beautiful my voice was.

—*Walter Turnbull*

There are advantages in beginning music study at this time. There is rapid progress at the outset because both mind and body find it easy to grasp the basics of reading and technique. The first books are completed quickly, especially if progress is measured by the pace of younger learners. It often happens that a child who begins study at this age may accomplish in a few months what a six-year-old beginner achieves in two years. Since it is likely that a nine-year-old beginner may be more active in seeking instruction than a six-year-old, initial enthusiasm is strong. This is especially true if the nine-year-old is taking lessons in the same studio as her friends, or can join her friends playing in a band or orchestra.

There are some disadvantages, however, in beginning later. The rush of success enjoyed by most older beginners at the outset must eventually even out. This happens when the material is no longer so easy, or when the student catches up to what the average nine-year-old is doing. The student then finds that he may have to work harder or that learning new skills and pieces takes longer than it once did. While this does not discourage everyone, some children can be frustrated when the pace slows.

It also happens that some teachers use the same materials to teach beginners at almost any age. If the instruction books look babyish, or if the pieces seem juvenile, the ten-year-old beginner may be embarrassed to be heard playing the same music as the "little kids." While this problem may be resolved by switching to other materials (books and pieces appealing to older beginners are available), the teacher may not know of them or may choose not to use them. If a talk with the teacher does not bring about a solution, it is probably best to look for a teacher more in tune with the needs and interests of this age group.

The child who began music study earlier

If your child has studied music for several years, he can now begin to enjoy the fruits of that early labor. Efforts spent on learning to read music and coordinate basic movements can be directed to more satisfying, even if more demanding, tasks that promise greater rewards. It is easier to learn new pieces, and the pieces themselves seem more attractive because they are longer and sound bigger. He sees that a number of books and studies have been completed. He has a certain sense of arrival, and can feel proud and satisfied since many challenges have been met.

At this age your child experiences a growth spurt. Girls develop quickly at this time and are often bigger and stronger than boys of the same age. The growth spurt in boys usually takes place about two years later than it does for girls. At the end of the growth period, boys generally surpass girls in strength and endurance.

Fine motor control is easier, and making small and precise movements is gratifying because it demonstrates adultlike skills. Musically, this is the time when technical concentration changes from attending to basic posture and gesture habits to building speed, strength, and refinement. Your child probably likes to work at specific technical tasks and to keep track of measurable progress.

New directions

This is also a good time for your child to move in new directions since she is eager to help set goals and to develop the means to achieve them. Practice plans should result from a discussion between teacher and student, for example, rather than from the teacher's "orders." There may be some freedom in choosing pieces. Even if the teacher follows an established curriculum, it is possible to allow the student to select among many pieces that could suit the same purpose—for instance, to pick one sonatina from a group of four, or to choose a piece by Grieg rather than one by Schubert.

Your child may also want to explore different musical styles—perhaps improvisation, new age sounds, or electronic music—styles that he feels are more connected to his real world and that he can share with friends. In all these cases, he sees independence and choice as an indication of growing personal importance, and as a validation that his opinions count and can make a difference.

Classical culture may define the highest ideals of the human race, but the urge to individualism cannot be denied. . . . [It] is what motivates most of today's students.—Robert Ehle

Helping your child practice

Your role needs to change as well. This is the time to begin backing off. Allow your child more space—from removing your physical presence during the practice time and/or lesson to relaxing your supervision of practice in general. Give your child a little room to explore—accept your child's interest in new age music or buy computer software to stimulate your child's curiosity in music theory.

If she hasn't already begun to do so during the first years of study, your child should now assume some responsibility both for making a practice plan and for putting the plan into action. Making the plan is done with the teacher. Putting the plan into action is done at home and will probably require at least some supervision on your part. Just how much supervision you offer will depend on the level of independence your child has already gained or may need.

Listen, probably from a distance, to what your child does while practicing. Don't interfere if it seems that he is going about the practice session more or less in accordance with the teacher's suggestions, which are usually found in the notebook, in comments placed on the music itself, or summed up for you and your child at the end of a lesson. You

Deciding when a child needs to be supported in her thinking and when she must be given a chance to solve her own dilemmas is no easy task; learning is, and remains, an interactive process.
—Richard Landsdown and Marjorie Walker

might, however, show that you support his efforts with comments like, "I can tell that you are making progress by the way you practice," or "You work on your exercises and pieces like a pro."

I always wanted to know what made music. How you do it and why it sounds good. I always practiced, worked like hell.—Benny Goodman

What does good practice sound like?
The student:
- works at short sections without stumbling.
- repeats with pauses in between to assess.
- maintains quiet concentration.
- begins new tasks slowly and carefully.
- works up speed gradually and with control.
- varies tasks and allots time to each.

What does bad practice sound like?
The student:
- stops and starts in the same places.
- makes many repeats during which nothing changes.
- sighs and mutters.
- rushes through everything.
- plays items only once.
- remains silent, perhaps woolgathering.
- plays only favorites. Avoids the "hard stuff."

If students are to conceptualize, carry out, and present their projects effectively, they need to be guided . . . in the various phases and aspects of this activity.
—Howard Gardner

If it seems that your child is not following the teacher's directions, guidance is needed. One way to provide this is to help your child begin the practice session. Have her explain what she thinks she should do, then help her settle on the order in which she will do various tasks and estimate how much time each task will take. This guidance will not only show her how to structure music practice, but it will also demonstrate how to go about organizing any project that requires attention and effort. More is gained than just ensuring that the next music lesson will be prepared. The benefit to you (especially if you cannot play, or play well, yourself) is that you will gain a better understanding of what is required to improve certain technical skills or perfect the performance of a piece. You will develop the right kind of patience (not the grit-your-teeth kind) because you are beginning to appreciate the complexity of the entire process and may come to have new respect for what your child is trying to accomplish.

Many teachers include practice advice in their studio brochures or in special letters to parents.

Parents and students share the responsibility for deciding on a time for uninterrupted practice until the student is able to do so without parental supervision and discipline. This point of maturation and self-discipline varies with each student. Practice time should be a priority, and should remain free from distractions and interruptions by siblings, telephone, television, and the like.

Sandra Karsnia, Detroit Lakes, MN

Assignments, practice, and participation in studio activities are expected to have the same priority as homework, sports, and other activities. In order to make the best progress in music study, daily practice is recommended. To help develop self-discipline and good work habits, it is suggested that a regular time for practice be set aside each day. It is the responsibility of the parent to see that home practice and written assignments are carried out. We expect each student to keep practice records periodically, and request that parents read and sign the assignment book each week. Parents should talk with us if there are questions or problems.

Winborne-Shaw Piano Studio, Oshkosh, WI

Some teachers use a questionnaire to uncover how their students feel about practicing.

	1 = not at all 5 = very much
I like to practice hard new music.	1 2 3 4 5
I like to practice easy new music.	1 2 3 4 5
I like to polish music I am playing.	1 2 3 4 5
I like to memorize.	1 2 3 4 5
I like my parents to listen to or help me practice.	1 2 3 4 5
I like to practice technique and warm-ups.	1 2 3 4 5
I like to practice sight-reading.	1 2 3 4 5
I practice as much as I think I need to.	1 2 3 4 5
I could find more time to practice if I wanted.	1 2 3 4 5
I find my teacher's practice suggestions helpful.	1 2 3 4 5

Manduca Music Studios, Portland, ME

BACKING OFF

Now is the time to begin the weaning process by withdrawing your guidance of the practice period. This is not something that should be done "cold turkey." Saying "Starting next week, I'm not sitting in on your lessons anymore," or "Now that you're ten, don't expect me to help you practice!" is too abrupt. Most children, but especially those who are more dependent, need time to adjust to the *idea*, as well as the reality, of being without parental backup. You might say in June, "Beginning next September, I feel that you can handle your music lessons all by yourself. During the summer we'll experiment with how that might work." Many children also respond well when given an option, rather than an ultimatum. "When would you like me to stop coming to each lesson—next month, or in September?" The message is clear. You will no longer attend lessons. There is time, however, for your child to get used to the idea, and it may be easier for her to do so if she feels she has the freedom to decide for herself when she thinks she might be ready.

Sometimes it is the teacher who initiates the weaning. If your child's teacher suggests that you no longer sit in on the lesson and you are in agreement, talk over when would be the best time to start. Doing so gradually, or at a specified time, is a good way to back off without any fuss or bother. If, however, you are uncomfortable or in complete disagreement with the teacher's suggestion that your child can handle lessons on his own, that is a sensitive situation. Most teachers do not want to "get rid of" a parent whose presence is helpful and supportive. If the teacher suggests that you discontinue attending lessons, it may be that she is picking up on something that has escaped your notice.

Your child may feel caught trying to please two authorities. He may sense that you are critical even if you say nothing. He may feel pushed or babied just because you are there. Or it may be that the teacher feels the time is right for your child to strike out on his own. It often happens that a child begins to develop a personal relationship with the teacher and sees the teacher as an intermediary between the adult world and his own. Thus, being alone with the teacher has a special value in your child's eyes, and he may see himself as moving toward adulthood because he has an adult "friend." The teacher may be picking up on this, and that is why she recommends that you start backing off. Try to trust the teacher's judgment or, at least, grant her the benefit of the doubt. If you are hurt or confused by being asked to step aside in this way, be honest with the teacher about your feelings, but do not insist on having your way at the expense of your child's development. And, above all, do *not* discuss this in front of your child.

How to begin backing off

- Help get the practice started; then leave.
- Sit in at the end of practice, to help review.
- Guide the practice only on the day after the lesson, making sure things are correctly underway.
- Sit in on the practice right before the lesson, helping your child to pull it all together.
- Sit in on the practice both the day after and the day before.
- Be an audience rather than a judge.
- Help your child formulate good questions to ask the teacher, rather than provide answers yourself.
- Videotape a home performance. Watch and discuss it together with your child.

SOME RED FLAGS

Eagerness to learn, which is quite natural when a child is younger, may begin to dull as tasks become more difficult, expectations rise, and the support systems at school and at home may appear more matter of fact.

Teachers may now be more critical and demanding while, at the same time, your encouragement in the form of help with practice and homework may be less frequent or entirely absent (perhaps because it is being given to younger siblings). You expect your child to be more self-sufficient, and yet you may want her to remain obedient to rules that no longer seem reasonable and just to her. Her give-and-take with authority is undergoing subtle change during these years, partly because learning to get along is becoming less a matter of pleasing you and other adults, and more a matter of gaining acceptance by her peer group.

Another kind of backing off is for you to cease being the practice policeman. Do not allow your child to make *you* responsible for whether he practices or not. Your child must learn that practicing is his job, and that the consequences of not practicing (embarrassment, discomfiture, or fear of going to the lesson) stem from his own lack of discipline or organization. While it may be relatively painless to let this happen for a week or two (and that may be enough to make the point), it is likely to become an unpleasant controversy if carried out for longer periods. Don't be trapped back into the policeman role just to get things rolling again. If your child continues to skip practice and this does *not* become an issue at the lesson (where the teacher is likely to bring matters to a head), it may help for you and your child to discuss the matter of practice. Remember, however, that such a discussion will be valuable only if you are truly willing to listen to what your child says, and allow a little leeway for him to stretch and discover how to act responsibly.

A talk with your child about how to improve his practice, however, may not produce the expected results. Each of you may have very different ideas of what music lessons are "for," and what "music" really is. In such a case, talking with the teacher may be more helpful than trying to settle the matter at home. It is one of the teacher's tasks to help sort out priorities, intentions, and results. Remember that a parent often sees changes in practice habits before these differences become apparent at the lesson. The parent may, or may not, understand that the problem relates to all aspects of the child's life, not just the music lesson. The child may be unhappy at school, may be trying to cope with social challenges, or may be affected by illness (his own, or that of a family member). On the other hand, the teacher may be fully aware of inadequate or unfocused practice, and may be biding time or switching the focus in order to keep your child's interest by encouraging her to explore new activities, such as improvising, playing jazz, or working with a computer program—things you may not know about or with which you disagree.

There are no perfect parents! What's important is that you keep moving in the direction of good parenting.
—Virginia Satir

If you speak with the teacher, remember two things: Make an appointment to do so (or agree on a good time to phone) and converse without your child being present (or within earshot). A teacher will appreciate your concern and is likely to work together with you to sort matters out, to consider changes that could be made (such as working on different repertoire), or to make adjustments of other kinds. Teachers can be enlightened by what they learn about home conditions and parent attitudes as a result of such discussions, and thereby are better able to deal with your child both as a person and as a learner. If your child's teacher is unwilling to discuss such issues, or does not make reasonable changes and adjustments in light of new information uncovered by such talks, this may be a sign that it is time to change teachers.

The teacher may also serve as a sounding board for your own ideas about music study, and may help you examine these in the light of current music pedagogy. The music teacher you had as a child, for example, made it clear that playing "popular" music was out of the question, or a waste of time. Your child's teacher, however, may not only be comfortable with including such music in the curriculum, but may be enthusiastic in using it to teach harmonization as well as to supply motivation.

Time to quit?

If your child began music study at a very young age, he may find that the excitement and novelty of lessons has diminished or evaporated, and may express a desire to quit music lessons for that reason. You, of course, want to reinforce his sense of responsibility and perseverance, and fear that stopping now would be equivalent to fostering just the opposite. Assess this situation seriously and honestly. Do not insist, for example, that lessons continue no matter how your child feels. Keep in mind that what prompts the desire to quit may not always be what it seems and may stem from a number of factors, most of them not apparent to your child.

It may be true that your child is disinterested in music study, and that now is the time to stop. It sometimes happens that a youngster who quits plays more than ever because making music is no longer a burden or a must. If you had hoped that your child might play for pleasure, then you might win the war even if you lose this particular battle. On the other hand, forcing your child to continue in order to teach perseverance may kill the musical urge, even to the point where playing will always carry overtones of drudgery or compulsion.

Some aspect of music study may be at the root of your child's frustration. A ten-year-old pianist, for example, who is never involved in group or ensemble playing, may find practicing lonely just when the importance of her social world is beginning to expand. All that may be necessary to keep music study going is to have the teacher arrange for her to play duets or to collaborate with a friend who plays a clarinet or cello. Your child might dislike the teacher, the pieces, certain practice routines, or playing in a recital. The reason can only be uncovered by attention to what your child says, and does not say. None of these reasons indicates a dislike for music, only frustration with aspects of the instruction. Teachers, pieces, routines, and performance obligations can all be changed.

A nine-year-old boy who had studied for two years was reluctant to practice. He even said to his parents, "Why are you making me do this?" After talking through the matter together, both parents and teacher agreed that this child had a flair for music and really enjoyed it. Since they weren't ready to "abandon ship," they devised a joint strategy.

The teacher spent several weeks "at play" with this boy. During lessons they improvised, played duets, and did some computer and CD-ROM work together. No practice was expected. In a few weeks he asked, "Could we go back to the way things were?" They did—almost. New material especially appealing to the boy was chosen and the teacher entered him in auditions that provided a specific goal.

At the same time, things also changed at home. The boy was given an allowance for the first time. To earn it, he was expected to do certain chores *and* he was expected to practice. This combination of bending somewhat to the boy's wishes and raising expectations worked!

What is most important is that you and the teacher discuss the situation, and do so within a reasonable amount of time. Don't let a problem fester for several months before discussing it. Remember that you are likely to pick up on your child's frustration before the teacher may notice it because you see the whole of your child's life patterns. Knowing *when* to take action, however, is not always simple. Keep in mind that your child's progress is never straight up or down.

Making comparisons

At this age, your child becomes aware of her own place in the world, how she "rates," and what her "role" is. Part of this stems from what goes on at home. Comparisons made there can have far-reaching effects.

Comments you make may hurt, confuse, or stigmatize your child. On the other hand, comparisons can have positive effects. "Didn't Jamie play great last week in the master class? I'm sure you'll be right up there with him very soon!" It really all depends on the emotional tone in which the comparison is couched. Young children often admire those slightly older, and make their own quiet comparisons as a way of testing whether or not they "measure up." If you catch yourself making public comparisons, just make sure that your comments do not carry negative overtones or tip the scales unjustly or unfairly as do those below.

"Kari, why do I always have to get after you to practice? I never have to remind Sean."
Sean may have an entirely different learning style and personality. Working by himself may be easy and what he really wants to do. Kari may need help getting started, or may find it hard to keep organized. A parent may not be responsive to individual differences.

"Ginny, I wish you played pieces like Bill did when he was ten. They sounded so big and impressive."
Bill may have bigger hands and greater physical coordination than Ginny. Bill might also have played a different instrument, or have had a different teacher. Ginny may not like the kinds of pieces Bill played and is very happy playing what she does. A parent may criticize a child for something over which the child has no control.

"Well, Jon is the sportsman in the family. No music for him. Julie is the sensitive one. She plays so beautifully."
Jon likes sports, but he also may enjoy music. He would be happy to play the drums, but his mother wanted him to take violin lessons. A parent may cast a child in a certain role, and the child, willingly or not, is groomed to fill that role. Jon may never get a chance to study or make music, and may grow up believing he is unmusical.

Your child is also aware that comparisons and ratings are common in the world beyond the home. Report card grades, scores, and lists of winners are part of every classroom scene. So also are informal labels, such as "the brain," "the teacher's pet," or "the big goof-off." Some music studios also foster comparison, as is the case when race scores are colorfully posted on bulletin boards. Your child may come to believe, correctly or not, that the teacher likes students in proportion to how well they perform. Your child must learn that there is a difference between being loved for who he *is* and being admired for what he *does*. It is likely that a child senses this disparity earlier, but the years from nine to twelve are those in which an expanding social world shines a strong light on peer differences.

Once again, you may contribute unwittingly to the score keeping. Asking questions (usually of the teacher) such as, "How did he do?" or "Is Jane where she should be right now?" sends the message to your child that you are checking to see if he measures up. Although these questions indicate a kind of parent involvement, they also imply that the parent's concern may be driven by comparison to others rather than by whether or not the child is doing his personal best.

Sometimes the teacher may offer a summary of the lesson by saying to the parent at the end, "Meg played her pieces very convincingly today. There has been real improvement from week to week." Don't spoil the situation by rejoining, "Well, it's about time!" or "That's great, but she still has a long way to go." Just give Meg a hug.

Recitals and auditions are situations fraught with comparison pitfalls for parents, teachers, and peers alike. Peers may be thoughtless. "Too bad you had an accident right in the middle!" or "I can't believe Jerry got such a high score. He just rushed through everything." Teachers are apt to try to support each child in the right way, but even they display preferences with remarks like "That was a stunning performance!" (said to only one child but within earshot of all the others). Your child may have to cope with such comments, no matter how generally supportive any teacher or peer group may be. You have no control over that. But you *do* control your own response to your child's (and her peers') performances, and you can help your child put comments by others in perspective.

These are years in which your child can be very sensitive about performing in public, even if that "public" is just Aunt Margaret. When your child was younger, and especially when playing and taking lessons were new for him, performing on call was often fun and resulted in attention and praise. Now, however, your child may begin to feel manipulated, or may feel awkward and uncomfortable with his physical growth. He is also struggling a bit to free himself from you, and part of this may manifest itself in wishing to be asked (instead of told) to do things, especially things that may put him on the spot.

Choosing a good time to ask is also important. Asking in front of Grandma, "Would you like to play your new pieces for Grandma?" is just as devastating as being told to play. Ask that question before Grandma arrives. Shyness or unpreparedness can then be discussed in private. Your child values being treated with respect for his feelings.

Recital jitters

Preparing for an upcoming recital generates a certain amount of excitement. You can offer support in a number of practical ways.

Before the recital

- help your child choose special, but comfortable, clothes.
- have your child practice in these clothes.
- play preparation games with your child.
- refer to the recital as a time to share and celebrate.
- avoid remarks such as "Are you nervous?"

The day of the recital

- don't overschedule family events for that day.
- try to maintain a generally calm home atmosphere.
- don't have your child play the recital pieces to warm up. Instead, he may use exercises (such as scales) or improvise.
- treat the performer to a bubble bath.
- do deep breathing exercises. Perhaps, inhale saying I am; exhale saying O.K.

*What **not** to say after a recital*

- "Why did you play so fast?"
- "Now you know you'll have to practice harder."
- "No one noticed that you had a memory slip."
- "I thought I told you to smile."
- "Well, you really looked nice at least."
- "Were you nervous?"
- "I think you played better than anyone else."
- "I'll bet you're glad it's over."
- "Well, do you think you deserve that ice cream?"

Even comments that seem positive such as, "No one noticed that you had a memory slip" are not effective because it is likely that the memory slip was obvious. Your child rightly does not believe such a remark. What helps is to tell the truth without calling attention to what went wrong—for example, "I was impressed by the way you handled things." The slip goes unremarked; the fact that she carried on despite the difficulty is what's applauded. Likewise, telling your child that he played better than anyone else seems supportive, but the underlying message is that comparisons were made and that his playing was judged, not enjoyed. Comments that seem empathic like "Were you nervous?" or "I'll bet you're glad it's over" also cloak a prejudicial inference that your child should have been nervous, or should regard a recital as an ordeal, rather than as a time for sharing. Here the hidden message is that *you* were nervous and are glad the recital is over. Your child picks up on this and now feels that, at the next recital, he must cope with your nerves as well as his own. Just as with comparisons, the emotional tone of your comments may carry greater weight than what is said. Your child needs to know that she is loved no matter what happens.

> *What to say after a recital*
> - "Your part in the program was very special to me."
> - "I appreciate what it took to get this ready."
> - "You really played with energy."
> - "I was impressed with the way you handled things."
> - "You gave it your best. I think you were wonderful."
> - "This was another milestone. Congratulations."
> - "Ice cream all around. Let's celebrate!"

Notice that good after-recital comments carry no "buts"—for example, "I enjoyed your performance, but I wished you would have smiled at the end," or "You really played with energy, but why did you rush through everything?" Your immediate after-recital reaction should be positive and supportive. If some things went wrong or the playing was less than perfect, your child knows this and cannot do anything about the results now. Later, when things are calm and normal, the teacher is likely to discuss the "buts." This is not parent territory.

If a treat was promised, have it, no matter what happened. Playing in a recital or audition *is* an event and deserves celebration. Don't spoil the hot fudge sundae by talking about how to improve or hashing over small details of the performance. Follow even a positive comment such as, "You gave it your best," with an endorsement—"I think you were wonderful." If left to stand alone, "You gave it your best" may come off as meaning, "Well, despite all the problems you had, you tried." That is a very lukewarm pat on the back. Performing in public is a special test. The performer is vulnerable, and lack of support, or criticism, especially coming right after a performance, really hurts.

The right teacher

What kind of teacher works well with children of this age? These are characteristics you will want to note.

> *The elementary teaching specialist*
> - adapts technical training to the growing child.
> - provides comprehensive technical training.
> - gives clear practice and performance guidance.
> - has a good sense of humor.
> - appreciates the child's expanding social world.
> - encourages exploration in keeping with a student's interest.
> - responds to different learning styles with flexibility.
> - knows how to encourage and support independent learning.
> - allows the student some latitude and freedom.
> - provides opportunities for peer-group interactions.

The teacher who is successful with children from nine to twelve years old, just like the teaching specialist at the primary level, guides the child to explore, and is sensitive to the child's own learning style, especially because it is more clearly defined at this stage. There are characteristics associated with the teacher at this level, however, that deserve special mention.

Posture and physical habits

Although physical change in children of this age group is easy to see, not all music teachers deal with issues relating to the growth spurt with insight and flexibility. The proportions of arm and torso length are in a state of flux during these years. The graceful six-year-old may now appear ungainly and self-conscious. Children (especially girls) who grow tall quickly are apt to slump. Postures in relation to the instrument that were comfortable for the younger child may need adjustment as the child grows. The teacher must be alert in this regard and make sure that the student understands how to make these adjustments and how important it is to do so.

You must reinforce your child's awareness of posture habits, not just because good posture looks better, but because inappropriate postures are often the root causes of physical problems that afflict the performer at later stages. Because many bad physical habits, not only posture, go unchecked during the growth-spurt years, it is vital that the teacher, parent, and child are cautious and alert during this formative stage.

Thinking really begins in the body.—Thomas Armstrong

Choice is the essence of responsibility. When students make choices, especially publicly, it is evident that they are, to an important extent, determining their behavior. This helps them to feel intrinsically motivated, positive, and accountable for their learning.

—*Raymond Wlodkowski and Judith Jaynes*

At this age, your child may only want to play fast and loud. Children nine to twelve years old are able to deal with fine motor control to a degree that was not possible earlier. These are good years to do serious technical work. Many people—even some teachers, unfortunately—equate technique with scales and repetitious drills. These activities play a role in developing technique, but that role may be exaggerated, or emphasized at the expense of developing techniques that produce more refined and subtle musical results. Repetitious drills, however, are just what many children this age enjoy because they permit the child to revel in doing things that now seem achievable, if not easy. Fingers can make finer motions, growth extends the range of movement, and stronger muscles make power and endurance possible.

A careful teacher watches that the technical regimen provides a comprehensive approach. The most important aspect of teaching technique is awakening the ear, getting your child to *hear* differences between effect and variations of sound brought about by physical action. The second, equally important, element is guiding your child to be aware of how her arm or wrist *feels* when the gesture is natural and effective. These are precisely the years when things may go wrong, technically speaking, because your child may be "working" to produce sounds and effects in inappropriate, even harmful, ways. The teacher who is informed and vigilant in this regard often uses audio- and videotapes to illustrate beautiful sounds and natural gestures.

At this age, your child wants to help run the show and make the rules. The ideal teacher involves your child in helping to make plans and set goals. Planning might begin with short-term projects, such as devising a week's practice procedures or outlining a system to learn a new piece efficiently. Seeing quick rewards as a result of good planning enables your child to stretch the time frame and attempt to deal with projects that may take longer, such as preparing for a program or working toward an audition.

The wise teacher allows your child some voice in selecting pieces. Several pieces can always be found that will serve the same purpose or teach the same skills or styles. If your child chooses a piece, she has a sense of ownership about it. Given some freedom, she may decide to work on two pieces instead of one. Even if your child makes a "wrong" choice, opting to work on something that is beyond reach or too long, she learns from that experience just which factors need to be taken into account when the time to choose comes again. As a result, she gains a degree of self-knowledge that might never be reached if the teacher always advises or intervenes. The teacher also gains insights into your child's tastes by noting the choices and discussing the reasons that prompted them. A vital offshoot of these freedoms—to plan and to choose—is that your child begins to accept some accountability for the entire process of music study and acquires some appreciation for the realities involved in keeping commitments.

One of the gang

Children from nine to twelve years old are joiners. Teams and clubs are magnets that draw most children into an extended social orbit, one that includes a peer, as well as a family, group. Your ten-year-old wants to "belong," and membership in a group outside the family is part of that goal. The music lesson, on the other hand, is often an isolated experience, especially if the lesson is private. The music practice period is another lonely ordeal. These are terrible years to be practicing by yourself when your friends are outside playing ball together. The piano student feels this isolation most deeply; string and wind players generally have the opportunity to play, and sometimes practice, as part of a group.

To offset the aloneness your child may feel while practicing, it may help for you to be around—reading, computing, or doing other quiet tasks. Every so often, take time to be a real audience. This, of course, demonstrates your interest and support, but it also shows that listening is a worthwhile activity. If you can't always be present physically while your child practices, suggest that he audiotape a practice session or two. Later, when you do have time, listen to it with him.

When to practice

Together with your child, take a look at when practice is scheduled. If time for practice conflicts with after-school group activities such as soccer practice, scout meetings, or "hanging out," work out another time to practice, perhaps in the morning before leaving for school. Short intense practice periods are generally more useful than longer practice sessions because remaining on-task for an extended time often dissolves into mindless repetition or meandering. Have your child try a 20-minute practice period before school coupled with a 15-minute practice right after dinner. Use the early practice to work on technique, cleanups, and new pieces. The later session can be used to check on the results of the morning's work or to "perform." This kind of plan means that practice does not compete with peer-group activities and, for that reason, it may be done more willingly or with less distraction.

One of the reasons that friendships are formed more easily around this age is the child's growing ability to see another person's point of view.
—Richard Landsdown and Marjorie Walker

When you engage in a learning experience with your child, you have the opportunity to gain insight into how you learn, and you may be surprised by how much your child can teach you.
—Thomas Armstrong

Some teachers use a group teaching approach, believing that peer interaction has educational and social benefits, and that children learn from observing each other as well as from watching the teacher. The group need not be large; it may consist of four to six children, or two students may work as partners. Teachers who give private lessons often supplement them with studio classes to teach related skills such as music theory, to work with ensembles, or to hold informal recitals.

Technology in the studio

Some music teachers have studios containing electronic equipment as well as standard instruments that enable students to have computer lab time, to drill notes and rhythms, to play with background accompaniments, or to notate original compositions. Time for this is often scheduled immediately before or after the lesson. While such activities may be nongroup in appearance (the student interacts only with the program or sequencer), a group atmosphere is sometimes experienced because children may work with various pieces of equipment at the same time, but may stop now and again to share discoveries or successes with those around them. Many computer programs are game-like, and students enjoy pitting skills against a computer (a pseudosocial experience that is often quite real to the child) or competing with other students in the same studio.

Some children think computers are alive, some think they are not, others settle on "sort of."—Sherry Turkle

However a teacher arranges for group experiences, these interactions are vital in order to give the music student a sense of community and an awareness that other children are taking lessons, having similar problems, succeeding, and enjoying what they do. Young wind and string players have an edge over pianists because ensemble experience, such as playing with a small group or in a band or orchestra, is usually an intrinsic part of the instruction. No matter what instrument your child plays, or in what kind of setting lessons take place, she should be able to talk with other children who take music lessons because her experience cannot be shared elsewhere, often not even in the home.

Music as an outreach

Just as your child needs opportunities to interact with others involved in studying and making music, so also he needs to realize that music can be an outreach to those who don't play or sing. Too often music is confined to the lesson, the rehearsal, the recital, and the practice period, as if it were something special and outside everyday life. A child who never fits his music-making into a bigger picture may get a skewed notion of music as culture.

There are many ways in which your child may be helped to see that she can contribute to the pleasure of others by sharing her music-making skills, however simple these may be. Music teachers are likely to arrange some of these experiences, but there are numerous things *you* can suggest and organize to help your child relate music-making to real life.

If your child is studying with an independent teacher, help her fit music into her school life. The classroom teacher may not know that your child plays an instrument and might be willing to arrange for your child to play for classmates, perhaps as part of sharing time, if she were aware of that possibility. There are other activities the classroom teacher may suggest, such as playing holiday music for sing-alongs, or performing a minuet or tango (that your child might be studying) during a history or geography class. It is important for you to play a proactive role in your child's educational life, and finding ways to establish a liaison between home, school, and music studio is just one way to make effective connections.

It would not be out of place for you to suggest that the classroom and music teachers converse with the idea of finding ways to correlate music with daily school life. That may not have been necessary a decade or two ago, when music educators in the classroom were plentiful. Now, however, many school systems have cut back music as well as other arts programs to such a point that there is very little fine arts education in the classroom.

Music as a gift

Help your child videotape performances of favorite pieces as learning them is completed. This may be done over the course of several months, and may include spoken introductions, anecdotes about incidents that occurred while learning the piece, comments about why the piece is a favorite, and so on. When a small program has accumulated, give the tape as a gift—for Mother's Day, to Grandpa on his birthday—or use it as a highlight at a family get-together. There are several benefits. The recipient is honored and pleased because the gift is personal. You have a family keepsake and a real proof of progress. Your child has the opportunity to choose the music, plan the tapings, and see a finished product. If tapings are made over a period of time and with a degree of naturalness, your child learns how to prepare to play "live" without the stress of playing many pieces at once or facing up to a more formal recital atmosphere.

Music-making has obvious social functions. Playing for a holiday or birthday sing-along, a religious service, a scout meeting, or as part of at-home "jamming" are common examples. Yet too often these days we rely only on audiocassette and CD players to furnish the music for everyday use and entertainment, and overlook the fact that even very young and less experienced players can contribute music for at least some of these occasions. If you can play an instrument or sing a little, make music with your child. It doesn't matter if the results aren't perfect. What counts is that music-making becomes a shared, normal experience, one that could be as natural as playing ball or hiking together.

There are other social uses of music that would allow your child to see music-making as a less lonely, more purposeful activity. You, or you and the teacher, could arrange for your child and his friends to play for children confined to the hospital or for an informal get-together in a senior center or nursing home. You could help your child organize a neighborhood backyard or recreation room benefit concert, from which the modest profits could be donated to a worthwhile charity. Be creative in concocting some way to relate music-making to whatever may be meaningful or useful in your particular situation. In one city, for instance, children in various neighborhoods set up a plan, called "practice for pets" in which they were paid for the amount of time they practiced. The proceeds were donated to local animal shelters. Children who made especially large "contributions" had their names inscribed on plaques that were hung prominently in the city pounds.

Extra programs and special events

In all large cities, and in most good-sized ones, there are programs offered at community arts schools, preparatory music departments, church and temple schools, and recreation centers that provide classes or workshops that may be either more specialized or more wide-ranging than what is usually part of studio or school music instruction. Music theory and master classes, music and movement activities, and smaller ensembles, such as trios and quartets, are found in most preparatory departments attached to colleges and universities and in community arts schools. These schools and centers also provide many other activities such as artist recitals, folk song performances, screenings of films about music and musicians, slide and lecture presentations (for children and for adults), and a host of other festivals and concerts. Sometimes these are classes or series that extend over a few weeks or months; sometimes they last a day or weekend, or are offered as a summer workshop.

How do you find these places? Ask your music teacher or school music instructor, call the music department of your local college, consult your local or state arts councils, contact a professional organization for music teachers, look in the phone book under headings such as "music instruction," "schools," "performing arts," and the like, and look for articles in the human interest or style sections of your newspaper (especially small, local papers) that often feature stories about events, festivals, and concerts that take place in these schools and centers.

Most newspapers also run calendars toward the end of the week or on weekends that list what concerts, workshops, classes, and programs are available for certain age or interest groups. Sometimes the listings are quite specific—music, pop, rock, country, folk, traditional, jazz, blues, new age, children's events, children's theater and dance, auditions, and so on. Sample a few of these with your child. Both of you are likely to meet others with similar interests and questions at such events, and often information passed along from such sources is helpful and practical.

Summer specials

Summertime is rich with possibilities for reaching out. Your child's own teacher or school is likely to offer summer specials such as group sessions, sight-reading marathons, music history or appreciation classes, computer camps, and composition and improvisation workshops. Local schools and centers already mentioned also provide a menu of such offerings. There are, in addition, a significant number of music camps held throughout the United States. Not every camp is appropriate for every child. There are several ways that you can find out which might be best for your own child.

The most obvious is to contact the camps that have the greatest appeal to you or your child (whether because of teachers, locale, size, or price) and request information, including a list of former camp attendees. You might wish to contact parents whose children attended a particular camp to inquire about things you need to know, which a brochure might not divulge. Consult the librarian in the reference room of your local library for summer camp listings. Your child's music teacher is a further source of information about which camps might be right for your child; the teacher may even be on the faculty of such a camp herself.

If your child's teacher is not on the faculty of the camp your child attends, your child will study for a while with another instructor. There are both advantages and disadvantages to this arrangement. It may take time to adjust to the new teacher's style or grasp the new teacher's expectations. The kind of give-and-take that usually occurs between a teacher and student who see each other regularly over a long period of time can seldom develop during the course of a week or two. On the other hand, a different teacher may offer a fresh way of looking at things, or may uncover and try to develop a skill, such as an ability to improvise, that has gone unnoticed in the home, school, or studio.

Lessons are likely to be more frequent than is usual during the school year; in most camps each child receives two lessons a week. In addition, practice time is set in the schedule and may even be supervised. Ear training, sight-reading, or musicianship classes are also programmed into the day's activities. All this makes for a greater concentration on music study than your child may be accustomed to back at home. For most children, this is often stimulating, partly because everyone else in the camp is similarly involved, and partly because there are fewer distractions. Nonetheless, some children at this age get homesick, some feel snowed under by the steady pace of playing and instruction, and some (especially if the camp activities or the peer group is not challenging enough) get bored. In any case, your child makes important personal discoveries and gets a chance to try his wings in a setting that requires him to stretch a little. He meets new people, both adults and children, and often makes new friends. For someone at this age, these are healthy steps.

Choosing the camp

A word of caution. Some camps are tailor-made for this age group, but some are not. First-time campers who are nine to twelve years old often do best in a program separate from older teens. Most camp brochures make clear what musical and recreational activities are designed for the campers. Some camps have performance levels, as well as age groups, in mind. This is usually spelled out in a brochure or during a phone call, but that is not always the case. Your child may be over- or underprepared for what the camp offers or what the teachers in the camp expect. It is important to know the degree of your child's intensity and interest with regard to music. Is she ready for 100 percent music immersion, or better suited to a situation where proportionately equal time is given to music and other activities? There are camps for each type of child.

Still other camps are for young professionals, and the child's musical ability is screened by means of an audition. Camps that require an audition tape are clearly looking for specific performance levels. The audition is a double safeguard. The scope of camp activities can be maintained; the fledgling camper who is not yet ready for certain challenges is protected.

Questions to ask as you search for a summer camp
- How good a performer do you expect my child to be?
- What is the daily camp schedule?
- What is the balance between music and other activities?
- What is the age range of those attending the camp?
- What are the sleeping, eating, and social arrangements?
- Who supervises camp activities?
- What are the qualifications of the supervisors?
- What are the practice rooms like?
- Is practice time supervised?
- How are teachers and classes assigned?

Questions that a camp director might ask you
- Has your child ever been away from home before?
- Has your child ever been to any other kind of camp?
- How much does your child usually practice every day?
- How well does your child adjust to new people and places?
- How does your child handle criticism or correction?
- What is your child's current repertoire?
- How much performing has your child done?
- Does your child have certain dietary or health needs?

What parents can do

Going to a summer camp may certainly stimulate your child's interest in music at this age, but even more important is the range of enrichment activities and resources you provide throughout the year.

Family listening time. Arrange a family listening time, each person choosing his favorite music. Relax and enjoy what each family member selects.

Family music time. Create a family music time during which family members play for each other or together and combine their assorted skills in playing, singing, or dancing. The type of music may vary, depending on family interests, the season, the current mood, and the like.

Duets. If you play an instrument or sing, work on a duet with your child.

Movies. Rent a movie with a music-related focus for family viewing. Invite your child's friend(s). Don't forget the popcorn!

Concerts/recitals. Plan to attend a concert or recital together. Prepare by listening to some of the repertoire beforehand. If possible, choose a program in which gifted young soloists are performing.

Dance programs. Plan to attend a colorful ballet or dance program together. Prepare by reading the story and listening to the music (perhaps dancing to some of it yourself!). *The Nutcracker, Swan Lake,* and *The Firebird* are choices that help make the connection between music and dance.

Resources. Use a resource like Barlow's *Happy Listening Guide* to give focus to a listening experience.

Books and Music. Buy music or books about music as gifts for your child. You may want to read some of these together, particularly if you select one that is a general history appropriately written for this age group. A book such as *Bach, Beethoven, and the Boys* can provide a few shared laughs as well as information.

Software and CD-ROMs. After consulting with the teacher, purchase software or CD-ROMs that might be helpful supplements to music study. Some CD-ROMs make good family browsing material.

Three Points of View

Keep in mind that the members of the child-parent-teacher triangle are different people. You, your child, and your child's music teacher each have points of view about music study. In some cases, these may be similar; in others they may be quite distinct. It helps to consider some usual points of view not because each child, parent, or teacher will have exactly these opinions or attitudes, nor because awareness of different viewpoints will magically erase the differences. The value of such reflection is to put yourself in another's place and, in that way, try to appreciate what has meaning and worth to someone else. Your child cannot do this. Your child's music teacher should be able to do this, but is separate from the daily routine that you and your child share as members of the same family. *You* are the go-between and referee. How clearly you understand these nuances and how honestly you deal with them will affect your child's success regarding music study.

Your child's point of view

- "Music study should be fun."
- "Music is more fun if I play it with others."
- "It's embarrassing when Mom asks me to play for other people."
- "I think I'd like to practice alone, but I'm not sure if I can."
- "Practice is getting in the way of playing and being with my friends."
- "I like to help pick the pieces and goals."
- "I care a lot about what my friends think of me and what I do."
- "I'd like to try some computer music programs, or play cool music."

Your point of view

- "I'd like my child to have every opportunity; music is just one of these."
- "My child should enjoy playing and be reasonably successful."
- "I'd like my child to persevere through routines and challenges."
- "You can play soccer *if* you continue violin lessons."
- "I wish my child could practice more on his own."
- "I'd like my child to play for others, even if it isn't perfect."
- "My child should play music that I recognize and enjoy."
- "I'm tired of driving to so many lessons, rehearsals, and events."

The teacher's point of view

- "Now is the time to hang in there; things are starting to sound good."
- "This is an excellent time to work on technique."
- "I think you should increase your practice time."
- "I can hardly wait to assign this new book."
- "What about playing in an audition?"
- "I have this wonderful piece for your next recital."
- "We need to work for a more refined sense of style."
- "I wish you would listen to more classical music."

Compare these views. Some juggling and balancing will be necessary.

Each person has a different focus.

- Your child has a single focus—himself and what gives him pleasure and self-esteem.
- Your focus is wider—how music helps your child and how that fits into his total growth.
- The ideal teacher's focus is both on the child and the music; each is important.

Each person wants music study to be pleasurable.

- Your child is looking for fun and excitement.
- You want your child to enjoy playing music that sounds good to you.
- The teacher hopes that the beauty of music and success will generate pleasure.

Each person has opinions about playing in public.

- Your child probably has mixed emotions about this, depending on the circumstances.
- You want others to see how well your child is doing, even if the results are not so polished.
- The teacher regards performance as important and seeks the highest possible standards.

Each person cares about practice time.

- Your child may find this lonely and may be unclear about how to follow through.

- You would like your child to learn greater self-reliance and self-direction.
- The teacher regards practice as necessary and expected.

Each person may be interested in a different kind of music.

- Your child likes music that pleases himself and his friends.
- You like music that sounds familiar.
- The teacher probably upholds classical "standards," or has ideals of "quality" music.

Each person reacts to new musical outlets.

- Your child is looking to explore music that relates to his real world.
- You must juggle everyone's schedule and feel the increasing demands on your time.
- The teacher is thinking in terms of rehearsals, auditions, and concert attendance.

No one can tell you how to achieve balance in your own family life. Some juggling will be necessary, if only at times. Communication, however, will help to smooth out differences and confusions. Since you see how all aspects of your child's life must interact, don't hesitate to speak or inquire when necessary. You are more likely to find solutions if you ask questions or raise issues. Remember that your progress in parenting, like your child's in learning, is never straightforward. Be ready for the rises, dips, and plateaus. They are all part of being human.

HIGHLIGHTS

☆ These are make-or-break years with regard to music study.
☆ If your child is beginning music study now:
   This is a good time to begin study of brass and wind instruments.
   There are ways you can help your child to select an instrument.
   Studying through school is attractive because it often involves playing in a group.
   There is usually rapid progress at the outset of study at this age.
☆ If your child is continuing music study begun earlier:
   This is a good time to expand your child's musical outlets.
   Because of the growth spurt, this is also a good time to zero in on developing technique.

Your role is beginning to change; now is the time to start backing off.

Your child should begin to develop a sense of independence and self-reliance.

☆ With regard to practicing:

Your child still needs some guidance and support.

You should have some idea of what good and bad practice sounds like.

You should not be the "practice policeman."

You may need to discuss the matter of practice with your child and the teacher.

☆ If your child is having problems:

Try to uncover the real source of the problem.

Your child's progress is never consistent; there are rises, dips, and plateaus.

Be careful of making unjustified or unthinking comparisons.

You can help your child to perform by preparing and responding positively.

☆ A good teacher for this age group:

Handles the development of technique with care and insight.

Shows your child how to practice independently in very concrete ways.

Encourages your child to explore new areas and make choices.

Realizes the importance of the peer group at this age and provides group interaction.

☆ Music must be a part of your child's real world:

You can help your child make a gift of music to a relative or friend.

You can encourage your child to play for the pleasure of others, not just in a recital.

Your community is a resource that you and your child can tap together.

Your child might be interested in attending a summer music camp.

CHAPTER RESOURCES

The resources listed below are appropriate for the age group discussed in this chapter. Age recommendations are listed only if an item has more narrow appeal. Some items have wide appeal and are listed in the chapter resources of more than one chapter.

Take special note of Part IV, "General Resources," for a listing of books, recordings, movies, games, teaching aids, CD-ROMs, and catalogs.

BOOKS FOR YOU

Armstrong, Thomas. AWAKENING YOUR CHILD'S NATURAL GENIUS: ENHANCING CURIOSITY, CREATIVITY, AND LEARNING ABILITY. Los Angeles: Tarcher, 1991.

A natural outgrowth of the author's *In Their Own Way*, here Armstrong examines specific learning styles in greater depth. Among these are chapters on math, art, music, science. Giftedness, computer learning, special eduation, Montessori, Waldorf, and superlearning are also discussed and, often, criticized. The text is broken up by the insertion of lists, headings, and rich and diverse quotations.

Bigler, Carole L. and Valerie Lloyd-Watts. MORE THAN MUSIC: A HANDBOOK FOR TEACHERS, PARENTS, AND STUDENTS. Athens, OH: Ability Development, 1979.

Although written for those involved in Suzuki piano training, all parents will find the introductory chapters helpful. Especially useful are the chapters entitled "The Role of the Parents in the Education of Their Children," "The Role of Parents and Relatives at Lessons and at Home," and "Parental Aids: Motivating Students." Specific guidelines for assisting with practice are stated clearly.

Campbell, Virginia F. PUZZLING, PATTERNING, PRACTICING: A GUIDE TO MORE EFFECTIVE PIANO STUDY. Chapel Hill, NC: Hinshaw, 1985.

A concise pamphlet of suggestions for effective practice. Useful for teachers and parents with children nine to sixteen years old.

Canter, Lee and Lee Hausner. HOMEWORK WITHOUT TEARS. New York: Harper & Row, 1987.

This parent's guide for motivating children to do homework and to succeed in school has a good-humored approach. Chapter 10, "Solving the Seven Most Common Homework Problems," will ring a responsive chord for parents struggling to guide their children in music practice. Includes helpful long- and short-range planning charts.

Gardner, Howard. FRAMES OF MIND. New York: Basic Books, 1985.

This book has already become a classic since Gardner's theory of multiple intelligences, introduced in this work, has attracted many followers. Musical intelligence is discussed more from the standpoint of the composer of music than the performer. Gardner speaks of how one perceives music in relation to the functions of the brain, and he also addresses unusual talents, such as that of the idiot savant. While the reading style is friendly, the general tone of the book is serious.

Gardner, Howard. THE UNSCHOOLED MIND: HOW CHILDREN THINK AND HOW SCHOOLS SHOULD TEACH. New York: Basic Books, 1991.

Gardner asks how we can help students move beyond rote learning to achieve genuine understanding. He makes a strong case for restructuring schools, using the latest research on learning as a guide. Here are new ideas about education—from the world of the young child as "natural learner" to the adolescent's search for meaning. A serious, provocative book.

Satir, Virginia. THE NEW PEOPLEMAKING. Mountain View, CA: Science and Behavior Books, 1988.

Written by a pioneer in family therapy, this book explores all facets of family living and interaction, from self-worth to the family of the future. The writing style is direct, humorous, and right on target. Each chapter is full of useful advice that is sometimes framed in diagrams, conversations, or anecdotes.

Wlodkowski, Raymond J. and Judith Jaynes. EAGER TO LEARN: HELPING CHILDREN BECOME MOTIVATED AND LOVE LEARNING. San Francisco: Jossey-Bass, 1990.

The authors speak directly to parents about understanding and supporting a child's desire to learn. The writing style is practical, listing specific steps that parents can take. Discussions are often handled in a question-and-answer format. Especially useful are the chapters entitled "Building a Positive Parent-Teacher Relationship," and "Encouraging Effort and Perseverance," as well as the resource section that includes such information as how to prepare for a parent-teacher conference. There are also two videos, called "Motivation to Learn," associated with this book. (See Videos listed below).

BOOKS FOR YOU WITH YOUR CHILD

Barlow, Amy. HAPPY LISTENING GUIDE. Secaucus, NJ: Summy-Birchard, n.d.

A booklet that gives helpful hints on improving music listening. Could be used by parents and students during live or recorded performances. There are sample listening charts, checklists of "what to listen and watch for" during performances, pages to note favorites, and an autograph page. For parents with children six and older.

Cohn, Amy L. FROM SEA TO SHINING SEA: A TREASURY OF AMERICAN FOLKLORE AND FOLK SONGS. New York: Scholastic, 1993.

This treasury of folk songs and stories covers the entire history of America from the time before the early settlers to the present. There are generous color illustrations and easy piano scores for the songs. A family browser. All ages.

Krull, Kathleen. GONNA SING MY HEAD OFF. New York: Knopf, 1992.

Folk songs for children, collected from all regions of the United States, are beautifully illustrated by Allen Garns with an introduction by Arlo Guthrie. Piano accompaniments require ability to play melodies with simple chords. All ages.

BOOKS FOR YOUR CHILD

Ardley, Neil. MUSIC. New York: Knopf, 1989.

This book about instruments shows them in color photographs. The photographs are outstanding not only for their precision and clarity (at times showing the instrument disassembled), but also for the extremely wide scope of instruments included. The range of percussion instruments depicted is unusual, as is the inclusion of modern amplified instruments. Ten and older.

Buettner, Stewart and Reinhard G. Pauly. PORTRAITS: GREAT COMPOSERS— GREAT ARTISTS. Portland, OR: Amadeus Press, 1992.

An art historian and a musician/scholar have collaborated to create a unique book, an annotated collection of musicians' portraits. The portraits of great composers through the ages are artistically significant, by major artists, from a painting of Martin Luther by Lucas Cranach the Elder to a sculpture of George Gershwin by twentieth-century artist Isamu Noguchi. An outstanding work. Students will enjoy seeing portraits of composers they are studying. Eleven and older.

Donald, Dave. BACH, BEETHOVEN, AND THE BOYS. Toronto: Sound and Vision, 1986. (359 Riverdale Ave., Toronto, Canada, M4J 1A4).

The subtitle, "Music History as It Ought to Be Taught," suggests the tongue-in-cheek writing style. Dates and facts are completely accurate, but the anecdotes and cartoonlike illustrations focus on offbeat incidents and information. Only in a book like this would you find out that Haydn's wife used his manuscripts to line cake tins, Schubert's friends called him "Tubby," or that Wagner's pet poodle ran away from home. A good dose of music history in an easy-to-swallow form. Ten and older.

Erlewine, Michael and Scott Bultman. ALL MUSIC GUIDE. Corte Modera, CA: Miller Freeman c/o BMR Associates, 1984. (21 Tamal Vista Blvd., Suite 209, Corte Madera, CA 94925).

Comprehensive and authoritative guide to all genres of music, organized in twenty-seven categories. "Music Map" shows at a glance how a particular music style developed, identifies each style's major players, and traces who influenced whom. Eleven and older.

Helpern, Mark. *SWAN LAKE*. Boston: Houghton Mifflin, 1989.

An absolute treasure of a book written in elegant prose by a prize-winning author. The illustrations by Chris Van Allsburg are magical. A perfect introduction to the story of *Swan Lake* as preparation for seeing the ballet and hearing the music by Tchaikovsky. Eleven and older.

Hoffman, E. T. A. *NUTCRACKER*. New York: Crown, 1984.

The magnificent illustrations of Maurice Sendak illuminate the delights of Hoffman's story in this rich and tantalizing tale. Good preparation for seeing the Tchaikovsky ballet. Five to eleven years old.

Hughes, Langston. JAZZ (UPDATED AND EXPANDED BY SANDFORD BROWN). New York: Franklin Watts, 1982.

A history of jazz from its beginnings to 1980s jazz rock. Included is information on the African roots of jazz, work songs and spirituals, jazz forms, jazz instruments, and jazz singers, with separate attention paid to Louis Armstrong and Duke Ellington. Major artists are mentioned, and there are a number of photographs. A good way to introduce and/or explain jazz as a separate style. Ten and older.

Koch, Karen. MY OWN MUSIC HISTORY. Trenton, IL: The Music Studio, n.d. (422 N. Maple St., Trenton, IL 62293).

A hardback, loose-leaf notebook that presents the periods of music history. Each period has its own color. There is a time line of composers, milestones of music history, great composer color seals, and more. The composer biography sheets are unique; the student writes about the pieces he is playing and how these "fit in" with music history. Eight and older. Best done with a teacher's help.

Krull, Kathleen. LIVES OF THE MUSICIANS: GOOD TIMES, BAD TIMES (AND WHAT THE NEIGHBORS THOUGHT). San Diego: Harcourt Brace Jovanovich, 1993.

These brief biographies are written with rare charm, partly because they recount very human aspects of the musician's life ("what the neighbors thought" gives you a clue), and partly because these bits of information relate directly to a young reader's life (for instance, the fact that Beethoven liked macaroni and cheese, that Brahms left his clothes on the floor when he went to bed, or that Ives had a cat named Christofina who ate asparagus). The choice of musicians is also uncommon. Scott Joplin, Woody Guthrie, Gilbert and Sullivan, and Nadia Boulanger are there with Bach, Beethoven, and Mozart. This is a quality book. Parents will enjoy it as much as the kids. Ten and older.

McLeish, Kenneth and Valerie McLeish. THE OXFORD FIRST COMPANION TO MUSIC. New York: Oxford University Press, 1982.

Specially designed for young children, this book uses large type, has hundreds of illustrations, and covers all kinds of music, including Oriental, African, pop, and jazz music. Six and older.

Mundy, Simon. THE USBOURNE STORY OF MUSIC. London: Usbourne, 1980.

A highly illustrated, almost cartoonlike history of music from ancient times to the present (contemporary, classical, and popular music). Appealing thumbnail sketches of each period. Ten and older.

Nichols, Janet. AMERICAN MUSIC MAKERS: AN INTRODUCTION TO AMERICAN COMPOSERS. New York: Walker, 1990.

Biographies of ten American composers, written in a friendly style, that are of interest to young readers. What is most refreshing, however, is the choice of composers—Louis Gottschalk, Charles Ives, Ruth Crawford Seeger, George Crumb, and Philip Glass, to name half. There is a brief suggested listening list, a glossary, and a few ideas for further reading. Ten and older.

Nichols, Janet. WOMEN MUSIC MAKERS: AN INTRODUCTION TO WOMEN COMPOSERS. New York: Walker, 1992.

Biographies of ten women composers who were born between 1619 and 1947. The book offers the young female reader a gallery of role models, and draws attention to the fact that these composers were, in turn, influenced by other musical women and needed their own role models in order to succeed. Included are Fanny Mendelssohn Hensel, Clara Wieck Schumann, Ellen Taaffe Zwilich, and Laurie Anderson. Unfortunately, many of the recordings are not easy to locate. Ten and older.

Sommer, Elsey. THE KIDS' WORLD ALMANAC OF MUSIC: FROM ROCK TO BACH. New York: World Almanac, 1992.

Trivia information, arranged by chapters. References range from Bach to nicknames of groupies. Also included are the basics of music theory and information about inventors of musical instruments. Offbeat fun. Ten and older.

Tames, Richard. FRÉDÉRIC CHOPIN. New York: Franklin Watts, 1991.

A good biography, done in slightly larger print on good-quality paper. It includes many photographs (some in color) of Chopin, important people in his life, and cities in which he lived and performed. The details of Chopin's life, such as his relationship with George Sand, are dealt with honestly. Ten and older.

Tatchell, Judy. UNDERSTANDING MUSIC. London: Usbourne, 1990.

This book is crammed with assorted information. Definitions of musical styles (including folk, ethnic, jazz, rock, and pop), information about instruments, listening suggestions, pictures of performers, and a survey of composers and what kind of music they wrote are presented along with instructions on how to read music. There is also information on learning to play an instrument. Ten and older.

Van der Meer, Ron and Michael Berkeley. THE MUSIC PACK. New York: Knopf, 1994.

An exciting multimedia introduction to musical creation that allows you to see and hear how sound is produced and turned into music. Fold-out spreads feature playable pull-out and pop-up instruments, three-dimensional views of various instruments, a booklet on musical notation, and an interactive world music map. A 70-minute CD with twenty musical masterpieces is included. All ages.

VIDEOS

AFRICAN AMERICAN TALENT SHOW. GPN. 800-228-4630.

Uniquely gifted African American youngsters who are studying and planning careers as classical concert artists are showcased in this well-filmed documentary. Comments by several of the young performers on their goals and hopes for the future make this tape especially valuable.

AGAINST THE ODDS: LUDWIG VAN BEETHOVEN. Films for the Humanities. 800-257-5126.

The focus in this short biographical film is on Beethoven's ability to compose in spite of his increasing hearing loss. Extremely well produced. Though expensive, it gets its message across remarkably effectively. Eight and older.

ANDRÉS SEGOVIA: SONG OF THE GUITAR. Teldec Video. 212-399-7782.

An evocation of Spain in exquisite travel scenes, and a tribute to the life of this master guitarist with beautiful, sensitive performances.

BEETHOVEN LIVES UPSTAIRS. The Children's Group. 800-456-2334.

A dramatization centering around Christophe, a ten-year-old in nineteenth-century Vienna, whose mother rents the rooms "upstairs" to Beethoven. The boy learns to accept Beethoven's odd habits as well as his music. There is no condescension in this presentation. It offers a superior evocation of the era as well as Beethoven's music. Eight and older.

THE COMPETITION. GPN. 800-228-4630.

This encounter investigates competitions as an important learning experience and an opportunity for self-evaluation. Young performers on the violin, piano, and flute are featured.

THE FIDDLE SHOW. GPN. 800-228-4630.

Master artist-teacher Joseph Gingold, a young performer, and a group of violin students demonstrate the agility and fitness necessary to make music with the violin.

LEONARD BERNSTEIN'S YOUNG PEOPLE'S CONCERTS SERIES WITH THE NEW YORK PHILHARMONIC. Music in Motion. 800-445-0649.

Ten videos of twenty-five digitally remastered programs originally broadcast from 1958 to 1970. Topics include What Does Music Mean? What Is Classical Music? What Is Sonata Form? What Makes Music Symphonic? There is a book of Bernstein's lectures taken from these videos. A remarkable series from a great communicator.

MOTIVATION TO LEARN: HOW PARENTS AND TEACHERS CAN HELP. GUIDELINES FOR PARENT-TEACHER CONFERENCES. ASCD (Association for Supervision and Curriculum Development). 703-549-9110.

These videotapes have been prepared in conjunction with the book *Eager To Learn*, by Wlodkowski and Jaynes. Tape One is for parents and teachers. In the first segment, we see an unmotivated boy (of middle-school age) at various times in his day. A parent-teacher conference involving this boy makes up the second segment. Interdependent roles of parent and teacher are discussed. Tape Two is primarily for teachers and contains edited parent-teacher conferences dealing with student motivational problems. Although these videos are designed with workshop presentation in mind, parents would find them useful as examples of real-life coping strategies.

MUSIC ANIMATION MACHINE. Stephen Malinowski. 510-235-7478.

As you listen to the music of a wide range of classical composers, a graphic color representation scrolls by, showing how the music is structured and contoured. These conceptual elements take shape before your eyes. There is nothing quite like this presentation, and even sophisticated musicians are captivated. Children who play beyond beginning levels would get the most out of this approach. Ten and older.

ORCHESTRA! INTRODUCTION TO THE ORCHESTRA. UPPER STRINGS. LOWER STRINGS. BRASS. PIANO. PERCUSSION. MAESTRO. THE ART OF CONDUCTING. Films for the Humanities. 800-257-5126.

Conductor Sir Georg Solti and Dudley Moore introduce viewers to the instruments. The orchestra is comprised of talented young people from around the world. The young musicians discuss their reasons for choosing a particular instrument. A splendid opportunity to hear all the instruments separately and together. The tone is informal, the dress is casual, and Moore is entertaining. Ten and older.

THE PIANO SHOW. GPN. 800-228-4630.

Features three young pianists in different stages of musical development who excel in different musical styles. A fourth pianist provides a stunning example of what discipline and hard work can accomplish. Concert pianist Leon Fleisher is a special guest.

PROKOFIEV: THE PRODIGAL SON. Films for the Humanities. 800-257-5126.

A breathtaking portrait of one of the twentieth century's musical giants. Superb musical performances are interwoven with film clips of the life and times of the composer and dramatic presentation of events from his life. A thoroughly professional production.

TRYIN' TO GET HOME: A HISTORY OF AFRICAN AMERICAN SONG. Heebie Jeebie Music. 510-548-4613.

Written and performed by Kerrigan Black, this is a stirring performance and a musical record of an important part of American musical heritage.

WE REINVENT THE CIRCUS. NOUVELLE EXPERIENCE. SALTIMBANCO. Cirque du Soleil. 800-727-2233.

This combination of acrobatics, costumes, music, and effects is truly a spectacle. The circus is taken to new heights of creativity and fantasy, and the Montreal-based ensemble provides excitement way beyond the entertainment level. Music, performed live, plays a major role in these productions.

CD-ROMs

Call the telephone number of each company to ask for a catalog. Check system requirements before ordering. Ask for a try-before-you-buy arrangement.

MUSICAL INSTRUMENTS. Microsoft Home. 800-426-9400.

This provides wonderful access to information about more than 200 instruments. There are four ways to navigate: "Families of Instruments," "A–Z of Instruments," "Instruments of the World," "Musical Ensembles." You can see how the instruments work, hear musical examples, and "play" limited pitches on each instrument. There is reference to jazz, rock, classical, and other ensembles. For Macintosh and Windows. All ages.

THE MUSICAL WORLD OF PROFESSOR PICCOLO: THE FUN WAY TO LEARN ALL ABOUT MUSIC. Opcode Systems. 415-856-3333.

Includes reading music, fun musical games, music history, music notation, and musical instruments data. It is a self-paced interactive course in music theory and musical styles, with excellent graphics. Macintosh and Windows.

THE ORCHESTRA: THE INSTRUMENTS REVEALED. Time Warner New Media. 800-482-3766.

Based on Benjamin Britten's *The Young Person's Guide to the Orchestra*, this program invites the user to see and hear the instruments of the orchestra and learn how they are played. Also included: a conducting lesson, an orchestration lab, a pronouncer, biographical information, a glossary, and a time line. Macintosh. Ten and older.

ROCK, RAP, AND ROLL. Paramount Interactive. 415-812-8200.

A colorful, easy-to-use CD-ROM in which the user assigns instruments, vocals, and sound effects to the keyboard and screen. The user can add his own voice and sing along.

SO I'VE HEARD. The Voyager Company. 800-446-2001.

A sweep through the masterpieces of Western classical music with music critic Alan Rich. This five-volume series combines essays, both witty and wise, with lavish illustrations for the eye and ear in dozens of artworks and audio examples. Volume 1: *Bach and Before*. Volume 2: *The Classical Ideal*. Volume 3: *Beethoven and Beyond*. Volume 4: *Romantic Heights*. Volume 5: *Here and Now*.

The Adolescent Years

What you will find in this chapter

- The adolescent from twelve to fifteen
- The adolescent from fifteen to eighteen
- Why these are special years for music study
- The teen who begins music study now
- The teen who began music study earlier
- Strategies to encourage continued study
- The teen considering a music career
     Planning ahead. Variety of musical choices.
- Competitions
- Summer camps
- Teens and technology
- Music enrichment in the public schools
- The right teacher for your teen
- Time to change teachers?
- Time to quit?
- Practice problems and support
- Physical cautions about technique
- How to react to teen music
- Three points of view
- Highlights
- Chapter resources

"*A*DOLESCENECE is is a disease from which I think I have recovered." So begins the saga of one college student. What of these transition years? Certainly for the teen, they are among the most mercurial, dramatic, challenging, terrifying, and thrilling years of life so far. At no other time in your role as a parent has the thought of the daunting choices been more fraught with danger or filled with so many exciting possibilities. As we explore the world of adolescence, that very special time when the young person has one foot on either side of childhood, the terminology immediately changes. We can no longer refer to this young offspring of yours as your "child," although that relationship will be true throughout your life. The years of developing a sense of independence and separation have arrived, whether parents like it or not.

You have to do your own growing no matter how tall your grandfather was.
—Abraham Lincoln

Establishing his own identity, or ruminating over the possibility of doing so, becomes a major preoccupation for your teen. The transition is challenging for both of you. These are the years when you must redefine your relationship with your child, whom we shall hereafter refer to as your "teen" out of respect for his need not to be viewed as a child ever again, no matter how many times that label may be accurate.

Adolescence is known as a time of "storm and stress," and the challenges that face teens on every front—physical, social, emotional, and cognitive—are difficult for them and their families. One of the remarkable things about music study is that it can have the power to focus energy positively, to build the self-esteem that so often is shaky in the teen years, answer social needs in an affirmative way, and provide attainable goals.

Before we explore these positive benefits of music in the life of your teen, let's examine the classic profile of the adolescent.

The adolescent from twelve to fifteen

The adolescent from twelve to fifteen

- has reached puberty (practically all girls and many boys).
- has many aspects of behavior influenced by growth spurt and puberty.
- experiences trauma from abrupt shift to a larger school (middle schoolers).
- feels somewhat awkward, due to self-consciousness at sudden growth.
- is concerned about physical appearance and sex roles.
- strongly desires to conform to peer standards.
- highly values acceptance by peers.
- shows growing independence and has initial thoughts about identity.
- is still likely to obey rules out of respect for authority or to impress others.
- is in generally good health, but has poor eating and sleeping habits.

Teenagers are maddeningly self-centered, yet capable of impressive feats of altruism. Their attention wanders like a butterfly, yet they can spend hours concentrating on their own involvements. They are often lazy and rude, yet they can be loving, and when you least expect it, helpful.
—Mihaly Csikszentmihalyi and Reed Larson

Though conformity may be a new form of security on the stormy sea of adolescence, there is diversity as well. Variations in physical growth, hormonal inheritance, relationships within the family, and patterns of early childhood development all influence the climate in these fragile, dynamic, and crucial years. As tenuous as the onset of adolescence may be, the remaining years of adolescence from age sixteen to eighteen have their own particular qualities.

What is it like to be a teenager in today's world? What do teenagers do and think, and how do they feel about themselves and their changing world?

The early teenage years present the shock of entry into the transition, but it is the older teen who must face the first serious choices in life, and they all come cascading at once. "What do you want to be when you grow up?" is a question often asked of the young child. Now it becomes an urgent refrain, not always welcome to teenage ears. What career? What college? What partner? What personality? What hairdo? What values? What shoes on Saturday night? Questions become a jumble of the immediate and the long-range. Sometimes there is denial of the probing issues, but eventually every teen and family must face them.

When you look at the following definition of the late teen years, keep in mind the diversity you can expect from your own teen.

The adolescent from fifteen to eighteen

> ### The adolescent from fifteen to eighteen
> - has almost reached physical maturity.
> - is often interested in sex.
> - is influenced by parents in long-range plans.
> - is influenced by peers in more immediate decisions.
> - has anxiety about friendships (girls more than boys).
> - may have emotional disorders, most commonly depression (more frequent in girls than boys).
> - is capable of engaging in formal thought, but may not use this capability.
> - may engage in unrestrained theorizing, be threatened by possibilities, and be subject to adolescent egocentrism.

These generalizations don't take into account the most outstanding characteristic of the adolescent years, the variability among teenagers and within any one teenager. If you step back and observe, rather than challenge a passing attitude or mode of behavior, you are allowing your teen an opportunity to become a new, more mature self, which is what these years are all about. The fact that teenagers in general, and your teenager in particular, may be "trying on" various roles for size may make it difficult to identify which self is at the core of an observed behavior. By stepping back a bit, you are giving your teen's uniqueness a chance to emerge.

Why these are special years for music study

If life from the cradle on has been filled with music, with shared family support, and enrichment activities, there should be some continuation of these values as your child makes the journey from childhood to adulthood. There may be a need similar to the two-year-old's to "do it myself," as well as a need for privacy, a sense of separation and individuality, no matter how close the family unit has been. You may no longer be the most significant person in your teen's life at this time, and that can hurt.

The child you once accompanied to lessons will probably do better without you. In fact, if your teen is still dependent on your presence, that is more cause for concern than if he wants you to stay away.

The child who needed your support during practice should now be well on the way to fruitful independent study. From the moment of birth, the sense of independence should gradually be established. Listening and practice habits should be well ingrained, if your child has had good instruction from the preschool or elementary school level.

The times of crisis are generally the times of change in the school pattern. Going from lower to upper elementary school is a mild, but not too traumatic, shift. Going from upper elementary school to junior high or middle school is a significant change. It is an abrupt shift from being the oldest, biggest, most sophisticated in the smaller school environment to being the youngest, smallest, and least knowledgeable in a larger school. This is the time that many music students begin to feel the pressure of academic demands. Some will have the capacity to carry both academics and music. Some will crumble under the burden. Parents and teachers should be sensitive to this transition by lessening the load for those who are oppressed by the changes. By responding with understanding to the new pressures and adjustments, you are more likely to help your teen bridge the gap successfully.

How does all of this psychological jargon translate to your teen and music lessons?

If you have come aboard at this chapter, you are probably the parent of a young person who is bordering on adolescence, and has one of three possible musical needs. You have a teen who:

- has always loved music, but who is asking for lessons for the first time.
- has studied for several years, but with the advent of heavier academic pressure, a more active social life, and definitely more active hormones, is considering whether to continue music study.
- is becoming more and more heavily engrossed in music to the point that he is beginning to think about the possibility of making music a career.

We deal with each of these musical needs in this chapter. In some ways, we hope that the parents of a much younger child have looked ahead to see some of the possibilities of these teen years. No one arrives at adolescence without an important history. The early years have been a prelude to these transition years. You can seldom create sudden miracles of industry, focus, balance, and enthusiasm.

Oh, to be only half as wonderful as my child thought I was when he was small, and only half as stupid as my teenager now thinks I am.
—Rebecca Richards

Definition of adolescence: A Kind of emotional seasickness.—Arthur Koestler

The teen who begins music study now

It doesn't happen every day, but there is the teen who either has resisted formal lessons offered earlier and now finds a reason for wanting to learn, or who suddenly requests lessons. Usually it is a teen who is involved in music through school activities, through active listening to music, or from observing peers who can play. Parents are sometimes skeptical of these "late" requests, thinking that this may be just another whim or passing fancy.

Some of these late bloomers are among the most focused, challenging, and interesting students to teach. For one thing, independent study habits have been established. The student is usually articulate enough to give important feedback to the teacher in terms of what is or is not understood. The rate of progress, compared to a younger beginner, is often much faster.

The message is clear in any case: *It is never too late to learn.* If your teen requests lessons, say a hearty yes, making sure that you have agreed on a certain investment of time (a year is a fair amount of time for testing interest and industry). Clarify what you and the teacher expect in terms of effort, then enthusiastically support that effort, even rewarding outstanding progress or organization of time with a gift of music (a recording, a subscription to a music magazine, or a trip to a concert, perhaps with a special friend).

The teen who began music study earlier

What of the teen who began study as a preschooler or in elementary school? What is to be done when academics, social life, and all the previously mentioned pressures of these years begin to overwhelm your teenager? The crisis usually arrives at the onset of junior or senior high school. Your teen is struggling with more homework, more deadlines, more pressure to get high marks to get into a good college. Suddenly, time management can be a problem. Add to this the desire on the part of some teens to extend their social lives, extracurricular efforts, or leisure, and you have the makings of a real dilemma.

How can you help your teen sort out the important from the unimportant? How can you help her arrive at her own decision about continuing music lessons after considering all the possibilities? There are several questions that can be put to your teen, or that the teacher, after consulting with you, can present. (Sometimes you are the best one to have the "heart-to-heart." Sometimes the teacher can be a helpful assistant in reaching this delicate decision.) The following is a possible parent script.

> ### Questions to ask your teen
> - Do you enjoy your music lessons?
> - Do you enjoy the music you are studying?
> - Do you like your teacher?
> - Is the work too easy?
> - Is the work too hard?
> - If you could change anything about your lessons, what would it be?
> - Do you think you would miss music in your life if you stopped studying?
> - Are you willing to discuss your feelings about lessons with your teacher?
> - Is there anything that we [parents] can do to help?

I have found the best way to give advice to your children is to find out what they want and then advise them to do it.—Harry S. Truman

By giving your teen an opportunity to examine the seeds of discontent in regard to music study, you and the teacher are acknowledging one of the most important skills required of the adolescent—the art of making choices. Up to this time, there has been little or no choice. The young person has everything laid out for him: what subjects to take, what food to eat, and what clothes to wear. Now there is a choice. Music is an elective. It should be a joyous one, even though it may sometimes require effort. It is your job to discover the underlying cause of the discontent.

There are a number of issues that may be at the core of the problem:

- The teen may feel isolated while practicing, in which case the growing desire for social contacts may need to be addressed.
- An increasingly heavy academic burden may be alleviated by lightening the music assignment for a short time.
- A change of materials may be in order.
- The socially conscious teen may need new reasons for pursuing music.
- It may be time to change teachers.

No matter what the reason for the difficulty, one thing is clear. The solution must be reached by your teen, in cooperation with you and the teacher. The energy and commitment must come from the student, guided by the adult members of the team. The cooperation you will need from your teen is similar to the time in his childhood when you needed his energy to push his foot into the shoe. A limp or rigid limb defeated the purpose. Teens have to have their own reason for study, and it must be their firm commitment, not limp agreement or begrudging compliance, that will make continued study worthwhile and fruitful.

Strategies to encourage continued study

There are several strategies that can be useful when teens have doubts about continuing lessons.

Answering social needs. The skill to use solitude to pursue goals independently does not come easily to adolescents. For the teen who lacks such skills, solitude is nothing more than a frightening vacuum. The social aspects of making music with others answer some basic teenage needs. This is especially true for pianists, who have less opportunity to play in band, orchestra, or other ensemble activities.

The public school music teacher can be a key figure in helping to arrange musical ensemble opportunities. If your teen is shy about announcing his aptitude and interest, you may have to let the school music teacher know (in private, of course, to avoid embarrassing your offspring). The school music teacher can encourage participation in ensembles, chorus accompanying, multimedia and other technology projects, musical theater, or jazz combos, any of which may answer these social needs.

The independent instrumental or vocal teacher can add duet and other ensemble literature to the student's repertoire. Community music schools and music preparatory schools also offer these enrichment opportunities.

Adolescents are more likely to enjoy an activity if they feel they've made the choice to do it.—Jane Conoley

Lighter load. If your teen gets obvious pleasure from studying and playing the instrument, but still feels overwhelmed by trying to fit practice into the schedule, you may want to discuss the possibility of a shorter assignment with the teacher. It often helps if the teacher enlists the student's opinion in selecting only one or two favorite pieces to work on for a while. Changing the expectations can somehow make a huge difference. More challenge can be introduced at a later date when the teen has become accustomed to the heavier academic demands.

Change of repertoire. To answer the teen's changing tastes and emotional needs, the teacher may have to assign new material. Teens often like music that has a rich, full sound. Music that is expressive, dramatic, and romantic also rings a responsive note. Some teens do best with shorter, less demanding goals. Others thrive on longer works that offer more challenge. It only takes one piece that the teen is in love with to turn the tide.

Outreach. Experiences that psychologists call "flow" experiences are those that produce a feeling of fulfillment. Sports, arts, and many other enjoyable pursuits allow the teen to experience the blend of goals, thoughts, and emotions. But the ability to find enjoyment is not enough to ensure that a person will grow up to make the most of his or her potential. Teens involved in outreach programs develop a sense of self-worth and maturity that the sole pursuit of personal skills and pleasure cannot produce.

Every culture must find ways of engaging its youth in the responsibility of being adults. Stated simply, the issue is: How can we help adolescents to like the world into which they are born?
—Mihaly Csikszentmihalyi and Reed Larson

How can a teen become active in such projects? A teacher, principal, or community youth service bureau may be able to arrange for the teen to become a mentor for younger students. This project has the double advantage of turning the teen into a role model for the younger student, while giving the teen a glimpse of a possible new path in music as a teacher. Often this tutoring results in better practice habits for the older student because teaching the process clarifies it.

A special goal. Many colleges consider not only the student's SAT scores, grades, and extracurricular activities, but also skill in an art form carried through an entire school career. If a teen has invested five or six years in music study, working to make the best possible videotape to submit with a college application can prove to be a fruitful project. A videotape is evidence of the broad scope of interests and accomplishments. Preparing the tape can occupy a good part of sophomore and junior years of music study. It is possible to produce such a tape in any number of ways:

- Opt for high-fidelity recording at a professional recording studio.
- Plan multimedia productions with paintings, scores, and biographical and/or historic data to complement the pieces played.
- Tape informally, playing several pieces in a different venue: one at a lesson, one at home, one at a recital or formal concert.
- Simply record a program at home or at the teacher's studio.
- If a student is involved in ensemble playing (duets, chamber music, jazz or other combos), it is worthwhile to include these along with solo performances.
- Original compositions should also be considered as part of the sub-

mitted program, either in performance or score form, although the combination of score and performance is preferable.

• Tapes should not be more than 10 to 15 minutes in length, unless a particular school has suggested a lengthier entry.

Note that the project to make a videotape does not apply to students who plan to enter college as music majors. They are expected to audition in person. See the discussion of the career- oriented teen later in this chapter.

Benefit concert. If your teen is the questioning type, reasons for continuing study may come up. Your teen may ask, "Why music?" Often the argument will go something like this. "I'm not going to be a concert artist. Why do I have to practice and perform? I don't want to be on display the way I used to be when I was younger."

Every child is an artist. The problem is how to remain an artist once he grows up.
—Pablo Picasso

If your teen has this or a similar reaction, it may help to supply a different reason for having music in her life. The fact that she will be sorry to have quit when she is thirty will not register. Long-range goals for teenagers generally extend to the next weekend or next month.

Instead, if your teen has a sense of social responsibility, she can be encouraged to plan a special project that turns music into a gift. She can choose a worthy cause, and (with the help of the teacher) prepare a benefit program to be performed for invited guests. It may take a whole semester or season to plan for and work on such a program, but it gives a different meaning to practice, and turns the goal into a cause the teen believes in, not goals set by parents or the teacher. This project can be done alone or in cooperation with other teens. Publicity and design of programs adds other creative avenues to explore. Besides, it also looks good on your record.

The teen considering a music career

What of the teen who has decided that music is one of the most important things in life, an all-consuming passion?

The focused teen

- welcomes hard work and is open to experience.
- is better prepared to sustain and expand interests.
- is comfortable spending more time alone or with family than most teens.
- spends less time socializing, and more in productive activities with peers.
- economizes attention and diverts energy into developing his or her talent.
- is less sex-stereotyped.
- has a more conservative orientation toward sex and to the opposite sex.
- has a stable home environment that provides support and stimulation.
- engages in productive activities at school and performs well there.
- has satisfying short- and long-range goals.
- may have difficulty finding kindred spirits.

In an excellent book, *Talented Teenagers: The Roots of Success and Failure*, the authors ask,

> What are we to make of a person who is oriented to hard work but who pays attention to ideas and sensations because they are interesting? who is warm and cooperative with other members of the family and yet is strongly independent? who spends more time with the family and more time alone than the average teen? who likes those teachers best who demand hard work but are also fun? who acts a bit like an artist and a bit like a scientist? who enjoys the moment and yet looks ahead to the future? who feels skillful and yet feels challenged? Such a person is, like a good bottle of wine, complex and surprising, multidimensional, and likely to improve with age.

No matter how ideal that profile sounds, however, life is not always a bed of roses for the talented teenage musician. With an artistic nature often comes extreme sensitivity, which is a blessing and a curse. The emotional changes that underlie moving, artistic performances can cause mercurial mood swings, not always pleasant for the teen to live with or control. Parents and teachers who remain calm in these times have the best chance of helping to quell the storms more quickly. You can become the "port in the storm."

Another challenge for the talented teen is self-induced pressure to be perfect, or as close to it as possible. The good news is that the talented teen has developed an admirable ability to critique herself, yet she may be her own severest judge. As long as self-praise accompanies the criticism, a balance should be possible. This is a gray area for parents and teachers. Teens can smell false praise a mile away. When asked "How does that sound?" be very sure that the teen really wants an answer. The question is like one a wife might ask her husband. "How do I look?" Nine times out of ten, the desired answer is "You look great." Ask your teen what particular details he wants you to listen for (balance, dynamic shading, note accuracy, or other details). Do your best to give honest feedback. Otherwise, be an appreciative audience, letting the teen and teacher work out the critical details.

Planning ahead

The teen who plans to enter a college or conservatory needs to begin planning much earlier than the average teen. The following statement from the Music Teachers National Association *Book of Policies, Letters and Forms,* gives a clear indication of this need to prepare early.

> If any family has a child considering a performance career, they should discuss it with the teacher as soon as possible. These students need a commitment to practice time far greater than for other careers in music (i.e., music education, music therapy, music librarian, etc.). Without proper training and this early dedication of time and considerable effort, they cannot expect to be accepted into the performance programs of any college, university, or music school. This is not a decision to be made in the senior year of high school. It must be made earlier.
>
> from the studio of Ruth J. Carder, Belpre, OH

In preparation for applying as a performance major, it is helpful for your teen to send away for catalogs of several music schools by ninth or tenth grade, check the entrance requirements, and use the highest level of these requirements he is capable of as a guide to repertoire, theory, and the like. *The Performing Arts Major's College Guide* and the *Schirmer Guide to Schools of Music Throughout the World* are helpful resources. The wider the variety of musical experiences in your teen's education the better. Training in theory, music history, ensemble, composition, and improvising should be combined with frequent listening to recordings in a wide variety of musical styles. The young musician who has listened to many recordings is storing a lexicon of aural memories that will be invaluable later on.

There is always the possibility that a student is a "late bloomer." The importance of music as a career may not be so obvious when a student is thirteen or fourteen years old. Of course, early decision about a music career choice makes the preparations smoother, but students who have a later awakening can also consider applying to college as music majors.

One student we know was unfocused and generally unorganized during early adolescence. Schoolwork and practicing were difficult. Even remembering a coat on a cold winter day could be a problem. In her senior year, she had an epiphany. She decided to make a videotape to accompany her college applications. Suddenly she was focused completely. Her love of music, which was never in doubt, triumphed over her past inability to concentrate. She took complete charge of her practicing, producing a videotape that enabled her to be accepted at a fine school as a music education major.

Variety of musical choices

It is important to keep in mind the wide variety of choices open to someone contemplating a career in music. The teen is well advised to

A good musician is someone who says 'How can I contribute?' A musician who says 'I want to become a soloist,' is immediately less of a musician, because that's not what music is about. You want a certain status. That's great if you have the talent, and you go and do it, and you're lucky. But if that's your first priority, you really missed the boat.

—*Yo-Yo Ma*

try his hand at a number of musical activities such as accompanying, teaching, recording engineering, editing, scoring and orchestration, multimedia, conducting, and chamber music. Planning for a multifaceted career in music is much more realistic than deciding that only one goal will do (as soloist, orchestral first chair, or whatever). The preparation is like getting ready for a trip. It is better to take more than you need than to run out. By considering the multiple roles that a musician's life can take, and preparing accordingly, your teen will be in a better position to make important career choices in the years ahead. Two videotapes are especially revealing in giving portraits of the variety possible in a music career—*Critical Stages* and *Ashkenazy Observed.*

If your teen spends a great deal of time practicing, the school music department may be able to assist in arranging a schedule that allows for early dismissal for practice and lessons. Even one extra hour can make a difference in fitting in sufficient practice. The school music teacher, if informed of a teen's keen focus on music, may arrange for some in-school performances to give the teen more concert experience.

In addition, schools in some communities give credit for private music study. Procedures vary from state to state, and even from town to town, and there are some localities where no such program exists. One example of successful local procedures follows:

- The private teacher's credentials must be approved by the school.
- The private teacher gives an evaluation and grade at the end of each quarter.
- These grades are entered into the student's record.

If your teen is motivated by grades, this can be a helpful arrangement. If your school does not have such a program, perhaps you can spearhead such a project. There are precedents throughout the country. The Music Teachers National Association and Music Educators National Conference may be able to assist you.

Competitions

For the career-oriented student, auditions are essential. For other teens, they can be a worthwhile adjunct to study. It is helpful to put them in perspective as good goals, valuable feedback, and rich growth opportunities. Whether or not a student plans a career in music, auditions can be strong motivators. By working to perfect a group of pieces, students who accept the challenge become more focused in their practice. For the career-oriented teen, experience performing in informal recitals, formal concerts, and auditions of increasing difficulty all prepare him for college or conservatory entry and beyond. Teachers accustomed to preparing students as music majors will be well informed about competition possibilities.

Summer camps

Your teen may be talented, but unsure about whether she wants a career in music. She may have a number of interests and talents. The music camp experience can be a deciding factor in whether your teen pursues a career in music. This is an opportunity for total immersion into the world of music with others of similar persuasion.

Here is a series of questions that may help your teen decide about the importance of summer music camp.

Why summer music camp?
- Meet friends with similar interests.
- Preview living away from home.
- Learn about a particular campus or geographic area.
- Sort out future schooling and career choices.
- Find out what it is like to focus primarily on music.
- Find out how you feel about intense, extended practice.
- Discover the rewards of practice.
- Work hard, learning to delay gratification.
- Gain skills and knowledge from experienced faculty.
- Have performance opportunities that build confidence.
- Be inspired and motivated by distinguished teachers and guest artists.
- Experience the cooperative efforts in chamber music.

Questions to ask about camps
- How old are the counselors, and how many campers does each counselor supervise?
- What activities are required? Do campers have a choice of special activities?
- How often do campers take trips and what transportation is provided? At extra charge?
- What medical services are available at the camp and nearby?
- Does the camp provide references of parents whose children attended the camp?

Teens and technology

Music students at any stage or level of involvement can find enrichment and interest in all that music technology has to offer. This is especially true for teenagers, both those who need a shot in the arm during a lag in interest, and those for whom technology is a passion. Technology includes computers, sequencers, synthesizers, CD-ROMs, CD players and tape recorders, samplers, drum machines, video cameras and VCRs, and other electronic equipment.

For the reluctant student, the computer can fill gaps in music skills at the student's own pace in a patient, nonthreatening environment with frequent feedback on progress. Open-ended technology (such as CD-ROMs, videodiscs, and computer networks) allows students to follow their own interests, quickly accessing and exploring a vast amount of musical information. The interactive nature of some programs is often a welcome change of pace during a downward curve in effort and enthusiasm.

The student with a passion for technology who has a combination of musical and technological ability, has notably different needs. We have an obligation to prepare these students who have multiple aptitudes for paths in music that will include past traditions, but also teach techniques for dealing with new sounds. For these students, music study with technology offers a glimpse of possible careers as composers, orchestrators, arrangers, sound engineers, and designers of multimedia, new instruments, and music software.

What is now available to make music learning better?

Music is the happy marriage of mathematics and art, of the hyperrational and the ineffable.

—Newsweek
Technology '95 issue

Music software. Allows a student to drill or receive tutorial help in ear training and developing music concepts through computer programs that reinforce learning through repetition in linear progression until a predetermined level of mastery is reached.

CD-ROM software. Allows students to explore musical parameters such as composition, form, and expression in an unstructured way, while gathering information related to composers, cultural, and historical influences.

Word processing and database programs. Useful for organizing and communicating ideas about music.

Sequencing and music-printing programs. Organize and communicate musical sounds and structures.

Samplers. Let students experiment and make music with sounds recorded from the real world (such as nature sounds, voices, cityscapes, and the like).

Multimedia controller programs. Allow the user to organize and communicate with words, still and moving images, and music, all in the same package.

Synthesizers. Help students compose, learn orchestration, and play duets and concertos with accompaniment.

Digital keyboards. Can support students in practice techniques by adjustments in tempo, repetition of segments that need improvement, and instant playback capabilities so that students can evaluate their performances.

MIDI (Musical Instrument Digital Interface). A device that allows the computer to have a dialogue with most of the above components, and opens a world of performance and composition possibilities.

And what can we expect in music's future? According to composer Tod Machover, director of the experimental media facility at the MIT Media Lab, the following are among the major changes that technology is likely to bring to the music field in the next five to ten years:

- Musical instruments themselves will continue to evolve. It will eventually be possible for all acoustic instruments to become connected to synthesizers and computers as only electronic keyboards are at this point. Further, totally new instruments will appear, allowing performers to shape sound with conducting-like gestures, the human voice, and perhaps, even brain waves!
- Musical instruments will increasingly have some intelligence built in, and will be able to respond somewhat independently to the player, making up an accompaniment, improvising a response, or perhaps suggesting an interesting melodic theme to the budding composer. Such instruments will take forms ranging from musical "assistants" to "music games" and "music toys," and will be designed for both professional virtuosi and musical amateurs.
- Computer networks, such as the Internet and World Wide Web, will become ever more popular for music exchange as the speed and quality of network technology improves. Network music activities will include long-distance learning and coaching, marketing services that guide "preference profiles," on-line jam sessions and

concerts, and group compositions that invite the participation of hundreds or thousands of network creators.

- Music itself will have an ever-widening definition, as computer recording, editing, and synthesizing techniques make it possible to bring many different kinds of sounds together. Such music will combine recognizable instruments with electronic timbres, spoken and sung voices, natural sounds, and elements we can't yet imagine. Listening to experimental composers, to adventurous movie sound tracks, or to popular music forms such as rap and techno gives some idea of where this hybrid music might be heading.

- Music will increasingly be part of a multimedia environment, with images designed for most musical experiences. This trend will lead to a new kind of music notation which is more like computer animation, and will also lead to a new field of computer visual design to accompany music that will start where Disney's *Fantasia* left off. In fact, musicians and listeners of the future might have to be vigilant to make sure that music does not become "background music."

All of these speculations imply that today's music students should consider learning fundamental underlying concepts of computer music technology, in addition to specifics of a particular synthesizer or software package, so as to be able to adapt easily to a landscape that will continue to evolve for a long while. How can we prepare our young people for such a world? The work has already begun. In a 1995 Music Teachers National Association survey of over 400 music teachers who use technology, teachers were asked how parents and students reacted to their use of technology in teaching. The responses were overwhelmingly affirmative.

At the beginning of the century, technology was like a big train breaking everything, a killing machine. It was really an adversary to nature. But today we see that technology and nature are not so far apart.—Renzo Piano

"Students can evaluate their own progress."
"Students are more aware of their own strengths and weaknesses."
"Invigorating, exciting, rewarding."
"Students become musically literate in a shorter time."
"Parents love the extra options and being part of a studio on the cutting edge."
"I often use technology as a reward and motivator."
"This is the electronic age. Students must be exposed to technology."
"The possibilities for encouraging creativity in sound are enormous."

If you and your teen want this kind of training, it is important to find teachers who are knowledgeable about technology. This may be an instrumental or vocal teacher, the high school music teacher, or it may be necessary to find a separate teacher or class to help round out the training. The Music Educators National Conference, Music Teachers

National Association, and the Association for Technology in Music Instruction are good sources for finding teachers and schools that specialize in music teaching with technology. All are listed in "Chapter Resources" at the end of Chapter Six, "Choosing the Teacher."

As to the selection of equipment, it is best to choose a technologically astute teacher who can advise you on software and hardware. Don't underestimate the technological sophistication of your teen. If you are already a computer family, you know the problems of obsolescence. The equipment you buy today may be outmoded within a week, a month, or a year. However, you are fortunate to be entering this arena now; costs have decreased considerably. Even if you choose equipment that doesn't do the ultimate task, but is adequate for the time being, you can replace it later without too much financial burden.

Planning equipment purchases wisely isn't easy. Selecting equipment "on approval," leasing, or renting it also may be viable options. Rapid technological obsolescence is a condition of our times, and as long as we tell ourselves that we can add components gradually and that we don't have to have the latest "toy," but can wait until its worth is established, we can get aboard the technology train without fear. Those who do are in for a thrilling ride.

Music enrichment in the public schools

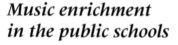

Today's music students are fortunate in the amount of support and enrichment they receive from the public schools. Not only do the band, orchestra, jazz ensembles, choruses, and musical theater provide vehicles for music students to perform, but they create a social atmosphere so important in teen life. The camaraderie of marching in a band at football games and in parades can be invaluable. Often, school chamber ensembles and orchestras have intramural performances that allow students to be challenged by new performance environments. Many schools have electronic music courses of some kind, though the problems of earmarking money to update equipment are often not easy to solve in today's "tough-on-the-arts" economy.

Public school music teachers can be most receptive to the ardent music student, making opportunities for extra performances and accompanying assignments as well as giving general moral support. As a parent, do whatever you can to encourage the growth of the music program in your local schools. Your support will be greatly appreciated by the music teachers and by your teen.

The right teacher for your teen

What qualities should the teacher of the adolescent possess?

Empathy. There are times when a teen may need to use lesson time to talk out problems, rethink priorities and scheduling, or sort out ideas. Parents should understand that an occasional lesson spent on personal matters is not wasted. If teacher and student have a good rapport, this dialogue can be a significant help in your teen's sorting-out process. The teacher whose agenda is focused only on music, or who has little experience with teenage students, may consider this a waste of time. Even the most understanding of teachers, however, must be able to distinguish the real need for heart-to-heart dialogue from the need of the student to stall.

Flexibility. Proms, exam crunch, a school performance, or participation in a major sporting event can assume major proportions in the life of some teens. The teacher who honors these occasions in the student's life, yet still challenges the teen to accomplish her musical best, is most likely to bring that teen through the adolescent years still involved in music. Some teachers have a "swap" list that allows students who wish to be listed to make their own arrangements for changing lesson times. This flexibility on the part of the teacher lets the teen pursue these new and increasingly important-to-them events, and opens the way for teenage flexibility as well.

Acceptance and respect. It helps if the teacher understands the necessity for some teens to try various passing fads in dress, fashion, and music. Accepting the reality of the teenage need to conform, while still respecting the underlying persona, gives reassurance during this period of exploration.

Teachers and parents who are sensitive to some teens' need to listen to and play "their" music are again facing a reality, the current music fashion. For teens who have a need to share this interest, it is helpful if the teacher is willing to listen to this music, occasionally making it part of the assignment.

A sense of humor. The teacher who has a strongly developed sense of humor is greatly appreciated by most teens. Much can be accomplished with a light touch that would sink like a lead balloon if handled seriously. Of course there are times when the teen is in a dark mood, and that can only be eased by quiet listening.

A sense of drama. To reach some teenagers, the teacher needs to provide a sense of drama and excitement. If the teacher can call upon a heartfelt passion for the music, plus a sense of adventure in exploring new and challenging territory, the contagion can be powerful. The drama is increased if the teacher can ignite a burning curiosity, not only about the music, but about the literature, art, history, and other significant influences on the music being studied. Especially significant to teens are a composer's human characteristics.

Special insight for the older beginner. The teacher of the older beginner needs to be especially sensitive to musical and emotional needs. The music must not be "babyish." A sensitive teacher will choose duets or simple ensemble pieces that allow the student to sound his age. The teacher should take into consideration the size and abilities of the growing hands and body and plan materials accordingly. The teacher who works best challenges the student's capabilities, respects growing maturity by enlisting the student's help to some degree in choosing materials, monitors the rate of progress carefully, and listens to clues from the teen. Teachers who specialize in working with older beginners will be aware of the wide variety of repertoire choices available.

Challenge for the career-oriented teen. The teacher of the career-oriented teen must have the musical knowledge and career experience to guide and challenge the teen who has aspirations to become a musician. The teacher should be aware of competition and performance opportunities that will prepare the student for the rigors of auditions and college entrance music exams. It helps if the teacher is also a performer in order to better assist the student in concert preparation and decorum.

The teacher of the career-oriented teen should have an eclectic knowledge of music and the related fields of literature, art, drama, world history, and dance to cross-reference and help illuminate the study of the music repertoire.

The teacher should be sure that the career-bound music student is well trained in music-related subjects (theory, harmony, music history, composition, and improvisation), and be willing to help the student arrange special classes in these subjects if he is not equipped to teach them himself.

Time to change teachers?

Even the most dedicated teen may hit a plateau. If you notice a waning effort on your teen's part, it could be that your teen needs a different teacher for this span of time, one who employs the right balance of challenge and expectations. Observe carefully over an extended period of time, asking yourself whether the teacher who was right for your child in the younger years is still the right one for your teen.

Before you consider a change, you and the teacher should meet to discuss the situation. Together you may want to assess just how much progress your teen has made in music. If a considerable amount of skill has been achieved, this is a good reason to encourage continuing.

It sometimes happens that a student has been with a teacher for too long. If your teen began study in elementary school or earlier, and continues with the same teacher, that teacher may have made the necessary adjustments to your teen's changing needs. If not, your teen may profit from a different point of view.

The teacher may have expertise in working with all age groups, or may specialize in a particular age group. If it is important for your teen to have peers within the music environment and there are few other teens in the studio, that might be another reason to consider a change.

Teens who have studied for a number of years need teachers who know and play advanced literature well. It is especially helpful if the teacher performs. By entering into the practicing, preparing, and performing mode, the teacher has much more to share with the student.

There may be some students who require a particular type of teacher as a role model in these transition years. A teen may especially need a strong male or female model now. Some teachers are able to tune in to the needs of either male or female students. If this is not the case, you may have to consider changing teachers.

Making a change should be done with the utmost diplomacy. The teacher should be informed of your intentions as far in advance as possible. Spring is a good time to give notice. This allows the teacher to fill that slot. The teacher will appreciate a gracious note or gesture of thanks for the years of shared music and experiences.

Time to quit?

When you have explored all the alternatives (change of literature, change of focus or goals, and change of teacher), all to no avail, the only choice may be to let your teen stop lessons. If training has been good, your teen will have the resources to return to music at some point, either to resume study later on, or to become part of the future audience. Your teen may become a parent in later life, and will have to struggle with the same dilemmas that you have faced. This may be small consolation, but your guidance now projects not only to your children, but to the generations that follow.

A memorable experience illustrates this. A young woman called to inquire about lessons for her sons. At the time, the teacher had no openings during after-school hours. "Oh, no!" she literally cried. Then after a pause she said, "Well, will you teach *me*?"

The teacher asked the woman for information about herself. "When I was a child, I took piano lessons for about eight years. When I entered high school, I began to develop other interests, and to have other distractions. My mother said, 'If you don't practice, I'm going to give the piano away.' "Well," the young woman continued, "I didn't, and she did! She actually gave my piano away! I was shocked, but there was no turning back. Now I have just moved to the area. The first thing I did after we bought a house was to purchase a piano. I can't wait for music to be back in my life."

A morning hour was found for the young woman to have lessons. By the next season, her sons had begun to study, and music had reentered her life. So if your teen does decide to stop lessons, it may not be the end of music in her life, just a hiatus while she regroups her priorities.

Children begin by loving their parents; as they grow older, they judge them; sometimes they forgive them.
—Oscar Wilde

Practice problems and support

Practice represents different challenges to the three categories of teens we have been discussing. The teen who begins as an older beginner will be learning the language of music, at the same time acquiring practice skills. Because the older beginner has already learned some of the techniques of independent study and has the ability to concentrate, practice skills should come quite easily, especially if the teacher is careful to list all the steps to accomplishing each musical task. Parents can support this new endeavor by being an appreciative audience and by praising effort and time well spent.

For the teen who studied previously, practice *is* the problem—how to schedule the extra time or how to concentrate when so many other ideas are flooding the mind. We have discussed some of the techniques for making the schedule less oppressive. Parents can help in other ways.

What parents can do to help teens with practice

- Protect study and practice time by insisting that no calls be taken until work has been completed.
- Keep the house as quiet as possible during practice time.
- Compliment your teen on a job well done, or time well organized.
- Help your teen make a schedule that indicates not only work time, but leisure (sports, games, and socializing) and maintenance time (eating, transportation, chores, and errands).
- Help your teen make choices in the use of time, so that he is neither overscheduled nor underchallenged.
- Help your teen make practice a priority, not just something that is squeezed in.
- Help your teen to understand that practice is:
  an art.
  an organizational skill.
  a continual process.
  a group of specific tasks.
- The payoff is that practice enables your teen to play the music he enjoys.

The teacher can assist with a number of other specific practice techniques. Be sure to tell the teacher, in private, of your observations of your teen's work habits. Sometimes teachers are not aware of what students do at home. Your input can be valuable in helping the teacher to focus your teen's practice routine. Some of the suggestions concerning practice made in Chapters Two and Three for younger students may also be helpful for your teen.

Burton Kaplan, who leads a retreat for advanced students and professionals who want to maximize their practice skills, gives the following suggestions for reaching achievable practice goals. Your teen may find these ideas helpful. Pass them on directly, or mention them to the teacher, who may be in a better position to present them.

Tips for achieving artistic success in practicing

- Pick a practice goal that is not too hard (leading to frustration).
- Pick a practice goal that is not too easy (leading to boredom).
- Select a passage to improve.
- Choose ONLY ONE quality you will aim to improve (intonation, tone, rhythm, coordination, expression).
- If unsuccessful after two or three tries, simplify the goal until it is achievable without physical strain.
- Ways of simplifying goals:
  - change tempo (fast passages slower; slow passages faster)
  - remove the rhythm, play only the pitches
  - remove the pitches, play only the rhythm
  - design a better fingering
  - take a smaller portion to work on
  - simplify or redesign phrasing
  - lower the intensity of emotional expression, playing with 75%, 50%, or 25% emotion
  - sing the phrase; then try playing it, imitating the phrasing and emotional nuances of your voice
  - without making sounds, finger the actual instrument as if playing the music (rhythm and notes); coordinate this "ghost" playing with the metronome beat.
- If you can't improve a passage as described above, change your expectations entirely. (Go to another passage. Try again later.)
- Congratulate yourself if you succeed.
- REMEMBER: BETTER IS PERFECT and perfect is irrelevant!

It may take years to form the practicing habit. The length of time doesn't matter. The important thing is to allow the impulse to root and blossom in its own natural growing cycle.
—W. A. Mathieu

Physical cautions about technique

Another set of observations is important. Does your teen ever complain of eyestrain or headaches? If so, check practice area lighting, making improvements if necessary. If improved lighting doesn't help, make an appointment for your teen to have an eye exam.

Does your teen complain of pain or muscle tension after practicing? If there are signs of pain or tension, your teen may be using her body incorrectly. As the literature gets more challenging for students who have not developed adequate technical facility, there is a tendency to misuse the body, sometimes causing irrevocable damage. An ardent teen, especially, may strain the technical mechanism. *Pain should never*

be ignored. Your teen should share the difficulty with the teacher. If a solution is not quickly found, there are a number of resources that you should investigate. The earlier the problem is identified, the less the likelihood of permanent injury.

There is much controversy about how to treat physical injury due to misuse or overuse in practicing. Not only are instrumentalists at risk, but singers must be aware that by forcing the voice in a choir, by imitating rock stars, or by singing without training, they can put the voice in jeopardy.

Prevention is always the best policy. If the student is already involved in formal study, it is the teacher's responsibility from the very beginning of training to see to it that no abuse occurs. If injury is suspected, questions arise about whether to seek musical, medical, or relaxation solutions to the problem.

- Musical solutions are found by having the teacher address the problem after careful observation. In some cases, it may be necessary to change to a teacher who has a carefully worked out philosophy concerning technical training or, in extreme cases, to one trained to deal with injured musicians.
- Medical solutions can be found at more than forty Performing Arts Medicine centers throughout the country.

- Alexander technique, Feldenkrais technique, and other systems for training the mind to control the body are alternative ways of addressing the problem.

According to Dr. Alice Brandfonbrener, a leader in performing arts medicine at the Medical Program for Performing Artists at the Rehabilitation Institute of Chicago, "Nothing awful is going to happen" if concerned parents wait before taking action in the treatment of observed injury. She states further, "Do not gravitate to the first advice you are given. A second opinion is definitely worthwhile."

The following list is by no means complete, but should help you begin your search if you suspect that your teen is experiencing serious physical problems while practicing.

STRESS MANAGEMENT RESOURCES

AMERICAN CENTER FOR THE ALEXANDER TECHNIQUE, 129 West 67th Street, New York, NY 10023. 212-799-0468

Alexander technique is a structured system employed by those in many disciplines to use the body in a stress-free, efficient manner. Musicians and dancers have found the technique to be especially helpful. The retraining takes place in classes as well as in private sessions with licensed instructors. The American Center for the Alexander Technique is a training center for Alexander teachers throughout the country. The North American Society of Teachers of the Alexander Technique is a professional society of Alexander teachers. Either group gives teacher referrals.

THE FELDENKRAIS GUILD, 706 Ellworth Street, Albany, OR 97321. 800-775-2118

Feldenkrais technique is a system of training the mind to control the body in a synchronized fashion. The focus is somewhat different from Alexander technique in that there is more emphasis on individual exploration of mind/body processes. The method is used by those in a number of fields, including music. Sessions are either in classes or in private sessions with licensed instructors. A number of audio- and videocassettes describing the method are available.

MEDICAL PROBLEMS OF PERFORMING ARTISTS, Philadephia: Hanley & Belfus, 210 South 13th Street, Philadelphia, PA 19107. 215-546-4995

This quarterly journal is dedicated to promoting occupational health in the performing arts. It is directed to physicians, performers, and teachers, and includes research articles on the biology of music-making. Although specialized, it may be helpful for those with performance-related injuries.

PERFORMING ARTS HEALTH MEDICINE CENTERS

There are a number of medical centers throughout the country that deal with performing artists' injuries. Diagnosis of damage is done by videotaping performance patterns, doing other diagnostic tests, and then prescribing therapy to change incorrect physical habits, or otherwise treat the condition. (See listings in "Chapter Resources" section.)

THE TAUBMAN INSTITUTE, Medusa, NY 12120. 518-239-4284

Taubman has been responsible for helping many injured musicians discover the source of their difficulties. At the Dorothy Taubman Institute in Amherst, MA, musicians gather each summer to study her technique. A number of musicians throughout the country have been trained by her to teach young musicians the most efficient use of the body in an injury-free manner. Videotapes of master classes are available.

How to react to teen music

Extraordinary how potent cheap music is.—Noel Coward

There is an area of distress for parents that is in no way as serious as physical injury, yet it can cause tension within the family. There are few parents who escape the problem of how to respond to their teens' taste in popular music.The decibels increase with each century and decade. The songs of unrequited love may have a different tune, but the message is the same through the ages. The sound palette has grown from the Renaissance lute to today's drum machine and throbbing bass line.

What are stressed parents to do about music that speaks to their teen, but is disturbing to them? You might try the following, though there are no guarantees of effectiveness.

At a family listening time, or at your request, sit down with your teen and listen to some of his music. Have him describe what he likes about the music. Ask him to guide your listening. What sounds especially intrigue him? What message in the songs excites or moves him? Which vocal sounds appeal? Are there chord progressions that are of interest? Is there something hypnotic and therefore attractive about the rhythm? Does your teen consider this good music to dance to, dream to, or study to?

By entering into your teen's listening world and by asking questions, you may open the door to your teen's more focused listening. If you're lucky, your teen may ask you what *you* think of the music. Find at least two things you honestly do like—perhaps the driving, tribal beat, or the gentle, hypnotic melody. Then, if you find the beat or melody too repetitive or if the words are not to your taste, you can at least share your point of view. You might even end up playing some of the music that you listened to as a teen or some of your current favorites. Be prepared for shocked surprise at how square it now sounds, but remember that your history and taste are definitely worth sharing.

The following account illustrates how one family dealt with their children's taste in music. When the children were quite young, all of them studied classical music on at least one instrument and improvised or played by ear—everything from folk to "their" music. The family used to play a guessing game when they tuned in to the middle of a piece of music on the radio. "Is that Bach or Mozart? Bartók or Chopin? Is it Russian, French, or German? Is that a wind quintet or quartet? Which Beethoven symphony is that?" After a few years, everyone was pretty good at spotting more and more detail. Praise was always lavish for good guesses.

Well, turnabout is fair play, and when the children were teenagers, the parents began to be quizzed by their teens. "Is that the Rolling Stones, the Grateful Dead, or the Beatles? Is that Judy Collins or Joan Baez?" The praise, "Very good, Mom!" was equally lavish if the parents guessed right (which, by the way, wasn't nearly as often as the children had responded correctly to guessing the parents' music).

Three points of view

No matter how much empathy you have for your developing teen, you
are bound to see the world differently.

Your teen's point of view

- "Time alone is hard. I like being with my friends."
- "I like adults who have a sense of humor."
- "I want to take charge of my own practicing and studying."
- "I like being challenged, but not in everything."
- "I appreciate it when my parents and teachers treat me as an
  adult."
- "Music is important to me, especially music I like."
- "Performing is sometimes fun, but often makes me nervous."
- "Though I know I should be planning for the future, it's
  scary."

Your point of view

- "I like to help my teen deal with the difficulties of daily life."
- "I know there needs to be a change in the relationship with
  my teen."
- "I'm proud when my teen takes responsibility for his own
  practice."
- "I worry about the challenges that face my teen in a world of
  rapid change."
- "I know that more decision-making has to transfer to my
  teen."
- "I hope music will continue to enrich my teen's life."
- "I want my teen to enjoy performing."
- "I hope my teen will make sound choices in career and
  relationships."

The teacher's point of view

- "Learning takes time. Keeping focused on goals helps."
- "I enjoy students with enthusiasm, independent spirit, and curiosity."
- "Practice time requires problem-solving skills that teens can learn."
- "Students are under pressure and I want to help them learn to budget time."
- "Independent practice is an important skill."
- "Attending concerts, museums, and dance programs adds dimension to study."
- "Performing is a means of sharing and testing a musician's personal best."
- "Studying music should be a challenge, a privilege, and a pleasure."

As we compare these views, there are some points at which they converge, but it requires adult sensitivity to modify goals to suit teen needs.

Each person has a different focus.

- Teen focus is on peers, while fear for the future may cause an avoidance of advanced planning.
- You are concerned about impending teen career choices and teen preparation for adult life.
- The teacher wants to increase challenges, and develop the student's independent effort and personal best.

Each person wants music to be a valued part of teen life.

- Your teen hopes that music will be a social asset and an emotional uplift.
- You want your teen to take obvious pleasure in musical pursuits.
- The teacher hopes that the beauty of the music is the chief motivation for teen effort.

Each person relates to public performance differently.

- Your teen enjoys perfoming if peer feedback is positive, but may be anxious if overchallenged.
- You are proud of your teen's growing ability to make music.
- The teacher sees performance as an important motivating goal and has high standards.

Each person cares about practice in varying degrees.

- Your teen may find practice an intrusion on social life, sports, or academic work.
- You hope that by this time your teen is self-motivated, needing no prodding from you.
- The teacher expects practice and hopes the teen has assimilated independent practice techniques.

Each person may have different tastes in music.

- Your teen may like making her own choices, including current peer favorites.
- Your tastes may be similar in some music, but you may have difficulty with the latest teen sounds.
- The teacher hopes to develop the broadest musical taste, cutting across all styles and periods.

The dilemma during the teen years is not only in the area of music. It cuts across all disciplines. This teen with one foot on either side of childhood wants to make independent decisions. The parent and teacher have more insight into the challenges that lie ahead. The more dialogue between you and your teen the better. The more you relate to the adult in your teen, the more adult he will become. Ultimately, the most fervent hope of parents and teachers is that somehow they will have helped to cultivate a love of music that will last a lifetime. The following anecdote amply illustrates that goal.

Michael, a fifteen-year-old piano student as well as varsity soccer player, expressed his fervent feelings for music in a speech on the occasion of his religious school confirmation.

"There is no other time in my life when I feel more spiritual than when I play the piano. For those of you who do not play an instrument, I can tell you that creating music is one of the most powerful feelings in the world. I know that without music I would have many feelings that I would be unable to express. Today I will play for you a Chopin Nocturne that was composed about a hundred and fifty years ago in Warsaw, Poland. I've chosen it because I feel that it is one of the most beautiful classical pieces that I have ever heard. As you are listening, think about the possibility that some of our ancestors from many generations ago may have listened to this very same piece and enjoyed its beauty."

HIGHLIGHTS

✰ This is a hard transition time for most adolescents.

It is a time of anxiety, confusion, mood swings, and physical change.

Establishing a new and more mature identity is a challenge.

In most cases, peers become a more dominant influence than parents or teachers.

Career decisions must be made.

✰ These are important years in music study, since they determine the degree of musical involvement and skill in adult life.

✰ There are three types of teens involved in music study, each with different challenges.

The teenage beginner makes rapid progress at first, needs pieces that sound hard.

The teen who began study at an earlier age may have conflicts about continuing because of increased academic demands, new interests, and changing tastes.

The teen who has aspirations for a career in music needs to plan ahead.

There are a variety of career choices. As many as possible should be explored during these pre-college years.

✰ Teachers of teens should be empathetic, flexible, accepting, and have a sense of humor and drama.

✰ Teachers of the older beginner need to choose age-appropriate material and involve the student in making choices.

✰ Teachers of stressed teens can use a number of strategies for encouraging continued study:

Do projects that involve other teens.

Use the assistance of a public school music teacher to add enrichment.

Lighten the assignment for a short time.

Change repertoire to match student's changing interests and needs.

Do projects with new goals—the teen could tutor younger students; do a benefit concert.

Try projects using technology.

✰ Teachers of career-oriented students need to offer challenges such as auditions, performance opportunities, and early preparation for college entry.

✰ Competitions and auditions can be strong motivators for some students. They are essential preparation for the career-oriented student.

✰ Summer camp experiences can help teens decide about careers in music.

✰ If all attempts at igniting enthusiasm for study fail, it may be necessary to help your teen gracefully stop lessons for the time being.

✰ Practice challenges vary with each type of teen student. Teens should be gaining more independence and skill in practicing. Parents can do little in terms of specific help, but can create a quiet environment for work, and help the teen handle an increasingly complicated schedule.

☆ Parents should observe their teen for signs of eyestrain or body pain as a result of practice. There are a number of sources for seeking relief. Pain should never be ignored. It is a serious sign of misuse and can cause permanent damage.

CHAPTER RESOURCES

The resources listed below are appropriate for the age group discussed in this chapter. Age recommendations are listed only if an item has more narrow appeal. Some items have wide appeal and are listed in the chapter resources of more than one chapter.

Take special note of Part IV, "General Resources," for a listing of books, recordings, movies, games, teaching aids, CD-ROMs, and catalogs.

BOOKS FOR YOU

Caviezel, Sandy et al. DIRECTORY OF SUMMER MUSIC PROGRAMS. 6716 East-side Dr. NE, Tacoma, WA 98422. 206-927-3269.

An annual description of over 400 national and international summer music programs, organized geographically. There is infomation on tuition, camp size, age range, deadlines, and focus.

Csikszentmihalyi, Mihaly and Reed Larson. BEING ADOLESCENT: CONFLICT AND GROWTH IN THE TEENAGE YEARS. New York: Basic Books, 1984.

What is it like to be an adolescent? What do teenagers think and care about? This survey of seventy-five teenagers records their thoughts and feelings, which are frequently amusing and invariably revealing. The authors analyze the data to provide an original document of great value to parents and educators.

Csikszentmihalyi, Mihaly, Kevin Rathunde and Samuel Whalen. TALENTED TEENAGERS: THE ROOTS OF SUCCESS & FAILURE. New York: Cambridge University Press, 1993.

This volume reports on a study of over two hundred talented teenagers, examining why some succeed and others fail to develop their abilities. The book includes charts and graphs, but the overall tone is direct and friendly. Of special interest are the chapters entitled "What Are Talented Teenagers Like?" (athletes, musicians, and artists are lumped together); "How Families Influence Talent Development;" and "Schools, Teachers, and Talent Development." This is a powerful book since, despite the research appearance, it "tells it like it is."

Gardner, Howard. FRAMES OF MIND. New York: Basic Books, 1985.

This book has already become a classic since Gardner's theory of multiple intelligences, introduced in this work, has attracted many followers. Musical intelligence is discussed more from the standpoint of the composer of music than the performer. Gardner speaks of how one perceives music in relation to the functions of the brain, and he also addresses unusual talents, such as that of the idiot savant. While the reading style is friendly, the general tone of the book is serious.

Satir, Virginia. THE NEW PEOPLEMAKING. Mountain View, CA: Science and Behavior Books, 1988.

Written by a pioneer in family therapy, this book explores all facets of family living and interaction, from self-worth to the family of the future. The writing style is direct, humorous, and right on target. Each chapter is full of useful advice that is sometimes framed in diagrams, conversations, or anecdotes.

Wlodkowski, Raymond J. and Judith Jaynes. EAGER TO LEARN: HELPING CHILDREN BECOME MOTIVATED AND LOVE LEARNING. San Francisco: Jossey-Bass, 1990.

The authors speak directly to parents about understanding and supporting a child's desire to learn. The writing style is practical, listing specific steps that parents can take. Discussions are often handled in a question-and-answer format. Especially useful are the chapters entitled "Building a Positive Parent-Teacher Relationship" and "Encouraging Effort and Perseverance," as well as the resource section that includes such information as how to prepare for a parent-teacher conference. There are also two videos, called "Motivation to Learn," associated with this book. (See Videos listed below.)

BOOKS FOR YOUR TEEN

ABOUT BEING A MUSICIAN

Hart, Mickey and Jay Stevens. DRUMMING AT THE EDGE OF MAGIC: A JOURNEY INTO THE SPIRIT OF PERCUSSION. San Francisco: Harper San Francisco, 1990.

The percussionist for the Grateful Dead describes his discovery of the historical and spiritual heritage of the drum.

Salmon, Paul G. and Robert G. Meyer. NOTES FROM THE GREEN ROOM: COPING WITH STRESS AND ANXIETY IN MUSICAL PERFORMANCE. New York: Macmillan, 1992.

This book should be meaningful to serious performers. Achievement as a performer at all levels can be aided by access to educational, medical, and psychological resources that, when coupled with genuine ability and hard work, can help performers refine their skills, cope with stress more effectively, and limit the probability of physical or psychological impairments both on and offstage.

Wolff, Virginia E. THE MOZART SEASON. New York: Henry Holt, 1991.

A novel about Allegra Shapiro's twelfth summer during which she prepares for an important violin competition. The reader learns about Allegra's world—the violin lessons, family relationships, peer interaction and competition, and the mysteries and turmoil of growing up. A good example of how music can be a major part of a young person's life.

BIOGRAPHY

Bonis, Ferenc. BÉLA BARTÓK: HIS LIFE IN PICTURES AND DOCUMENTS. Budapest, Hungary: Kossuth Printing House, 1972.

For those who are studying Bartók, this is a marvelous, very alive document, filled with pictures from the Bartók archive and documents that give a sense of immediacy.

Buettner, Stewart and Reinhard G. Pauly. PORTRAITS: GREAT COMPOSERS—GREAT ARTISTS. Portland, OR: Amadeus Press, 1992.

An historian and a musician/scholar have collaborated to create a unique book, an annotated collection of musicians' portraits. The portraits of great composers through the ages are artistically significant, by major artists, from a painting of Martin Luther by Lucas Cranach the Elder to a sculpture of George Gershwin by twentieth century artist Isamu Noguchi. An outstanding work. Students will enjoy seeing portraits of composers they are studying.

Goffstein, M.B. A LITTLE SCHUBERT. Boston: David R. Godine, 1984.

A whimsical story with pictures—short, sweet, and charming. A delightful gift for Schubert lovers.

Krull, Kathleen. LIVES OF THE MUSICIANS: GOOD TIMES, BAD TIMES (AND WHAT THE NEIGHBORS THOUGHT). San Diego: Harcourt Brace Jovanovich, 1993.

These brief biographies are written with rare charm, partly because they recount very human aspects of the musician's life ("what the neighbors thought" gives you a clue), and partly because these bits of information relate directly to a young reader's life (for instance, the fact that Beethoven liked macaroni and cheese, that Brahms left his clothes on the floor when he went to bed, or that Ives had a cat named Christofina who ate asparagus). The choice of musicians is also uncommon. Scott Joplin, Woody Guthrie, Gilbert and Sullivan, and Nadia Boulanger are there with Bach, Beethoven, and Mozart. Parents will enjoy this as much as the kids.

Nichols, Janet. AMERICAN MUSIC MAKERS: AN INTRODUCTION TO AMERICAN COMPOSERS. New York: Walker, 1990.

Biographies of ten American composers, written in a friendly style, that are of interest to young readers. What is most refreshing, however, is the choice of composers—Louis Gottschalk, Charles Ives, Ruth Crawford Seeger, George Crumb, and Philip Glass, to name half. There is a brief suggested listening list, a glossary, and a few ideas for further reading.

Nichols, Janet. WOMEN MUSIC MAKERS: AN INTRODUCTION TO WOMEN COMPOSERS. New York: Walker, 1992.

Biographies of ten women composers who were born between 1619 and 1947. The book offers the young female reader a gallery of role models, and draws attention to the fact that these composers were, in turn, influenced by other musical women and needed their own role models in order to succeed. Included are Fanny Mendelssohn Hensel, Clara Wieck Schumann, Ellen Taaffe Zwilich, and Laurie Anderson. Unfortunately, many of the recordings are not easy to locate.

Nicholson, Stuart. ELLA FITZGERALD: A BIOGRAPHY OF THE FIRST LADY OF JAZZ. New York: Charles Scribner, 1994.

A look at the personal life as well as the seven-decade award-winning career of one of the most accomplished jazz singers of this century.

Tames, Richard. FRÉDÉRIC CHOPIN. New York: Franklin Watts, 1991.

A good biography, done in slightly larger print on good-quality paper. It includes many photographs (some in color) of Chopin, important people in his life, and cities in which he lived and performed. The details of Chopin's life, such as his relationship with George Sand, are dealt with honestly.

Thompson, Wendy. COMPOSER'S WORLD SERIES: BIOGRAPHIES OF BEETHOVEN, HAYDN, MOZART, AND SCHUBERT. New York: Viking, 1991.

These elegant, richly illustrated books are written by a British musicologist. The writing style is factual but flowing. The human details included should appeal to the young reader. Excerpts of the composer's music (always in piano score, and sometimes quite extensive) are included. There is a listing of the composer's works detailed enough to give the reader some idea of the scope of his writing without being overly detailed.

Venturi, Piero. GREAT COMPOSERS. New York: Putnam, 1988.

The author writes, "This is not a history of music. It is an invitation to understand the works of famous musicians of all time, in the context of the time and place in which their talents unfolded and with an emphasis on their artistic personalities." He has done this with stunning illustrations.

COLLEGE GUIDES

Everett, Carole J. THE PERFORMING ARTS MAJOR'S COLLEGE GUIDE. New York: Macmillan, 1994.

This practical book sheds light on the college admissions process, and offers advice from beginning the search through the completion of the application. It provides helpful information about auditioning, researching teachers, and asking useful questions. A selected listing of performing arts programs notes schools and conservatories with strong programs in particular fields.

Uscher, Nancy. SCHIRMER GUIDE TO SCHOOLS OF MUSIC AND CONSERVATORIES THROUGHOUT THE WORLD. New York: Schirmer Books, 1988.

Comprehensive guide with geographical listings of schools of music, colleges, and universities with preparatory divisions. Detailed description of facilities and services.

FAMILY RESOURCES

Erlewine, Michael and Scott Bultman. ALL MUSIC GUIDE. Corte Madera, CA: Miller Freeman c/o BMR Associates, 1984.

Comprehensive and authoritative guide to all genres of music, organized in twenty-seven categories. "Music Map" shows at a glance how a particular music style developed, identifies each style's major players, and traces who influenced whom.

Fowler, Charles. MUSIC! ITS ROLE AND IMPORTANCE IN OUR LIVES. New York: Macmillan/ McGraw-Hill, 1994.

Written as a high school text, this beautifully illustrated book is filled with musical examples and suggested listening activities. It covers the full range of music history from earliest times, and includes sections on world music as well as thorough coverage of twentieth-century music. A set of CDs accompanies the text. Expensive, but worthwhile if you have no access to a thorough music history course. Excellent college preparation for the serious music student.

Kendall, Alan. THE CHRONICLE OF CLASSICAL MUSIC: AN INTIMATE DIARY OF THE LIVES AND MUSIC OF THE GREAT COMPOSERS. London: Thames & Hudson, 1994.

This diary-style chronology is rich in color pictures, photographs, and information. In a clever, but complicated, cross-reference system, the user may check out key people and works; key places; and issues, events, and themes. The intense focus (often on just a few years) helps the reader to appreciate the multitude and variety of coeval events. A great family browser.

Raeburn, Michael And Alan Kendall. THE HERITAGE OF MUSIC. New York: Oxford University Press, 1989.

A four-volume encyclopedic history of Western music from its beginnings to the present. Combines an authoritative text with abundant and beautiful illustrations. It is written for music lovers and for serious students.

Sadie, Stanley and Alison Latham. MUSIC GUIDE. Englewood Cliffs, NJ: Prentice-Hall, 1987.

This comprehensive volume is a resource for students and all music lovers. The scope of the volume is enormous, ranging from early chapters that cover the fundamentals of music to a history of modern times. The last chapter gives serious consideration to jazz and popular music. A set of six audiotapes is available to accompany the text. Especially valuable for serious teenage music students.

Schwartz, Elliott and Daniel Godfrey. MUSIC SINCE 1945. New York: Schirmer Books, 1993.

Meant for the serious music student, this book fills a real gap in the history of music in the twentieth century. Among the topics: new aesthetic approaches, nonwestern influences, multimedia, the electronic revolution. Selected bibliography and discography.

Sommer, Elsey. THE KIDS' WORLD ALMANAC OF MUSIC: FROM ROCK TO BACH. New York: World Almanac, 1992.

Trivia information, arranged by chapters. References range from Bach to nicknames of groupies. Also included are the basics of music theory and information about inventors of musical instruments. Offbeat fun.

Tatchell, Judy. UNDERSTANDING MUSIC. London: Usbourne, 1990.

This book is crammed with assorted information. Definitions of musical styles (including folk, ethnic, jazz, rock, and pop), information about instruments, listening suggestions, pictures of performers, and a survey of composers and what kind of music they wrote are presented along with instructions on how to read music. There is also information on learning to play an instrument.

Van der Meer, Ron and Michael Berkeley. THE MUSIC PACK. New York: Knopf, 1994.

An exciting multimedia introduction to musical creation that allows you to see and hear how sound is produced and turned into music. Fold-out spreads feature playable pull-out and pop-up instruments, three-dimensional views of various instruments, a booklet on musical notation, and an interactive world music map. A 70-minute CD with twenty musical masterpieces is included.

Willoughby, David. THE WORLD OF MUSIC. Dubuque, IA: William C. Brown, 1993.

This guide to music listening, although written for college-level students, is eminently suited to the serious talented teen who wants a comprehensive overview of world music literature that includes traditional folk, religious, popular, Western European, and world music. The beautifully illustrated text is accompanied by a set of audiocassettes or CDs.

FAMOUS MUSIC STORIES

Helpern, Mark. *SWAN LAKE*. Boston: Houghton Mifflin, 1989.

An absolute treasure of a book written in elegant prose by a prize-winning author. The illustrations by Chris Van Allsburg are magical. A perfect introduction to the story of *Swan Lake* as preparation for seeing the ballet and hearing the music by Tchaikovsky.

Price, Leontyne. *AIDA*: BASED ON THE OPERA BY GIUSEPPE VERDI. San Diego: Harcourt Brace, 1990.

Opera diva Price, known throughout the world for her portayal of Aïda, tells this powerful love story of a royal princess from the princess's intimate point of view. Caldecott medalists Leo and Diane Dillon have created vibrant paintings that give both characters and events a dramatic immediacy.

Rosenberg, Jane. SING ME A STORY. New York: Thames & Hudson, 1989.

The librettos of fifteen of the most popular operas are presented with colorful illustrations in this lavishly printed book. There is a delightful introduction by Luciano Pavarotti. An excellent gift for a junior or senior high school student or an ardent adult opera lover.

INSTRUMENTS

Ardley, Neil. MUSIC. New York: Knopf, 1989.

This book about instruments shows them in color photographs. The photographs are outstanding not only for their precision and clarity (at times showing the instrument disassembled), but also for the extremely wide scope of instruments included. Captions attached to the photographs provide a wealth of information and bits of special interest. The range of percussion instruments depicted is unusual, as is the inclusion of modern amplified instruments.

Gill, Dominic (ed.). THE BOOK OF THE PIANO. Ithaca, NY: Cornell University Press, 1981.

An elegant and authoritative book that deals with many kinds of pianos, the history of pianos, and piano makers. Specialists in various areas have contributed chapters. The book is designed for the serious (but not necessarily professional) reader. The chapters on the jazz piano, the popular piano, and unusual pianos are captivating. Although not really a "coffee table book," this one has the size and quality. This would be a wonderful gift for a serious young pianist.

THE HISTORY OF MUSIC

Beránek, Vratislav. THE ILLUSTRATED HISTORY OF MUSIC. London: Sunburst Books, 1994.

This picture-rich book (color and black-and-white) is not presented chronologically but in interestingly grouped categories such as "Music for Pleasure," "The Stage Resounds with Dance," and "Canned Music." The writing style is friendly and conveys much diverse information. This history includes Schubert and Streisand as well as Handel and "Hair." This is a something-for-everyone book.

Donald, Dave. BACH, BEETHOVEN AND THE BOYS. Toronto: Sound and Vision, 1986. (359 Riverdale Ave., Toronto, Canada, M4J 1A4)

The subtitle, "Music History as It Ought to Be Taught," suggests the tongue-in-cheek writing style. Dates and facts are completely accurate, but the anecdotes and cartoonlike illustrations focus on offbeat incidents and information. Only in a book like this would you find out that Haydn's wife used his manuscripts to line cake tins, Schubert's friends called him "Tubby," or that Wagner's pet poodle ran away from home. A good dose of music history in an easy-to-swallow form.

Hughes, Langston. JAZZ (UPDATED AND EXPANDED BY SANDFORD BROWN). New York: Watts, 1982.

A history of jazz from its beginnings to 1980s jazz/rock. Included is information on the African roots of jazz, work songs and spirituals, jazz forms, jazz instruments, and jazz singers, with separate attention paid to Louis Armstrong and Duke Ellington. Major artists are mentioned, and there are a number of photographs. A good way to introduce and/or explain jazz as a separate style.

Mundy, Simon. THE USBOURNE STORY OF MUSIC. London: Usbourne, 1980.

A highly illustrated, almost cartoonlike history of music from ancient times to the present (contemporary classical and popular music). Appealing thumbnail sketches of each period.

PRACTICE AIDS

Campbell, Virginia F. PUZZLING, PATTERNING, PRACTICING: A GUIDE TO MORE EFFECTIVE PIANO STUDY. Chapel Hill, NC: Hinshaw, 1985.

A concise pamphlet of suggestions for effective practice. Best used with guidance of teacher.

Kaplan, Burton. THE MUSICIAN'S PRACTICE LOG. New York: Perception Development Techniques, 1985. (Box 1068, Cathedral Station, New York, NY 10025)

This guide to efficient practice gives specific tips and allows one to assess one's own practice profile and keep a practice diary. For serious students or those who would like to improve their practice skills. Highly recommended. For teens with help of parent or teacher.

VIDEOS

AFRICAN AMERICAN TALENT SHOW. GPN. 800-228-4630.

Uniquely gifted African American youngsters who are studying and planning careers as classical concert artists are showcased in this well-filmed documentary. Comments by several of the young performers on their goals and hopes for the future make this tape especially valuable.

AGAINST THE ODDS: LUDWIG VAN BEETHOVEN. Films for the Humanities. 800-257-5126.

The focus in this short biographical film is on Beethoven's ability to compose in spite of his increasing hearing loss. Extremely well produced. Though expensive, it gets its message across remarkably effectively.

ANDRÉS SEGOVIA: THE SONG OF THE GUITAR. Teldec Video. 212-399-7782.

An evocation of Spain in exquisite travel scenes, a tribute to the life of this master guitarist with beautiful, sensitive performances.

ASHKENAZY OBSERVED: EPISODES FROM THE LIFE OF A WANDERING MUSICIAN. Teldec Video. 212-399-7782.

This is an account of the life of a touring concert artist in rehearsal and performance, balancing a hectic travel schedule with career and family. This is an Important video for any student contemplating a career as a performing artist.

CHICK COREA: ELECTRIC WORKSHOP. DCI Music Video Inc (CPP Belwin). 800-628-1528.

In this tape, Corea highlights his approach to synthesizers and gives the viewer glimpses of his way of improvising and composing, showing the steps he takes to realize a piece.

CHICK COREA: KEYBOARD WORKSHOP. DCI Music Video Inc (CPP Belwin). 800-628-1528.

Chick Corea is the winner of six Grammys and innumerable other awards. In addition to being a performer of outstanding quality, he is a gifted and articulate teacher. This should be an inspiring tape for teenage students who are experimenting with jazz.

THE COMPETITION. GPN. 800-228-4630.

This encounter investigates competitions as an important learning experience and an opportunity for self-evaluation. Young performers on the violin, piano, and flute are featured.

CONCERTO! SH Productions Inc. 800-336-1820.

In this three-tape series, pianists Claude Frank, Lillian Kallir, and their daughter, violinist Pamela Frank, each rehearse a Mozart concerto with an orchestra conducted by Ian Hobson. A unique feature is the dialogue between the performers and conductor about how to perform these works. Especially valuable for teenagers who are working on concerto literature. Spirited performances.

CRITICAL STAGES. VideoPhases. 1280 Hanley Industrial Ct., St. Louis, MO 63144. 314-963-8840.

This video won an Emmy for outstanding writing. It portrays gifted students and their teachers. The facts of musical life from the initial stages of finding the right instrument and teacher, to the changing circumstances of study, to the realities of career-building are all well documented. Passionate student performances at each critical stage make this a thought-provoking and inspiring video.

DIGITAL MUSICAL INSTRUMENTS AND THE WORLD OF MIDI. Red Pohaku Productions. 1621 Dole St., #100, Honolulu, HI 96822.

A clear demonstration for the novice of the world of MIDI. Defines controller, MIDI, multitimbral, patch, port, sequencer, tone module, track, and other pertinent data. Joseph Rothstein is the articulate presenter.

DOROTHY TAUBMAN: THE CHOREOGRAPHY OF THE HAND. The Taubman Institute, Medusa, NY 12120. 518-239-4284.

This video documents a master teacher's views on proper use of the body in piano playing. Other tapes are of detailed master classes on specific major works of the piano literature. (Beethoven, Liszt, Chopin, Mendelssohn).

THE FIDDLE SHOW. GPN. 800-228-4630.

Master artist/teacher Joseph Gingold, a young performer, and a group of violin students demonstrate agility and fitness necessary to make music with the violin.

FOUR AMERICAN COMPOSERS: JOHN CAGE. Mystic Fire Video. 800-292-9001.

For those wishing to gain insight into the music of the twentieth century, this extremely well-made tape will be a revelation. John Cage has profoundly influenced musical and performance art. This videotape covers the wide scope of his experiments and the wide range of his influence. The other composer portraits in the series are of Philip Glass, Meredith Monk, and Robert Ashley.

HOW YOUR PIANO WORKS. JMC Productions, Box 2415, W. Brattleboro, VT 05303. Designed for pianists of all levels, from beginning to professional, this video gives a thorough presentation of how a grand piano works. It includes a valuable reference section on piano problems with a discussion of piano care and maintenance.

IN CELEBRATION OF THE PIANO: AN ALL-STAR TRIBUTE TO STEINWAY. Music in Motion. 800-445-0649.
Hosted by Van Cliburn, this Steinway tribute features twenty-six pianists including Lazar Berman, Alfred Brendel, Ruth Laredo, and Rudolph Serkin. A dazzling finale features Schumann's *Carnaval* divided among twenty-one pianists. A rare display of pianism.

JACQUELINE DU PRÉ: ELGAR CELLO CONCERTO. Teldec Video. 212-399-7782.
The artistry of Du Pré is equaled by her courage when, in her adult life, she is stricken with multiple sclerosis. An inspiring video, both in musical and human terms.

LEONARD BERNSTEIN'S YOUNG PEOPLE'S CONCERTS SERIES WITH THE NEW YORK PHILHARMONIC. Music in Motion. 800-445-0649.
Ten videos of twenty-five digitally remastered programs originally broadcast from 1958 to 1970. Topics include What Does Music Mean? What Is Classical Music? What Is Sonata Form? What Makes Music Symphonic? There is a book of Bernstein's lectures taken from these videos. A remarkable series from a great communicator.

MUSIC ANIMATION MACHINE. Stephen Malinowski. 510-235-7478.
As you listen to the music of a wide range of classical composers, a graphic color representation scrolls by, showing how the music is structured and contoured. There is nothing quite like this presentation, and even sophisticated musicians are captivated. Children who play beyond beginning levels would get the most out of this approach.

NELITA TRUE AT EASTMAN: PORTRAIT OF A PIANIST-TEACHER. Alfred Publishing Company. 800-292-6122.
This four-volume series will be helpful to serious piano students as they observe this charismatic teacher in action. Volume 1: *Portrait of a Pianist-Teacher.* Volume 2: *The Studio Lesson.* Volume 3: *Technique through Listening.* Volume 4: *Principles of Style for the Young Pianist.*

THE PERFORMER PREPARES: 100% COMMITMENT. Pst . . . Inc. 214-991-7184.
A Robert Caldwell performance workshop, based on the book of the same name. Deals with ways of overcoming performance anxiety.

THE PIANO SHOW. GPN. 800-228-4630.
Features three young pianists in different stages of musical development who excel in different musical styles. A fourth pianist provides a stunning example of what discipline and hard work can accomplish. Concert pianist Leon Fleisher is a special guest.

PROKOFIEV: THE PRODIGAL SON. Films for the Humanities. 800-257-5126.

A breathtaking portrait of one of the twentieth century's musical giants. Superb musical performances are interwoven with film clips of the life and times of the composer and dramatic presentation of events from his life. A thoroughly professional production.

THE TROUT: AN HISTORIC COLLABORATION OF DANIEL BARENBOIM, ITZHAK PERLMAN, PINCHAS ZUCKERMAN, JACQUELINE DU PRÉ, AND ZUBIN MEHTA. Teldec Video. 212-399-7782.

The rehearsal interplay among these great musicians is as beguiling as the actual performance of one of Schubert's greatest works.

TRYIN' TO GET HOME: A HISTORY OF AFRICAN AMERICAN SONG. Heebie Jeebie Music. 510-548-4613.

Written and performed by Kerrigan Black, this is a stirring performance and a musical record of an important part of American musical heritage.

WE REINVENT THE CIRCUS, NOUVELLE EXPERIENCE, SALTIMBANCO. Cirque du Soleil. 800-727-2233.

This combination of acrobatics, costumes, music, and effects is truly a spectacle. The circus is taken to new heights of creativity and fantasy, and the Montreal-based ensemble provides excitement way beyond the entertainment level. Music, performed live, plays a major role in these productions.

CD-ROMs

Call the telephone number of each company to ask for a catalog. Check system requirements before ordering. Ask for a try-before-you-buy arrangement.

ALL MY HUMMINGBIRDS HAVE ALIBIS. The Voyager Company. 800-446-2001.

Morton Subotnick, a leading contemporary composer, speaks informally about two of his works, and lets the user join him on an exploration of how the title work and *Five Scenes from an Imaginary Ballet* were created. Five musical "scenes" accompany the images and text by Max Ernst. For the sophisticated user who wants to be in touch with the use of technology in composition. Macintosh.

CD TIME SKETCH: COMPOSER SERIES. Electronic Courseware Systems. 800-832-4965.

This four-disc series includes *A Portrait of Bach: Toccata and Fugue in D minor; A Portrait of Beethoven: Symphony #5; A Portrait of Brahms: Symphony #3;* and *A Portrait of Mozart, Symphony #40.* Each disc includes a performance in addition to the analysis of the work. Although designed for music instructors, serious teens and adults will find these valuable. For Macintosh and IBM/PC.

A GERMAN REQUIEM: THE GREATEST CHORAL WORK OF THE ROMANTIC ERA. Time Warner New Media. 800-482-3766.

With English and German texts. The user can see an analysis while listening, see the score, and explore the background of this Brahms masterwork.

MULTIMEDIA BEETHOVEN: THE *NINTH SYMPHONY*. Microsoft. 800-426-9400.

Explores the structure, the instruments, and the cultural, social, and political events that surrounded Beethoven as he created the Ninth Symphony. You can hear and see the score, clicking the mouse at any point to investigate the work from a number of points of view. Macintosh and Windows.

MULTIMEDIA MOZART: *THE DISSONANT QUARTET*. Microsoft. 800-426-9400.

Allows the listener to explore individual instruments of the quartet, noting how they function alone and how they blend to create the whole. Browse the historic background of eighteenth-century Europe in this video, audio, and encyclopedic world. Macintosh and Windows.

MULTIMEDIA STRAUSS: *THREE TONE POEMS*. Microsoft. 800-426-9400.

The Cleveland Orchestra performances of tone poems of Richard Strauss *(Don Juan, Death and Transfiguration, Till Eulenspiegel)* is the core of this CD-ROM. The accompanying information includes "Inside the Score," "Pocket Audio Guide," "Master Orchestrator," and "The Prankster Game" (based on *Till Eulenspiegel*) in which the listener is challenged to match themes. Macintosh and Windows.

MULTIMEDIA STRAVINSKY: *THE RITE OF SPRING*. Microsoft. 800-426-9400.

An innovative ballet gave *The Rite of Spring* visual expression. This CD-ROM explores the dance background and the artistic milieu that influenced its creation. The imaginative musical exploration is by Robert Winter. Macintosh and Windows.

MUSICAL INSTRUMENTS. Microsoft. 800-426-9400.

This provides wonderful access to information about more than 200 instruments. There are four ways to navigate: "Families of Instruments," "A–Z of Instruments," Instruments of the World," "Musical Ensembles." You can see how the instruments work, hear musical examples, and "play" limited pitches on each instrument. There is reference to jazz, rock, classical, and other ensembles. For Macintosh and Windows.

MYST. Broderbund Software. 415-382-4400.

This interactive disc allows for intuitive virtual exploration and problem solving. Graphics are stunning and sound is used in intriguing ways. It is for those who enjoy paying attention to detail, collecting information, and solving mysteries. Macintosh and Windows.

THE ORCHESTRA: THE INSTRUMENTS REVEALED. Time Warner New Media. 800-482-3766.

Based on Benjamin Britten's *The Young Person's Guide to the Orchestra*, this program invites the user to see and hear the instruments of the orchestra and learn how they are played. Also included: a conducting lesson, an orchestration lab, a pronouncer, biographical information, a glossary, and a time line. Macintosh.

PUPPET MOTEL: LAURIE ANDERSON WITH HSIN-CHIEN HUANG. The Voyager Company. 800-446-2001.

Navigate a world saturated with performance artist Laurie Anderson's dynamic presence and interact in a variety of ways. Play four "juiced-up" electronic violins, connect the dots to create your own constellation, hear performances of *Down in Soho* and excerpts from *Stories from the Nerve Bible*.

ROCK, RAP, AND ROLL. Paramount Interactive. 415-812-8200.

A colorful, easy-to-use CD-ROM in which the user assigns instruments, vocals, and sound effects to the keyboard and screen, and can add his own voice and sing along.

SO I'VE HEARD. The Voyager Company. 800-446-2001.

A sweep through the masterpieces of Western classical music with music critic Alan Rich. This five-volume series combines essays and illustrations for the eye and ear in dozens of artworks and audio examples. Volume 1: *Bach and Before*; Volume 2: *The Classical Ideal*; Volume 3: *Beethoven and Beyond*; Volume 4: *Romantic Heights*; Volume 5: *Here and Now*.

ORGANIZATIONS

Magic Mountain Music Farm. Burton Kaplan, Director. RD 1, Box 48, Morris, NY 13808. 607-263-2304, 212-662-6634.

A retreat for advanced students and professionals who want to maximize their practice skills.

The following is a set of resources for those seeking help due to physical injury from music practice or seeking advice on its prevention. Several sources can provide referrals throughout the country.

American Center for the Alexander Technique. 129 West 67th Street, New York, NY 10023. 212-799-0468.

The Arts Medicine Center [referral service] at Thomas Jefferson University Hospital. Dr. Robert Sataloff, Director. 1721 Pine Street, Philadelphia, PA 19103. 215-735-7487.

Cumulative Trauma Disorder Consultants. Columbia Presbyterian East Side (Practice in Music Medicine). Dr. Emil Pascarelli, Director. 16 East 60th Street, New York, NY 10022. 212-326-3348.

The Feldenkrais Guild. 706 Ellworth Street, Albany, OR 97321. 800-775-2118.

Medical Problems for Performing Arts (quarterly journal). Hanley & Belfus. 210 South 13th Street, Philadelphia, PA 19107. 215-546-4995.

Medical Program for Performing Artists at Rehabilitation Institute of Chicago. Dr. Alice Brandfonbrener, Director. 345 East Superior Street, Room 1129, Chicago, IL 60611. 312-908-2787.

North American Society of Teachers of the Alexander Technique [NASTAT]. Box 517, Urbana, IL 61801. 800-473-0620.

Performing Arts Clinic Brigham & Women's Hospital, Brigham Medical Group. Dr. Michael Charness, Director. 45 Francis Street, Boston, MA 02115. 617-732-5771.

Performing Arts Health Network. Box 566, New York, NY 10101. 212-246-0557.

The Taubman Institute. Medusa, NY 12120. 518-239-4282.

University of California Health Program for Performing Artists. Dr. Peter F. Ostwald, Director. 401 Parnassus Avenue, 3rd Floor, San Francisco, CA 94143. 415-476-7373.

IMPORTANT
CHOICES

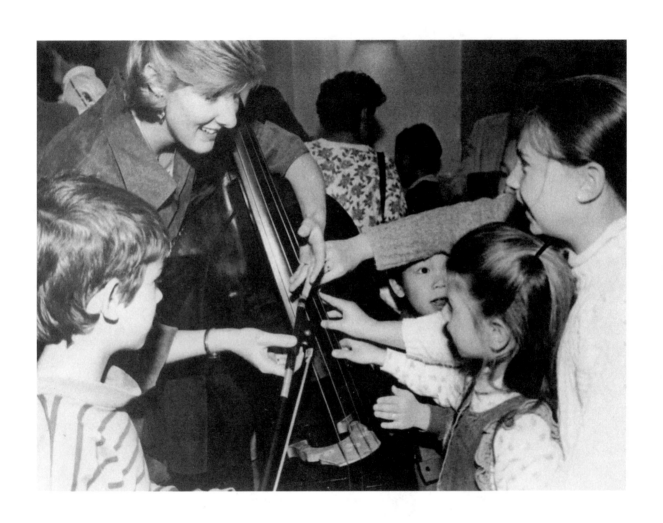

Choosing an Instrument

What you will find in this chapter

- If your child is under six
- If your child is between six and nine
- If your child is ten or older
- A look at all the instruments
- Physical features
-     How do I play it? Where do I play? When do I start?
-     What is special about each instrument?
- How to use the charts
- String instruments
- Woodwind instruments
- Brass instruments
- Percussion instruments
- Keyboard instruments
- Guitars
- Harp
- If you think your child should sing
- Electronic instruments
- How to sample the instruments
- A friend for life
- Highlights
- Chapter resources

*F*INDING an instrument for your child is something like helping him find a friend.

Instruments have personalities, just as your child does. You know your child. This chapter will tell you about the instruments and how to make a good match between your child and an instrument.

Making music in a certain way is a very personal choice. Tastes differ considerably. Some children love holding a violin or cello, feeling the vibrations as they move the bow across the strings, changing each sound as they form it. For other children, even those who are very musical, this is awkward or unattractive. Some children enjoy being alone at a keyboard, can cope with two-staff reading, and like the idea that they can play the melody and harmony at the same time. Others feel that playing the piano is mechanical or too complicated.

The world of music is a kaleidoscope of sound.
—Neil Ardley

The point is that most of us enjoy making music chiefly (perhaps only) in a certain way—bowing, blowing, strumming, drumming, singing, or pushing down keys. Don't think that if your child considers playing a piano, cello, or flute unappealing, she is unmusical or disinterested in making music. She may just need to find an instrument she's attracted to and comfortable with.

A good starting place is to discover what type of instrument attracts, or might attract, your child. Suggestions for doing this will be offered later in the chapter. Once you have an idea of what general "family" of instruments seems right, sifting through the several instruments in each group is easier than trying to compare several different instrument types at the same time.

You may know little about instruments, much less how to introduce options to your child. What follows should give you a start. Keep in mind, however, that this is only a start. Nothing can take the place of hearing, seeing, and handling instruments, or speaking with people who love them and play them well. Another caution: Guidelines can only be general. There will always be exceptions. Learn all you can from general information, but don't be afraid to venture beyond. Your child may surprise you.

If your child is under six

Age is a factor in matching children with musical instruments. A very young child has distinctive physical and mental abilities. While these are considerable, limitations exist. In order to play an instrument, a child must be able to hold or reach it comfortably. At this age, therefore, certain instruments are too large. Some instruments are made in smaller sizes, but many are not. The child must also be capable of producing sound in the way required by the instrument. The lung power and lip control necessary to play wind and brass instruments, for example, is beyond many young children.

It is also true that teaching methods designed for the young child (Suzuki study, for instance) usually enlist the time and talents of the parent in order to carry on and support the instruction. Parents are often asked (at times required) to attend lessons, take part in lesson activities, and supervise home practice sessions.

A child at this age may demonstrate strong attraction to a specific instrument, sometimes to the point of becoming insistent about it. If your child longs to play the violin, for example, chances are good that this will work out. A strongly motivated child finds ways to overcome drawbacks (if any exist), and may surprise everyone with his resolve and tenacity once instruction begins.

Most children, however, are impressionable and look to parents or others in authority to lead and support them. If your child shows no special interest in a particular instrument, it would be advisable to enroll her in a preschool music and movement class. Other ways to introduce instruments to your child will be discussed later in the chapter.

I heard an introduction to the instruments of the orchestra (on the radio) and when they got to the cello, I fell in love with it . . . something within the instrument spoke to me. I told my mother, "I want to make that sound."
—*Jacqueline Du Pré*

If your child is between six and nine

Many children begin music study at this time because they are bigger and stronger, not only because they have greater concentration and cognitive powers. The range of instruments that children between six and nine can play is wider, of course, although much depends on how quickly your child has grown, and where in that time frame your child is. It is probably true that a child as young as six or seven can play any instrument to which he is attracted provided that the instruction is given by a professional teacher who understands both the instrument and the child. (Not every teacher fits this description.)

Many instruments are made in smaller sizes, and small-size instruments are available for sale or rental. Where this is not the case (with wind and brass instruments, for example), the child may yet be able to handle a particular instrument if his physical capabilities are not too far out of line with what the instrument requires, and if the teacher knows how to bring him along in a way that is natural and gradual. A qualified instrumental teacher may also sustain a child's interest in a specific

Any real learning experience you engage in with your child benefits both of you.
—Thomas Armstrong

kind of instrument by recommending study on a similar instrument (for instance, a folk harp instead of a pedal harp, or a cornet instead of a trumpet) until the child is ready to cope with playing the instrument of first choice.

This is an age where a discussion about whether or not to study a musical instrument makes some sense. A child at this age has a better, although still uncertain, understanding that study and lessons will entail responsibility and that going to lessons and practicing will have to be fitted into the schedule. Wanting to play a particular instrument (the guitar, clarinet, or keyboard, for instance) may be more strongly motivating than just "taking music lessons."

If your child is ten or older

A child wishing to begin music study at this point is often motivated to do so in order to be part of a group—the school orchestra, a neighborhood band, or a gospel choir, for example. For some young people, working and playing within such a group develops self-esteem, reveals latent personality traits, or even stimulates interest in a career. Music plays an important role in the lives of preteens and teens. Being able to play music, as well as listen and dance to it, is a powerful lure for taking lessons at this age.

It is not only what we do that determines the pattern of our lives, but also whom we choose to associate with.
—Mihaly Csikszentmihalyi, Kevin Rathunde, and Samuel Whalen

This is also an age at which some young players like to branch out. They might wish to play a second instrument, often one that puts them in touch with music different from what they've been playing. A pianist, for example, wants to play in an orchestra, and so takes up the oboe. A preteen instrumentalist may develop an interest in songwriting and may get a digital keyboard with a MIDI interface that enables her to notate or arrange music. A young singer may begin to dream of making music a career and comes to understand that learning to play the piano will further that goal. This is the age of self-discovery, and many teens learn that expressing one's individuality through music-making is a powerful way of communicating what often cannot be said in words.

A look at all the instruments

No matter what the age of your child, knowing something about a wide variety of instruments gives you information and background that you can use as your child grows or changes. What follows is a survey of many instruments. They are grouped, in most cases, by "family." For each instrument there is a description of its physical features; how it is played; where it is played; when instruction on it usually begins; and what makes each instrument special.

Physical features. In addition to describing the physical characteristics of the instrument itself, this section offers a very general sketch of the physical abilities needed by the player. You get only a glimpse of what the instrument is like, but it may help you begin to answer the question: "Does my child 'fit' this instrument?"

How do I play it? Because the player's physical relationship to the instrument influences how he feels about playing it, you must consider this. It is your child, of course, who will have the experience, but you already know the physical actions and reactions he enjoys or dislikes. Answer the question: "Will my child enjoy this activity?"

Where do I play? Each instrument can be played solo, but some are more satisfactory solo instruments than others. Some instruments, likewise, are usually played as part of a group. Group types also vary considerably. Playing in an orchestra is not the same as playing in a jazz combo or rock group. Note where each instrument usually plays, and ask if these environments will suit your child. Consider too that where one plays affects the practice environment. Group practice or rehearsal appeals to some children, but not others. Your child may prefer to work alone.

Different instruments are also associated with different kinds of music even though any sort of music may be played on most of them. Because the survey lists usual places that each instrument plays, this seems to imply that each plays only certain kinds of music. Don't take this too literally. While some connections are true—for example, strings with classical music and symphony orchestras, electric guitars with jazz and rock groups—keep in mind that these associations are also stereotypes. Today harpists and violinists may play in jazz combos and classical guitarists work in folk settings.

Some instrumentalists will always be needed and welcomed. If you can play the bassoon, oboe, viola, or French horn, for example, you never have to search long for a group that wants you. The story is quite different if you play the flute, clarinet, saxophone, or piano. The larger number of such players does not matter so much when forming student ensembles, but at advancing levels, the competition for scholarships and recognition is considerable.

A word of caution about the "Where do I play" comments. Do not take them to mean that the beginner performs in these groups, or plays as a soloist, in the first years of instruction. In some cases, that may be true. In many cases, however, it may take a player a number of years to reach the point where performing in the roles and groups listed is likely. These charts offer you and your child the chance to see what *might* lie ahead. Ask: "Where will my child want to play?"

When do I start? This is a question that plagues most parents. A general overview can't provide answers to questions that concern your child's personal readiness. Much will depend on factors that vary from child to child, as much as on factors that fluctuate during your own child's developmental stages. Ask: "Does my child seem ready for this instrument?"

What is special about each instrument? In some sense, each instrument is special. What is unique about each instrument is not always easy to describe, but it is at the heart of why a person plays one instrument rather than another, or why a person feels that a certain instrument suits him. Some instruments require great dedication if the player is to succeed at beginning stages because they are difficult to play. Some instruments play music that has "solo" written all over it, while music for others is likely to be cast in a supporting role. Some instruments make specific physical demands on the player's hand span, breath control, or lip formation. On some instruments it takes longer to acquire a good sound, while on others playing well may require the ability to read more complicated music, to improvise, or to do several things simultaneously.

The charts below attempt to show the special characteristics of each instrument. As long as you read what is special about each instrument with a measure of impartiality and a sense of curiosity, you may find it useful to ask: "Does this sound like my child?"

How to use the charts

The chart for each instrument gives you a quick look at the instrument and what it takes to play it. Read through all the charts (if no instrument has yet been chosen or your child does not seem to gravitate toward any particular instrument), or just those that interest you. You may know, for instance, that your child wants to play a wind instru-

By the time my voice changed, I was already into the oboe. I've been fanatical about the oboe ever since. I fell in love with the sound of it, as many people do. I liked playing it, too, physically. I have the right personality for it, kind of tenacious. That's what the oboe takes.—Allan Vogel

ment, but is unsure which. In this case, examine all of the woodwind and brass groups in order to gain a general overview.

Next to each chart, a small list allows you to match your child with the instrument. Check the box that seems to come closest. (In some cases, you may not be sure.) When you finish your survey, gather instruments listed as "likely" or "possible" to form your short list.

At this point, the most important thing is to gain direct experience with the instruments. Listen to recordings or videotapes, go to a music store, arrange to visit a band or orchestra rehearsal at your local school, look up an instrument maker or repair shop, and speak with teachers and students who play the instruments.

If your child is old enough, it would be a good idea to go through the survey together. This opens up opportunity for discussion, provides your child with a sense of self-direction, and gives her an idea of how to research anything that is unfamiliar or confusing.

Note: Do not choose an instrument on the basis of these charts alone. The charts offer only basic facts, and cannot substitute for hands-on experience and talking to people who play the instruments well.

String instruments

All string instruments are "personal." The player makes the sound in a very direct manner, and controls the quality of the sound with the bow and the left-hand fingers. No string instrument is easy to play, and this is especially noticeable at the beginning. Progress is likely to be slow since learning to produce good sound and accurate pitch takes sensitivity, time, and much careful practice.

At the outset, instruments are usually rented. This is done through the teacher, the school, a music store, or an instrument repair shop. The price depends on the quality. The player must also have a bow and a case, generally included in the rental. The instrument requires protection from temperature extremes, light cleaning after each use, care in transporting, repair of bow and replacement of strings, and guarding against dropping or accidents.

Early instruction may be done in groups, but satisfactory progress generally requires individual instruction. Most string students participate in ensembles or student orchestras, even at an early age. Players who persevere through the early years of instruction often remain lifelong players, and making music with a few friends (even in amateur groups) continues to satisy.

*It is exciting to play in
an orchestra. When everyone
plays together it is like a wall
of different, beautiful sounds
around you.*
—Elizabeth Sharma

STRINGS

VIOLIN

Physical Features No valves, slides, frets, or keys to help child produce pitch. Instrument is supported between chin and collarbone. Can be played standing or sitting. The bow is as important as the violin itself. Correct, balanced position is challenging to learn and must be supervised.

How Do I Play Player makes strings vibrate by drawing the bow across them. Left-hand fingers "stop" the strings to determine pitch. Right hand may also pluck the strings.

Where Do I Play Solo. Orchestra. Small ensembles.

When Do I Start As young as three, but four or five is better. Violins are also made in three-quarter, half, quarter, eighth, and sixteenth sizes. Smaller instrument requires a smaller bow.

What Is Special Need good sense of pitch both to tune and play. The player must be persevering because producing good tone will not come quickly.

MY CHILD
Likely   ( )
Possible   ( )
Doubtful   ( )
Certainly Not   ( )

VIOLA

Physical Features Larger size than violin. Sounds lower than the violin. Left arm must reach further than when playing the violin. Can be played standing or sitting. For all else, see Violin.

How Do I Play See Violin.

Where Do I Play Solo. Orchestra. Small ensembles.

When Do I Start Around eight or nine (strictly on the viola), but may transfer (often later) from the violin.

What Is Special Need good sense of pitch both to tune and play. Player will always be in demand, but parts are often supportive and less "showy."

MY CHILD
Likely   ( )
Possible   ( )
Doubtful   ( )
Certainly Not   ( )

CELLO

Physical Features Much larger than the viola. The "tenor" string instrument. Instrument is played while sitting, supported on the floor and between the knees. The bow is somewhat heavier and larger.

How Do I Play See Violin. The left hand also uses the thumb for stopping higher pitches.

Where Do I Play Solo. Orchestra. Small ensembles.

When Do I Start As young as four or five. Smaller-size cellos are made, and are available for sale or rental. All sizes of student instruments are more expensive than violins. May transfer from another instrument, but most cellists begin on this instrument.

What Is Special Player needs good stretch between the left-hand fingers. Cello parts are often expressive and demand a sense of drama and poetry.

MY CHILD
Likely   ( )
Possible   ( )
Doubtful   ( )
Certainly Not ( )

DOUBLE BASS

Physical Features A comparatively large instrument. Played while standing, or sitting on a high stool. Bow is heavier and larger. Need large left hand with wide spaces between fingers. May need and use a dolly or wheel to transport.

How Do I Play See Violin. Right hand often plucks the strings.

Where Do I Play Solo. Orchestra. Jazz, pop, country, bluegrass combos, many others.

When Do I Start Often as a teenager. May begin earlier, and many now start in "young bassist" programs. Double basses are made in smaller sizes, down to one-tenth size. Player must be big enough to hold and control the instrument. Often transfer from another instrument. This may be a second instrument.

What Is Special Bass ensemble parts are supportive, but modern players play much solo music. The only string instrument that is a usual part of jazz and other combos.

MY CHILD
Likely   ( )
Possible   ( )
Doubtful   ( )
Certainly Not ( )

Woodwind instruments

Woodwind is the traditional name for this group of instruments even though some of them are not made of wood. The woodwinds have undergone many changes (such as from wood to metal) and improvements (such as the addition of finger keys) in the last few centuries, many of these in an effort to make the instruments easier to play. All of them have ancestors in ancient instruments, except for the saxophone, which is only about 150 years old.

Children may begin with group instruction on these instruments, often in conjunction with a school band or orchestra, but it may be better to work with someone who plays and teaches the instrument well even at the outset. First instruments may be rented from the school or—on the recommendation of the private teacher—from a music store. Rentals are generally reasonable. If your child is wearing braces or retainers, these will not interfere if she is properly instructed.

The instruments are disassembled before being placed in cases. Reeds are needed for the oboe, clarinet, bassoon, and saxophone. Caring for the instruments includes protection from temperature extremes, cleaning and drying after each use, and cautious attention when assembling and disassembling. Prices for new instruments vary, depending on the quality of the instrument. Bassoons and oboes can be costly, and saxophones are usually more expensive than clarinets. Quality student instruments are available at reasonable prices.

Some instruments such as the alto flute, piccolo, English horn, and bass clarinet, are not included in this survey because these are usually begun as an offshoot from study on the "main" instrument.

Winds—especially the flute, clarinet, and saxophone—are popular choices, and most of them are versatile in the sense that they are at home in many settings, from local dance halls to renowned concert stages.

WOODWINDS

FLUTE

Physical Features Most often made of silver. Need a good left-arm stretch. A curved headjoint model is available for slightly younger or smaller players.

How Do I Play Player purses lips and blows controlled stream of air over open hole. Only wind instrument on which sound is produced without direct contact with the player's mouth. Player needs good manual dexterity.

Where Do I Play Solo. Concert band. Marching band. Orchestra. Jazz combos. Small ensembles.

When Do I Start As early as five or six (if flute with curved headjoint is used).

What Is Special Flute sounds are often soft, but they can be penetrating and dramatic. Flutists are abundant, and competition for scholarships and positions is keen.

MY CHILD
Likely   ( )
Possible   ( )
Doubtful   ( )
Certainly Not   ( )

OBOE

Physical Features The treble double-reed instrument. Need very good breath control.

How Do I Play Player's lips fold over teeth around two narrow reeds. Air is blown between the blades of the reeds. Fingers manipulate keys.

Where Do I Play Solo. Concert band. Orchestra. Small ensembles.

When Do I Start May begin from ten to twelve, but often start in junior high or older. Often transfer from another instrument.

What Is Special The player must be determined because the instrument is difficult to play. Oboe players are often in demand. A unique and beautiful sound. The oboe often plays solos within the ensemble.

MY CHILD
Likely   ( )
Possible   ( )
Doubtful   ( )
Certainly Not   ( )

MY CHILD
Likely   ( )
Possible   ( )
Doubtful   ( )
Certainly Not   ( )

CLARINET

Physical Features A single-reed instrument. An instrument with a very wide range. Player needs a high degree of coordination.

How Do I Play Player has mouthpiece inside the mouth. Blow to vibrate wide reed clamped to mouthpiece. Fingers manipulate keys.

Where Do I Play Solo. Concert band. Marching band. Orchestra. Jazz combos. Small ensembles.

When Do I Start Between eight and eleven. When fingers are able to span spaces between the keys, and when finger pads are able to cover the open holes.

What Is Special The clarinet is versatile and has a wide range with special qualities in each register. The clarinetist can play in many musical settings.

MY CHILD
Likely   ( )
Possible   ( )
Doubtful   ( )
Certainly Not   ( )

BASSOON

Physical Features The bass double-reed instrument. A heavy instrument. Player needs strength, although a seat strap helps support the instrument.

How Do I Play Player's lips fold over the reeds. Air is blown between the blades of the reeds. Fingers manipulate keys. A larger hand size is helpful.

Where Do I Play Concert band. Orchestra. Small ensembles.

When Do I Start Junior high, but may start younger. Often transfer from another instrument.

What Is Special The bassoon can be clownlike, but also serious and intense. Bassoonists are often in demand.

SAXOPHONE

Physical Features This is a family of instruments: Soprano/Alto/Tenor/Baritone. A quite heavy instrument, depending on the type and pitch level. Player needs strength, although neck strap helps support the instrument.

How Do I Play Player has a relatively large mouthpiece in the mouth. Blow air over the reed, similar to the clarinet. Fingers manipulate keys.

Where Do I Play Concert band. Marching band. Jazz combos. Small ensembles. Player often solos in jazz combos.

When Do I Start Junior high or older, but can also begin at ten. Can begin on alto sax around nine, then change to larger sax later on. Can transfer from the recorder or flute since the fingering is similar.

What Is Special The saxophone is the most "modern" of the winds and has a penetrating sound. The saxophone is especially suitable in jazz and other combos.

MY CHILD
Likely ( )
Possible ( )
Doubtful ( )
Certainly Not ( )

RECORDER

Physical Features This is a family of instruments: Sopranino/Descant/Treble/Tenor/Bass. Children usually play the descant recorder. Instrument is small and light. Little physical energy is required.

How Do I Play Player has mouthpiece in mouth. Blow air into the tube. Fingers cover the open holes.

Where Do I Play Solo. Recorder ensembles.

When Do I Start Six and older.

What Is Special The sound is gentle and refined and the recorder can be played by young children. Advanced recorder players specialize in playing music from earlier historic periods.

MY CHILD
Likely ( )
Possible ( )
Doubtful ( )
Certainly Not ( )

Brass instruments

This is a large and ancient group of instruments. Horns of all kinds have been associated with a number of activities, not all of them musical. They are commonly linked to religion, hunting, celebrating, and the military. As a group, they are often considered loud instruments, although each of the modern brass instruments can be played very softly. They are distinguished by the fact that they have cup-shaped mouthpieces. The player's lips might be said to function as the vibrating "reed."

Just as with winds, children often begin study of a brass instrument as part of a "like" group (for example, all trumpets, or all horns) and change to private study after the beginning stages are past. The first instrument is usually rented through the school or a music store.

What instrument makes you think of kings and queens? The festive, regal-sounding trumpet.—Rosmarie Hausherr

The instruments are sturdier than many of the woodwinds, although they too must have care and protection, especially from bumping or denting. There are no reeds, however, and the chief concern is keeping the moving parts oiled and cleaned. Since there are few valves or pistons (as compared to the greater number of keys and moving parts on woodwinds), there is less need for repairs and adjustments. Music for brass instruments, especially at the outset, is quite simple, and most children have no trouble reading or playing it. In all cases, the price for a new instrument depends on its quality.

There are other instruments not listed that are part of extended brass "families"—such as C and D trumpets, flügelhorn, bass trombone—and are played as second instruments by those who play the instruments surveyed here.

BRASS

TRUMPET

Physical Features The "soprano" brass instrument. Need firm teeth and gums. With good breath support, the greater back pressure needed to play shouldn't matter. Consult your dentist if your child wears braces.

How Do I Play Player blows, or buzzes, into the mouthpiece. Notes are produced by creating larger and smaller openings in lip/mouth positions. Right-hand fingers operate three valves that also affect pitch.

Where Do I Play Solo. Concert band. Marching band. Orchestra. Jazz and pop combos.

When Do I Start Around ten.

What Is Special Music for the trumpet generally stands out in any group. Trumpeters may play many different kinds of music.

MY CHILD
Likely   ( )
Possible   ( )
Doubtful   ( )
Certainly Not   ( )

CORNET

Physical Features Like a trumpet with a deeper tone. Light to hold and play. Need firm teeth and gums. Produces a different kind of tone than the trumpet.

How Do I Play See Trumpet.

Where Do I Play Solo. Concert band. Marching band. Jazz combos.

When Do I Start Could begin as early as seven or eight, if teeth and gums are firm and permanent teeth are in. A good preparatory brass instrument.

What Is Special The cornet is no longer quite so popular, but is good for younger players. The cornet is most at home in bands.

MY CHILD
Likely   ( )
Possible   ( )
Doubtful   ( )
Certainly Not   ( )

MY CHILD
Likely   ( )
Possible   ( )
Doubtful   ( )
Certainly Not ( )

BUGLE

Physical Features Light to hold and play. Simpler construction than trumpet or cornet. Can be with or without valves.

How Do I Play Player blows, or buzzes, into the mouthpiece. Notes are produced by creating larger and smaller openings in lip/mouth positions. If there are valves, using these also affects pitch.

Where Do I Play Solo. Drum and bugle corps.

When Do I Start See Cornet.

What Is Special The bugle is commonly associated with military bands. It is not an instrument that one goes on to "study."

MY CHILD
Likely   ( )
Possible   ( )
Doubtful   ( )
Certainly Not ( )

FRENCH HORN

Physical Features An instrument with elaborate, tightly-wound tubing. Lip positions are extremely sensitive. Player needs excellent sense of pitch to produce good tone, accurate pitch.

How Do I Play Player blows, or buzzes, into the mouthpiece. Notes are produced by creating larger and smaller openings in lip/mouth positions. Left-hand fingers operate three valves that also affect pitch. Right hand, in bell, helps to support the instrument. Relationship among pitch, lips, and valves is important.

Where Do I Play Solo. Orchestra. Small ensembles. Concert band.

When Do I Start Could begin as early as ten. Often transfer from another instrument, especially other brass instruments such as cornet or trumpet. Can also transfer from flute. Keyboard background is helpful to reinforce pitch reference.

What Is Special The player must be dedicated, since the instrument is challenging to play. French horn players are always welcome since there are not very many of them.

BARITONE

Physical Features Looks like a small tuba. Lighter to hold and play than a tuba. Large mouthpiece.

How Do I Play See Trumpet.

Where Do I Play Concert band. Marching band. Solo.

When Do I Start Nine to ten, or older. Good preparatory instrument for learning the lower brass.

What Is Special Music for the baritone is generally easy, and the instrument is fun to play. Gets many solos to play in concert bands.

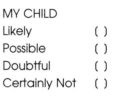

MY CHILD
Likely   ( )
Possible   ( )
Doubtful   ( )
Certainly Not   ( )

MY CHILD
Likely ( )
Possible ( )
Doubtful ( )
Certainly Not ( )

TROMBONE

Physical Features Light to hold and play, but long. Player needs excellent sense of pitch. Right arm must be long enough to manage the slide (but children grow quickly).

How Do I Play Player blows, or buzzes, into the mouthpiece. Notes are produced by blowing, with careful positioning of the slide. No valves or independent finger work are involved.

Where Do I Play Solo. Concert band. Marching band. Orchestra. Jazz combos. Small ensembles.

When Do I Start Could begin as early as nine or ten.

What Is Special Trombones sound mellow, but can also be assertive and dramatic. Trombonists get to play many different kinds of music.

MY CHILD
Likely ( )
Possible ( )
Doubtful ( )
Certainly Not ( )

TUBA

Physical Features A very large instrument.

How Do I Play Player blows, or buzzes, into the mouthpiece. Notes are produced by creating larger and smaller openings in lip/mouth positions. Right-hand fingers operate three or four valves.

Where Do I Play Concert band. Orchestra. Small ensembles. Marching band (Sousaphones [modified tubas] are used in marching bands).

When Do I Start Could begin as early as ten. Must be big enough to hold the instrument (but there are ways around this). Desire, not the age, is half the battle.

What Is Special While tubas often call forth smiles, they can be played very sensitively. Advanced players can make the instrument sound amazingly versatile.

Percussion instruments

Drumming and tapping seem to be universal instincts. Keeping the beat is something that people do spontaneously—at parades, rock concerts, folk festivals, and listening to car radios. Why then should your child study to play the drums when doing so appears natural and easy? Perhaps a beginning answer to this question lies in considering the precision and subtlety with which drumming can be done and the variety of sounds that drumming includes. Further answers may be found in examining the instruments known collectively as percussion.

Percussion, which derives from making sound by striking (percussing), includes many more instruments than drums. Some of the tuned instruments are familiar, even though you may not have thought of them as percussion—instruments such as the marimba, vibes, and xylophone. Tuned drums, called kettledrums or timpani, are also well known, but most people do not appreciate what skill it takes to tune and play them.

Parents sometimes feel that playing drums is not musical. They wish, instead, that their child might play the piano, or violin, or clarinet. Yet, the drummer is often a highly sensitive person whose sensitivity expresses itself in rhythms rather than melodies or chords. If your child is constantly drumming on things around home or fidgets and experiments with sticks and spoons, consider drum lessons. The child who fidgets also often flits from one activity to another, and that is exactly what percussion players do—changing mallets, sticks, and instruments as a matter of course. Parents of young percussion players must also have some tolerance for noise, since that will be a factor.

Initial costs are minimal, and practicing is done on drum pads. Beginning rental sets can include a variety of things, such as a snare drum, a drum pad, and occasionally even a small xylophone. It is not always easy, however, to find a teacher who can take your child beyond the basics. You must persevere and ask questions.

We all enjoy making rhythmic sounds from an early age, and this is why there are more percussion instruments in the world than any other kind of instrument.
—*Elizabeth Sharma*

Some instruments are called idiophones, meaning "own sound." An amazing variety of percussion instruments, producing an equally amazing range of crashes, bangs, chimes, thumps, knocks, rattles, and rasps belong to this category.
—*Alan Blackwood*

PERCUSSION: NONTUNED INSTRUMENTS

SNARE DRUM

Physical Features Need physical energy. Need flexible wrists. Need noticeable sense of rhythm.

How Do I Play Fingers loosely hold the sticks. Rhythms are controlled by fingers, hands, and arms. Player may practice on a drum pad, although practice on a drumhead is preferable.

Where Do I Play Concert band. Marching band. Orchestra. Jazz combos. Drum and bugle corps.

When Do I Start May start as early as six. Usually start around eight or nine.

What Is Special Drumming seems to be a release of energy, but doing it well requires concentration.

MY CHILD
Likely ( )
Possible ( )
Doubtful ( )
Certainly Not ( )

DRUM SET

Physical Features Combination of several instruments arranged around the player. Need high physical energy. But a child who seems to lack energy may be energized by playing the drum set. Need superior coordination, but playing the drum set will also help to develop it.

How Do I Play Player often does different things simultaneously. Player uses both hands and feet.

Where Do I Play Jazz combos. Rock groups. Dance bands.

When Do I Start Junior high or older. Preparation by playing the snare drum is advantageous.

What Is Special Playing the drum set is not as easy and "natural" as it may look. A skilled drummer is welcomed in most musical ensembles.

MY CHILD
Likely ( )
Possible ( )
Doubtful ( )
Certainly Not ( )

PERCUSSION: TUNED INSTRUMENTS

TIMPANI

Physical Features These are tunable drums (kettledrums) that come in sets, two or more. Need great coordination and acute sense of pitch. Instruments are tuned either by turning screws or by adjusting with a pedal.

How Do I Play Fingers loosely hold the sticks. Rhythms are controlled from the wrist. Player's skill includes tuning.

Where Do I Play Orchestra. Concert band. Drum corps.

When Do I Start Junior high or older. Seldom the first instrument. Often transfer from another instrument. Choral or keyboard background is helpful.

What Is Special Playing timpani is a very special form of drumming. Timpanists must be able to tune while playing.

MY CHILD
Likely   ( )
Possible   ( )
Doubtful   ( )
Certainly Not   ( )

XYLOPHONE

Physical Features Set of hardwood or synthetic bars, arranged similar to a keyboard, placed on a stand. Played while standing. Need great coordination and flexible wrists.

How Do I Play Player reads music from the grand staff (like a pianist). Player may hold more than one stick in each hand.

Where Do I Play Solo. Orchestra. Concert band. Drum corps.

When Do I Start Junior high or older. Must be tall enough to see and reach the entire instrument. May transfer from the keyboard.

What Is Special May be a first choice, but is usually learned as part of becoming a percussionist.

MY CHILD
Likely   ( )
Possible   ( )
Doubtful   ( )
Certainly Not   ( )

MY CHILD
Likely ( )
Possible ( )
Doubtful ( )
Certainly Not ( )

VIBRAPHONE

Physical Features Set of metal bars, arranged similar to a keyboard, and placed on a stand. Bars have vibrating "fans" below. Has a damper pedal like the piano. Played while standing. Need great coordination and flexible wrists.

How Do I Play See Xylophone. This is seldom a first instrument.

Where Do I Play Solo. Dance band. Jazz combos.

When Do I Start See Xylophone.

What Is Special "Vibes" have a distinctive sound and are popular as a solo instrument. Much piano music and music written specially for this instrument can be played on it.

MY CHILD
Likely ( )
Possible ( )
Doubtful ( )
Certainly Not ( )

MARIMBA

Physical Features Set of hardwood or synthetic bars, arranged similar to a keyboard, placed on a stand. Bars have tubular resonators below. Played while standing. Need great coordination and flexible wrists.

How Do I Play See Xylophone. This is seldom a first instrument.

Where Do I Play Solo. Dance band. Jazz combos. Ethnic combos.

When Do I Start See Xylophone.

What Is Special Much classical and popular music can be played on the marimba.

Keyboard instruments

The keyboard is so well known that introducing it seems unnecessary. Everyone has seen and probably touched one at some time. It appears easy to play, and piano teachers are easy to find, unlike teachers for some other instruments. Parents often regard it as a logical first choice because training on it can prepare one for many other musical experiences.

It may be hard to appreciate that "keyboard" is a generic name, like woodwinds or strings. There are many kinds of keyboards—piano, organ, harpsichord, to list the obvious—and to these must be added the electronic instruments—such as the digital piano and the synthesizer. Most people mean piano when they say "keyboard," but that may depend on age. To many young people, keyboard is an electronic instrument, not the piano in Grandma's living room. Keep this is mind when you talk to your child about "piano" lessons.

Only the piano and digital piano are listed, but it is important to understand that these are not the same instrument. The digital piano (one whose sound is produced electronically rather than by hammers striking strings) is not just a newer, or a cheaper, piano. It may look similar, but it requires a different touch, and it offers a different set of possibilities to the player.

Most musicians would agree that it is best to begin on the piano and include, or transfer to, a digital piano at some future point. A modest, but growing, percentage of piano teachers now have digital as well as "acoustic" pianos in their studios. If you have interest in these newer instruments for your child, seek out such a teacher and direct specific questions to her.

KEYBOARDS

PIANO

Physical Features Many sizes and types of pianos. Need good eye-hand coordination and mental agility. Need independence of hands and fingers.

How Do I Play Entire body participates in playing, even though it appears that the fingers do all the work. Feet should rest on the floor or on a stool.

Where Do I Play Solo. Small ensembles. Accompanist. Orchestra.

When Do I Start May start as early as three or four. Often begin around six.

What Is Special The pianist can play any kind of music. The pianist must be able to read many more notes simultaneously than other players. Practicing may be lonely, but the pianist may have varied performance roles, such as playing in small ensembles or working as a collaborative artist (accompanist).

MY CHILD
Likely   ( )
Possible   ( )
Doubtful   ( )
Certainly Not   ( )

MY CHILD
Likely   ( )
Possible   ( )
Doubtful   ( )
Certainly Not   ( )

DIGITAL KEYBOARD

Physical Features See Piano. Offers great variety of sounds and effects. May practice with headset. May hook up to a computer.

How Do I Play See Piano.

Where Do I Play Solo. Keyboard ensembles. Small ensembles. Jazz, pop, and rock groups.

When Do I Start See Piano.

What Is Special Many types of digital pianos are available, ranging from simple to complex. This instrument seems to invite the player to experiment and create. Often paired with a computer for composing or arranging.

Guitars

The guitar, like the keyboard, is a familiar instrument. "Guitar" is also a generic name. It includes instruments as dissimilar as the ukulele and the bass guitar. "Guitar" often splits into two main camps. The sounds of a classical guitar evoke associations with Spain or folk music. The electric guitar, however, belongs to an altogether different world. No one doubts that the classical and electric guitar are separate instruments, yet "guitar" is used to identify each of them. If you speak to your child about guitar lessons, be sure that you are talking about the same thing.

Guitars are sometimes referred to as fretted instruments. Frets are metal strips fixed on the fingerboard that mark positions for "stopping" the strings. They aid the player in producing correct pitch, which may give the idea that the guitar is easier to play than is actually the case. Tuning the guitar is a tricky job in itself, and people who think they can teach themselves to play sometimes damage the instrument just by tuning it improperly.

Many inexpensive used guitars are available, but seek advice from someone who plays a guitar well before purchasing an instrument. (Watch out for warped necks and tuning pegs that don't hold.) Because electric guitars require amplifiers, safety issues surrounding the use of voltage must be considered.

The classical guitarist lives in a quieter world than does the electric guitarist, and for those who play electric guitars it is often the group scene, as much as the instrument, that is the attraction. Some guitarists, however, switch between, or live in, both worlds. While most teachers specialize, there are some who can teach all styles, responding to the changing interests of a young guitarist.

GUITARS

CLASSICAL GUITAR

Physical Features Acoustic nylon-string guitars are used for classical playing. Acoustic metal-string guitars are used for folk, bluegrass, and so on.

How Do I Play Left hand "stops" strings to alter the pitches. Right hand strums/plucks strings; there is also "finger style" picking with the nails. Played seated. Left leg is elevated on a footstool; the left thigh supports the guitar.

Where Do I Play Solo. Guitar ensembles. Small ensembles. Accompanist.

When Do I Start When child can hold instrument easily; when left hand has some finger stretch. There are also three-quarter, half, and one-quarter size guitars. The ukulele may be played by the very young.

What Is Special The guitarist can play a wide variety of music. The guitarist can be a complete performer; there is no need for an accompanist. It is not easy to find a good guitar teacher, one who can go beyond the basics.

MY CHILD
Likely   ( )
Possible   ( )
Doubtful   ( )
Certainly Not   ( )

MY CHILD
Likely   ( )
Possible   ( )
Doubtful   ( )
Certainly Not   ( )

ELECTRIC GUITAR

Physical Features Instrument can be solid and rather heavy. There are also hollow-body electric guitars. Need coordination and mental agility.

How Do I Play May use a pick instead of fingers. Left-hand reach/technique different from classical. May be played standing or sitting. A strap helps support the instrument. Sounds are amplified electronically, and it is easy to play loud. Can play single line and chords.

Where Do I Play Solo. Pop/rock groups. Folk groups. Jazz combos. In schools that have a stage band or swing choir, a guitar chair is often available.

When Do I Start May begin as early as ten or eleven. Good to have previous experience with nylon-string guitar, for left-hand development.

What Is Special The electric guitar is associated chiefly with pop and rock music. Although there are many good players, finding a good teacher is not easy.

MY CHILD
Likely   ( )
Possible   ( )
Doubtful   ( )
Certainly Not   ( )

BASS GUITAR

Physical Features Larger and heavier than the electric guitar. Easier to play than the electric guitar, but requires a longer left-hand finger stretch. Need some understanding of electricity and voltage.

How Do I Play See Electric guitar. Plays single lines and double stops.

Where Do I Play Pop/rock groups.

When Do I Start Junior high or older.

What Is Special Bass guitarists do not usually get "solo" opportunities. Although there are many good players, finding a good teacher is not easy.

Harp

Although the harp is an instrument with strings, it does not really fit into any group, and thus is treated separately here. In some ways, the harp is also a family of instruments since there are many different kinds of harps—such as folk, Irish, Celtic, nonpedal, and pedal harps—and many different sizes of harps. Young players often begin on a folk or Irish harp because these instruments are smaller and do not have pedals, which are used to raise and lower the pitches of the strings. They are also less expensive than the standard pedal harp. Many harp teachers, however, do not regard playing folk harps as the only, or best, way to begin. In addition, some harpists choose to play Irish or Celtic harps and do not regard playing these instruments as stepping-stones to playing anything else.

The harp itself is a beautiful instrument and more versatile than you might think. Like the piano, it is a self-contained instrument, and you will see or hear harpists in many places such as in symphony orchestras, chamber groups, folk groups, churches, restaurants, or jazz combos. An attractive feature of playing the harp is that you can make beautiful sounds right from the beginning. A skilled harpist can play almost any kind of music. (There is even new age music for harp these days, although you need to look for it.)

There are some challenges if your child is interested in playing a harp. The first is to locate a harp, so that your child will have some idea of its actual size and what the physical reality of playing it is like. (You are unlikely to find a harp in a local music store or school band room.) The second is to locate a teacher. These challenges can probably be solved in a single act—arranging to visit a professional harpist at a nearby college or in a local symphony, or even by speaking to the harpist who plays in a restaurant—at which time, your child will both see and hear the harp, and you will have an opportunity to discuss matters relating to instruction and how and when your child might have an opportunity to try out the instrument.

Because there are many different kinds of harps, the purchase price of a new harp will vary considerably. Depending on the size of your community, it may be possible to rent a harp. It is also true that in larger communities you will find a greater number of professional harpists who offer harp instruction. While transporting a harp is a bit of a problem, it is no more difficult than transporting other larger instruments, such as a double bass or marimba. (Of course, double bass players and harpists do not drive Mazda Miatas!) You should also be aware that your child will not need to transport a harp to the lesson, since at the lesson the teacher's harp will be used.

HARP

MY CHILD
Likely   ( )
Possible   ( )
Doubtful   ( )
Certainly Not   ( )

Physical Features A (relatively) large instrument, depending on the type of harp. Need coordination between hands and feet to play a pedal harp.

How Do I Play Player tilts harp toward body. Both hands pluck the strings. Feet control raising and lowering of pitches by means of foot pedals.

Where Do I Play Solo. Orchestra. Small ensembles. Jazz combos. Folk groups.

When Do I Start May begin as early as six or seven. There are smaller harps, and it may be possible to rent one. It helps to have studied the piano first.

What Is Special Becoming a skilled harpist is likely to require both determination and devotion. Harpists can play many different kinds of music and can perform in many settings.

If you think your child should sing

Most young children love to sing, and it is easy to be captivated by the charm of child voices. If you feel that your child's voice is special, you may be inclined to seek voice lessons. You must realize that, in this case, the singer *is* the instrument. The child voice, like everything else about the child, is largely undeveloped and, if not interfered with, will mature with time. Pushing or straining a young voice beyond its natural capacities is highly dangerous. Some voice teachers are hesitant to work with a child; some will not even consider accepting a student until well into the teens. You probably know that outstanding talents like Beverly Sills and Lea Salonga both studied and sang publicly early in their lives, but you may not be aware that a great number of promising child voices have been injured by misuse or overuse. This is an area in which you must be cautious.

That does not mean, of course, that your child should receive no vocal training. Professional voice teachers, however, do not agree when voice training should begin, or even whether early voice training is helpful or harmful. Those who do believe in working with young voices feel that as long as the singing technique and the repertoire is age-appropriate, the young voice actually benefits from receiving training that guards against voice abuse and, perhaps, even channels parental and student ambitions.

If you feel that your child has an exceptional voice, try to find a teacher that is a genuine professional with experience in working with young voices. Inquire at your local college or community school. Speaking to voice teachers on those faculties ought to help in locating an appropriate instructor. You should know that not everyone who conducts a musical theater production is capable of providing vocal instruction and, while involvement in musical theater is exhilarating and may be worthwhile, it is often not the best place to cultivate a young voice.

Another way of providing vocal training for your child is to enroll him in a singing group, such as a children's choir. Those who direct these groups are generally highly qualified, and know how to cultivate the child voice in a way that is healthy and beneficial. Children's choirs often develop the child's capacity to read and understand music (as well as to sing) through classes and rehearsals that devote time to sight-singing, vocalizing, and breathing as well as to learning the music for programs. Membership in such a group also offers the child an opportunity to become part of a musical community, and often—by identifying with the success of the group—to develop a high degree of self-esteem. In some preeminent children's choirs, however, membership is by audition or invitation only. It is also true that many children's singing groups are composed of several choirs, and belonging to a certain choir may require an audition.

Vocal talent is an innate gift. If a child has talent and a strong desire to learn how to sing better, then instruction by a knowledgeable singing teacher will strengthen the vocal mechanism rather than harm it.—Robert Edwin

Electronic instruments

It is common to hear electronic instruments referred to as instruments of the future, or the future of music described as the electronic age. In fact, electronic instruments have been in use for half a century. Today we live in a sea of electronic sound. Music that sounds "live" on commercials and computer games, for example, is most often produced electronically. A century ago, families gathered around the parlor piano to sing, much as they flocked around the bandshell in the park to join in holiday festivities. Today, someone turns on an audiocassette, switches to MTV, or buys a CD. It is a different way of relating to music. In some ways, music has become like instant soup; we buy it packaged, consume it with little or no preparation, and are largely unaware of what it contains.

There is a variety of electronic equipment with which to make and/or enjoy music. This includes instruments, hardware, software, and assorted amplifying and hookup equipment. By definition, an electronic instrument has a sound source that is electronic rather than acoustic. Many instruments (such as pianos, flutes, violins, or guitars) can be electronic, which means they must be plugged in and need amplification if the sound is to be heard. Here we discuss only some keyboard instrument types because many students use these as beginning electronic instruments. (Electric guitars are mentioned in the section on guitars.)

The digital piano has built-in amplification (onboard speakers) and can be played rather like a piano. Depending on the model, there may be from sixty-one to eighty-eight keys and one to three pedals. Some keys are touch-sensitive, which means that the speed of the key's descent will result in different tone and volume quality (as happens on an acoustic piano). Low-end models are less apt to offer this feature. In some cases, the degree of sensitivity is adjustable. Touch-sensitivity is desirable, since the player has much more direct musical control of the sound.

When shopping for an electronic instrument, you will hear about MIDI, an acronym for Musical Instrument Digital Interface. MIDI is a feature that allows instruments to communicate with each other via cable connections, and recently instrument manufacturers have agreed on a standardization of this feature allowing for easy communication among all instrument types and brands. MIDI makes it possible for a player to store and edit musical data, to layer it in "tracks," and, in some cases, convert musical information into conventional notation. Most digital pianos have some MIDI features.

A synthesizer is another electronic musical instrument whose best and chief use is to create unique sounds, although it can also simulate conventional instrument sounds. It may have piano keys, but it is not played like a piano. Its purpose is to generate and process audio signals, and it does this in complex ways. In general, the more costly the synthesizer, the more variety there will be in the synthesizer's capabilities to manipulate sounds.

A sequencer, another piece of electronic equipment, is really a special kind of computer. It is a device that processes MIDI data. Like a tape recorder, it records and plays back sounds, but (unlike a tape recorder) it can also change (edit) pitches, rhythms, and speeds. Just as a word processor is more sophisticated than a typewriter, so a sequencer exceeds the uses and functions of a tape recorder. Some electronic keyboards have onboard sequencers; in other cases, sequencers may be small, stand-alone pieces of equipment; or sequencing functions may be incorporated with computer software.

There is an instrument called the MIDI piano which is not a digital piano, but an acoustic instrument with an onboard sequencer. This sophisticated and costly instrument is used chiefly by professionals for creative, archival, educational, and medical research applications.

Even from these brief descriptions, you can see that electronic instruments offer unique features. Depending on the model, a digital piano may make available any number of sounds. It can sound like a violin, trumpet, harpsichord, vibraphone, or many other instruments, and it can also can make noninstrumental sounds. It can offer the player different kinds of supports; it may, for example, provide chords or rhythm backgrounds. It may also be a source of sound effects (bells, whistles, laughter, thunder, and so on). One major sound difference between the piano and digital piano is that, on an acoustic piano, the kind of sound is predictable; on a digital piano, however, there is always constant choice and selection of sounds. While it is true that a digital piano is often less expensive than one that is acoustic, this is not always the case. A secondhand upright may cost much less than even a semisophisticated digital keyboard.

Electronic instruments can be used in varied ways. They can serve as solo instruments, allowing the performer to demonstrate special skills. They are instruments on which to create because they invite exploration and, through MIDI and computer hookups, can produce notated scores. They are instruments on which to practice because they are portable and capable of being played with headsets. They are a new kind of ensemble instrument because they can produce a variety of mixable sounds and effects.

Beyond choosing a particular model or make of electronic instrument, however, you may want to consider the educational implications of having your child begin on a digital piano. With an electronic instrument it is possible to bypass much of the process of music making. Buttons and dials can provide almost everything—pitch, rhythm, melodies, chords, sound effects, styles, and instrumentation. They can do what was traditionally the skill of the musician—they can change key, provide introductions and endings, harmonize, and, to a degree, even create original music. Therein lies what some consider the danger. The "soup analogy" is once again apt. If you feel your child should know that it takes real vegetables and broth to make soup, then you will agree with those who contend that music, like soup, should be "made from scratch." Only when you know the materials and the process can you evaluate and appreciate the shortcut.

There is, however, another perspective with regard to electronic instruments. In a way, they attempt to imitate acoustic instruments. But they also make sounds that are unique to them. How to play these instruments so that music for them goes beyond imitation or substitution is just beginning to develop. These instruments foster experimentation. While a young player might hesitate to fool around on a piano or with a violin, exploring seems to be the order of the day on electronic instruments. People with minimum skills dive in without misgivings because so many effects, sounds, and styles are available with the push of button or the twist of a dial. Sometimes, in the process, they become truly inquisitive and seek to find out about the "real vegetables." But whether they dig deeper or remain content with quick effects, they have become involved with making music, and could be discouraged if they had to do it all from scratch.

If your child is interested in electronic instruments and music, it might be wise to find the teacher first, and purchase or rent the instrument after. Someone who uses electronic as well as acoustic instruments is in the best position to answer questions. Many high school music programs use digital pianos, computers, and MIDI hookups, and speaking to these music teachers may be a good source of information. Those who teach privately may also have digital instruments and computer labs.

Your search for information about electronic instruments will be similar to the process of buying a computer. There is much to learn, and it may take time to sift through the possibilities and choices. Just as in any rapidly changing market, instruments, sizes, options, and degrees of sophistication (not to mention prices) will remain in flux. You will need to sort out your own priorities and make decisions based on usefulness and practicality. It is easy to be overwhelmed by the "bells and whistles."

How to sample instruments

Giving your child a hands-on experience with an instrument may be no trouble at all; the instrument may be in your own home, or in that of a neighbor or relative. When this is not the case, or when you wish to have your child exposed to several instruments so that an informed choice can be made, you must take action.

Depending on your circumstances, and the size of the city or town in which you live, the following suggestions should help. Not all suggestions provide hands-on opportunities, but exposure to many different instruments, even just hearing and seeing them, is stimulating. Once your child manifests an attraction to specific instruments, it will be easier to find ways to give your child a chance to feel, hold, or play the instruments.

An important fact to keep in mind, however, is that seeing an instrument should always be connected with hearing it, and—to the extent possible—hearing it played well. Photographs or museum exhibits are only an introduction and, in some cases, may even be misleading. Your child should be attracted to the *sound* of the instrument, not only its size or shine.

How to sample instruments

- Watch a videotape. (See "Chapter Resources" and "General Resources.")
- Listen to an audiotape or CD. (Once again, check the resource sections of this book.)
- Attend a symphony or band concert. The group need not be professional.
- Attend recitals. Look for those including a variety of instruments.
- Visit museums with instruments displayed; if available, rent the audiotape.
- Check your local newspaper for weekend current events. These often involve instrumental group performances that are free.
- Sit in on a rehearsal of a local school band or orchestra.
- Contact the school music teacher or band director.
- Contact teachers of the instruments that interest your child.
- Investigate the presence of a community arts school in your area.

A friend for life

Choosing an instrument for your child requires careful thought. You and your child will devote time and effort learning to play the instrument. You will spend money on the instrument and its upkeep, on lessons and materials, and may even have to rearrange your home somewhat in order to place the instrument or make practice possible. Beyond all of this, however, the most important fact to keep in mind is that you introduce your child to a new companion, one that may be a friend for life. That doesn't always happen, but when it does, the rapport between player and instrument becomes a true relationship, one in which it is possible for the player to speak in a special voice and, sometimes, even to become someone else.

HIGHLIGHTS

☆ The relationship between player and instrument is very personal.

☆ If your child is under six:

There is a limited number of instruments available to your child.

It is important that your child be physically ready to play the instrument.

You may need to help your child find a suitable, appealing instrument.

Your own time and talents will be called upon in order to help your child succeed.

☆ If your child is between six and nine:

Almost any instrument is possible if your child is physically ready and interested.

It is important to find a teacher who understands both the instrument and the child.

Involve your child in making decisions about the instrument and taking lessons.

☆ If your child is ten or older:

Taking music lessons often goes along with wanting to be part of a group.

Playing in a group may develop self-esteem and even point to career directions.

It may be time for your child to play another, or a different, instrument.

☆ In checking out which instrument your child should play, think about whether your child:

"Fits" the instrument physically.

Is likely to enjoy the physical sensations associated with the instrument.

Will want to play in the environments most likely for that instrument.

Is at an appropriate age to begin playing the instrument.

Is "suited" to what makes the instrument special.

☆ String:

Instruments are satisfying but difficult to play.

Players have opportunities to be soloists or to play in groups.

Music is largely classical. The double bass, however, fits in jazz and many other combos.

☆ Woodwind:

Instruments vary with regard to playing difficulty—some are easy, some challenging.

Players have opportunities to be soloists or to play in many different kinds of groups.

Music is varied, from classical to pop/jazz.

☆ Brass:

Instruments are sturdier than woodwinds.

Players have less opportunities to solo, but are frequent band and orchestra "stars."

Music is varied, from classical to marching bands.

☆ Percussion:

Instruments include more than drums.

Players are usually members of groups or bands. Some percussion can be solo instruments.

Instruments can figure in any kind of music imaginable.

☆ Keyboard:

Instruments include many types; the most common are piano and digital piano.

Players are usually soloists and loners, although they can perform with others.

Music is varied, from classical to rock, depending on the instrument.

☆ Guitar:

Instruments include many types; the most common are classical and electric guitar.

Players may be soloists or work in groups; some switch between classical and electric.

Players can play any kind of music on either kind of guitar.

☆ The harp:

Is also a family of instruments; there are many kinds and sizes of harps.

Is a versatile instrument, and harpists play in many different settings.

Player can play any kind of music, from Renaissance to new age.

☆ The child voice:

Is the instrument.

Must be trained, if at all, with great caution and only by those qualified to do so.

May be trained in singing groups and children's choirs.

☆ Electronic instruments:

Are numerous, varied, easily portable, but require amplification.

Can imitate other instruments, but can also generate unique sounds and effects.

Invite experimentation and creativity.

☆ You can sample instruments with your child in a number of different ways:

Hands-on experience is the best.

Visiting rehearsals, recitals, and performances is valuable.

Speaking with players and teachers of the instruments is important.

Using video- or audiotapes may be practical and easy.

CHAPTER RESOURCES

Take special note of Part IV, "General Resources," for a listing of books, recordings, movies, games, teaching aids, CD-ROMs, and catalogs.

BOOKS FOR YOU

Elliott, Barbara et al. GUIDE TO THE SELECTION OF INSTRUMENTS WITH RESPECT TO PHYSICAL ABILITY AND DISABILITY. St. Louis: Distributed by MMB, 1982.

Designed to aid the teacher and therapist in the selection of an appropriate instrument for a student with physical handicaps. Describes which physical abilities are involved in playing each instrument, as well as the specific physical limitations that might affect playing a particular instrument. Full-body and close-up photographs (of adults) show playing positions on standard instruments. Dense with charts, lists, and text, but offering unique information. A good resource for both parents and teachers.

BOOKS FOR YOU WITH YOUR CHILD

Danes, Emma. THE USBOURNE FIRST BOOK OF MUSIC. London: Usbourne, 1993.

For young children this is a colorful introduction to music with suggested activities to encourage active involvement in all aspects of music, from listening to sounds and making simple instruments to dancing, performing, and composing. Four to eight years old.

Drew, Helen. MY FIRST MUSIC BOOK. New York: Dorling Kindersley, 1993.

This delightful book is full of exciting musical instruments to make at home. There are step-by-step photographs and simple instructions. Colorfully illustrated. Three to nine years old.

Hausherr, Rosmarie. WHAT INSTRUMENT IS THIS? New York: Scholastic, 1992.

The great charm of this book is the photography (half in color, half in black and white). The color photographs are unique in showing small children of all races playing and reacting to instruments. Black-and-white photographs are shots from real life of varying instrumentalists such as folk singers, country fiddlers, and concert and rock performers. The text is minimal, each instrument being introduced by a question (What instrument looks like a shiny boa constrictor with a wide-open mouth?). The answer and brief overview is on the next page. This is a book to savor for its beauty and quality rather than for informational content. Read with younger children. Can be read alone by children eight and older.

Hayes, Phyllis. MUSICAL INSTRUMENTS YOU CAN MAKE. New York: Franklin Watts, 1981.

An activity book with simple, effective ideas. For each item there is a recipe: what you need and how to do it. A brief introduction to each "instrument" provides a perspective and some background information. Useful to parents with children four to six years old.

BOOKS FOR YOUR CHILD

Anderson, David. THE PIANO MAKERS. New York: Pantheon Books, 1982.

This explains and illustrates how a grand piano is made. It is a picture book with minimal text. The photographs are excellent (all taken in the New York Steinway factory), and show detailed steps in the manufacturing process as well as close-ups of many piano parts. Eight and older.

Ardley, Neil. MUSIC. New York: Knopf, 1989.

This book about instruments shows them in color photographs. The photographs are outstanding not only for precision and clarity (at times showing the instrument disassembled), but also for the extremely wide scope of instruments included. Captions attached to the photographs provide a wealth of information and bits of special interest. The range of percussion instruments depicted is unusual, as is the inclusion of modern amplified instruments. Ten and older.

Arnold, Caroline. MUSIC LESSONS FOR ALEX. New York: Clarion Books, 1985.

The charm of this book lies in its photographs by Richard Hewett. This is the story of Alex, a little girl who decides to take violin lessons. The text covers the first year of her study, including how her instrument is purchased, and how she practices and rehearses, and concludes with her first recital. The photographs are of many people beside Alex, and depict with realism and poetry the world of the young violinist. Larger-size print. Eight and older.

Blackwood, Alan. MUSICAL INSTRUMENTS. New York: The Bookwright Press, 1987.

This slight book gives a quick overview of many instruments, from alpenhorn to synthesizer. The large-size print and writing style is tailored to the young reader. There are many color photographs of various instruments and ethnic groups, from Peruvian panpipes to a pop concert. Six to eight years old.

Blackwood, Alan. THE ORCHESTRA. Brookfield, CT: The Millbrook Press, 1993.

This is a thorough and broad introduction to the orchestra. The last section depicts a day in the life of an orchestra (in this case, the London Symphony Orchestra), including information and pictures about rehearsals, concert halls, transporting an orchestra, and glimpses into the daily life of orchestra musicians. The graphics, layout, and pictures are outstanding. Most illustrations are in color which adds to the book's attractiveness. An encyclopedia of information for a bargain price. Ten and older. Could be read to a younger child.

Gill, Dominic (ed.). THE BOOK OF THE PIANO. Ithaca, NY: Cornell University Press, 1981.

An elegant and authoritative book that deals with many kinds of pianos, the history of pianos, and piano makers. Specialists in various areas have contributed chapters. The book is designed for the serious (but not necessarily professional) reader. The chapters on the jazz piano, the popular piano, and unusual pianos are captivating. Although not really a "coffee table book," this one has the size and quality. This would be a wonderful gift for a serious young pianist. Teenagers and parents.

Hart, Mickey and Jay Stevens. DRUMMING AT THE EDGE OF MAGIC: A JOURNEY INTO THE SPIRIT OF PERCUSSION. San Francisco: Harper San Francisco, 1990.

The percussionist for the Grateful Dead describes his dicovery of the historical and spiritual heritage of the drum. Teenagers and parents.

Krementz, Jill. A VERY YOUNG MUSICIAN. New York: Simon & Schuster, 1991.

This engaging story of a gifted young trumpet player is a perfect book for the elementary-age student who is getting ready to choose an instrument. The superbly photographed illustrations add to the appeal. Seven to eleven years old.

Kuskin, Karla. THE PHILHARMONIC GETS DRESSED. New York: Harper & Row, 1982.

A delightful and unusual view of orchestra members preparing for performance. The illustrations and simple text follow various musicians from their homes to the concert hall. This is a picture book the entire family will enjoy. Four to nine years old.

Martin, Bill, Jr. THE MAESTRO PLAYS. New York: Henry Holt, 1994.

This picture book for preschoolers combines the writing virtuosity and humor of Martin with the brilliant illustrations of Vladimir Radunsky. The text is an invitation for the child to play with and move to the pulsating, adverb-rich words. Who can resist this "Maestro" and his merry musicians? Three to five years old.

Rubin, Mark and Alan Daniel. THE ORCHESTRA. Buffalo, NY: Firefly Books, 1992.

This picture book is an illustrated introduction to music and to the orchestra. In simple language, the families of instruments are described and charmingly illustrated. Five to eight years old.

Sharma, Elizabeth. LIVE MUSIC! BRASS; KEYBOARDS; PERCUSSION; STRINGS; THE VOICE; WOODWINDS. New York: Thomson Learning, 1992.

A brief overview of each group of instruments and the voice. Many photographs (most in color) and other illustrations and drawings. Especially rich is the inclusion of photographs and information about widely divergent music-making styles—from Australian aborigines playing didgeridoos to rock musicians. Also welcome is a book about the human voice with photographs ranging from a family singing at a seder to Aretha Franklin performing in concert. Eight and older.

Tatchell, Judy. UNDERSTANDING MUSIC. London: Usbourne, 1990.

This book is crammed with assorted information. Definitions of musical styles (including folk, ethnic, jazz, rock and pop), information about instruments and the science of sound, listening suggestions, pictures of performers, and a survey of composers and what kind of music they wrote are presented along with brief instructions on how to read music. There is also information on choosing and learning to play an instrument. This is a miniencyclopedia. Ten and older.

Walther, Tom. MAKE MINE MUSIC! Boston: Little, Brown, 1981.

Instructions for making many types of instruments. The scope is broad, from making a gutbucket to constructing a nonhuman vocal tract. The instructions are detailed and presented in black-and-white diagrams. Emphasis is on learning about the properties and varieties of sounds by hands-on experience with the way things make sounds. A child who loves to tinker (with a good bit of parental help) may enjoy this book. Ten and older.

VIDEOS

DIGITAL MUSICAL INSTRUMENTS AND THE WORLD OF MIDI. Red Pohaku Productions. 1621 Dole Street, #100, Honolulu, HI 96822.

A clear demonstration for the novice of the world of MIDI. Defines controller, MIDI, multitimbral, patch, port, sequencer, tone module, track, and other pertinent data. Joseph Rothstein is the articulate presenter.

EARLY MUSIC EDUCATION WITH SUZUKI. Films for the Humanities. 800-257-5126.

The film follows a three-year-old boy and his mother as they begin Suzuki training in violin, and shows classes, lessons, scenes at home (with sibling interruptions), and a festival at which Suzuki himself interacts with a group of over a hundred violin students. Will be informative to those with an interest in Suzuki training. Six and older, especially Suzuki students and parents.

THE FIDDLE SHOW. GPN. 800-228-4630.

Master artist/teacher Joseph Gingold, a young performer, and a group of violin students demonstrate agility and fitness necessary to make music with the violin.

HOW YOUR GRAND PIANO WORKS. JMC Productions. Box 2415, W. Brattleboro, VT 05303.

Designed for pianists of all levels, from beginning to professional, this video gives a thorough presentation of how a grand piano works. It includes a valuable reference section on piano problems with a discussion of piano care and maintenance.

LEONARD BERNSTEIN'S YOUNG PEOPLE'S CONCERTS SERIES WITH THE NEW YORK PHILHARMONIC. Music in Motion. 800-445-0649.

Ten videos of twenty-five digitally remastered programs originally broadcast from 1958 to 1970. Topics include What Does Music Mean? What Is Classical Music? What Is Sonata Form? What Makes Music Symphonic? There is a book of Bernstein's lectures taken from these videos. A remarkable series from a great communicator.

ORCHESTRA! INTRODUCTION TO THE ORCHESTRA. UPPER STRINGS. LOWER STRINGS. BRASS. PIANO. PERCUSSION. MAESTRO. THE ART OF CONDUCTING. Films for the Humanities. 800-257-5126.

Conductor Sir Georg Solti and Dudley Moore introduce viewers to the instruments. The orchestra is composed of talented young people from around the world. The young musicians discuss their reasons for choosing a particular instrument. A splendid opportunity to hear all the instruments separately and together. The tone is informal, the dress is casual, and Moore is entertaining. Ten and older.

THE PIANO SHOW. GPN. 800-228-4630.

Features three young pianists in different stages of musical development who excel in different musical styles. A fourth pianist provides a stunning example of what discipline and hard work can accomplish. Concert pianist Leon Fleisher is a special guest.

TUBBY THE TUBA. Paul Tripp and George Kleinsinger. Live Entertainment, Van Nuys, CA. Available from educational retailers.

The enchanting tale of the winsome little tuba who tires of only being able to sing "oompah," *Tubby the Tuba* is a delightful musical fantasy. In the process of searching for his own identity and voice, he encounters all the instruments of the orchestra. The animation is graced by the voices of Dick Van Dyke, Pearl Bailey, Cyril Ritchard, and other notables.

CD-ROMs

Call the telephone number of each company to ask for a catalog. Check system requirements before ordering. Ask for a try-before-you-buy arrangement.

MUSICAL INSTRUMENTS. Microsoft. 800-426-9400.

This provides wonderful access to information about more than 200 instruments. There are four ways to navigate: "Families of Instruments," "A–Z of Instruments," "Instruments of the World," "Musical Ensembles." You can see how the instruments work, hear musical examples, and "play" limited pitches on each instrument. There is reference to jazz, rock, classical, and other ensembles. For Macintosh and Windows.

THE ORCHESTRA: THE INSTRUMENTS REVEALED. Time Warner New Media. 800-482-3766.

Based on Benjamin Britten's *The Young Person's Guide to the Orchestra*, this program invites the user to see and hear the instruments of the orchestra and learn how they are played. Also included: a conducting lesson, an orchestration lab, a pronouncer, biographical information, a glossary, and a time line. Macintosh. Ten and older.

Choosing the Teacher

What you will find in this chapter

- Why begin music lessons?
- What makes a good music teacher?
    Qualifications. Human qualities.
    A complete music curriculum.
- Teaching with technology
- Prioritizing musical goals
- Music learning environments
- Directory of sources for finding a teacher
- Cautions
- You the consumer
- A script for the first phone interview with an independent teacher
- First meeting with the teacher
- Visit to a music school
- Escape clause
- When you want to change teachers
- A perfect match for your child
- Highlights
- Chapter resources

*H*AVING decided that it is time to select a music teacher for your child, how will you go about it? Certainly with the same care and research that you would use to select a family physician or purchase a car.

There are similarities in choosing a doctor or music teacher. In both cases, you have every reason to expect qualified, educated individuals, and you want technical and interpersonal skills to be equally balanced. In some ways, of course, choosing a music teacher is not like choosing a physician. Music study is not a matter of life and death. While no one ever died of musical malpractice, many have been turned off for life by making the wrong choice.

When buying a car, most people research cost, reputation, comfort, and reliability. The car must meet your standards as confirmed by *Consumer's Report* or other guides. You also want to be sure you won't be "taken for a ride" by incompetent maintenance personnel. Some of the same factors are important when looking for a music teacher.

This chapter explores criteria for finding a teacher. It may take you as long or longer than the selection of a doctor or a car, but your choice can make or break your child's chances of having a lifelong love affair with music.

Why begin music lessons?

Before you read further, you may want to question your motives for seeking music lessons for your child.

Has your child asked for lessons frequently for a long period of time?

If your child has asked for lessons not just once or twice, but persistently over a fairly long period of time, you have good reason to begin your search for a teacher. An anecdote highlights the issue. Husband-and-wife concert artists vowed that they would not coerce their only child to study music. Therefore, they made a pledge that their child would have to ask, beg, plead, perhaps even cry for lessons before they responded to her request. That child, in fact, grew up to be an outstanding concert artist in her own right. The parents wanted to be absolutely sure that the desire for lessons came from the child rather than from their own hopes and ambitions.

Sometimes children request lessons, but parents may have to "prime the pump" by making an appealing case for beginning lessons. This may include taking your child to concerts, playing videotapes that show children earnestly playing instruments, or reading books that highlight the enchantment of music lessons. Whatever you do, be sure that you are following your child's dreams and wishes rather than your own.

Do you want to try lessons to test your child's musical skills?

You may suspect that your child has special musical talent and feel that music lessons will be a test of this ability. This may be an opportunity to try the musical waters, but be equally sensitive to the fact that it is easy to exploit your child or have false expectations. In general, good music educators steer away from labeling students as talented and gifted too soon, realizing that it is a combination of aptitude, industry, and sustained effort that make the musically gifted individual. Only time, positive parental support, and excellent teaching can achieve satisfactory results.

Is the rapport your child has with the teacher important to you?

The human qualities that become so important in the one-to-one relationship between teacher and student are especially important in music lessons. If you find the combination of musical competence and personal style that matches your child's needs, you will have done a great job. Does your child need a teacher who is lighthearted and playful, or demanding and challenging? Searching for these qualities becomes especially important if your child has special needs.

When you are dealing with a child, keep your wits about you, and sit on the floor.
—Austin O'Malley

Is it important to you to have a teacher who is well known?

There is nothing wrong with seeking a teacher who either by word of mouth or other publicity is considered a "name." If the teacher of note is willing to accept your child, you may indeed be flattered. Just be sure that the personality match between child and teacher is as it should be. Some teachers with impeccable credentials expect their students to "produce" for them. This may not be a plus for your child.

There are some highly trained teachers who have a conservatory model as a goal for their students. This means that they expect the same high level of performance and industry from their students that they achieved in their own childhood. This may be exactly what some students need. They may thrive on benign discipline and the challenge to reach a personal best. On the other hand, the child who needs nurturing, enhanced self-esteem, and calm may do better with a teacher who is informal, relaxed, and reassuring.

Is price an important consideration in your selection of a teacher?

Whether you are on a tight budget or merely accustomed to shopping for the lowest bid, price may be an important priority. As with your doctor, the quality of training, as well as human characteristics, should take precedence over cost. If your budget is tight, you should be aware that many teachers and community music schools offer partial or full scholarships if there is genuine need. Ask about fees and scholarship possibilities at the time of the first in-person meeting, not during a preliminary phone inquiry.

There are no bargains in music lessons. Teachers set their fees based on training, experience, and regional economic conditions. If you find a very low rate, you probably should be suspicious of the quality of what you will receive. There is no substitute for quality, either in the teacher or the instrument you select. One of the biggest errors that parents can make is to settle for less quality until they see whether lessons will "take." This is like giving your children inferior food until you are sure they like to eat!

Is convenience a factor in your choice of a teacher?

Certainly if you are a working parent, or if you have other siblings to care for, convenience may be a factor in your choice. Is the teacher within walking distance? Will the teacher come to the house? How far will you have to travel? You may be fortunate enough to have a remarkable teacher right in your community or neighborhood, but sometimes you may have to travel to find a quality teacher. Before you place convenience too high on your priority list, sacrificing quality for convenience, consider carefully.

Is your primary concern the quality of the teaching?

If your priority is musical standards, begin by checking the training and experience of the teacher, by having knowledge of what an excellent curriculum should be, and by observing the teacher in action. You will then be well prepared to select the most musically and personally qualified teacher for your child.

What makes a good music teacher?

When you begin your search for a teacher, the choices open to you are many and exciting. Don't be surprised to find that things have changed quite a bit since you were a child. What are these changes? What qualifications can you expect from a well-trained music teacher?

What has changed

- Teacher training is more rigorous.
- Teacher certification is often part of credentials.
- There are teacher specialists for preschool, special needs, gifted, and so on.
- The music curriculum includes a wider range of subjects.
- Group instruction offers new learning possibilities.
- Fees have risen to reflect increased training and status of the music-teaching profession.

What can you expect of a well-qualified music teacher?

A well-qualified teacher has

- a love of teaching.
- a degree in music (minimum: bachelor's).
- experience in performance.
- experience in teaching.
- interpersonal skills.
- diagnostic skills.
- knowledge of learning theory and varied learning styles.
- a well-equipped studio.
- an acquaintance with a wide variety of music literature.
- membership in local or national professional societies.
- possible certification by a professional society.
- possible additional training in pedagogy (the art of teaching), or a combination performance/pedagogy degree.
- possible training in specialties to prepare for work with preschoolers, the gifted, or those with special needs.
- possible affiliation with a community arts school.

**IMPORTANT
CHOICES**

*I love to teach as a
painter loves to paint, as a
singer loves to sing, as a
strong man rejoices to win
a race.—William Phelps*

What is the professional training of a music teacher? Basic requirements at college or conservatory are for a bachelor's degree, though
training may extend to the master's or doctorate level. Emphasis may be
on performance, whether as a soloist, chamber artist, or orchestral
musician. Among the other specialties are jazz studies, recording arts,
conducting, music history, and composition. There is a recent trend
among music majors to pursue a degree in pedagogy (the art of teaching). The curriculum for a pedagogy degree includes supervised practical experience in teaching. The music teacher may combine teaching
with performing, conducting, composing, writing, or lecturing. She may
choose to teach independently or be affiliated with a community music
school, college, or university. Qualified teachers will often have membership in professional societies and be actively involved in workshops
and teacher conferences to ensure professional growth.

The hallmark of a quality teacher, however, is not merely an expertise in music. The teacher should have musical, educational, and interpersonal skills and resources. The richness of the mix is what is valuable. These teachers look to expand student horizons and to have
students develop an open, curious attitude. One should expect not only
an experienced performer and teacher, but also a caring individual who
is concerned with the student's development and who has excellent
diagnostic skills to assess the best way for a particular student to learn.

QUALIFICATIONS

*The ideal condition would
be, I admit, that men should
be right by instinct; but since
we are all likely to go astray,
the reasonable thing is to
learn from those who can
teach.—Sophocles*

There is a growing trend for teachers to become certified. There are
teachers who do not have certification or belong to professional societies. They may be fine teachers who are not joiners or who do not wish
to go through the certification process. There is no legal requirement
that independent music teachers become certified.

Certification requirements vary for each organization. Teachers may
have to show notarized proof of their degrees, and demonstrate teaching skills before a carefully selected panel of peers. If the certification is
in group work, the teacher must demonstrate her skills by teaching a
class.

Certification for public school teaching has a different set of requirements from individual teacher certification, and may vary from state to
state. This includes training in classroom techniques, psychology, and
general music subjects.

If you are checking certification credentials, you may want to ask
what certification requirements are. Do teachers merely pay a membership fee? Do they undergo particular training or fulfill specific requirements? How rigorous is the process?

It is important to emphasize that whatever recommendations you gather, whatever credentials you are given, you will still have to make a judgment about what you think the personal chemistry will be between your child and a particular teacher.

HUMAN QUALITIES

Assessing human characteristics will be one of the biggest challenges as you search for just the right teacher. All the degrees, professional affiliations, and special training in the world will not compensate for certain personal qualities. Your child's first teacher is especially important. At the early stage, this intimate one-on-one relationship can shape attitudes and instill a love of music along with correct playing, good practice habits, and artistic values. When you first meet the teacher in person, ask whether you may visit a recital, class, or lessons. If you are turned down, you should probably cross that particular name off your list.

A COMPLETE PROGRAM

In addition to teacher qualifications, you should know what program of study a teacher or school has to offer. The full range of skills on all instruments is offered as part of a community music school curriculum. Public schools as well as music schools offer experience in band, orchestra, and chamber music. Independent music teachers may incorporate musicianship study into the private lesson, or schedule weekly, biweekly, or monthly classes. You may have to search for this rich mix of choices. It is the ideal, but well worth seeking.

Menu for a well-balanced curriculum

To have music as a lifetime skill, one should be trained
- to read music fluently.
- to play the instrument with physical ease and technical skill.
- to have a well-trained ear.
- in musical structure and history.
- to know a wide range of musical styles.
- in harmony, analysis, and improvisation.
- in ensemble playing.
- to perform in formal and informal settings.

Teaching with technology

A music environment equipped with technology offers possibilities of thinking about sound in new ways. It allows for a broadened curriculum, and is increasingly part of the training of young musicians. A typical studio will have a computer connected to a digital keyboard or synthesizer. There may be a video component to combine sound and image. One of the advantages of such a studio is that it extends the capabilities of both student and teacher. There are features that aid practicing, and provide drills in theory, ear training, improvisation, and composition, and even provide ensemble experience.

Image is a great instrument of instruction.—John Dewey

Other technological enhancements further extend curriculum possibilities. When students videotape lessons, they learn a great deal from seeing and hearing their own performances. In addition, CD-ROM is becoming an increasingly effective tool for students to do independent study in a wide variety of music topics from analysis of specific compositions to the exploration of musical instruments and music history. There is a growing amount of impressive educational music software available for music enrichment. Students with some of this technology at home can profit from these tools. Teenage students, especially those with computer "smarts," find this environment especially intriguing. Careers in audio engineering, composing, arranging, multimedia, to name a few, are spawned here.

The Music Educators National Conference, Music Teachers National Association, and the Association for Technology in Music Instruction are all good sources for finding teachers and schools that provide music technology instruction. (A directory of sources is presented later in this chapter.)

Prioritizing musical goals

You have checked your initial reasons for seeking music lessons and considered teacher qualifications and curriculum. Now what about your musical goals for your child?

Do you want your child just to have fun with music?

If this is your main goal, but the teacher has expectations of a high level of performance, you could be disappointed. If demands on you and your child are in keeping with your wishes, that is fine, but if the child is not ready for such challenges, a more demanding teacher will soon project the feeling that somehow your child has failed. For this child, it is better to find a teacher who is flexible and willing to give your child a well-rounded music curriculum suited to interests and needs, without sacrificing quality, but not demanding only superior performance.

Neither you nor your child should expect that music lessons will be all fun and games. Neither should they be dull and dreary or a constant chore. There is effort involved, and there is an investment of time. Just as you guide and encourage homework standards, you can help with the shaping of music practice.

There has been a recent rash of offerings claiming that with practically no effort, one can be playing an instrument in no time at all. Be wary of such promises. They are unrealistic and misguided. Competent music teachers who love teaching are anxious to share their love of music to help your child achieve lifetime competence. They will help your child to feel pride in achieving a musical goal *even if it takes some effort.* The benefits resonate beyond music-making. They extend to the empowerment gained through accomplishment.

Do you hope your child will become a professional musician?

Occasionally the parent may have aspirations for the child to be a professional musician. The parent may be a professional musician and wants the same or even higher musical goals for the child. Or the parent may be a music lover who wishes to fulfill his own fantasies through the child. For parent or child with early dreams of a life in music, there are several good books and videotapes that describe the life of a musician. The video, *Critical Stages,* is especially good at depicting a day in the life of a musician.

Are music lessons just one of many extracurricular activities?

Are music lessons equated with a host of other skills that you feel are important so that your child has "everything"? Remember that more is not necessarily better as you seek enrichment options for your child. Many parents try to include sports and training in at least one art form along with academics. What will happen to the precious dream time that should also be an inalienable right of childhood? And how can overscheduled youngsters do justice to all of these enrichment activities? The most common criticism that music teachers make of parents is that they overschedule their children, creating an environment that produces many who are "jacks-of-all-trades and master of none." Parents and teachers owe it to students to help them make intelligent, careful choices as they select extracurricular activities. Beware the "hurried child". If quality of performance begins to slip in any area, or if there is no time for tranquillity, it is the adult role to help prioritize choices.

Do you hope to provide your child with music literacy?

If your goal is to find the most enriching training available, the teachers you choose should provide an up-to-date program to give your child skills for a lifetime. Consider the teacher's credentials, the ambiance of the studio, the response of other parents and students who study with that teacher, and, above all, the personal qualities of the teacher.

You have considered teacher qualifications, curriculum, practical, and musical priorities. Your next set of decisions has to do with the varied musical environments in which music lessons take place.

Music learning environments

> ### *Music learning environments*
> - The convenience of the teacher who makes house calls
> - The variety of subjects and enrichment in a community music school
> - The cooperative music studio combining some features of the private studio and the music school
> - The peer stimulation of group lessons
> - The intimate environment of the independent music studio
> - The easy access to music and instruments when lessons are at a local music store
> - The public school opportunity for study of orchestral/band instruments, chorus, and other large group activities
> - The technology-equipped studio that extends the ways of thinking about sound
> - The innovative programs and technical support of a college preparatory department
> - The challenge of the conservatory preparatory division

Each environment has its pros and cons. After you browse the following, noting which environments seem best suited to you and your child, you may want to select several to visit so that you can observe the differences in person.

LESSONS IN YOUR HOME

DESCRIPTION

Many young teachers get their start by giving lessons in the home, especially before they are able to equip an independent studio.

PROS

- Convenience for working parents or those with very young siblings.
- Opportunity for the teacher to know your environment.

CONS

- Distractions by other activities in the house (disruptive sound of television, telephone, crying babies, other siblings).
- No access to library of teaching materials.
- Enrichment items seldom on hand: visual aids, video equipment, computers.
- Precludes the feeling that lessons take place in a special place at a special time just for the student.

LESSONS AT A COMMUNITY MUSIC SCHOOL

DESCRIPTION

Community music schools certified by the National Guild of Community Schools of the Arts accept students at all ages and levels, serve the needs of a wide range of interests, must have quality faculty and adequate facilities, have a community outreach program, and offer scholarships.

PROS

- Programs for preschool, average-age, adults, gifted, special needs, and professionals.
- Musicianship courses available to all enrolled students.
- Chamber music, band, orchestra, chorus, jazz ensembles.
- Many student recitals and artist faculty concerts.
- Easy to change teachers if first choice proves unsatisfactory.
- Teachers act as support group for each other.

CONS

- Tight scheduling may not allow for the same dialogue with parent and child, or flexibility of scheduling as in a private studio.
- Ambiance may not be as aesthetic or informal as in a private studio.

LESSONS IN A COOPERATIVE MUSIC STUDIO

DESCRIPTION

By teachers sharing rental space, secretarial and management services, and specialized expertise, possibilities are expanded through studio recitals, chamber music, and musicianship classes, some of which are easier for the cooperative than for the independent teacher to arrange.

PROS

- Teachers act as support group for each other.
- By pooling resources, range of services and viewpoints is expanded.
- Pooling of finances may facilitate adding equipment.

CONS

- Physical equipment may be limited.

GROUP INSTRUCTION

DESCRIPTION

Either in a private studio or at a school. Growing number of teachers opt for specialized training in group techniques in one of these formats:
- Small group (two to four) plus partner or individual lessons.
- Large group (five to eight) plus partner or individual lessons.
- Individual plus weekly or monthly group class.

PROS

- Increased incentive and encouragement when students play for peers.
- Teachers present same core material to group of students of similar ability.
- Students learn to listen attentively by hearing partner play the same works.
- Cost of group lessons is somewhat less than for private lessons.

CONS

- Rate of progress may be slower than with private lessons.
- There is less attention to the individual.
- If not grouped according to ability and needs, results may be unsatisfactory.

LESSONS IN THE INDEPENDENT STUDIO

DESCRIPTION
From simple setup in the teacher's living room to studios with several instruments, computers, electronics, classroom space, visual aids, and library resources.

PROS
- The intimacy of a one-on-one environment.
- In the best studios, a variety of equipment and materials is close at hand.
- May have more flexible scheduling policies than schools.

CONS
- May lack the variety of enrichment classes, such as musicianship, theory, chamber music, and other subjects available at music schools.
- Concert and performance opportunities may be fewer than at a school.

LESSONS AT A MUSIC STORE

DESCRIPTION
Some music stores offer lessons at the time of purchase of an instrument. There may be a director of the instructional department, or studio space may be available for individual teachers as independent contractors.

PROS
- A number of instruments at the student's disposal.
- Library of materials easily at hand.

CONS
- Priorities in a music store are generally retail sales.
- Teaching standards may be lower than in some other environments unless there is a separate department with quality control of teachers and educational principles.
- Noise from the retail division of the store, and from other studios, if not properly soundproofed.
- May be less aesthetic than some other environments.

LESSONS IN THE PUBLIC SCHOOL

DESCRIPTION

Introductory instruction given on a wide variety of instruments. Teachers will probably recommend a specialist for private lessons after a short period, unless the teacher's specialty is on the instrument the child has chosen.

PROS

- Child can experiment with learning an instrument without great cost or pressure.
- Especially helpful if this is a second instrument.
- Enjoyment provided by learning with peers.
- School concerts are good music performance goals.

CONS

- If the instrument of choice is not the specialty of that particular teacher, student can progress only to the level of teacher's knowledge.

LESSONS IN A TECHNOLOGY-EQUIPPED STUDIO

DESCRIPTION

Studio typically has several keyboards, synthesizers, and computer inter-connected to make a complete music workstation. Most often found in piano and guitar studios, some college preparatory music departments, and a few community music schools.

PROS

- Musicianship skills are enhanced.
- Composition and improvisation opportunities are increased.
- Provides training in practice skills.

CONS

- There may be extra lab fees.
- Added expense if student wants software and equipment at home.

UNIVERSITY OR COLLEGE PREPARATORY DIVISION

DESCRIPTION
- Like community music school, has open enrollment for students at all levels.
- May require entry audition and testing.
- See *Schirmer Guide to Schools of Music and Conservatories Throughout the World* and *The Performing Arts Major's College Guide* in " General Resources."

PROS
- Often experimentation with new curriculum ideas.
- Experiments in multimedia and other new technology.
- Good support from university technology department.
- Musicianship classes, chamber music, and frequent recitals are available.

CONS
- Child might be taught by an undergraduate or graduate student in a practice teaching situation rather than by a master teacher, though master teacher may act in a supervisory role.
- May be more costly than other types of study.

CONSERVATORY PREPARATORY DIVISION

DESCRIPTION
- Selective enrollment for students at the intermediate and advanced levels.
- Requires entry audition and testing.
- See *Schirmer Guide to Schools of Music and Conservatories Throughout the World* and *Performing Arts Major's College Guide* in "General Resources." Serious practice and dedication are expected.

PROS
- Faculty of distinguished artists.
- Musicianship classes, chamber music, and recitals are available.
- Exposure to peers with equal enthusiasm and focus.

CONS
- Environment can be highly competitive and less nurturing than some young students require in the formative years.
- May be more costly than other types of study.

Directory of sources for finding a music teacher

The following directory lists a number of professional societies and reference materials, each with a particular focus to help you narrow your choices. By contacting those that represent your main interests, you should be able to assemble a workable list of teachers. Not every organization is represented here. For instance, if you are researching a particular orchestral instrument, you may contact the Music Teachers National Association, but there are also professional societies for almost every instrument. Ask your librarian for the *Encyclopedia of Associations*.

To use the directory, first scan the "Source" and "Focus" categories to identify those groups that interest you. The "Ask for" category suggests information to request. Armed with brochures and data from these sources, you will be one well-informed parent!

AMERICAN ORFF-SCHULWERK ASSOCIATION
Box 391089
Cleveland, OH 44139
216-543-5366

FOCUS   Early childhood music curriculum.

DESCRIPTION
Trains teachers/students in group music-making techniques.
Uses special Orff instruments. See Chapter One.

ASK FOR
Brochure describing Orff curriculum and list of Orff teachers.

AMERICAN STRING TEACHERS ASSOCIATION (ASTA)
1806 Robert Fulton Drive
Reston, VA 22091
713-476-1316

FOCUS   String training.

DESCRIPTION
Supports high standards in string performance and teaching.
Competitions for students.
Annual conferences, workshops for teachers.

ASK FOR
Name of your state ASTA president for teacher referrals.

ASSOCIATION FOR TECHNOLOGY IN MUSIC INSTRUCTION (ATMI)
c/o Barbara Murphy, Technology Directory Editor
Michigan State University School of Music
East Lansing, MI 48824
E-mail: 21798BAM@msu.edu

FOCUS Source for active exchange of ideas for users of technolgy in music instruction.

DESCRIPTION

Provides a forum for the exchange of ideas among developers and users of music technology.

Maintains extensive directory of music technology information including an annually updated listing of hardware and software.

Provides consultation help for new users.

Publishes a newsletter.

ASK FOR

Technology Directory, newsletter.

Referrals of teachers and schools in your area involved in technology-based music instruction.

CENTER FOR MUSIC AND YOUNG CHILDREN
217 Nassau Street
Princeton, NJ 08542
800-728-2692

FOCUS Early childhood music and movement curriculum.

DESCRIPTION

The Center for Music and Young Children formed Music Together®, a program for infant, toddler, preschool, and prekindergarten children, a research-based curriculum strongly emphasizing parent/caregiver involvement. Includes materials for home use. See Chapter One.

ASK FOR

Parent materials, catalog, teacher referral.

DALCROZE SOCIETY OF AMERICA (DSA)
c/o Anne Farber,
161 West 86th Street
New York, NY 10024
800-471-0012

FOCUS   Early childhood music curriculum.

DESCRIPTION
Trains teachers, performers, and others of all ages in eurhythmics, defined
  as the integration of rhythmic movement with ear training and impro-
  visation.
The basis for most rhythm/movement programs.
Listening and creative aspects of responding to sound are emphasized.
See Chapter One.

ASK FOR
Brochures, videos, and teacher referral.

KINDERMUSIK® INTERNATIONAL
Box 26575
Greensboro, NC 27415
800-628-5687

FOCUS   Early childhood music curriculum.

DESCRIPTION
Structured, sequential, flexible approach to teaching music concepts to
  groups of children age eighteen months to seven years.
Four-semester curriculum.
Extensive teacher training. See Chapter One.

ASK FOR
Brochures, video, and teacher referrals.

MUSIC EDUCATORS NATIONAL CONFERENCE (MENC)
1806 Robert Fulton Drive
Reston, VA 22091
800-336-3768

FOCUS   Music-teaching standards.

DESCRIPTION
A voluntary, nonprofit organization representing all phases of music edu-
cation in schools, colleges, universities, and teacher- education institu-
tions.
Powerful lobby and advocate for music.
Program of accreditation for public school music teachers.
Affiliated organizations: American String Teachers Association, National
School Orchestra Association, International Association of Jazz Educa-
tors.

ASK FOR
List of publications and pamphlets, advice on technology, and other music-
education–related information.
Advice on music advocacy in your community.

MUSIC TEACHERS NATIONAL ASSOCIATION (MTNA)
The Carew Tower
441 Vine Street, Suite 505
Cincinnati, OH 45202
513-421-1420

FOCUS   Music-teaching standards for all instruments and voice.

DESCRIPTION
Professional organization of over twenty-five thousand college, university,
and independent music teachers that supports the highest standards in
performance and teaching.
Membership is open to all persons engaged in music teaching.
Annual conferences for teachers.
Annual auditions for students at state, division, and national levels.

ASK FOR
List of certified teachers. Name of state MTNA president and district chair-
person for teacher referral.

NATIONAL ASSOCIATION FOR MUSIC THERAPY (NAMT)
8455 Colesville Road, Suite 930
Silver Springs, MD 20910
301-589-3300

FOCUS   Services for children with special needs.

DESCRIPTION
Resources for those trained in working with the learning disabled, those
   with behavioral, emotional, motor, or neurological disorders. See Chapter Nine for additional sources.

ASK FOR
Teacher referrals.

NATIONAL ASSOCIATION OF TEACHERS OF SINGING (NATS)
2800 North University Boulevard
Jacksonville, FL 32211
904-744-9022

FOCUS   Vocal training.

DESCRIPTION
Professional society of voice teachers.
Sponsors workshops and national conferences for voice teachers.
Auditions and competitions for students.

ASK FOR
Teacher referrals.
Advice on proper age to begin voice training.

NATIONAL GUILD OF COMMUNITY SCHOOLS OF THE ARTS (NGCSA)
Lolita Mayadas, Director
Box 8018
Englewood, NJ 07631
201-871-3337

FOCUS   Forum for community music schools.

DESCRIPTION
Organization of community schools of the arts with rigorous standards for
member schools, based on faculty quality, curriculum, facilities, community outreach, and other criteria.

ASK FOR
Names of accredited community music schools in your area.

NATIONAL PIANO FOUNDATION (NPF)
4021 McEwen Street, Suite 105
Dallas, TX 75244
214-233-9107

FOCUS   Provides information, encourages study of piano.

DESCRIPTION
Develops educational programs, activities, and materials related to the
study of the piano. The educational arm of The Piano Manufacturers
Association.

ASK FOR
A full listing of brochures and videos.
Among the most helpful brochures:
How to Help Your Child Succeed at the Piano
Consumer's Guide to Buying a Piano
Piano for Preschoolers
Piano for the Handicapped

ORGANIZATION OF AMERICAN KODÁLY EDUCATORS (OAKE)
Glenys Wignes, Director
1457 S. 23rd Street
Fargo, ND 58108
701-235-0366

FOCUS   Early childhood music curriculum.

DESCRIPTION
Established to provide communication and training for Kodály educators.
A music-readiness program. Emphasis on singing, symbol recognition,
and creativity. See Chapter One.

ASK FOR
Parent brochure, video, and list of Kodály centers and teachers.

THE PERFORMING ARTS MAJOR'S COLLEGE GUIDE
Everett, Carole J. New York: Prentice-Hall/Macmillan, 1994.

FOCUS   Major music, dance, and drama schools.

DESCRIPTION
A reference book that lists programs at colleges and conservatories world-
wide.
Gives audition advice.

ASK FOR
Purchase book or ask your local librarian.

SUZUKI ASSOCIATION OF THE AMERICAS (SAA)
Box 17310
Boulder, CO 80308
303-444-0948

FOCUS   Early instrumental music training.

DESCRIPTION
Program of early instrumental training for violin, viola, cello, harp, guitar, piano, and flute, taught by imitation.
Teacher training with certification.
Active parent participation. See Chapter One.

ASK FOR
Brochures, list of books, and videos for parents.
List of trained Suzuki teachers in your area.

SCHIRMER GUIDE TO SCHOOLS OF MUSIC AND CONSERVATORIES THROUGHOUT THE WORLD
Uscher, Nancy. New York: Schirmer Books, 1988.

FOCUS   Major music schools.

DESCRIPTION
Comprehensive reference book with geographical listing of schools of music, conservatories, colleges, and universities with preparatory divisions.
Detailed description of facilities and services.

ASK FOR
Purchase or ask your local librarian.

YAMAHA INTERNATIONAL, MUSIC IN EDUCATION
6600 Orangethorpe Avenue
Buena Park, CA 90622
800-722-8856

FOCUS   Early childhood musicianship and instrumental training.

DESCRIPTION
A six-year program to develop performance, composing, and improvising
   skills in children four years old and older.
Teacher training program and certification.
Parent participation for several years. See Chapter One.

ASK FOR
Regional office manager as well as a brochure and videotape on the Junior
   Music Program.

YOUNG MUSICAL ARTISTS ASSOCIATION (YMAA)
Scott McBride Smith, Director
30 Goldenbush
Irvine, CA 92714
714-262-0540

FOCUS   The gifted young pianist and chamber musician.

DESCRIPTION
YMAA G.I.F.T. Institute (Guiding, Identifying, Fostering Talent).
Network of teachers and researchers with expertise and interest in work-
   ing with the gifted student.
Summer enrichment program.

ASK FOR
Brochure of programs and list of affiliated teachers.

In addition to the national/worldwide organizations listed above, there are several local sources that might be helpful.

LOCAL MUSIC TEACHERS ASSOCIATIONS

Provide a dialogue for teachers within a given geographic radius.

Provide performance opportunities for students and teachers.

Association brochures that give teacher credentials.

Provide teacher brochures that state studio policies and course descriptions.

Check library reference room, *Yellow Pages,* or local arts council.

Note: Teacher membership in local, state, and national professional societies is a sign of involvement in continuing education.

PUBLIC SCHOOL MUSIC TEACHERS

Are often aware of individual music teachers of quality within the community.

LOCAL COLLEGE AND CONSERVATORY MUSIC DEPARTMENTS

Often have placement bureaus that list graduates.

Do not provide ratings of teaching ability or match child to teacher.

May accept more advanced students.

May recommend other qualified local teachers.

LOCAL SYMPHONY ORCHESTRA MUSICIANS

May teach, but often only more advanced students.

May have helpful teacher recommendations.

Are an excellent source for finding a teacher of more unusual instruments.

YELLOW PAGES

Lists some community music schools and independent music teachers (see "Music Instruction," "Musicians").

WORD OF MOUTH

Is one of the most common ways to find a teacher.

Can provide information as to whether students of a particular teacher are enthusiastic and committed to lessons.

Cautions

Beware of the friendly neighbor down the street who once took music lessons for a few years and has decided to teach in spite of a lack of professional training. You may be exceptionally lucky in finding a gifted teacher this way, but you will more likely sacrifice quality for convenience. The idea that one can choose any old teacher or instrument to see if the lessons "take" is courting disaster.

Beware of claims such as:

- Learn to play in ten easy lessons.
- No practice drudgery required.
- Low-cost lessons in your home.

Also, beware of unprofessional advertising flyers on store or community bulletin boards and left at your door.

Although you may find the names of qualified teachers on a store bulletin board or in a leaflet left in your mailbox, chances are that reputable qualified teachers will not use these means of announcing availability. Most typically, teachers will send a card or brochure announcing the opening of their studio, will perform locally at concerts that are announced in the press, or will belong to professional societies (many of which have referral services). Music stores sometimes allow music teachers to display flyers or brochures, but you will still need to verify credentials as described above.

Armed with information on teacher qualifications, learning environments, and curriculum, as well as having considered your own reasons for wanting to give your child music lessons, you are ready to make the first inquiry calls. During your preliminary search, make the first visit without your child. Your early work should help you narrow the choices before you involve your child.

You the consumer

The phone interview is your opportunity to sense whether you are on the right track with a particular teacher. You should be as brief and courteous as possible. If this is a busy, well- qualified teacher, the evaluation works both ways. The teacher will probably ask you questions about your needs and interests, making a first assessment of your goals.

A script for the first phone interview with an independent teacher

The call should take no more than ten minutes.

"Hello. My name is —, and I'd like to inquire about music lessons for my child. Is this a convenient time to talk?" *(Teacher will either ask you questions, or you should briefly describe your child.)*

"My child is _____ years old, in the _____ grade, is the _____ [youngest, oldest, only child] and is a beginning student [*or has studied for — years*]." (*Describe your child's interest and involvement in music to date. Is your child a novice who is enthusiastic about sound? Has your child had previous training? Was it satisfactory?*)

"May I ask you a few questions about your program?" (*The teacher will be ready to discuss the program with you or suggest that she mail you a brochure with information about her background, training, experience, studio policy, fees, and curriculum.*)

Assuming that the teacher is ready to discuss the program on the phone, there are a variety of questions you may wish to ask:

- "Do you use a particular method or have a special philosophy?" (*Answers may vary from listing the materials used to the statement that teachers prefer to suit the method to the student's needs.*)
- "Do you offer musicianship classes? If so, how often are they held?" (*Classes held weekly are ideal, monthly only adequate. They should include theory, harmony, improvisation, composition, ear training, and sight-reading.*)
- [If you have special requirements, ask:] "Are there classes for [*the gifted*] or [*the child with special needs*] or [*early childhood*] or [*and so on*]?" (*This is your opportunity to discuss your child's special requirements. Describe your child's personality characteristics. Wait for the in-person interview to ask how the teacher would handle specific problems.*)
- "How much parental involvement do you expect? Could I sit in on lessons from time to time?" (*Teachers of the very young often welcome parent participation. Some teachers of older students encourage parent participation, either at the lessons or in practice support. Others take a different attitude and expect the lessons to be between teacher and student.*)
- "Are there any other questions I should have asked you?" (*If you are comfortable with the responses, and the teacher has openings, ask for an in-person interview. If there are no openings, ask for other teacher referrals, or ask to be put on a waiting list.*)

Do not discuss money or teacher credentials on the phone. Not everyone will agree, but in our opinion, on the phone, it is better to establish whether you and the teacher have a beginning rapport. Wait for the in-person interview to ask about credentials, scholarships, and fees. If the stated fee is beyond your budget, it is proper at that time to ask if there are any scholarships or partial scholarships available. Not all teachers or schools will request your most recent tax return, but be prepared to supply a copy as proof of need.

First meeting with the teacher

At a first in-person interview, the teacher will collect personal and musical data and do some musical games to assess student attention and readiness for lessons, aptitude for music study, as well as attitude. If you are changing teachers, your child should be prepared to play a few pieces, and to bring his most current music books and notebook. The teacher will probably ask about both parent and student goals in relation to music, and share her own goals and expectations.

Most teachers have a printed studio policy that describes the teacher's credentials, curriculum, fees, policy about attendance, illnesses, and makeup lessons. This is the time for the teacher to state what is expected of parents and children in terms of parent participation and student practice. If they haven't already been answered, you may wish to ask the following questions.

What do you recommend as the length of weekly lessons? *(For young students, two half-hour instrumental lessons a week are ideal. For average-age students (six to nine), a 45-minute lesson is appropriate. Most older beginners, intermediate, and advanced students can profit from an hour lesson.)*

How many lessons are there per year? *(The typical season is from 32 to 42 weeks.)*

What are your expectations for student practice? *(The age of the student, level of advancement, and ability to concentrate are all considerations. You can assume that if the teacher expects an hour or two of practice daily, this is a rigorous studio. Be sure the child is ready for that degree of commitment before enrolling.)*

Are there special summer classes? *(Some teachers offer summer sessions. Special courses might include music history, musicianship skills, ensemble, or technology.)*

What is the tuition? Are scholarships or partial scholarships available? *(If money matters have not been covered, now is the time. See Chapter Seven for a discussion of typical fees.)*

Are there frequent student recitals and performance workshops? *(The more opportunities for performance the better. One recital a year is not enough.)*

Do your students participate in auditions, competitions, and/or festivals? *(Some students thrive on these out-of-studio challenges. Others do best without pressure. If the teacher participates in out-of-studio events, are they compulsory for all students?)*

Do you use technology in your studio? If so, what kind? *(The teachers who use technology in teaching are the pioneers. They are on the cutting edge of the future of music education. Typically these studios include computers, digital keyboards, video, and perhaps CD-ROM. Within ten years the number of teachers using technology will increase severalfold.)*

What do you do if a student hits a plateau or shows signs of waning interest? *(Answers are varied, but it's important to know that most students hit plateaus. It is the job of the teacher, in cooperation with the parents, to discover the cause, whether too much pressure, the need for a change of repertoire, or a growth phase.)*

May I visit a lesson, class, and/or recital of your students? *(The answer should be a hearty "YES" or cross this name off your list.)*

May I have the names of other parents whose children study with you? *(If supplied, ask parents to describe the degree of their children's enthusiasm for music.)*

Assuming that you have permission to visit a lesson, class, or recital, what should you be looking for? Depending on curriculum, some observations will be more appropriate than others.

Observing the teacher in action

- Does the teacher give frequent, specific, and honest praise?
- Does the teacher make positive corrections?
- Does the teacher have a sense of humor?
- Are activities varied and appropriate to the child's age?
  For the young student, a mixture of songs, movement, and so on.
  For the older student, a blend of technical and musical skills.
- Are new pieces carefully prepared at the lesson?
- Is the child encouraged to ask questions?
- Is more than one way used to explain, if the student doesn't understand?
- Are visual aids used?
- Is the room large enough? Is it attractive?
- Does the teacher tailor instruction to fit the child's needs?
- Does the teacher provide specific, attractive practice assignments?
- For all instruments, is there emphasis on proper hand and body placement?
- For instruments other than piano, is there instruction in breathing (for winds and brass), intonation, tuning?
- For voice students, does the teacher take time to warm up the voice?
  Is the repertoire varied to include songs in different languages?
  Are sight-singing, vocal technique, breathing, and intonation part of the structure?
- Do materials seem appropriate for the age of the student?
- Is there mention of care of the instrument?
- Does the teacher allow phone calls or other interruptions during a lesson?
- Is there good rapport between teacher and student?

When you teach, for me it is a great work, very difficult, very doubtful. You cannot be a teacher if you have not a need of understanding, the love for the personality of the other. He is a human being and you can help him in one way or another . . . and that is in you a fascination. It makes for me a great event. He has understood.
—*Nadia Boulanger*

It is especially important to note the ambiance of the studio and the rapport between student and teacher. If you attend a recital, note the interaction among the parents. Are they cordial to each other? Are they supportive of children other than their own? Do students look as if they are engrossed and enjoying the performance environment? How well do the students play? If a student has a performance mishap, how does the teacher handle it? The response should be positive—a smile and praise for the effort, or an invitation to try again right then with some on-the-spot teacher support. Here is a perfect chance to see whether this is a studio for "stars" or whether each type of student is encouraged. You may want to ask parents how long their children have studied with that teacher. The retention rate among fine teachers is generally high.

Visit to a music school

If some of your calls include music schools, the procedure is slightly different. You may request a school brochure and ask brief questions about availability of the kind of program in which you are interested. When it is time for an in-person interview, it will probably be with the director or dean of students, who will answer detailed questions and make suggestions for a program of study for your child. If the responses please you, ask for an appointment to visit in person. *Do not take your child to the preliminary interview.* Narrow the choices before the child is involved. If this is a conservatory preparatory school, your child is probably not a beginner, has studied for at least three or more years, and will be expected to audition either for one teacher or a panel of teachers.

Escape clause

Whether the interview is with an independent music teacher, a community music school, or other program, you may need time to consider all that you have seen and heard. Have a sentence or two ready that allows you some time. Try "Thank you for seeing us. May I call you in a few days after my husband/wife and I discuss it?" or "I would like to call you in a day or two after my child and I discuss how ready she is to meet the requirements you outlined." Do not feel pressured to select a teacher or program until you have time to compare your careful research data.

Don't be surprised if the teacher also has an escape clause that allows her time to consider whether your child will thrive in her studio. One studio includes the following questions to parents with the registration form to help the teacher assess parent values and commitment.

TEACHER QUESTIONNAIRE FOR PARENTS

Please circle items that reflect your feelings about your child's music study.

Our child is studying music:

    A. mainly because he/she wants to.

    B. because we all want this.

    C. because we want him/her to, but he/she does not resist lessons.

    D. at our insistence, and resists having lessons.

E. We feel regular practice (six to seven days weekly for a specified amount of time) is essential.

F. My child is very busy and practice is irregular, and we feel this is okay.

G. Practice is important, but other things occasionally take precedence.

H. My child finds school work demanding and cannot practice as much as we would like.

I. We expect minimal practice.

J. We are willing to accept responsibility for encouraging regular practice, for reading the assignment each week, for supporting activities involved in music study, and for communicating with the teacher when there are problems or questions. (Please note that parents who are not willing to accept this responsibility generally should not expect more than a minimum amount of progress during the year.)

K. We feel that this experience is between student and teacher, with little or no parental involvement necessary.

L. Please list the extracurricular activities in which your child is involved: scouts, specific sports, drama, and so on. List during what part of the year they occur.

M. What do you feel that we teachers should know about your child? How can we assure a satisfactory experience for this student?

N. List the music your family owns that you think might be suitable for your child(ren) to use. Include all current lesson books that the student has not completed.

                                from the Winborne-Shaw Studio, Oshkosh, WI

When you want to change teachers

If your child is not a beginner, but ready for a change of teacher, the same care for matching personal qualities applies. Does your child need more or less structure and challenge? What kind of teacher will bring out the best in your child? Should you be seeking someone with specialized training?

Sometimes you will be the one to sense the need for a change. Sometimes it may be your child or teen who makes the request. Do not rush to change. Ask to sit in on a few lessons to observe the situation. Share your concerns with the teacher in a phone or in-person teacher/parent conference. Be tactful in describing your concerns. If you have not noticed significant improvement after several months, you are justified in seeking a different learning environment. Use the same procedures as you did in the beginning. Make calls. Interview teachers without your child. When you have collected data, share it with your child, and decide together which teachers you will visit.

If you are transferring because of a geographic move, an organization like the Music Teachers National Association can be most helpful in providing a list of certified teachers in your new location. If your child had a close relationship with a teacher before the move, the adjustment may be difficult, especially if your child is wishing for a clone of the old teacher. It is best to encourage your child to be open to change, and to look forward to the new teacher with a sense of adventure. Choose the most qualified teacher you can find, be supportive of the new teacher, as well as patient and positive as your child makes the adjustment. It can take as much as a year or more for the transfer of allegiance to take place.

A perfect match for your child

The student/teacher match is sometimes compared to a good marriage. We stress that matching your goals, your child's expressed goals and needs, and the teacher's goals must be similar or there is little hope for a successful pairing. Consider your choices carefully because the relationship with the music teacher may be one of the most significant in your child's life.

HIGHLIGHTS

☆ Understand your motives in seeking music instruction for your child:

Your child asked for lessons.

You want to test your child's aptitude for music.

Someone else has spotted musical interest or aptitude in your child.

You would like to give your child every opportunity.

☆ A well-qualifed teacher:

Loves teaching.

Has at least a bachelor's degree.

May be a generalist, dealing with all levels and types of students.

May be a specialist in a particular age group or student type.

Is able to diagnose the student's musical, physical, or personal problems.

Knows how to adapt to the student's learning style.

Has a well-equipped studio.

Knows a wide variety of music literature.

Is good at selecting the right material for each student.

Often is a member of local or national professional societies.

Often is certified by a professional society.

Has good interpersonal skills.

☆ A good music program for early childhood:

Encourages good listening skills.

Builds rhythmic understanding, often through movement.

Increases attention span.

Aids motor coordination.

Uses whole-body and multisensory experiences.

Provides group games and social interaction.

Often expects adult participation.

☆ A good music program for advancing students makes sure they:

Read music fluently.

Play an instrument with skill and ease.

Have knowledge of musical structure and history.

Know a broad range of musical styles.

Have experience in ensemble playing.

Have training in harmony, analysis, improvisation, and composition.

Have formal and informal performance opportunities.

Have opportunities to enter festivals and competitions.

☆ It helps to know what you want your child to get out of music study:

Chiefly amusement?

To achieve professional goals?

One of many enrichment choices for your child to try?

Training for lifetime skills?

☆ Consider the best environment for your child's lessons:

The intimate environment of the independent studio.

The peer stimulation of group lessons.

The variety of subjects and enrichment in a community music school.

The public school opportunity to be part of a band, orchestra, or chorus.

The cooperative studio that may combine aspects of the independent studio and the school.

The college preparatory division that may have innovative programs and technical support.

The conservatory preparatory division that can challenge the gifted.

Your own home that offers convenience, but may be distracting for the child and lack enrichment facilities.

The local music store with easy access to music and instruments.

The technology-equipped studio that extends ways of thinking about sound.

☆ The "Directory of Sources for Finding a Music Teacher" can help you choose:

For early childhood:

American Orff-Schulwerk Association

Center for Music and Young Children (Music Together®)

Dalcroze Society of America

Kindermusik® International

Organization of American Kodály Educators

Suzuki Association of the Americas

Yamaha International, Music in Education

For instrument and voice training:

American String Teachers Association

Music Educators National Conference

Music Teachers National Association

National Association of Teachers of Singing

National Guild of Community Schools of the Arts

National Piano Foundation

The Performing Arts Major's College Guide

Schirmer Guide to Schools of Music and Conservatories Throughout the World

Particular Programs:

Association for Technology in Music Instruction

National Association of Music Therapy

Young Musical Artists Association G.I.F.T. Institute

Some local sources that may help you find a teacher:

      Local music teacher associations
      Public school music teachers
      Local college and conservatory placement bureaus
      Local symphony orchestra conductors and musicians
      Yellow Pages
      Word of mouth
☆ Beware of:
      Teachers without adequate training
      Promises of quick and easy success
      Unprofessional announcements of available lessons
☆ It helps to have:
      A list of prepared questions for phone inquiries
      A list of extra questions for an in-person interview
☆ On a visit to a lesson, class, or recital, observe:
      Ambiance
      Specific teacher skills
      Rapport between teacher and students
      Facilities
      Thoroughness of the curriculum
☆ Remember that you are the consumer. The research time it takes before you
make your choice is absolutely worth it.

CHAPTER RESOURCES

Take special note of Part IV, "General Resources," for a listing of books for all ages, recordings, movies, games, teaching aids, and catalogs.

BOOKS FOR YOU

**Armstrong, Thomas. AWAKENING YOUR CHILD'S NATURAL GENIUS:
ENHANCING CURIOSITY, CREATIVITY, AND LEARNING ABILITY.** Los
Angeles: Tarcher, 1991.
    A natural outgrowth of the author's *In Their Own Way*, here Armstrong examines spe-
cific learning styles in greater depth. Among these are chapters on math, art, music,
and science. Giftedness, computer learning, special education, Montessori, Waldorf,
and superlearning are also discussed and, often, criticized. The text is broken up by
the insertion of lists, headings, and rich and diverse quotations.

242

IMPORTANT
CHOICES

Elkind, David. MISEDUCATION: PRESCHOOLERS AT RISK. New York: Knopf, 1993.

Elkind shows us the very real difference between the mind of a preschool child (how it works) and that of a school-age child. He makes clear how much young children can and do learn when they are presented with developmentally appropriate parenting practices and education. And, in turn, he shows how early miseducation can cause permanent damage to a child's self-esteem by blocking natural gifts and potential talent.

Everett, Carole J. THE PERFORMING ARTS MAJOR'S COLLEGE GUIDE. New York: Prentice-Hall/Macmillan, 1994.

This practical book sheds light on the college admissions process, and offers advice from beginning the search through the completion of the application. It provides helpful information about auditioning, researching teachers, and asking useful questions. A selected listing of performing arts programs notes schools and conservatories with strong programs in particular fields.

Gardner, Howard. THE UNSCHOOLED MIND: HOW CHILDREN THINK AND HOW SCHOOLS SHOULD TEACH. New York: Basic Books, 1991.

Gardner asks how we can help students move beyond rote learning to achieve genuine understanding. He makes a strong case for restructuring schools, using the latest research on learning as a guide. Here are new ideas about education—from the world of the young child as "natural learner" to the adolescent's search for meaning. A serious, provocative book.

Healy, Jane M. ENDANGERED MINDS: WHY OUR CHILDREN DON'T THINK. New York: Simon & Schuster, 1990.

The message here is that electronic media, unstable family patterns, fast-paced lifestyles, and other reflections of current society change not only how a child thinks, but also affect his actual brain structure. Healy presents research in the neuropsychology of learning and attacks popular opinions—for example, that watching *Sesame Street* aids your child's learning or that day care programs give a child a head start in school. Not Sunday afternoon reading fare, but written in friendly language, with many helpful anecdotes.

Uscher, Nancy. SCHIRMER GUIDE TO SCHOOLS OF MUSIC AND CONSERVATORIES THROUGHOUT THE WORLD. New York: Schirmer Books, 1988.

Comprehensive guide with geographical listings of schools of music, conservatories, colleges, and universities with preparatory divisions. Detailed descriptions of facilities and services.

Wlodkowski, Raymond J. and Judith Jaynes. EAGER TO LEARN: HELPING CHILDREN BECOME MOTIVATED AND LOVE LEARNING. San Francisco: Jossey-Bass, 1990.

The authors speak directly to parents about understanding and supporting a child's desire to learn. The writing style is practical, listing specific steps that parents can take. Discussions are often handled in a question-and-answer format. Especially useful are the chapters entitled "Building a Positive Parent-Teacher Relationship" and "Encouraging Effort and Perseverance," as well as the resource section that includes such things as how to prepare for a parent-teacher conference. There are also two videos, called "Motivation to Learn," associated with this book. See annotation under Videos.

The Economics of Music Study

What you will find in this chapter

- Budget for music lessons
- What do lessons cost?
- Other fees

  Registration, library, computer.

  Music purchase. Festivals and competitions.

  Accompanist fees and arrangements.

  Audition travel. Enrichment.

- Budget for onetime purchase
- The instrument

  Where to look. The trial period.

  Rental. Rental with option to buy.

  Buying an instrument.

  Comparing costs. Advice and opinions.

  Insurance, appraisals, and warranties.

  Maintaining the instrument.

- Practice environment and equipment
- Caution! No photocopying
- Highlights
- Chapter resources

*A*s YOU consider the economics of music study, a prime question will be whether to choose the teacher or the instrument first. In our estimation, it is better to know the instrument your child wants to study, but to wait for the actual purchase or rental until you have selected a teacher. The teacher will then be able to give you valuable opinions about instrument makers, sources for purchase, rental, maintenance, and a variety of other options that are unique to your location.

Once you have selected a teacher, you will need to make decisions about the instrument. Will you rent or purchase? Will you choose a brand name? And what of hidden costs?

The budgets listed in this chapter include most items you will need to consider. The cost of an instrument and lessons themselves will be your biggest expenses. The specific price of each item has been left blank for you to fill in after you do some calling and shopping. We will go over each item, describing choices, but not exact figures because fluctuation in the economic climate as well as regional differences will affect each item on the budget.

Budget for music lessons

Ongoing expenses are those that you can expect to incur on a yearly basis. These include music lessons and fees. Later in the chapter you will find a budget for onetime purchases, those items that, once purchased, do not have a yearly carrying fee.

*Yearly Budget
Ongoing Expenses*

• Lessons	$_____
• Registration, computer lab, library fees	_____
• Instrument rental	_____
• Insurance	_____
• Maintenance and repair	_____
• Accessories (strings, rosin, reeds, cork grease, slide oil, other)	_____
• Annual cost of buying music	_____
• Festival and competition fees	_____
• Audition travel expenses	_____
• Enrichment	_____
• Other	_____
• Yearly total	$_____

What do lessons cost?

The cost of music lessons in this country is governed by a number of factors. Tuition varies with the training, experience, and reputation of the teacher, and is affected by regional differences. Urban lesson fees are generally higher than those in rural or small-town areas. According to a recent *New York Times* survey of the cost of private lessons, estimated hourly rates for one-on-one instruction in the New York City area are from $25 to $125 an hour, depending on instructor training and experience. Rates will vary in other parts of the country. East and West Coast fees are generally higher than those in other regions.

Bargaining for tuition is not considered good form. In fact, discussing fees is best left to an in-person interview with the teacher or school music director after the preliminary phone conversation. Most teachers request payment in advance by the month, semester, or year for a season of 32 to 42 weeks. A few have special summer programs to encourage continuity in study, for which there is an extra fee.

If you have any financial concerns, discuss them at your first meeting. That is the time to inquire about availability of scholarships. Most schools of music have some provision for scholarships based on need. Some private teachers have a sliding scale to accommodate those under financial stress. If asked, be prepared to provide an income tax statement to prove need.

A 1989 nationwide survey of approximately two thousand independent music teachers by the Music Teachers National Association Foundation, indicated the following general statistics about music teachers' business practices.

> ### Independent music teacher survey
> - Seventy percent of the teachers offer private lessons of different lengths (30, 45, 60 minutes).
> - Fees increase proportionately for different lesson lengths.
> - Those teaching in rural areas and towns tend to charge less than those in cities.
> - More than seventy-five percent have a written studio policy statement.
> - Twenty-five percent never offer makeup lessons.
> - Thirty-three percent will make up lessons if 24 hours' notice is given.
> - Most teachers collect tuition in advance by the month, semester, or year.
> - The majority do not refund unused tuition.
> - Teachers raise fees commensurate with cost-of-living increases.
>
> From *The MTNA Foundation Survey of Independent Music Teacher Income and Lesson Fees, 1989.*

These general statements give only a partial picture of lesson fees in this country. One must also consider the environments in which lessons take place. Chapter Six reviews the environment possibilities (lessons at schools or independent studios, group or private lessons, lessons with technology, at a music store, or in your home). Check several environments to determine which best suit your educational goals and budget. Rates are affected not only by training, experience, and reputation of the teacher, but also by other factors.

> ### Factors affecting lesson fees
> - Services included in the tuition
> - Length of lessons
> - Number of weeks per season
> - Inclusion of musicianship classes
> - The curriculum offered
> - Computer lab
> - Ensemble/chamber music classes
> - Performance opportunities

Teacher quality makes a big difference in whether your child will have a good musical experience. Choose the best teacher that you can afford. The criteria for judging teacher qualities, the curriculum, and teaching environments are thoroughly outlined in Chapter Six. These factors should take precedence over seeking bargain lessons.

Other fees

Registration, library, and computer fees

Some teachers charge a onetime registration fee to reserve space in their studios. Others have an annual registration fee that covers costs for music, auditions, and other extras. If the teacher has a lending library, a library fee may be charged. Computer fees may be absorbed into the tuition, or a small additional charge may be added.

Music purchase

Your child's teacher should be able to give you a rough estimate of the cost of materials (music books, etc.) for a particular season. Studio policy might read, "Last year the average music charge was about $__, and the range was $__ to $__." Students learn at different rates, and have peaks and valleys in their progress. The teacher may not be sure whether your child is ready for a learning spurt or a plateau, but he should be able to give you a "ballpark" figure to pencil into your budget. Our estimate is that the cost of music for a beginning student will rarely exceed $50 in the first year.

As your child progresses to play the major literature, the expenditures will gradually increase. Purchases will include works that become part of your child's permanent music library. It is worthwhile to get well-printed, well-bound music editions that will last a lifetime. The teacher will usually have definite views on the best editions for particular composers' works.

As to actual purchase, teachers will either provide the music and bill you, or have you do the purchasing. If you do the purchasing, it is possible to order from your local dealer by phone, either using a credit card or establishing a personal account. Music can also be purchased from a mail-order house. The teacher may be able to suggest a few. One of the most exciting events for your child, however, is to let him accompany you to the music store, to browse through materials and make a wish list for the next visit.

Most teachers have a brochure stating their qualifications, curriculum, and business practices. The following excerpts are from studio policy statements published in the Music Teachers National Association's *Book of Policies, Letters and Forms.*

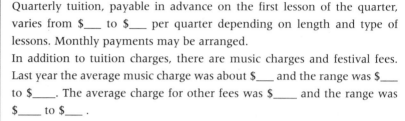

Quarterly tuition, payable in advance on the first lesson of the quarter, varies from $___ to $___ per quarter depending on length and type of lessons. Monthly payments may be arranged.

In addition to tuition charges, there are music charges and festival fees. Last year the average music charge was about $___ and the range was $___ to $____. The average charge for other fees was $____ and the range was $____ to $___ .

The bulk of these fees is payable with the Spring quarter bill. Since this causes that bill to be very large, you may make arrangements to pay it in installments prior to that time. Prompt payment is appreciated since I pay these added fees and music charges before billing you for them.

Some computer theory and/or tapmaster for rhythm is included in the group lessons. Additional work on these is available for a nominal fee.

From the studio of Jean Fox, Allentown, PA

Please note that tuition is a yearly fee, indicating a commitment to study for the entire academic year. For your convenience, the tuition may be paid annually, semiannually, or quarterly. In addition, a $___ registration fee (nonrefundable and not applied to tuition payment) should be enclosed with each student's registration form. This covers planning, supplies, and lending library; reserves the student's place in the studio; and recognizes our mutual commitment to a year of study. A late fee of $___ will be charged for payments received after the due dates.

Included in fees: 33 lessons (27 private and 6 small group), computer and tapmaster use, performance opportunities, theory worksheets, audition and festival opportunities.

Not included in fees: Music and audition fees. Deposit of $__ is made with the first tuition payment.

These policies are in accord with the recommended professional policies of the Music Teachers National Association (as well as state and local associations).

Winborne-Shaw Piano Studio, Oshkosh, WI

The policy concerning missed lessons is covered in most studio policy statements. Two examples follow.

Since rescheduling lessons is usually impossible, a swap list is available, making it possible for you to keep continuity in your private lessons when illness or conflicts arise. This list is available only to those requesting inclusion. Arranging the swap is your responsibility.

Refunds cannot be made for lessons canceled by the student.

Thirty weeks of lessons will be offered for Fall, Winter, and Spring quarters. Additional lessons are scheduled allowing for teacher cancelations. If other lessons are canceled by the teacher, you will receive a makeup.

From the studio of Jean Fox, Allentown, PA

No credit can be given for missed instruction. When appropriate, a makeup class will be given for students who have an excused* absence and given 24-hour notice. The makeup class will be held once a month and will focus on the current goals of the Studio (e.g., preparation for a tournament, festival, recital, etc.).

*An excused absence is student illness, student out of town, or family emergency.

A minimum of one month's advance notice must be given for any permanent change in schedule.

From the studio of Mary Gae George, Orange City, FL

A number of teachers offer various types of scholarships. Discuss scholarship possibilities at the first in-person interview with the teacher.

Responsible and deserving students will be given opportunity to assist with clerical duties at the Studio or serve as lab monitors. Credit at the rate of $____ an hour will then be applied toward their tuition.

This is an excellent way for students to learn business skills, and to better appreciate all that goes into the operation of a studio. In addition, they have the advantage of earning all or part of their own music tuition.

Parents may also take part in this program.

From the studio of Mary Gae George, Orange City, FL

Full-time and half-time assistant scholarships are available for students in need of financial assistance.

Manduca Music Studio, Portland, ME

In addition to the financial aspects of studio policy, many teachers include information about special opportunities within their programs, or offer advice about practice procedures or other musical matters. Note the following examples.

From December to March, each student will be required to perform in an outreach program either at a nursing home, medical facility, or day care center. These performances will be set up for you. You need only choose the date you prefer.

Manduca Music Studio, Portland, ME

I have scheduled a session for all students with a biofeedback, stress management professional to work with my students on performance anxiety, i.e., self-interference, self-judgments, and frustrations that take the joy out of playing and performing. Just as the end-product of the study of music is enjoyment, virtuosity, and inspiration, the actual process of learning can yield this same quality of experience. I think there would be a great deal of carryover from this to school, sports, etc.
This will replace one lesson.

From the studio of Judy Plagge, Wichita, KS

Our tuition fees take into consideration that we must provide all of our insurance, retirement, social security, and continuing education costs, as well as bear the expense of equipping and maintaining our studios, instruments, libraries, and other equipment and supplies. We find that we spend at least as much time in planning, study, scheduling, and other studio-related work as we do in actual lesson time.

Teaching is our profession, our business, and our art. We wish to present and live up to the policies that give us time and financial security to devote most of our energy to the creative act of sharing music with people.

We acknowledge our students' and their parents' place in a three-way relationship, and pledge to do our best to make music study a rich, growing experience for our students.

Winborne-Shaw Piano Studio, Oshkosh, WI

Festivals and competitions

There are a number of audition and performance opportunities available to students at the local, district, state, national, and international levels. Teachers enter qualifying students in a widening circle of these events to provide goals and challenges. Local music teacher groups often have yearly recitals or festivals requiring a modest audition fee, usually less than the cost of a single lesson. Local, regional, and national competitions are sponsored by professional societies such as the Music Teachers National Association and the National Federation of Music Clubs. Local symphony orchestras, opera companies, and chamber music groups hold auditions as well. Entry fees for competitive auditions at the local level rarely exceed the cost of a single lesson.

Serious students who enter state, division, national, or international competitions can expect somewhat higher entry fees. *Concert Artist Guild Guide to Competitions* lists worldwide competitions, their requirements, and entry fees.

Accompanist fees and arrangements

Those students who need a professional accompanist for auditions and competitions will find the range of fees at the same level as a midrange hourly lesson fee. Students should plan to budget for both rehearsal and audition time. The amount of time needed depends on the length and difficulty of the student program.

As in all other musical choices you make, get the best accompanist you can afford. The student's audition is greatly aided by a gifted collaborator. Conversely, a poor accompanist can ruin the audition of the best of players.

Mary Ann Brown, staff accompanist at The Juilliard School, has several suggestions directed to students (twelve years old and older) about making arrangements for an accompanist.

Advice to students on arranging for an accompanist

- Arrange for the accompanist well in advance of the audition date. (Joanne Procell, official accompanist for the Hoff-Barthelson Music School, confirms this and notes that few good, and therefore busy, accompanists will be available on short notice. Since you will be scheduling rehearsal as well as audition or performance time, this makes it doubly important to reserve early.)
- Allow for a rehearsal time at least 24 hours before the performance. This is especially important for singers and for wind and brass players, who need to conserve breath before an audition.
- Give the accompanist a clean copy (not a photocopy)of the score well in advance of the audition.
- If the accompanist has her own edition of the work(s) you are playing, check the score for differences.
- If you are under fifteen years of age, it helps to have a parent present to take notes during the rehearsal, if you are accustomed to having your parent present at lessons.
- Bring a pencil to the rehearsal and be prepared to work. Be open minded. There may be an exchange of ideas.
- Look at the accompanist's part. Listen to it beforehand if possible, so that you will be knowledgeable. You will be treated like a colleague, and you and the accompanist will have produced a real performance together.
- Confirm all travel arrangements with the accompanist, or have your parents do so. If a considerable distance is involved, you may be responsible for the accompanist's travel expenses, unless she is accompanying a number of students at the audition, in which case, you will share these expenses.

Most competitions and auditions allow the student to bring her own accompanist or to use the official accompanist of the competition. The same courtesies discussed above should be extended to the official accompanist. Each competition will have its protocol as to payment of the official accompanist. Usually this is a prepaid arrangement, with rehearsals scheduled by the sponsoring organization.

Although the preceding remarks have been addressed to the auditioning student, most often a teenager, it is wise for parents to participate in the audition arrangements with the child or teen. Parents, teachers, and students should read audition guidelines carefully to avoid last-minute mishaps.

Audition travel

When auditions require your child to go to state, national, or international sites, you may have travel expenses. This means that you will want to plan ahead as far as possible to arrange the best fares. Sometimes the sponsoring organization has arranged special air fares and room rates. In some cases, the sponsoring organization has a travel allotment to help subsidize auditioning students' travel expenses. Audition chairpersons can provide you with information, but you will be expected to make your own reservations, arriving well in advance of rehearsals and auditions to avoid last-minute travel difficulties.

Enrichment

The sky is the limit on enrichment items for your child, but before you make purchases, avail yourself of the local library. Books, recordings, CD-ROMs, and music software are all available at most local libraries. If they don't have an item on your list, they may be interested in ordering it. You should ask.

Other enrichment items might include tickets to concerts or ballets, trips to museums, a subscription to a music magazine, new music software, a beautiful edition of music, a song collection, a piece of sheet music, CD-ROMs, videos, or books.

Budget for onetime purchase

After assessing the cost of music lessons, peripheral fees, music purchase, and enrichment, there are considerations that pertain to instrument purchase and maintenance.

Budget for onetime purchase
- Cost of instrument $_____
- Instrument case (hard)   _____
- Instrument case (soft)   _____
- String instrument bow   _____
- Instrument appraisal   _____
- Practice room equipment:
  Lighting   _____
  Music stand   _____
  Music case   _____
  Music files or bookcase   _____
- Other   _____

- Onetime purchase total $_____

The instrument

Whether you purchase or lease, a common perplexing question remains, "How good does my child's first instrument have to be?" This question can't be answered simply, but it can be answered straightforwardly. Instead of looking for a minimum standard—"What is the cheapest instrument that would enable my child to get by for the time being?"—look at it from the top down. Ask yourself, "What is the best quality that I can afford right now?"

Examine the facts. If your child's first instrument is nearly a toy, or in poor condition, it will be difficult for her to sound good. That is not only demoralizing, but actually hinders progress. On the other hand, being able to play an instrument that sounds pleasing, even if not first-rate, contributes to self-esteem and is a great incentive to continue.

There are three grades of instruments to consider as you begin your search: beginner, student (high school and college non-music majors), and professional. One can always step up in quality as student needs change, as long as the initial instrument is of sufficient quality to create a pleasing musical experience.

Buying a good-quality instrument is also a wiser investment. Most instruments hold their value well unless real damage occurs or, in the case of electronic instruments, something better comes on the market. You do not lose money by buying as good as you can. If the instrument is kept in good condition, you are likely to get an almost even return for your dollar when the time comes to sell. In the meantime, your child

has played on an instrument of some quality and, while that is not easily measured, it is perhaps the wisest part of the investment. The Music
Educators National Conference has a booklet (*The Complete String Guide:
Standards, Programs, Purchasing, and Maintenance*) that describes standards
for purchase of string instruments. Local dealers have catalogs for each
instrument to help you begin your search.

In some cases, a parent could conceivably be willing to spend too
much on an instrument. This might happen, for instance, when buying
a violin, since costs may be anything imaginable. A teacher may feel
some responsibility for tailoring the cost of an instrument to the needs
of an individual student and, therefore, might advise against too great
an expenditure if the student's ability doesn't warrant such an outlay.

Where to look

There are several sources for finding an instrument.

The teacher. The most important recommendation is that made by
the teacher you have carefully selected. Ask the teacher's advice about
the relative merits of rental and purchase, names of tuners and repair
shops, and brand preferences.

Instrument rental and repair shop. A rental, repair, and/or
restoration shop suggested by the teacher or listed in the *Yellow Pages*
under "Musical Instruments" may have a full range of instruments or
specialize in winds, brass, strings, percussion, or keyboards.

Local dealer showroom. Here you will generally have a variety of
brands to choose from and support for repairs and maintenance, as well
as rental and purchase capabilities. The custom options of the specialized shop may not be available, but the hometown dealer is likely to
have a try-before-you-buy policy that allows you to rent a new instrument with an option to buy.

Piano tuner or rebuilder. A piano tuner may have rebuilt pianos,
or know about used pianos for sale. If the tuner or rebuilder is a member of the Piano Technicians Guild, such a skilled craftsperson is also in
a good position to help you evaluate the condition of a used piano.
There is usually a fee for the appraisal.

Mail-order catalog. This may be an especially viable method of purchasing digital keyboards and electronic equipment. You will still need

a knowledgeable teacher to guide your purchase. You may not have the service and maintenance support that a local dealer or specialized instrument shop can provide, but prices are generally competitive and the selection may be wider.

Classified advertisement.
Want ads in the local newspaper, and on bulletin boards in schools and supermarkets may advertise instru-ments for sale. If you consider buying in this way, it is important to have a teacher or instrument repair specialist look at the instrument before you buy. There may be a fee for such service, but it is as impor-tant as having your mechanic check a used car that you are thinking of buying. When you purchase from a private individual, you have no warranties, no service, and no recourse if the instrument proves unsat-isfactory. In the case of used drum sets, however, there are good and fairly safe buys.

The trial period

There are three categories to consider when you are arranging for an instrument for your child. You may rent, rent with an option to buy, or purchase the instrument. As you collect data on each of these alterna-tives, be sure you know what you are getting.

Unless you already have an instrument in your home or family, you will probably opt to lease or purchase a used instrument. In the minds of many parents, the first months of instruction are a trial period. They watch to see whether their children enjoy the activity, and if they make sufficient progress.

Often, how taking lessons was approached in the first place affects the outcome of the trial. If your child knows that a commitment need not be made and feels that getting out of it will be easy, it is more than likely that she will take that option the minute things become difficult or trou-blesome. In some way, you may have said as much. "If you don't like it, or if you don't do well, you won't have to continue."

It is better to make clear at the outset that there will be an investment of a definite time period. A year (or in some cases a semester) is a good rule of thumb. Two things are gained. A specific time commitment set-tles beforehand that music study is not like a video game—if you don't enjoy it, you stop or change. It also makes it possible for you and your child to get a more accurate feel for how things are going. It takes time to learn how to play an instrument and read music, and children develop at different rates of speed. Sometimes the beginning is slow going, but things become enjoyable and satisfying after a few obstacles are overcome. Conversely, whipping through the first books may give a false impression that there will be no, or few, challenges ahead. In a year, however, the assessment is likely to be more realistic.

Rental

Renting an instrument is not difficult, nor is it apt to be very costly. In most cases, you lease the instrument from a school, a music store, or an instrument dealer. Policies for this vary, so you need to inquire what is available in your school or community. Leasing usually includes normal repair, maintenance costs, and insurance. Pianos are hardly ever leased through a school, since most schools don't offer piano instruction as part of the music program. If you lease a piano, expect to pay cartage costs as part of the first payment. Some leasing arrangements provide an option to have payments go toward eventual purchase. This may be worthwhile if the instrument you buy is a good one. It makes less sense to enter into such an arrangement if the instrument is of minimum, or questionable, quality. You wind up buying an instrument that will have little value, either to you, or for resale.

Be sure you know what you are getting when you rent (or buy). Is a case included? What kind of case? A cloth case is less expensive, but it affords less protection for the instrument. It may be important for young students to have a lightweight fiberglass case (without a metal rim because a metal rim can harm the instrument, especially the varnish on string instruments). What accessories are included in the price? Bow and rosin for strings, new mouthpiece for winds, sterilized mouthpiece wrapped in plastic for brass, cleaning rod and cork grease for clarinet, slide oil and cleaning snake for trombone, cleaning cloth and rod for flute? Are accessory charges and insurance, maintenance, and repair charges part of the rental or additional?

Rental with option to buy

Merchants have varying plans for rental with an option-to-buy. Here are a few typical arrangements. One rental/repair shop states, "First-year rental fee goes toward purchase. The instrument is a new, entry-level instrument, and comes with case and manufacturer's warranty. There is some charge for insurance and accessories."

One major dealer describes rental with option to buy as follows: "Basic cost of the instrument is figured at 40 percent of list. The rental instrument is a new instrument, that, if listed at $600, would be sold for $350. The rental fee is $15 per month. After seven months the consumer has paid only $105. At the end of the year, he has a new instrument that he may purchase or return. Cost of insurance and warranty, bow for strings, and basic accessories for other instruments are included in the rental price."

This dealer continues, "There can be problems when you rent a new instrument with option to buy. The consumer may end up paying unnecessarily high insurance rates. When it is time for purchase, the cost of the instrument may be based on list price rather than on a discount offered by some dealers (as much as 40 percent of purchase price). The total cost may be much higher than outright purchase or better rental with option-to-buy arrangements."

A piano dealer states, "Pianos come with a one-year warranty, bench, and tuning as part of the rent-with-option-to-buy arrangement. This includes manufacturer's warranty. Rental of a new piano for six months is $50 per month. There is a $150 delivery fee each way. The six-month investment is $600. If the instrument is purchased, the cost of rental and delivery is absorbed."

Buying an instrument

If and when you decide to purchase, you will buy either a new, or a used, instrument. Just as when you purchase anything of value—a TV, refrigerator, or car, for instance—take the time to look carefully at what is available and what is essential in your situation. In the area of musical instruments, however, there are no consumer digests that give you a chance to do background comparison shopping. (Electronic keyboards, however, are sometimes covered in such guides.) You will need to rely on the advice and opinions of one who plays the instrument well (if you cannot do so yourself) because an instrument should be purchased on the basis of how it sounds, not on its name value or how it looks. The construction of most instruments is complicated, and only those who know the instrument are in a position to pass judgment on what is of value, what may be overlooked, and what may require only minimal repair.

There are obvious risks in buying a used instrument. The first of these is the physical condition of the instrument, and this is where you will need outside help. Don't hesitate to seek an expert—a teacher, a performer, or a technician—to play and evaluate the instrument for you, but be prepared to pay that person for the advice since they are giving time as well as expertise. It is wiser to pay a small cost for a pre-sale opinion than to buy an instrument only to find that it needs costly repair, or may even be beyond repair. Remember also that, unlike an automobile, a musical instrument is probably in better condition if it has been played regularly than if it has been untouched, or played only rarely.

If you buy a used instrument from an individual, there is no warranty. If you purchase a used instrument from a store or dealer, there may be a warranty, but you had better look into that carefully. One advantage of purchasing a used (or a new) instrument from a dealer or store is that servicing is generally available, if not directly from the dealer, then from some place the dealer uses. When you buy a used instrument from an individual, you are on your own when it comes to maintenance and repair.

If you have inherited or found a vintage piano, you may find it worth rebuilding. At anywhere from $1,000 to $15,000, restoration is expensive and can cost more than the piano is worth. The simplest way to find a good piano is to go directly to a restorer or dealer who sells rebuilt pianos. The cost of the rebuilding will be considerably less than the cost of that instrument new. (A refurbished Steinway sells for 25 to 30 percent less than a new one.) According to Sara Faust of Faust Pianos in Irvington, New York, once the piano has been well restored, it should look and feel as though it were new and, with maintenance, should last a lifetime.

The risks undertaken when purchasing a new instrument are the same as those encountered in buying any other new product. One thing is very different about buying a musical instrument, however. You are likely to know a great deal more about cars, TVs, or refrigerators than a violin, piano, or trumpet. Brand names make a difference, and each instrument has at least one name that means top of the line. Check out which these are (here your outside expert is again a trustworthy guide), even though you may not be interested, or able, to buy such quality. Knowing what is the best gives you a standard against which to judge everything else, and a name brand is in your favor at resale time.

When purchasing a student violin, however, it is not so useful to speak of brand names. Here, the "names" are those associated with factory- made (the cheapest) instruments such as Suzuki, Roth, Lewis, and so on. The concept of a brand name loses meaning when one speaks of better-quality student instruments, since there are probably thousands of makers. When choosing such an instrument, the teacher's input becomes crucial.

Comparing costs

When it comes to pricing an instrument, there is an instrument list price catalog for each type of instrument available from local dealers or from the National Association of Music Dealers. Do some comparison shopping. Like other big-ticket items, there is a list price and a discount price. Many dealers and mail-order houses sell instruments for as much as 40 percent of list. Compute the price based on list. In general, cost of instruments may be less in large urban areas than in small towns and rural areas because of the volume of business and competition.

Unlike dealing with tuition, it is appropriate to negotiate price when you are shopping for an instrument. You may not win, but you are better off trying.

Advice and opinions

The following provocative potpourri of advice and opinions from several dealers and repair shops concerns a few qualities to look for when choosing an instrument. You should check these opinions with the teacher and with reliable dealers and instrument rental/repair shops.

About string instruments

- Inexpensive bows made of fiberglass (*Glasser* bows) are fine for starters.
- *Dominant* strings are quality at entry level.
- Avoid steel strings.
- About plywood instruments: One source thinks that an entry-level cello should be plywood because other woods at this level are often not seasoned, and therefore prone to warp. The opposing view says to avoid plywood instruments, and those that do not have ebony finger boards, because plywood is not malleable and cannot be planed to make necessary adjustments.
- Get an instrument that is *well set up*. That includes a quality bridge, a sound post that fits, a fingerboard that is properly contoured with correct curvature, and pegs that fit properly—in other words, a custom setup even at the entry level.
- About wooden bows: Bows are graded by quality of wood. Brazilwood and Pernambuco are considered quality. One should check to see that the bow is straight, the wood strong and flexible, that it has the right weight and balance for the user. (Teacher evaluation is needed here.)

About winds and brass

- Flutes: One dealer prefers U.S. made entry-level flutes and states that they will be easy to maintain if the student does not bend the keys.

- Oboes, bassoons: One well-known music dealer thinks that oboes and bassoons at entry level should be plastic because at entry level, the quality of plastic is similar to wood. The opposing view says, "No plastic!"
- Clarinet: Plastic is all right for rental; for purchase, get wood.
- With rental wind instruments, it is important to get a new mouthpiece. Brass instruments should have a disinfected mouthpiece that is wrapped in plastic to assure its sanitary condition.

About percussion

- Be sure heads are put on correctly and evenly, but not too tightly, or rims will warp. Drums should be tuned at place of rental or purchase.

About cases

- Molded plastic or fiberglass is best because it is light and durable, but avoid metal rims that can damage the instrument, especially varnish on string instruments.

About pianos

- Buy a piano that is from a recognized manufacturer and has a solid warranty. Buy quality. Finance if necessary. The good-quality instrument will sound better, feel better, hold up better, need less service, and have better resale value should you want to sell or upgrade.

About buying used or rebuilt instruments

- Rebuilding a vintage instrument can be worthwhile if the builder is a skilled craftsperson and the instrument is of quality to begin with. A rebuilt piano, for instance, will have a new soundboard, new pins, dampers, felts, action, modern damper system, refinishing inside and out, plus work on plate and keybed.

Be on guard when buying a used instrument.
Before purchase:

- find out the cost of a similar new instrument.
- Take the serial number of the used instrument and check with the manufacturer to find out how old it is. (For instance, if you can buy a new clarinet for $350, and a used one is $250, the used instrument is not a bargain, especially since the cost of rejuvenating the used instrument could be close to $150.

Insurance, appraisals, and warranties

Whether the instrument you purchase is new or used, you must consider insurance. Insurance costs will vary greatly, depending on the quality and type of instrument. Instruments that are portable, and therefore exposed to loss, theft, or accident in transit, are subject to hazards that will not be attached to owning a piano, for example. Insurance for the instrument may be covered in your household policy, but this is something you should check. Often you must add the instrument to your homeowner's insurance policy and provide a written appraisal or a bill of sale.

Many dealers do not use "insurance." They call it comprehensive maintenance protection or maintenance and repair protection. The cost is typically $3 to $4 a month, and applies mostly to rental instruments.

When you arrange for insurance, you will need an evaluation from a reliable appraiser. Be sure that the appraiser you choose is a member of the American Society of Appraisers. Members' guidelines prohibit them from charging a percentage of the cost of the instrument. Appraisers' fees typically range from $50 to $125.

New instruments have their own warranty by the manufacturer. Used instruments will have the same warranty or a twelve-month warranty with a ninety-day exchange privilege. The warranty from the manufacturer protects you and gives you flexibility, should you wish to upgrade or sell the instrument. If you purchase from a private individual, there will be no warranty protection.

Maintaining the instrument

Keeping an instrument in good condition is a necessary counterpart to the lease or purchase. Different instruments require specific kinds of upkeep, but all instruments need to be protected from damage and tem-

perature extremes, and all need to be kept clean. Most instruments are tuned by the player, whereas pianos need to be tuned by a qualified technician at least twice a year. (Contact the Piano Technicians Guild for members in your community or ask your child's teacher for a recommendation.)

When an instrument is leased, the cost of basic repairs is factored into the lease arrangement. If you own the instrument, you assume responsibility for its maintenance. In most cases, your child's teacher will advise you when repairs are necessary, and might also suggest the best place to have these done. All repairs and reconditioning should be done by someone qualified. Music stores are likely to have, or know, qualified instrumental repair people. In some cases, repair people are highly specialized, and may have repair shops of their own. This is often the case with those who work with strings. In large cities, for example, you will find that almost all string players, professional and otherwise, go to one particular repair shop. Shops such as these are also excellent places to purchase instruments.

Part of maintaining an instrument includes care of it in your own home. This means protecting it from damage and accident. Caring for a larger instrument, such as a cello or harp, requires adequate space for storing and practicing. The placement of a piano often takes some consideration. The instrument should not be on an outside wall (because of climate variables), near heating or cooling systems, or too near the family TV, and preferably not in a room always in use, like a family room. Environmental climate control should be considered; perhaps some type of humidifier or dehumidifier equipment will need to be installed. Your instrument technician can advise you on the best system.

Placement of any instrument in a room with a door that can be closed to give privacy is ideal. In cases in which all of these criteria cannot be met, compromise is apt to include "house rules" that look after both the instrument and its player.

Practice environment and equipment

It is likely that you will need a music stand for your child unless he plays a keyboard. Music stands are either light, collapsible, and easily portable or heavier, solid, and not easily portable. Experienced players often prefer the sturdier model because it supports the music more securely, but will probably have need of the portable model as well.

You will also need to see that there is adequate lighting to read the music. (This is often difficult to achieve at a piano.) The best lighting comes over the shoulder of the player, either from a floor lamp or ceiling spotlight. A dimmer is an excellent feature to accommodate day and evening lighting requirements.

Portable instruments should be kept in cases, and the cases stored out of reach of siblings, pets, or visitors. Cases vary. Hard cases afford the greatest protection, especially for larger instruments such as the cello or double bass. Fiberglass cases have the virtue of being lightweight and sturdy. Prices for cases vary considerably. As your child continues to study and upgrades the instrument, you may want to consider upgrading the case as well.

A zippered music case or canvas bag in which to keep current music is especially helpful. Students are less apt to lose music enroute to lessons. If there is more than one sibling who takes lessons, it is wise to have cases of different colors.

As your child progresses and begins to accumulate a library of music and books, help her organize the literature by providing a music cabinet with narrow shelves or cardboard magazine files placed on shelves near the practice area. A student who continues study for more than four to five years will begin to acquire a considerable library of standard works to last a lifetime.

NO PHOTOCOPYING

It is worth noting that if we are to continue to have beautiful editions of great works and imaginative new materials for the early years of study, parents, teachers, and students should be aware that photocopying of music is illegal.

As you help your child to build a music library, share with him the importance of respect for intellectual and creative property. By complying with the copyright law, you are becoming a champion of composers' and publishers' rights.

As the library of materials continues to grow, if yours is a computer-literate family, try listing the library on a database. You might even add recordings and music software to the database. The works accumulated during the years of study can then be accessed to share with the next generation of young musicians.

The suggestions made in this chapter and in Chapters Five and Six present you with a large number of choices. We strongly recommend that you choose the best instrument you can afford because replacing a poorly chosen instrument may cost you money. It is equally, if not even more important to choose the best teacher you can afford. Choosing a less-than-qualified teacher can cost your child a lifetime of musical pleasure. Your research will be more than worth the time it has taken you.

HIGHLIGHTS

☆ Consider the economics of music lessons in this order:

Select the type of instrument your child wants to play.

Choose the best teacher you can afford.

With guidance from the teacher, begin a search for the instrument.

☆ Make two separate budgets:

One for items that are ongoing expenses.

One for items that are onetime purchases.

☆ Lesson fees are affected by:

Training, experience, and reputation of the teacher.

Regional differences.

Lesson length.

Type of lesson.

☆ If you need scholarship assistance:

Be prepared to present your latest tax return if you are requesting aid for economic reasons. Your child should be prepared to play an audition if you are requesting a scholarship based on your child's talent.

☆ Tuition varies. Check several learning environments and compare ambiance as well as services. Does the tuition include:

Lessons only?

How many lessons per season?

Musicianship classes?

Computer lab?

Ensemble?

Group or private lessons?

Registration fee?

Library fee?

Computer lab fee?

Audition and festival fees?

☆ The cost of buying music for a season is variable, depending on the student's learning curve. Costs increase as the student progresses. The teacher should be able to give you an estimate of the yearly cost.

☆ If your child enters certain types of auditions, you will need an accompanist. Fees vary. It is important to expect charges not only for performance, but also for rehearsal time.

☆ Tips for arranging an accompanist:

Make the arrangement well in advance.

Give the accompanist a clean, nonphotocopied version of the music.

Confirm travel arrangements. You may be responsible for the accompanist's travel expenses.

☆ Enrichment items include books, recordings, software, CD-ROMs, and concert tickets.

☆ Instruments should be leased or purchased on the basis of how they sound.

☆ Sources for finding an instrument include:

The teacher.

Instrument rental and repair shop.

Local dealer's showroom.

Piano tuner or rebuilder.

Classified advertisement.

Mail-order discounters.

☆ Lease, purchase, or option to buy:

Leasing an instrument is reasonable and easy.

Purchasing a new or used instrument requires advice and caution.

Leasing with an option to buy can also be risky. Be sure that the purchase price is based on a good discount and that insurance fees tacked on to the rental are not exorbitant.

☆ You assume maintenance and insurance costs when you purchase an instrument.

☆ Select the highest quality instrument that you can afford.

CHAPTER RESOURCES

American Society of Appraisers. Box 17265, Washington, DC 20041. 703-478-2228

Music Educators National Conference. 1806 Robert Fulton Drive, Reston, VA 22091. 800-336-3768.

Music Teachers National Association. The Carew Tower, 441 Vine Street, Suite 505, Cincinnati, OH 45202. 513-421-1420.

National Association of Music Dealers. 4020 McEwen, Suite 105, Dallas, TX 75244. 214-233-9107.

National Association of Music Merchants. 5140 Avenida Encina, Carlsbad, CA 92008. 800-767-6266.

Piano Technicians Guild. 3930 Washington, Kansas City, MO 64111. 816-753-7747.

The Woodwind and The Brasswind Catalog. 19880 Stateline Road, South Bend, IN 46637. 800-348-5003.

The following information was supplied by Sam Ash Music, Frank and Camille Piano Company, Cano Musical Instrument Company, Frank's Music Exchange, Van Hyning Percussion Services, White Plains Piano & Organ Company, Sylvia Woods Harp Center, and *The Woodwind and The Brasswind Catalog*. Most sources are in New York State. Prices as of

August, 1994, may not be indicative of all regions of the country, nor do they reflect possible market fluctuations. However, they allow comparison of relative costs for various instruments. The charts below are not all-inclusive, but list some of the most frequently played instruments.

INSTRUMENT PRICE CHART

INSTRUMENT	LOW PURCHASE PRICE ($)	MID-RANGE PURCHASE PRICE ($)	HIGH PURCHASE PRICE ($)	MONTHLY RENTAL FEE ($)
STRINGS				
Violin	200	300–550	1,000 and up	10.00–17.50
Viola	275	400–700	1,000 and up	10.00–17.50
Cello	500–600	800–1200	1,500 and up	10–20
Double Bass	900–1,100	1,500–2,500	3,000 and up	10–25
WINDS				
Piccolo	289--350	435–650	3,000 and up	9.50
Flute	300–350	500–1,000	4,000–10,000	7.50–10.00
Oboe	650	1,200–1,500	4,000–10,000	7.50–10.00
Clarinet	275–350	425–900	1,500–2,500	7.50–10.00
Bassoon	2,000	3,500	5,000 and up	10–30
Alto Saxophone	600–750	1,200–1,500	2,400–3,000	10–12
Soprano Recorder	5–15	60--125	250 and up	Seldom for rent
BRASS				
Trumpet	350–400	600–750	950–1,250	7.50–12.00
Cornet	350–400	600–750	950–1,250	10–12
French Horn	800–1,000	1,500–1,600	2,000–4,000	10.00–17.50
Baritone	1,200–1,400	200–2,400	2,600–3,500	10–15
Trombone	350–400	600–750	950–1,500	10–15
Tuba	2,000–2,800	3,000–3,500	4,000–16,000	10–15
Euphonium	1,200–1,400	2,400–2,800	3,000–4,000	10–15
PERCUSSION				
Snare Drum	90	150–200	300–400	10
Drum set	299–500	600–700	2,500–3,500	10

*otb = option-to-buy

INSTRUMENT PRICE CHART Continued

INSTRUMENT	LOW PURCHASE PRICE ($)	MID-RANGE PURCHASE PRICE ($)	HIGH PURCHASE PRICE ($)	MONTHLY RENTAL FEE ($)
PERCUSSION Continued				
Timpani (set of 2)	3,700	4,000–4,200	5,000–7,500	50 with otb*
Xylophone	1,000	1,600	2,700	50 with otb*
Vibraphone	2,200	3,700	4,500	50 with otb*
Marimba	1,900	2,500	5,250	50 with otb*
KEYBOARDS				
Piano, Spinet	New: 2,500–3,000 Used: 1,000–2000	3,000	3,800	50
Piano, Console	1,995–3,000	3,500	5,000	50
Piano, Studio	2,500	3,800	6,000	50
Piano, Grand	5,000	10,000	15,000 and up	
Digital: 61-key	160–1,350	375–1,700	—	60
Digital: 76-key	—	—	1,900–8,900	60
Digital 88-Key	1,600	2,000–2,500	7,000–45,000	60
GUITAR				
Classical Guitar	100	200–400	1,000 and up	35
Electric Guitar	189	400–600	1,000 and up	50
Bass Guitar	189	400–600	1,000 and up	—
HARP†				
Troubadour Harp	1,500	2,500	5,000	25–65
Folk Harp	750–1,500	2,000	4,000	20–60
Pedal Harp	8,000	—	27,000	50–125

*otb = option-to-buy

† This is a small representation of the available types of harps.

CHALLENGING
CHOICES

The Gifted Child

What you will find in this chapter

- About giftedness
- Recent theories of giftedness
    Musical intelligence. Musical talents.
    Ego strength. Originality.
    A talent seen early.
- Finding the right teacher
- Parents and the talented child
- The young talented child
    Protecting the talented child
- The talented child in the middle years
    Changing teachers
- The late-teen talent
- How it looks to your child
    The need to belong
- Special schools
- Summer music camp
- Music is a passion
- Music as an escape
- Beware of perfection
- Highlights
- Chapter resources

*I*F YOUR preschool child does most or all of the things listed below, you may be tempted to think that your child is musically gifted. Parents are usually pleased and excited by that possibility, even though they may have no special interest or talent in music themselves. It is also true that most parents have little or no idea how to foster such a talent and begin to search out experts for advice and guidance.

> ### *Your young child*
> - sings in tune.
> - asks to hear music.
> - pays attention whenever music is heard.
> - picks out tunes on the piano or other instrument.
> - moves rhythmically to music.
> - asks repeatedly to play a musical instrument.
> - shows great sensitivity to changes in music.
> - talks and asks questions about music.

It is possible that even if your preschooler acts in the ways described, she may not be specially gifted. Most children respond to music and many do so overtly, for example, by dancing, swinging, humming, or stopping to listen. Many also sing to themselves while playing, either inventing words and tunes or echoing those heard elsewhere. While these are good clues that a child is interested in music, they may not indicate exceptional ability.

Before you go off, therefore, to seek an expert to verify whether or not your child has special talent, it would be helpful to know a little about giftedness in general, and musical giftedness in particular. Then you will be better equipped to understand how your child might be tested, or what might lie ahead.

About giftedness

Those who study giftedness do not always agree on what it is. Research in this area, even the concept of something called an IQ, is barely one hundred years old, and theories to define giftedness have arisen for different reasons. In the United States, early interest in this subject centered around the work of Lewis Terman who developed probably the best-known "name brand" test for identifying intelligence, the Stanford-Binet. While no one has yet outdone Terman in terms of the quantity and longevity of his research (Terman and his associates studied 1,444 people over a period of forty years), his work is not without its critics. The current reservations about all standardized testing—race, gender, and socioeconomic bias, for instance—are similar to the criticisms first directed toward Terman. Although today there are many tests—some that assess achievement (such as the SAT) and some that assess potential (such as Gordon's *Musical Aptitude Profile*)—there is no surefire test that is universally regarded as completely reliable or conclusive.

Motives for identifying and supporting talent have also been political. The race into outer space (especially the Russian launch of Sputnik in 1957) changed American education in a way no educational reformer could ever have done. Science and mathematics became, almost over night, the rallying cries that energized school systems and funding organizations. Within a decade and a half, the United States Office of Education had an official definition of talent and giftedness. Efforts to identify the gifted and provide for them as part of public education have been on the increase ever since.

To prove his ideas, Terman began the granddaddy of all longitudinal psychological studies, the first scientific study that attempted to divine the origin and outcome of genius.—Joel Shurkin

---

UNITED STATES OFFICE OF EDUCATION DEFINITION OF GIFTEDNESS

1972 DEFINITION

Gifted and talented children are those identified by professionally qualified persons who by virtue of outstanding abilities are capable of high performance. These are children who require differentiated educational programs and services beyond those normally provided by the regular school program in order to realize their contribution to self and society. Children capable of high performance include those with demonstrated achievement and/or potential ability in any of the following areas:

1. General intellectual ability
2. Specific academic aptitude
3. Creative or productive thinking
4. Leadership ability
5. Visual and performing arts
6. Psychomotor ability

1978 REVISION

The gifted and talented are children and, whenever applicable, youth who are identified at the preschool, elementary, or secondary level as possessing demonstrated or potential abilities that give evidence of high performance capability in areas such as intellectual, creative, specific academic or leadership ability, or in the performing and visual arts, and who by reason thereof require services or activities not ordinarily provided by the school.

Because reasons for trying to define giftedness vary, it is not surprising that there are also many ways to identify it. A set point on the IQ scale (Terman's was 140) is only one way. Although the words "giftedness" and "talent" can be used interchangeably, usually someone who excels in verbal creativity is called gifted, and someone with a special artistic aptitude is referred to as talented. Thus we speak of musical talent, rather than musical giftedness.

Talent may also be viewed as a continuum that ranges from little or no talent, on one end, to evidence of genius on the other. Viewed this way, it is possible to state that each person has talent, but some have more than others. Where on that continuum does one pass the point that marks giftedness? It is difficult to say. This attitude toward talent may make a strong case for offering all children a stimulating education, rather than arranging challenging activities only for those singled out as gifted.

Recent theories of giftedness

Within the past few decades, theories about giftedness have expanded the scope of what marks the gifted person. One current expert in the field of gifted education, Joseph Renzulli, refers to a triadic model of giftedness. Three traits are critical: above-average (though not necessarily high) intellectual ability, a high degree of task commitment or motivation, and a strong creative sense. The latter two traits focus attention on the drive, stamina, and uniqueness of the gifted individual without subordinating these to whatever is the special talent. Other theorists include even broader factors, and suggest that five components overlap. High general intelligence is accompanied by special ability (a particular talent or aptitude), ego strength and dedication, supportive environment (home and school), and chance. This underscores the importance of the support structure that sustains the gifted person and the zeal and devotion that spur him, but concedes that unforeseen circumstances and opportunities play a role in developing a talent.

Many successful painters ruefully admit that the difference between them and the hundreds of artistic "failures" is not greater talent but contacts and accidental events that created visibility for their work—in short, blind chance.
—Mihaly Csikszentmihalyi, Kevin Rathunde, and Samuel Whalen

The gifted child has
- intelligence.
- ego strength.
- determination.
- creativity.

PLUS

The thriving gifted child has
- supportive family and teachers.
- persistence despite ups and downs.
- good luck.

Musical intelligence

Because intelligence is included in each theory of giftedness, it is noteworthy that the idea of multiple intelligences advanced by Harvard Professor of Education Howard Gardner proposes a special musical intelligence. He points out that recognition of pitch, rhythm, and timbre is basic to musical intelligence. He feels, however, that identifying these elements is just the beginning, that the person with musical intelligence grasps a great deal more. She is able to sense, for example, how motives and harmonies interact, or when phrases ought to come to a close; these abilities represent higher-level musical skills than just an accurate grasp of pitch and rhythm patterns.

If we accept Renzulli's triadic model, we can outline the characteristics of a musically gifted child with some clarity and greater scope. Qualities such as willpower and creativity are as telling and significant as special musical talents.

Musical talents

For the talented child, demonstrating all the skills in the list will not be difficult. Most of them are things the child does informally, even at an early age. Much depends, of course, on the home atmosphere. A home in which people sing, play instruments, and listen to music is more likely to awaken a child's musical instincts than one in which music is absent, or regarded merely as pleasant background to other activities.

Musical talents

Some or all of these may be present in varying degrees.

- **Pitch discrimination.** Singing in tune, matching pitches, "perfect" pitch. Remembering pitches sounded horizontally, as in a melody. Identifying pitches sounded vertically, as in a chord.
- **Rhythm discrimination.** Keeping the beat, repeating rhythms, and combining these skills. Sensing rates of speed (tempo) and changes of tempo.
- **Timbre discrimination.** Sensitivity to the sounds made by each instrument. Sensitivity to sounds within specific instrumental ranges.
- **Musical sensitivity.** Innate sense of phrasing and ways of making sounds. Innate response to dynamic (loud/soft) levels and changes.
- **Psychomotor skill.** Coordination to play a (specific) musical instrument. Strength and agility to play a (specific) musical instrument.
- **Desire to perform.** Delight in playing or singing, especially publicly.

It does happen, of course, that children with outstanding musical ability grow up in homes in which playing and singing are absent, or in which there is neither an instrument nor a music-friendly atmosphere. Where that is the case, however, it is more difficult for such abilities to come to light and less likely that, when discovered, developing the abilities will be encouraged and supported. Yet, unsupported but talented children often find ways to meet their own needs.

You may have noted the reference to perfect pitch—this is the ability to know, and perhaps name, exactly the note sounded. Don't make too much of this talent. It is not a magic blessing if present, nor is the lack of it a great loss. Many musicians do not have it, and many people with perfect pitch are not musical. The perception of pitch is a complex issue, and some musicians even claim that perfect pitch can be taught if training is begun early enough. A good musical education includes refining the ear, and even experienced musicians continue to develop this capacity. You should not be fooled into thinking that if your child has perfect pitch, you have a musical genius on your hands.

Ego strength

In describing personal traits of the talented child, it is evident that these not only propel him to ask for an instrument or lessons in the first place, but sustain and influence him throughout the study, practice, and performing that follow.

These factors mark the difference between a child with lively interest and talent, and one who goes on to become a successful performer or composer, if not a professional.

Ego strength

Some or all of these may be present in varying degrees.

- **Motivation.** Interest in music is a drive, not just a special pastime. Child is likely to beg for lessons insistently. Child often displays enthusiasm for a particular instrument.
- **Willpower.** Child is not satisfied with concessions or distractions. Ingenuity figures high in reaching a desired goal. Although easily teachable, the child can be headstrong.
- **Persistence.** Child enjoys concentrating and working on details. Child is willing to work long hours for remote goals.
- **Self-discipline.** Internal self-monitoring is innate, sometimes unhealthy. Inner strength can withstand setbacks and criticisms.
- **Dedication.** Child responds to the inspiration of beautiful sound. There is willingness to forgo other pleasures to reach a goal.
- **Single-mindedness.** Child is often absorbed while playing or practicing. Succeeding, or winning, may become all important.

These traits reveal a dominant personality. While they help the talented child succeed, the downside of these characteristics can create personal as well as learning difficulties. Whether or not the talented child is able to maintain a tolerable balance between forces that drive him internally and the envy, isolation, or adulation that often challenge him externally depends, to a large degree, on how his family upbringing has shaped and supported him as a person. We will return to this important subject later in the chapter.

Originality

There are other characteristics of a gifted person that can be detected early but remain potent as the person matures. They refer to qualities that reflect independence of spirit and give further evidence of ego strength.

Originality

Some or all of these may be present in varying degrees.

- **Creativity.** Finding and following a personal route is valued over ease. Uniqueness and variation is attractive and appreciated.
- **Divergent.** thinking Thinking and acting is nonconforming rather than conventional. There is less interest in right answers than in novel solutions.
- **Risk taking.** Taking a chance is stimulating rather than daunting. Curiosity is a strong driving force.
- **Problem solving.** Working out own solutions is gratifying. Challenge of solving a problem is likely to be a turn-on.
- **Intuitive acting.** There is a basic sense of self-reliance and trust of intuition. Often there is impatience with following rules and procedures.
- **Interest in process.** Things don't need to be black or white; gray areas are enjoyed. Pleasure is in the search and struggle rather than in the result.

The traits connected with originality seem positive, without possible downsides (unlike those dealing with ego strength, which could be seen as the sketch of a workaholic). Yet the appetite for exploration and variation driving an original thinker can produce frustrations, both for the thinker and those who try to guide him. Teachers often remark that they welcome the student who challenges, but the truth is that a nonconformist or original thinker makes most teachers uncomfortable. Such individuality is also likely to cause friction in the area of music where training based on apprenticeship (follow the master and do as you are told) has been the norm for centuries.

A profile of the musically talented child

Musical talent
- An ear
- Sensitivity
- Coordination
- Musical intuition

Motivation
- Willpower
- Persistence
- Self-trust
- Dedication

Originality
- Creativity
- Nonconformity
- Curiosity
- Risk taking

A talent seen early

At the outset of this chapter, we suggested ways to note special abilities in a preschool child because a unique feature of musical talent is that it is generally observed early in life. At the beginning, it may not be apparent in just which ways the talent will show itself most fully, nor is it possible to tell how great the potential is or how far a talent will go.

In most cases, the young child will play music with great ease, and it is therefore common that lessons focus on performance. No matter what a person becomes later—composer, conductor, educator, writer, historian (or doctor, banker, or politician, for that matter)—introduction to music study usually begins with learning to play an instrument. It may also begin with learning to sing, but because the voice develops later, only as the child matures physically, it is difficult to tell in the early stages whether someone will go on to become a great singer.

There are young composers. But childhood works (even of great composers like Mozart or Prokofiev), although considered remarkable, are not highly regarded as serious music. An eight-year-old can play a masterwork, but is not likely to write one. Yet musical creativity should be encouraged in the very young, not because it is apt to produce amazing pieces, but because it gives a young student a chance to experiment with sound and begin to learn something about music's grammar.

Of all the gifts with which individuals may be endowed, none emerges earlier than musical talent.

—*Howard Gardner*

Finding the right teacher

Are you concerned that you have a **gifted** *child, or a gifted* **child***? Concentrating on the latter can help your perspective.*

—Jacqulyn Saunders

Now that you have background information on giftedness and musical talent, you are ready to act. You may or may not have a gifted child. If your child shows any of the traits discussed, this child should have music lessons. Your first hope may be to have your child's talent "verified" by some music professional. Taking such an approach is not very productive because the extent of your child's abilities and how far his talents and energies will carry him can only be revealed with time. Searching for someone who will notice and remark on your child's special gifts may, in fact, lead to complications. You may be duped by false expectations; your child may feel manipulated or valued only for her gift.

The best procedure is to find a good teacher and begin the adventure. Chapter Six covers choosing a teacher, and the advice given there supplies answers for many questions that you might have. You may wonder, however, if there are certain teachers who specialize in working only with gifted students and how you might locate one of these.

In every area, a few teachers gain reputations for working with student "stars." In most cases the reputation is based on the fact that students from these studios win contests, play with orchestras, and perform in public a great deal. These teachers are well known in the local community, and some even have regional or national stature. Finding out who they are is generally not much of a problem. A call to your local college music department, to a community or magnet school, or to a professional music teachers' organization will supply these names.

If you intend to look for one of these teachers, there are a few things you should expect. The first is that you are apt to find that the studio roster is crowded; there is likely to be a waiting list. You may, however, be asked to come for an interview or audition. If your child is accepted, there may be qualifying conditions, such as insistence on serious and regular practice, dropping other activities to make more time for music, or participating in studio classes or competitive events. And, as you might expect, taking lessons will be expensive.

If your child is very young or a beginner, your main concern should be to find a qualified teacher, not necessarily one that is famous. In a study conducted by a University of Chicago research team, the formative years of twenty-one successful concert pianists were examined in light of their developmental experiences and how they felt about them. One factor was notable. The first teacher of each of these pianists was described as being "local, average" by 62 percent of the pianists, "better than average" by 24 percent, and "very good" by only 10 percent. The emotional response to the first teacher was also striking. In most cases, the memories were all positive, the teacher being described as someone who was kindly, patient, nurturing, and "good with kids." One pianist summed it up as, "I was crazy about this lady." It is obvious that beginning with a not-so-famous instructor did not hold back anyone's concert career.

It seems . . . that what was most important was to find a teacher who liked children and worked well with them.
—Lauren Sosniak

Once the pianist began to be noticed as special or outstanding, generally over a period of a few years and as a result of public exposure and success, search for a specialized teacher began. During the period the researchers called "the middle years," roughly from ten to sixteen, the pianists became aware of their own passion for music and demonstrated their dedication by intense practicing and concentration. The teacher was a highly regarded professional with whom the pianist often formed strong musical and human bonds. Attention was drawn to the fact that between teacher and student there had to be a special chemistry, and several pianists spoke of changing teachers (even if the teacher was an expert musician) to find that match.

In the late teens, the relationship between teacher and pianist more closely resembled mentorship. By this time the pianists were all working with master teachers. The teacher became a source of inspiration and a musical guide; the student was a devoted disciple and an avid learner. The teacher often was demanding and critical. "He would just intimidate you out of your mind." But the teacher was a renowned performer and therefore someone who "knew the ropes" in the professional world. The pianists knew that they had to be self-disciplined, resilient, and industrious. Ego strength was needed in the fullest.

THE EARLY TEACHER needs to be supportive and motivating, as well as qualified and reasonably demanding. The child's instincts need to be given some latitude in order that talent not be forced in one direction or the other. Public performing should generally be informal and competition downplayed.

THE MIDDLE-YEARS TEACHER should be a specialist, able to direct an exacting technical regimen, but also concerned to stimulate study of *music*, not just how to play the instrument. The repertoire must expand, but care must be taken that the student is not pushed. Public performance and competing will play a larger role. The student-teacher bond is apt to be strong. Career directions will be discussed, and choices made. The teacher will influence these.

THE MASTER TEACHER must be the consummate professional. Lessons will be intense and concentrated, even though they may not be regular. Personal feelings will not be spared, and criticism may often be severe. Emphasis is on perfecting work, be this composition or performance. Competition and public performance will play a major role. The individual must be self-directed and self-assured.

Parents and the talented child

So far we have considered the teacher's role and how this changes through a talented student's formative years. While the teacher is a crucial influence—technically, musically, personally—the child is growing as a person, as a member of a family, and as a citizen of the world. What happens within this person and to this person as a result of interactions with others is as important as the musical development. This is *your* role in your child's life. It is not enough to place your child in the care of an expert. No one but you can provide your child with the nurturing guidance needed to bring a young personality to maturity.

Raising a child with exceptional talent poses unique problems, but it also offers unusual satisfactions. The problems and satisfactions will not be the same in each family, but some elements and circumstances can be generalized. It may help to highlight these in terms of three growth periods in your child's life, much like the discussion centering on the teacher and the teacher's role. Keep in mind as you read these generalities that much will depend on the degree of talent your child has (which can be anywhere from above average to prodigy-level), and the ways in which the talent may ultimately manifest itself (a Yo-Yo Ma will not develop along the same lines as a Wynton Marsalis). Remember also

Contending with the effects of . . . success adds an extra dimension to the demands on these children's social and emotional development.
—David Feldman

that even a very gifted child will experience doubts and downtimes. No one's path is straight up.

The young talented child

When your child is young, preschool and a little beyond, your child's talent is likely to surprise, excite, and even intimidate you. You may find yourself torn between wishing to keep things "normal" by not making undue fuss over what your talented child can do, and trying to respect that talent by providing everything possible to promote it. It is not easy to maintain a balance that benefits your child without either spoiling or overwhelming her.

The young talented child needs
- encouragement and support.
- chances to choose what is of interest.
- help with practice.
- tangible rewards.
- time to play with friends.
- calm assistance with performances.
- to hear music as well as play it.
- to attend music and arts events.

Do not make the mistake of thinking that just because your child is talented, he will not need to be reminded to practice or helped while doing so. Often because many things come easily to such a child, he may never experience what it means to work in order to succeed, and is likely not to form good practice habits unless given both guidance and encouragement. It is also important for this child to have some choice in following what attracts him. An early interest in playing the piano may change to a fascination with composing, playing the oboe, or putting on neighborhood musicals. While arbitrary change of focus or instrument is not wise, neither is insistence on sticking with a certain instrument just because it was the original choice (which may not have been the child's).

Don't be concerned if, musically, your child is way ahead of you either in knowledge or skill. It is not necessary for you to be musical or to play an instrument yourself in order to provide what your child needs—guidance in how to manage time and energy, or how to cope with criticism and praise. A talented child is one who often reacts in extremes and mood swings. Because you are more experienced, you

Talent is best viewed as a developmental rather than as an all-or-nothing phenomenon. It is a process that unfolds over many years rather than a trait that one inherits and then keeps unchanged for the rest of life.
—*Mihaly Csikszentmihalyi, Kevin Rathunde, and Samuel Whalen*

Gifted kids may be one age emotionally, another age physically, and still another age intellectually.
—*Sally Walker*

can help your child sort out what the issues of real importance are. A talented child may also be a perfectionist, not only musically but in other areas as well. He may feel that he must succeed or be the best in everything just as when he plays or sings. This tendency can be especially dangerous if *you* are also a perfectionist, or if your child is made to feel that he is loved and valued only for his talent or only when he excels. It is easy for gifted children to confuse praise for the talent as the measure of self-worth.

You may also need to examine whether your child's success means more to *you* than to your child. While you may be willing to admit that some parents seek to live through their children, hoping that the children will achieve in ways a parent couldn't or didn't, it may be difficult for you to accept the fact that you could also fall into the same trap. This is not an issue you confront and settle once and forever. It recurs in sometimes surprising ways and throughout your child's entire development.

Protecting the talented child

A young child who performs outstandingly is charming and unique, and therefore often is the center of attention and adulation. Adults, teachers and parents included, may exploit such a child, parading her around and expecting her to perform on call. While the child does enjoy performing, and the praise that follows, she may begin to feel manipulated, if not abused. Stage mothers and pushy teachers are not fictions. There are so many true horror stories about children subjected to such treatment that it is painful to consider how easily a young child can be made to suffer for being remarkable.

Families differ in the degree to which they sidestep the limelight and also in the ways by which they seek to instill a sense of normality and regularity in their unusual children.

—Daivd Feldman

One of your difficult and most important roles is to protect your gifted child from such manipulation and exploitation. You will often wonder whether your child should perform so much, work with such concentration, participate in competitions, or be the subject of publicity. You and the teacher, you and your child, or you and your spouse may disagree about many of these matters. There are no easy guidelines to suggest ways around these pitfalls or answer the thorny questions. What you should weigh here is *your own* motivation in allowing or encouraging your child's public appearances.

At this point you will be contributing time and money in arranging for lessons, instruments, and extra rehearsals, classes, and recitals. This may involve travel to places in addition to the teacher's studio, and may also necessitate adjustment of the family schedule to allow for the events connected with music study. Other things, such as CDs, software, books, and tickets to concerts, ballets, and museums, will be needed or invaluable to foster your child's talent. You will find that these will enrich your own life, as well as that of the entire family. Paying for these may not always be easy. Supplying the needs of a gifted child may, and often does, require sacrifice of other conveniences or luxuries.

The talented child in the middle years

If your child's talent develops to the point where it becomes obvious that serious study is both necessary and desirable, you will be called upon to contribute in ways that go far beyond your beginning efforts and sacrifices. One of these is likely to involve money. You will probably need to buy a very good instrument for your child. No matter what the instrument, there will always be an upgrade of some kind without which your child will not be able to progress and develop. *Finding* that instrument may cost you as much in time and effort as paying for it when the time comes. Your child's teacher is apt to play a role in this process, usually by arguing for the necessity of having the instrument as well as by aiding you in the search-and-choose process.

A genius happens because his mother worked for the phone company to send him to school, or a grade-school teacher took dirt wages to teach him to write.

—Richard Rodriguez

The talented child in the middle years needs

- a very good instrument.
- an excellent teacher.
- a controlled practice environment.
- time to practice.
- transportation to many musical events.
- a compatible social group.
- support when performing or competing.
- some relief from other studies or duties.

Changing teachers

It is also likely that during these years, you will have to find a new teacher for your child. This may require both financial stretching and diplomatic juggling. A highly specialized teacher will command higher tuition. The appropriate teacher may not be conveniently located, and you may find yourself driving great distances not only for weekly lessons, but for many other events such as rehearsals, auditions, competitions, and recitals. In some cases, the entire family moves to another city to enable the talented child to be near those people and opportunities that will forward his training. (This happens in many fields, not just music—for example, in the training of young gymnasts, figure skaters, or tennis stars.)

CHALLENGING
CHOICES

My mother realized . . .
that I was playing better at
thirteen than most of the stu-
dents . . . and she figured that
there comes a point where you
outgrow the teacher.
—*from* **Developing Talent**
in Young People

The search for, and the transfer to, the new teacher may create another set of difficulties. It is possible that the transition may be smooth. The current teacher may realize that your child needs to move on and helps to locate the new teacher through professional networking. The new teacher and your child prove to be simpatico and everyone is pleased. That scenario, however, is not always the way it goes. The current teacher may not want to see your child move on. Your child may be the very best student she ever had, so it is understandable that letting go is difficult. With or without the assistance of other music professionals, the exactly right new teacher may be hard to find or, once having been found, is unwilling or unable to accept your child. It may also happen that another teacher hears your child, perhaps while judging a competition, and later, in informal conversation, convinces you and/or your child that something is missing, and that the missing something can be provided by study in his own studio. (This practice, although unethical, occurs more often than it should.) You decide to change, and need to find a tactful way to leave the old teacher. Making changes, especially those involving relationships, is a part of life, and the time for doing so often happens within these years. Both you and your child may struggle a little, but consideration and diplomacy can carry the day.

> *When you change teachers*
> • be direct and as fair as you can.
> • help your child write a sincere note of appreciation.
> • avoid criticizing the teacher or "telling tales."
> • be positive and courteous, even if this is difficult.

Your child now needs more time to practice, and to practice under favorable conditions. This could necessitate many adjustments. The entire family might need to accept practice in the wee hours of the morning, or might need to relinquish watching television or activities in certain parts of the house in order to afford quiet and privacy for the practicer. Although many gifted children excel both in music and in school, this is not always the case, and the time given to playing and practicing may require some accommodation with regard to maintaining a reasonable balance between practice and academic study. Practicing may involve rehearsals that could take place in numerous locations. Transportation becomes a scheduling factor. Weekends are often devoted to music-related activities. The commitment of one family member somehow becomes the commitment of the entire family.

The late-teen talent

If your child is in his late teens, most questions have already been answered, and the guidance your teen seeks and needs is provided largely by others. Although you are important in your teen's life, many professional decisions are no longer made in consultation with you. It is likely that you are still contributing heavily to your teen's financial support because a good music education takes many years and much money. You have also had many years of satisfaction and enjoyment as you watched your teen develop. Throughout the struggles and difficulties that lie ahead (and there will be many), you will yet be needed to provide counsel and comfort. Celebrate and be ready!

Terman found that the children in his sample seemed to be slightly larger, healthier, and better adjusted than the children in his control group. He did not attempt to explain why.—Joel Shurkin

The late-teen talent needs
- a master teacher.
- a great deal of practice time.
- a musical "family."
- wise career advice.
- money.
- good luck.

How it looks to your child

It is vital that you also take time to consider what being talented means to your child. Being talented brings satisfaction, of course, but it also gives rise to particular problems and confusions. As a parent, you may wonder if your talented child will be able to enjoy normal pleasures and relationships. Both research and experience show that your child's chances for turning out to be a happy, healthy, and well-adjusted person are above average, contrary to the popular caricature of the neurotic, sickly, and antisocial genius. This likelihood, in fact, was one of the discoveries made by Terman in his elaborate and exhaustive studies.

The talented child is generally aware that he is special. When he is very young, the talent is taken for granted since his limited experience offers little opportunity to compare himself with others. If the child studies privately, and therefore never hears anyone other than himself or the teacher play, it may be a while before he knows that other children cannot play as well, or that some children do not play a musical instrument at all. It doesn't take long, however, for him to realize that he is different, although just what this means cannot be put into words.

As pointed out earlier, traits associated with being gifted have upsides as well as downsides.

Traits of the gifted child

Upside The gifted child is usually	Downside The gifted child may also
• a quick learner. • a concentrator. • an independent thinker. • verbal. • original. • precise. • a problem solver.	• be a careless learner. • have tunnel vision. • be stubborn or determined. • be an introvert. • overfantasize. • worry or try to overachieve. • complicate things.

One can posit a pattern of growth for the young musical performer. Up till the age of eight or nine . . . the child proceeds on the basis of sheer talent and energy . . . but essentially does not expend undue effort.
— Howard Gardner

The child who learns music easily—whether this is a matter of reading music, playing with innate sensibility, or imitating readily—may go many years without "working" at anything. She may practice for hours on end, go through many books and pieces, and strive to perfect details, often with relative ease. It is as if deciding to do something means being able to do it. When the time comes to respond to a challenge, she may not know how to react since little or nothing in her past has forced her to proceed systematically or spend time trying. That is why the talented child must be taught how to practice and guided while doing so. This is obviously the teacher's responsibility, but it also requires some parental supervision of the home practice period.

The need to belong

An important need of the musically talented child is that he find friends like himself, other children who play very well and for whom music is a special love. This seldom happens in his school situation, although he may meet children gifted in other areas. Musical friends can be found in a number of places. Foremost among these is the teacher's studio. Although most gifted children study privately, a studio in which the teacher arranges for group activities offers the best chance for a talented child to get to know others with similar interests. Group activities such as theory and master classes, computer sessions, field trips to concerts, and summer camps enable your child to have fun with others who love music, but they also offer social and musical mirrors in which your child may compare himself to those who may play better or worse than he does.

Writers on giftedness stress how necessary it is for the child with exceptional talent to know that he is part of some group, that he "belongs" and is "accepted." One of the truly wonderful things about musical talent is that it usually transcends factors such as age and race. Older children often accept as equals young children who can play very well or exhibit other musical gifts. Because most studios include a mixture of children with various degrees of talent, it is likely that if your gifted child is young, he will see that he is beyond those his age. He will also hear and get to know some who play as well or better than he does. Although your child does not always make close, day-by-day friends as part of these experiences, he at least discovers a world in which others enjoy making, listening to, and talking about music.

Special schools

There are other ways in which your child can be introduced to a musical community. One of the principal values of having your child attend a magnet, community, or performing arts school is that in such surroundings students and teachers share common goals. It is also likely that a high percentage of the students will be better than average, if not talented. If your child plays the violin, she will see others playing pianos, clarinets, and guitars, and possibly also see children dancing, drawing, or acting. Recitals and arts events will be numerous, varied, and taken for granted. Teachers perform, so there are up-close models and people of inspiration. Visiting famous artists and specialists give workshops and master classes. There is likely to be a broad range of artistic styles represented. Even if your child attends such a school only one day a week for lessons or a theory class, it becomes obvious that the arts world is diverse and dynamic.

There are benefits to you as well. You also will see and hear other children and enrich your grasp of musical realities. You will discover "how things work" among musicians and artists. You will observe various teaching styles as you and your child attend master classes and recitals. You will join a network of parents sharing concerns and interests. You may learn as much as your child.

Summer music camp

Another valuable adventure would be for your child to attend a summer music camp. This experience will be short and intense (camps can offer from one- to eight-week programs), and is likely to be eye-opening and provocative (music occupies the entire day, practice may be supervised, and talent often abounds). Here will be the opportunity to play chamber music, attend high-level recitals, watch master teachers at work, and soak up music at the turn of every corner. Your child will be able to "talk shop" and exchange confidences with fellow campers who know just what he's talking about. A summer camp is often a good place to find out whether to devote a life to music. It can be a pre-professional testing ground.

Music is a passion

In the early years, high potential in (the performing arts) may be evidenced as much by passion as by skill.
—Jacqulyn Saunders

For a child with musical talent, involvement with music is emotionally important. For the child, it is not just a matter of having, or being able to demonstrate, something that sets her apart from others. Music is not something that she knows or does, so much as it is something that she feels and needs. Music is often her chief way of communicating and realizing a personal identity. She cannot put this into words, but this does not lessen the awareness that when playing or listening to music, she is happiest and at her best. It is wonderful to be on a pedestal—the talented child loves the applause—but she would still play and listen to music if there were no rewards or acknowledgement. Gaining approval is icing on the cake. It also contributes mightily to a sense of self-worth. Said one concert artist of the beginning years, "There was an awful lot of praise and an awful lot of attention. Play for the family, play for this one, play for that one. There was so much reward for performing that I've always loved it."

Your child also senses that there are rewards for you. Another artist reflected about his parents, "They would see that I was successful at what I was doing. In other words, when I was playing, people would enjoy it. They would appreciate it. Somehow I just had a talent to do this. That was enough to satisfy their sacrifice in some ways, and enough to satisfy their interest to keep me at it."

Music as an escape

Unfortunately, for some talented children, music is a means of escape. There can be many reasons for this, of course. Spending hours practicing or playing may be what he uses to cope with things he cannot understand or change—parents who argue, siblings who tease, or a neighborhood bully. He may also use music just as a refuge from the noise and disruption of a busy household. This is sound he can control and a world in which he is likely to be unchallenged. Escaping into music is surely better than using other means of avoiding reality, but withdrawal in this manner masks loneliness, insecurity, and perhaps anger. It may be difficult to determine whether your child's fervent attention to music is a sign of bliss or misery. If you are suspicious of hours spent in solo communion with the instrument, you will need to probe carefully and open a line of communication that can help you sort out what is going on. Many times your child will not even be aware that he is using music as an escape because he is, after all, also deriving pleasure from the same means.

At times your child's attention to music can be so absorbing (for reasons other than those just discussed) that you must find ways to divert her from single-minded tasks, such as playing the same piece over and over or pushing for greater and greater speed through technical studies. This is not to imply that you should offer milk and cookies or pull out the roller blades (though there will be times when this *is* the best solution). Music itself can be made to seem diverting. You could suggest that she play a favorite or new CD, tape her own playing and critique it, fool around with a music-related software program, or read a book about music. (Much will depend on your child's age and what interests her.) This might also be the time for you to sit down and play a music game with her. By being inventive yourself you are providing an example as well as a diversion.

An absorbed child might also be helped to break loose by extending his musical community. Speak with the teacher about arranging for some chamber music experiences or other music classes. What may be needed is for your child to enjoy music in the context of a wider social life. This may be a good time for him to become involved in music theater or to accompany a choral group. While these suggestions seem to be intensifying the attention to music, in reality they are showing your child how to make a more balanced, and more personally satisfying, use of his time.

Beware of perfection

While many parents wish they could entice their children to strive for perfection and pay attention to details, you are likely to have just the opposite challenge. The very nature of music study requires concentration and refinement, and the talented child often responds with an intensity and determination that is astonishing. It is evident that rewards (whether stickers, applause, or verbal approval) come when the piece or performance is "perfect" (even though it is admitted that this is never quite achieved). The personality feature that psychiatry calls the superego, the inner monitor and judge that is always on the alert, is very powerful in those who are gifted. The dilemma for them is that without a strong superego they cannot achieve or be successful, and yet, that is the very quality that can upset mental equilibrium or erode self-esteem if it dominates unhealthily.

One of your important roles is to aid your talented child in this struggle. You cannot do so, however, unless *you* accept imperfection yourself and make clear to him that he can make mistakes and fall short of goals—his own or those made by others—without upsetting his world or yours. It is very easy to let perfectionism get out of hand. A gifted child leaps and runs where other children gain ground steadily, and for this reason it is often tempting to keep the carrot far in front, to keep him reaching for challenge after challenge as if he were a racehorse being groomed to win the roses instead of a child who is allowed to experiment, stumble, question, or dawdle just like everyone else. Talented children also hit plateaus. There are downs as well as ups, and times of doubt amidst the shining hours.

The so-called bottom line is simple. You love your child just because she is your child, not because she is a budding Bernstein or a mini-Midori. She must know that she is accepted and cherished as readily when she breaks a glass, loses a tooth, gets a C+ in spelling, or has a memory slip as when she performs with panache, wins the contest, or impresses the world. The gift is not the reason for your love. It is your love that is the gift.

HIGHLIGHTS

☆ Experts do not agree on what giftedness is.
☆ Recent theories of giftedness suggest that:
  • Giftedness includes more than intellectual ability.
  • Giftedness includes ego strength, determination, and creativity.
  • Those who achieve also have supportive family and teachers and good luck.
☆ Characteristics of the musically gifted child include:
  • Musical talents: Pitch discrimination, rhythm discrimination, timbre discrimination, musical sensitivity, psychomotor skills, and desire to perform.
  • Ego strength: Motivation, willpower, persistence, self-discipline, dedication, and single-mindedness.
  • Originality: Creativity, divergent thinking, risk taking, problem solving, intuitive acting, and interest in process.

☆ The young talented child needs:
- Encouragement and support for effort as well as success.
- Tangible rewards and help with practice.
- Time to play with friends.
- An enriched musical world—books, videos, CDs, concerts, and so on.
- Opportunities to choose what is of interest.
- A teacher who is qualified, supportive, and motivating, who will give the child some latitude, and who will not push public performance and competition.

☆ In the middle years the talented child needs:
- A very good instrument.
- A controlled practice environment and time to practice.
- A compatible social group.
- Support when performing or competing.
- Transportation to many musical events.
- Some relief from other studies or duties.
- A highly qualified teacher who is a good technical coach, who stimulates the study of *music* (not just performing), who can wisely guide performing and competing routes, and who can provide good career advice.

☆ The late teen talent needs:
- A great deal of practice time.
- Wise career advice.
- Continued financial support.
- Good luck.
- A teacher who is a master teacher and performer, who is as much mentor as teacher, and who can navigate the professional performing and competing routes.

☆ As the parent of a talented child you must provide:
- Assistance in finding the right teacher(s).
- Support in practicing as well as performing.
- A good practice environment and good instruments.
- Times and ways in which your child can be "normal" and have fun.
- Protection from manipulation and exploitation.
- Financial support.
- Transportation and scheduling accommodations.
- Acceptance of him as a person, with perfections and imperfections.

☆ For your talented child, music:
- Is an emotional outlet and a means of communication.
- Is a means of giving pleasure and winning approval.
- May be an obsession or an escape.

☆ The musically talented child may find a peer group:
- In group activities in the teacher's studio.

- By participating in ensemble or chamber rehearsals and performances.
- As a result of meeting other performers at master classes, auditions, and competitions.
- In a special school such as a community, performing arts, or magnet school.
- In summer camps.

CHAPTER RESOURCES

The resources listed below are appropriate for the type of child discussed in this chapter. Age recommendations are listed only if an item has more narrow appeal. Some items have wide appeal and are listed in the chapter resources of more than one chapter.

Take special note of Part IV, "General Resources," for a listing of books, recordings, movies, games, teaching aids, CD-ROMs, and catalogs.

BOOKS FOR YOU

Alvino, James and the editors of *Gifted Children Monthly*. **PARENTS' GUIDE TO RAISING A GIFTED CHILD: RECOGNIZING AND DEVELOPING YOUR CHILD'S POTENTIAL.** Boston: Little, Brown, 1985.

Alvino has compiled this book from material published in the *Gifted Children Newsletter* (now *Gifted Children Monthly*). The issues examined include defining and identifying giftedness, parents' and grandparents' roles in cultivating giftedness, counseling the gifted child, troubleshooting, and parent advocacy for gifted children. There is a separate section on the visual and performing arts, and music is discussed in detail. An interesting inclusion is the chapter dealing with gifted girls as a neglected minority. The examples, anecdotes, checklists, and bibliographies are helpful.

Bloom, Benjamin S. (ed.). DEVELOPING TALENT IN YOUNG PEOPLE. New York: Ballantine, 1985.

An account of a study by a University of Chicago research team on the development of talented children. Subjects of the study include concert pianists, sculptors, tennis champions, research mathematicians, research neurologists, and Olympic swimmers. The chapters entitled "Learning to Be a Concert Pianist" and "One Concert Pianist" are engaging accounts of conversations with twenty-one pianists and their parents. The focus is on the early developmental years.

Csikszentmihalyi, Mihaly, Kevin Rathunde, and Samuel Whalen. TALENTED TEENAGERS: THE ROOTS OF SUCCESS & FAILURE. New York: Cambridge University Press, 1993.

This volume reports on a study of over two hundred talented teenagers, examining why some succeed and others fail to develop their abilities. The book includes charts and graphs, but the overall tone is direct and friendly. Of special interest are the chapters entitled "What Are Talented Teenagers Like?" (athletes, musicians, and artists are lumped together); "How Families Influence Talent Development;" and "Schools, Teachers, and Talent Development." This powerful book, despite the research appearance, "tells it like it is."

Feldman, David Henry with Lynn T. Goldsmith. NATURE'S GAMBIT. New York: Basic Books, 1986.

A study of six prodigies, boys of exceptional talent, via interviews with the boys, their families, siblings, friends, teachers, and peers. You may be most interested in the chapters that deal with the families, the choice of teachers, and the social and emotional issues in the lives of these boys. This is enjoyable reading, laden with anecdotes and samples of some of the boys' work.

Freeman, Joan (ed.). THE PSYCHOLOGY OF GIFTED CHILDREN. Chicester, England and New York: John Wiley & Sons, 1985.

A compilation of chapters by different researchers, the book offers an international perspective on the subject of giftedness. Of special interest is the chapter on musical giftedness by Rosamund Shuter-Dyson. Other chapters with unique viewpoints are "The Gifted Child As Exceptional" (an overview of many theories of giftedness, including Terman's and Renzulli's); "Emotional Aspects of Giftedness;" and "Evolution of Education for the Gifted in Differing Cultures."

Gardner, Howard. FRAMES OF MIND. New York: Basic Books, 1985.

This book has already become a classic since Gardner's theory of multiple intelligences, introduced in this work, has attracted many followers. Musical intelligence is discussed more from the standpoint of the composer of music than the performer. Gardner speaks of how one perceives music in relation to the functions of the brain, and he also addresses unusual talents, such as that of the idiot savant. While the reading style is friendly, the general tone of the book is serious.

Miller, Alice. THE DRAMA OF THE GIFTED CHILD. New York: Basic Books, 1981.

The author discusses how and why parents of gifted children sometimes foist their own ambitions and dreams on the children. Miller is an advocate for the child, and describes the personal and emotional scars that the child often carries for a lifetime. In many ways, this book shows the underside of what it means to be gifted. This is unstintingly honest writing.

Saunders, Jacqulyn with Pamela Espeland. BRINGING OUT THE BEST: A RESOURCE GUIDE FOR PARENTS OF YOUNG GIFTED CHILDREN. Minneapolis: Free Spirit, 1991.

The authors deal with recognizing giftedness in preschool children, although examples and anecdotes throughout extend the age level. This is very much a "hands-on" book, with lists, cartoons, and photos that lighten up the text. Each chapter concludes with suggested down-to-earth activities. The reading and source lists are wonderful. The section on music (within "Creativity Activities") is brief but accurate. Of special interest are "Making the Most of Your Home Computer" and "Choosing a Preschool."

Shurkin, Joel N. TERMAN'S KIDS. Boston: Little, Brown, 1992.

The author had unique access to the Stanford files of Lewis Terman, whose study of the gifted was extensive and groundbreaking. He provides background into the history of the study itself, but also extensive biographical pictures of some of the "kids" both early in their lives as well as now. This is fascinating reading because it depicts personalities, and shows that some of the gifted succeeded, while others painfully missed the mark.

Walker, Sally. THE SURVIVAL GUIDE FOR PARENTS OF GIFTED KIDS. Minneapolis: Free Spirit, 1991.

This was written as a complement to the several *The Gifted Kids Survival Guides* by Galbraith and Delisle. Information is offered in bits and pieces, lists, and cartoons. The book provides answers and strategies for coping with the problems and challenges of raising a gifted child. It suggests advocacy techniques and ways that parents can influence gifted programs. There is a good question-and-answer section and a useful bibliography.

PUBLICATIONS FOR YOU

GIFTED CHILD TODAY. Box 6448, Mobile, AL 36660-0448. 205-478-4700. Bimonthly.

GIFTED CHILDREN QUARTERLY. Published by the National Association for Gifted Children, 1707 L Street NW, Suite 550, Washington, DC 20036. 202-785-4268.

GIFTED EDUCATION PRESS QUARTERLY. 10201 Yuma Court, PO Box 1586, Manassas, VA 22110. 703-369-5017.

THE ROEPER REVIEW: A JOURNAL ON GIFTED EDUCATION. Box 329, Bloomfield Hills, MI 48303-0329. 810-642-1500. Quarterly.

BOOKS FOR YOU WITH YOUR CHILD

Bennett, Jill. NOISY POEMS. New York: Oxford University Press, 1994.

This picture book of twelve solidly noisy poems by James Reeves, David McCord, Elisabeth Coatsworth, and Jack Prelutsky will surely provoke a robust response. Excellent material for inspiring movement and original music. For the young child.

Chang, Nai Y. AN ILLUSTRATED TREASURY OF SONGS: NATIONAL GALLERY OF ART, WASHINGTON. New York: Rizzoli, 1994.

This beautiful volume presents traditional American songs, ballads, folk songs, and nursery rhymes by coupling each song (vocal line, words, simple piano accompaniment) with masterpiece paintings from the collection of the National Gallery of Art. The reproductions usually occupy an entire page.

Dunn, Sonja. BUTTERSCOTCH DREAMS. Portsmouth, NH: Heinemann, 1987.

This collection of chants comes alive, given rhythmical reading. As texts for creating original songs, they are best presented to children four to ten years old.

Fox, Dan and Claude Marks. GO IN AND OUT THE WINDOW. New York: Henry Holt, 1987.

This collection of songs of childhood is varied in moods and ideas. Each song is illustrated with paintings from the Metropolitan Museum of Art collection. Piano accompaniments require an ability to play melodies with simple chords. Ideal for family sings and for showing the correlation between art and music.

Hughes, Langston. THE SWEET AND SOUR ANIMAL BOOK. New York: Oxford University Press, 1994.

The publication of a lost manuscript by Hughes is an important event in American literature. With fanciful three-dimensional animals built especially for the book by young students from the Harlem School of the Arts, an introduction by Ben Vereen, and an afterword for older children and adults by Hughes scholar George Cunningham, this has potential to become a classic. Three and older.

Kaplan, Burton. THE MUSICIAN'S PRACTICE LOG. New York: Perception Development Techniques, 1985. (Box 1068, Cathedral Station, New York, NY 10025).

This guide to efficient practice gives specific tips and allows one to assess one's own practice profile and keep a practice diary. For serious students or those who would like to improve their practice skills. Highly recommended. For teens with help of a parent or teacher.

Koch, Kenneth and Kate Farrell. TALKING TO THE SUN. New York: Henry Holt, 1985.

An illustrated anthology of poems selected for young people and illustrated with art treasures from The Metropolitan Museum of Art. Presents an opportunity to correlate art, music, and literature. This exquisite book makes a wonderful gift. All ages.

BOOKS FOR YOUR CHILD

Arnold, Caroline. MUSIC LESSONS FOR ALEX. New York: Clarion Books, 1985.

The charm of this book lies in its photographs by Richard Hewett. This is the story of Alex, a little girl who decides to take violin lessons. The text covers the first year of study, including how her instrument is purchased and how she practices and rehearses, and concludes with her first recital. The photographs are of many people beside Alex, and depict with realism and poetry the world of the young violinist. Eight and older.

Beránek, Vratislav. THE ILLUSTRATED HISTORY OF MUSIC. London: Sunburst Books, 1994.

This picture-rich book (color and black-and-white) is not presented chronologically but in interestingly grouped categories such as "Music for Pleasure," "The Stage Resounds with Dance," and "Canned Music." The writing style is friendly and conveys much diverse information. This history includes Schubert and Streisand as well as Handel and "Hair." This is a something-for-everyone book.

Blackwood, Alan. THE ORCHESTRA. Brookfield, CT: The Millbrook Press, 1993.

This is a thorough and broad introduction to the orchestra. The last section depicts a day in the life of an orchestra (in this case, the London Symphony Orchestra), including information and pictures about rehearsals, concert halls, transporting an orchestra, and glimpses into the daily life of orchestra musicians. The graphics, layout, and pictures are outstanding. Most illustrations are in color, which adds to the book's attractiveness. An encyclopedia of information for a bargain price. Ten and older. Could be read to a younger child.

Bosseur, Jean-Yves. MUSIC. PASSION FOR AN ART. New York: Skira/Rizzoli, 1991. The history of art, from antiquity to the twentieth century, is depicted in works that include musicians and musical instruments. Each page offers vivid color reproductions, mostly of paintings and sculpture. The text describes music's place and function in different historic periods, and explains how the instruments and musicians reflect each artist's style, era, and understanding of music. An elegant volume.

Donald, Dave. BACH, BEETHOVEN, AND THE BOYS. Toronto: Sound and Vision, 1986. (359 Riverdale Avenue, Toronto, Canada, M4J 1A4).

The subtitle, "Music History As It Ought To Be Taught," suggests the tongue-in-cheek writing style. Dates and facts are completely accurate, but the anecdotes and cartoonlike illustrations focus on offbeat incidents and information. Only in a book like this would you find out that Haydn's wife used his manuscripts to line cake tins, Schubert's friends called him "Tubby," or that Wagner's pet poodle ran away from home. A good dose of music history in an easy-to-swallow form. Ten and older.

Erlewine, Michael and Scott Bultman. ALL MUSIC GUIDE. Corte Madera, CA: Miller Freeman c/o BMR Associates, 1984. (21 Tamal Vista Blvd., Suite 209, Corte Madera, CA 94925).

Comprehensive and authoritative guide to all genres of music, organized in twenty-seven categories. "Music Map" shows at a glance how a particular music style developed, identifies each style's major players, and traces who influenced whom.

Fowler, Charles. MUSIC! ITS ROLE AND IMPORTANCE IN OUR LIVES. New York: Macmillan/McGraw-Hill, 1994.

Written as a high school text, this beautifully illustrated book is filled with musical examples and suggested listening activities. It covers the full range of music history from earliest times, and includes sections on world music as well as thorough coverage of twentieth-century music. A set of CDs accompanies the text. Expensive, but worthwhile if you have no access to a thorough music history course. Excellent college preparation for the serious music student and family. Fourteen and older.

Galbraith, Judy. THE GIFTED KIDS SURVIVAL GUIDE: FOR AGES 10 AND UNDER. Minneapolis: Free Spirit, 1984.

This brief guide knows just how to talk to this age group. Information about being gifted comes cleverly packaged and delivers good advice (It's perfectly okay to be perfectly imperfect!) and speaks straightforwardly (Being left to wonder about yourself is a very uncomfortable feeling.). There are practical suggestions as well as many quotations from gifted kids themselves.

Galbraith, Judy and James Delisle. THE GIFTED KIDS SURVIVAL GUIDE I AND II. Minneapolis: Free Spirit, 1984, 1987.

These guides deal with attitudes, tests, and growing pains as well as items apt to touch the day-to-day lives of gifted kids, such as the heavy burdens of great potential, friendship and popularity, and even suicide and giftedness. The humorous, "cool" writing style manages to convey good advice very appealingly. Eleven to eighteen years old.

Helpern, Mark. *SWAN LAKE*. Boston: Houghton Mifflin, 1989.

An absolute treasure of a book written in elegant prose by a prize-winning author. The illustrations by Chris Van Allsburg are magical. A perfect introduction to the story of *Swan Lake* as preparation for seeing the ballet and hearing the music by Tchaikovsky. Eleven and older.

Hughes, Langston. JAZZ (UPDATED AND EXPANDED BY SANDFORD BROWN). New York: Franklin Watts, 1982.

A history of jazz from its beginnings to 1980s jazz/rock. Included is information on the African roots of jazz, work songs and spirituals, jazz forms, jazz instruments, and jazz singers, with separate attention paid to Louis Armstrong and Duke Ellington. Major artists are mentioned, and there are a number of photographs. A good way to introduce and/or explain jazz as a separate style. Ten and older.

Kendall, Alan. THE CHRONICLE OF CLASSICAL MUSIC: AN INTIMATE DIARY OF THE LIVES AND MUSIC OF THE GREAT COMPOSERS. London: Thames & Hudson, 1994.

This diary-style chronology is rich in color pictures, photographs, and information. In a clever, but complicated, cross-reference system, the user may check out key people and works; key places; and issues, events, and themes. The intense focus (often on just a few years) helps the reader to appreciate the multitude and variety of coeval events. A great family browser.

Krull, Kathleen. LIVES OF THE MUSICIANS: GOOD TIMES, BAD TIMES (AND WHAT THE NEIGHBORS THOUGHT). San Diego: Harcourt Brace Jovanovich, 1993.

These brief biographies are written with rare charm, partly because they recount very human aspects of the musician's life ("what the neighbors thought" gives you a clue), and partly because these bits of information relate directly to a young reader's life (for instance, the fact that Beethoven liked macaroni and cheese, that Brahms left his clothes on the floor when he went to bed, or that Ives had a cat named Christofina who ate asparagus). The choice of musicians is also uncommon. Scott Joplin, Woody Guthrie, Gilbert and Sullivan, and Nadia Boulanger are there with Bach, Beethoven, and Mozart. This is a quality book. Parents will enjoy this as much as the kids. Ten and older.

McLeish, Kenneth and Valerie McLeish. THE OXFORD FIRST COMPANION TO MUSIC. New York: Oxford University Press, 1982.

Specially designed for young children, this book uses large type, has hundreds of illustrations, and covers all kinds of music including Oriental, African, pop, and jazz music. Six and older.

Nichols, Janet. AMERICAN MUSIC MAKERS: AN INTRODUCTION TO AMERI-CAN COMPOSERS. New York: Walker, 1990.

Biographies of ten American composers, written in a friendly style, that are of interest to young readers. What is most refreshing, however, is the choice of composers—Louis Gottschalk, Charles Ives, Ruth Crawford Seeger, George Crumb, and Philip Glass, to name half. There is a brief suggested listening list, a glossary, and a few ideas for further reading. Ten and older.

Nichols, Janet. WOMEN MUSIC MAKERS: AN INTRODUCTION TO WOMEN COMPOSERS. New York: Walker, 1992.

Biographies of ten women composers who were born between 1619 and 1947. The book offers the young female reader a gallery of role models, and draws attention to the fact that these composers were, in turn, influenced by other musical women and needed their own role models in order to succeed. Included are Fanny Mendelssohn Hensel, Clara Wieck Schumann, Ellen Taaffe Zwilich, and Laurie Anderson. Unfortunately, many of the recordings are not easy to locate. Ten and older.

Onassis, Jacqueline (ed.). THE FIREBIRD AND OTHER RUSSIAN FAIRY TALES. New York: Viking, 1978.

Lavishly illustrated by Boris Zvorykin, this collection of fairy tales, especially *The Firebird*, is an excellent catalyst for a project on Stravinsky's work of the same name. A work like this helps to make the connection between literature, music, and dance. Eight and older.

Price, Leontyne. *AÏDA*: **BASED ON THE OPERA BY GIUSEPPE VERDI.** San Diego: Harcourt Brace, 1990.

Opera diva Price, known throughout the world for her portayal of Aïda, tells this powerful love story of a royal princess from the princess's intimate point of view. Caldecott medalists Leo and Diane Dillon have created vibrant paintings that give characters and events a dramatic immediacy. All ages.

Raeburn, Michael and Alan Kendall. THE HERITAGE OF MUSIC. New York: Oxford University Press, 1989.

A four-volume encyclopedic history of Western music from its beginnings to the present. Combines an authoritative text by leading authorities with abundant and beautiful illustrations. It is written for music lovers and for serious students. Thirteen and older.

Sadie, Stanley and Alison Latham. MUSIC GUIDE. Englewood Cliffs, NJ: Prentice-Hall, 1987.

This comprehensive volume is a resource for students and all music lovers. The scope of the volume is enormous, ranging from early chapters that cover the fundamentals of music to modern times. The last chapter gives serious consideration to jazz and popular music, A set of six audiotapes is available to accompany the text. Especially valuable for serious teenage music students. Thirteen and older.

Tatchell, Judy. UNDERSTANDING MUSIC. London: Usbourne, 1990.

This book is crammed with assorted information. Definitions of musical styles (including folk, ethnic, jazz, rock, and pop), information about instruments, listening suggestions, pictures of performers, and a survey of composers and what kind of music they wrote are presented along with instructions on how to read music. There is also information on learning to play an instrument. Ten and older.

Thompson, Wendy. COMPOSER'S WORLD SERIES: BIOGRAPHIES OF BEETHOVEN, HAYDN, MOZART, AND SCHUBERT. New York: Viking, 1991.

These elegant, richly illustrated books are written by a British musicologist. The writing style is factual but flowing. The human details should appeal to the young reader. Excerpts of the composer's music (always in piano score, and sometimes quite extensive) are included. There is a listing of the composer's works detailed enough to give the reader some idea of the scope of his writing without being overly detailed. Twelve and older.

Van der Meer, Ron and Michael Berkeley. THE MUSIC PACK. New York: Knopf, 1994.

An exciting multimedia introduction to musical creation that allows you to see and hear how sound is produced and turned into music. Fold-out spreads feature playable pull-out and pop-up instruments, three-dimensional views of various instruments, a booklet on musical notation, and an interactive world music map. A 70-minute CD with twenty musical masterpieces is included. All ages.

Venturi, Piero. GREAT COMPOSERS. New York: Putnam, 1988.

The author writes, "This is not a history of music. It is an invitation to understand the works of famous musicians of all time, in the context of the time and place in which their talents unfolded and with an emphasis on their artistic personalities." He has done this with stunning illustrations. Twelve and older.

Willoughby, David. THE WORLD OF MUSIC. Dubuque, IA: William C. Brown, 1993.

This guide to music listening, although written for college-level students, is eminently suited to the serious talented teen who wants a comprehensive view of world music literature that includes traditional, folk, religious, popular, Western European, and world music. The beautifully illustrated text is accompanied by a set of audio-cassettes or CDs. Fifteen and older.

Wolff, Virginia. THE MOZART SEASON. New York: Henry Holt, 1991.

A novel about Allegra Shapiro's twelfth summer during which she prepares for an important violin competition. The reader learns about Allegra's world—the violin lessons, family relationships, peer interaction and competition, and the mysteries and turmoil of growing up. A good example of how music can be a major part of a young person's life. Twelve and older.

VIDEOS

AFRICAN AMERICAN TALENT SHOW. GPN. 800-228-4630.

Uniquely gifted African American youngsters who are studying and planning careers as classical concert artists are showcased in this well-filmed documentary. Comments by several of the young performers on their goals and hopes for the future make this tape especially valuable.

AN EXCEPTIONAL CHILD: MUSICAL PRODIGY. Films for the Humanities. 800-257-5126.

The subject is a precocious eight-year-old whose week includes lessons in piano, violin, singing, tap dancing, ballet, swimming, speech, and harmony. The tape follows her typical week, and we hear from both her parents. The tape could be of interest to students eight to eleven years old who might see new possibilities of using time as they observe a highly motivated child in action. Eight and older.

THE COMPETITION. GPN. 800-228-4630.

Investigates competitions as an important learning experience and an opportunity for self-evaluation. Young performers on the violin, piano, and flute are featured.

CONCERTO! SH Productions Inc. 800-336-1820.

In this three-tape series, pianists Claude Frank, Lillian Kallir, and their daughter, violinist Pamela Frank, each rehearse a Mozart concerto with an orchestra conducted by Ian Hobson. A unique feature is the dialogue between the performers and conductor as they make decisions on how to perform these works. Especially valuable for teenagers who are working on concerto literature. Spirited performances.

CRITICAL STAGES. Video Phases, 1250 Hanley Industrial Court, St. Louis, MO 63144. 314-963-8840.

This video won an Emmy for outstanding writing. It portrays gifted students and their teachers. The facts of musical life, from the initial stages of finding the right instrument and teacher, to the changing circumstances of study, to the realities of career-building are all well documented. Passionate student performances at each critical stage make a thought-provoking and inspiring video.

DIGITAL MUSICAL INSTRUMENTS AND THE WORLD OF MIDI. Red Pohaku Productions, 1621 Dole Street #100, Honolulu, HI 96822.

A clear demonstration for the novice of the world of MIDI. Defines controller, MIDI, patch, multitimbral, port, sequencer, tone module, track, and other pertinent items. Joseph Rothstein is the articulate presenter.

THE FIDDLE SHOW. GPN. 800-228-4630.

Master artist/teacher Joseph Gingold, a young performer, and a group of violin students demonstrate agility and fitness necessary to make music with the violin.

FOUR AMERICAN COMPOSERS: JOHN CAGE. Mystic Fire Video. 800-292-9001.

For those wishing to gain insight into the music of the twentieth century, this extremely well-made tape will be a revelation. Cage has profoundly influenced musical and performance art. This videotape covers the wide scope of his experiments and the range of his influence. The other composer portraits in the series are of Philip Glass, Meredith Monk, and Robert Ashley.

MUSIC ANIMATION MACHINE. Stephen Malinowski. 510-235-7478.

As you listen to the music, you see a graphic color representation of how the music is structured and contoured. These conceptual elements take shape before your eyes. There is nothing quite like this presentation, and even sophisticated musicians are captivated. The music is all classical. Children who play beyond beginning levels would get the most out of this approach. Ten and older.

NELITA TRUE AT EASTMAN: PORTRAIT OF A PIANIST. Volumes 1–4. Alfred Publishing Company. 800-292-6122.

This four-volume series will be helpful to serious piano students as they observe this charismatic teacher in action. Volume 1: *Portrait of a Pianist-Teacher.* Volume 2: *The Studio Lesson.* Volume 3: *Technique through Listening.* Volume 4: *Principles of Style for the Young Pianist.*

ORCHESTRA! INTRODUCTION TO THE ORCHESTRA. UPPER STRINGS. LOWER STRINGS. BRASS. PIANO. PERCUSSION. MAESTRO. THE ART OF CONDUCTING. Films for the Humanities. 800-257-5126.

Conductor Sir Georg Solti and Dudley Moore introduce viewers to the instruments. The orchestra is comprised of talented young people from around the world. The young musicians discuss their reasons for choosing a particular instrument. A splendid opportunity to hear all the instruments separately and together. The tone is informal, the dress is casual, and Moore is entertaining. Ten and older.

THE PERFORMER PREPARES: 100% COMMITMENT. Pst . . . Inc. 214-991-7184.

A Robert Caldwell performance workshop based on the book of the same name. Deals with ways of overcoming performance anxiety.

THE PIANO SHOW. GPN. 800-228-4630.

Features three young pianists in different stages of musical development who excel in different musical styles. A fourth pianist provides a stunning example of what discipline and hard work can accomplish. Concert pianist Leon Fleisher is a special guest.

PROKOFIEV: THE PRODIGAL SON. Films for the Humanities. 800-257-5126.

A breathtaking portrait of one of the twentieth century's musical giants. Superb musical performances are interwoven with film clips of the life and times of the composer and dramatic presentation of events from his life. A thoroughly professional production.

THE TROUT: AN HISTORIC COLLABORATION OF DANIEL BARENBOIM, ITZHAK PERLMAN, PINCHAS ZUCKERMAN, JACQUELINE DU PRÉ, AND ZUBIN MEHTA. Teldec Video. 212-399-7782.

The rehearsal interplay among these great musicians is as beguiling as the actual performance of one of Schubert's greatest works.

CD-ROMs

Call the telephone number of each company to ask for a catalog. Check system requirements before ordering. Ask for a try-before-you-buy arrangement.

ALL MY HUMMINGBIRDS HAVE ALIBIS. The Voyager Company. 800-446-2001.

Morton Subotnick, a leading contemporary composer, speaks informally about two of his works and lets the user join him on an exploration of how the title work and *Five Scenes from an Imaginary Ballet* were created. Five musical "scenes" accompany the images and text by Max Ernst. For the sophisticated user who wants to be in touch with the use of technology in composition. Macintosh.

CD TIME SKETCH: COMPOSER SERIES. Electronic Courseware Systems. 800-832-4965.

This four-disc series includes: *A Portrait of Bach: Toccata and Fugue In D Minor; A Portrait of Beethoven: Symphony #5; A Portrait of Brahms: Symphony #3;* and *A Portrait of Mozart: Symphony #40.* Each disc includes a performance in addition to the analysis of the work. Although designed for music education instructors, serious teens and adults will find these valuable. For Macintosh and IBM/PC.

A GERMAN REQUIEM: THE GREATEST CHORAL WORK OF THE ROMANTIC ERA. Time Warner New Media. 800-482-3766.

English and German texts. The user can see an analysis while listening to the score and explore the background of this Brahms masterwork.

MULTIMEDIA BEETHOVEN: THE NINTH SYMPHONY. Microsoft. 800-426-9400.

Explore the structure, the instruments, and the cultural, social, and political events that surrounded Beethoven as he created the Ninth Symphony. You can hear and see the score, clicking the mouse at any point to investigate the work from a number of points of view. Macintosh and Windows. Fourteen and older.

MULTIMEDIA MOZART: THE DISSONANT QUARTET. Microsoft. 800-426-9400.

Listen to individual instruments of the quartet, noting how they function alone and how they blend to create the whole. Browse the historic background of eighteenth-century Europe in this video, audio, and encyclopedic world. Macintosh and Windows. Fourteen and older.

MULTIMEDIA STRAVINSKY: THE RITE OF SPRING. Microsoft. 800-426-9400.

An innovative ballet gave *The Rite of Spring* visual expression. Explore the dance background, and the artistic milieu that influenced its creation. The musical exploration is imaginatively done by Robert Winter. Macintosh and Windows. Fourteen and older.

MULTIMEDIA STRAUSS: THREE TONE POEMS. Microsoft. 800-426-9400.

The Cleveland Orchestra performance of tone poems of Richard Strauss (*Don Juan, Death and Transfiguration,* and *Till Eulenspiegel)* is the core of this CD-ROM. The accompanying information includes "Inside the Score," "Pocket Audio Guide," "Master Orchestrator," and "The Prankster Game," based on *Till Eulenspiegel,* in which the listener is challenged to match themes. Macintosh and Windows. Fourteen and older.

MYST. Broderbund Software. 415-382-4400.

This interactive disc allows for intuitive virtual exploration and problem solving. Graphics are stunning and sound is used in intriguing ways. It is for those who enjoy paying attention to detail, collecting information, and solving mysteries. Macintosh and Windows.

THE ORCHESTRA: THE INSTRUMENTS REVEALED. Time Warner New Media. 800-482-3766.

Based on Benjamin Britten's *The Young Person's Guide to the Orchestra,* this program invites the user to see and hear the instruments of the orchestra and learn how they are played. Also included: a conducting lesson, an orchestration lab, a pronouncer, biographical information, a glossary, and a time line. Macintosh. Ten and older.

PUPPET MOTEL: LAURIE ANDERSON WITH HSIN-CHIEN HUANG. The Voyager Company. 800-446-2001.

Navigate a world saturated with performance artist Laurie Anderson's dynamic presence and interact in a variety of ways. Play four "juiced-up" electronic violins, connect the dots to create your own constellation, and hear performances of *Down In Soho* and excerpts from *Stories From The Nerve Bible.*

ROCK, RAP, AND ROLL. Paramount Interactive. 415-812-8200.

A colorful, easy-to-use CD-ROM in which the user assigns instruments, vocals, and sound effects to the keyboard and screen. The user can add his own voice and sing along.

SO I'VE HEARD. The Voyager Company. 800-446-2001.

A sweep through the masterpieces of Western classical music with music critic Alan Rich. This five-volume series combines essays and illustrations for the eye and ear in dozens of art works and audio examples. Volume 1: *Bach and Before.* Volume 2: *The Classical Ideal.* Volume 3: *Beethoven and Beyond.* Volume 4: *Romantic Heights.* Volume 5: *Here and Now.*

ORGANIZATIONS

None of the organizations listed is concerned specifically with music (or performing arts) talent, but some have experts in these areas, and their publications and newsletters contain occasional articles on this subject.

American Association for Gifted Children. c/o Talent Identification Program, Duke University, 1121 West Main Street, Suite 100, Durham, NC 27701. 919-683-1400.

Association for Gifted and Talented Students. Northwestern State University, Natchitoches, LA 71497. 318-357-4572.

Council for Exceptional Children. The Association for the Gifted, 1920 Association Drive, Reston, VA 22091. 703-620-3660.

Gifted Child Society, Inc. 190 Rock Road, Glen Rock, NJ 07452. 201-444-6530.

National Association for Gifted Children. 1707 L Street NW, Suite 550, Washington, DC 20036. 202-785-4268.

World Council for Gifted and Talented Children. University of Toronto, Faculty of Education, 371 Bloor Street W., Toronto, ON, Canada M5S 2R7. 416-978-8029.

For associations for parents of gifted children listed by state, see Jacqulyn Saunders' *Bringing Out the Best* in Books for You above.

The Child with Special Needs

What you will find in this chapter

- Music therapy
- Trying to sort through labels and priorities
- Some basic hints
- The child with physical limitation

  Adapting instruments. Making movement easier. Listening and singing.
- The child with cognitive limitation

  Music as a language.

  Choosing instruments for the child with learning limitation.
- The child with a hearing loss

  Developing residual hearing. Music and hearing aids.

  Choosing instruments for the child with a hearing loss.
- The partially sighted or blind child

  Choosing instruments for the partially sighted or blind child.
- The child with a learning disability

  Multiple intelligences. The active child. The good side.
- Beyond this chapter
- Highlights
- Chapter resources

*I*F *YOU* have a child with special needs, you are busy coping with many adjustments to help him get through an ordinary day. You are probably meeting with medical and educational experts, who provide opinions and assistance that aid you in understanding your child's needs and challenges. None of these specialists, nor you yourself, are likely to give much thought to how music might contribute to your child's happiness and growth. Music is often regarded as an extra and, for children with special needs, an extra that may seem to be only remotely useful. It is important to remember that all children respond to music and enjoy taking part in activities that include it. A child with special needs is no different.

As you consider whether, and how, music may play a role in your child's life, keep in mind that, although some general recommendations are possible (and that is about the limit of what we offer in this chapter) the real focus must be on the needs of your own child. Her age, the home environment, and her specific physical and mental abilities determine what will be possible and useful for her as an individual. The variety of disabilities, and the complex way in which these are identified and dealt with, is as impressive as it is bewildering. Challenges faced by a child with Down syndrome are not those confronted by one with dyslexia. A child with hearing impairment trusts the use of different senses than a child who is blind. Here, more than anywhere, a child must be seen as unique. The course of action taken to aid each child is indeed a special education.

It may be encouraging, however, to know at least some of the ways that music may influence your child's development. Music therapists and educators have designed instruments and provide activities that enable children who are challenged in various ways to make and enjoy music. Even children with hearing impairments need not be denied access to the pleasures music offers.

This chapter can present only a limited sketch of what is available. Our main concern is to alert you to possibilities, organizations, and resources. Teaching music to children with special needs requires its own expertise, and you need to locate someone near you who can work with you to provide both guidance and instruction that will fit your child's particular circumstances.

Music therapy

We urge you to seek professional counsel early on. Your best move is to contact a music therapist. These are musicians trained to use music to influence changes in behavior as well as to work toward specific rehabilitative or therapeutic goals. A degree in music therapy provides intensive education in both music and medicine, and includes clinical training much like that of medical professionals.

The resources at the end of this chapter list professional music therapy associations which can provide you with local contacts as well as other information. You may already be working with special education teachers in your school district, and they are also likely to know how to help you contact a music therapist. Check your phone book, especially for county and city health care agency headings, and you will find listings such as "Children and Youth Services." Your neighborhood librarian can also assist you in researching useful resources. The music department in your local college may be able to offer a few practical leads, particularly if you ask to speak to someone in music education. Some colleges offer degrees in music therapy, and your local college may be one of these, or may be able to help you contact a college in the vicinity that has such a program.

Trying to sort through labels and priorities

It is likely that you already know a good bit about your child's disability. You learned this as a result of what was probably a painful process of examinations and tests. You have had to face your own personal difficulties in recognizing and ultimately accepting realities about your child. For many parents this journey involves periods of confusion, denial, guilt, and anger. Issues you face and the decisions you must make are often critical and stressful. It is far beyond the scope of this book to offer direct assistance to help you in this process. We can, however, point to ways in which, by encouraging and supporting your child, you may sort through your own priorities and gain a sense of direction.

When you first learn your child has a disability, you are starting at square one, but you will end up as an expert, capable of teaching others.
—Mark Batshaw, M.D.

Your child's condition is often given a name, a label, usually by the medical and educational specialists that you consult, or who work with your child. Identification of your child's condition may make it possible for him to receive treatment and educational services or obtain equipment enabling him to function with greater ease. But the label often changes into a stigma, and can sometimes be as much of a drawback as a source of information.

Dealing with labels is cumbersome, but if that were the only disadvantage, arguments against using labels would crumble. The harsher reality is that labels are often imperfect or restrictive. Even sadder is the fact that many children are mislabeled. The label, however, seems to stick, and the child can never get past what the label represents. As we recommend ways that music can be used as part of your child's special education, keep in mind that, although we may sometimes refer to commonly accepted labels, we do not assume that these categories are beyond argument.

Some basic hints

General advice can be given with regard to effective special education.

> ### *If you have a child with special needs*
> - learn as much as you can about your child's condition.
> - provide a safe and comfortable environment.
> - be sure to include time out for rest and relaxation.
> - be natural; avoid overprotection.
> - avoid negativity; positive comments build confidence.

> ### *When you work with your child*
> - realize that repetition may be necessary and important.
> - remove sounds and objects that might be distracting.
> - establish routines and cues that your child can rely on.
> - activate several senses, but not necessarily at once.

Because your child may need to interact with several people—a medical practitioner, special education teachers, perhaps a music teacher, and family members—the greater the similarity among the activities, routines, and cues used by all these individuals, the more likely it is that your child will succeed and become confident. Always remember, however, that each program must be fine-tuned to meet a child's unique needs. *Your child* might appreciate different stimuli. You are the constant in your child's life, so you bear the chief responsibility for synchronizing these various interactions.

In the discussion that follows, the groupings describe the limitation, impairment, or disorder rather than the names of particular conditions or diseases. We refer to physical limitation, for example, realizing that children with conditions as different as epilepsy, ataxia, spina bifida, and muscular dystrophy as well as children with Down syndrome or various degrees of mental retardation may each have some difficulty with motor skills and coordination. The suggestions referring to physical limitation, therefore, offer leads about music and movement that are generalized. Your child's specific condition must be considered. Some suggestions will be useful, some might work with adaptation, and a few might not be possible. These are not solutions or quick fixes. The goal is to give you ideas and fire your imagination.

The child with physical limitation

There are many types of motor disabilities that might relate to making music. Your child may have difficulty swaying or beating drums (gross motor movements), she may have trouble holding a pick or pushing down piano keys (fine motor coordination), she may not be able to play single piano keys or cover holes on a wind instrument (precise motor movements), or she may lack the energy to carry a drum or hold up a tonette (limited strength or endurance). But within that spectrum of

possibilities there are some things your child *can* do, just as there are many ways to help her use her body, no matter what her physical limitation.

Physical limitation may also result from an accident. Sometimes the degree of rehabilitation is uncertain in the early days of the recovery, and being able to play music, in whatever fashion, may contribute importantly not only to the outcome of the rehabilitation, but to the outlook and emotional well-being of the person injured. When he was quite young, Craig Chaquico, the former Starship electric lead guitar man, was in a serious accident that left him nearly immobile. A "guitar" of sorts was contrived to enable him to strum with one finger. By his own admission and testimony, this saved his spirit and kept him "reaching." Wherever Chaquico now tours, he always takes time to visit hospitals where injured children are recuperating, playing for them and often seeing to it that small guitars are added to the "medicine." Making music is a powerful motivator and curative.

> ### Do you know that
> - straps can be attached to fingers, palms, heads, wrists, and feet in order to play many percussion instruments?
> - clamp-on and bicycle-grip holders can be attached to many wind instruments to help hold the instrument?
> - bilateral handles and springs can be attached to bells and shakers to make them playable with minimum movement?
> - stands, frames, and tables are designed to angle and support instruments in order to make them easy to reach and hold?
> - picks of various sizes can be attached to dowels, straps, gloves, and thimbles to make strumming possible or easier?

Adapting instruments

Many adjustments and adaptations enable even a child with a more severe disability to play a wide variety of musical instruments. There are two especially useful resources that you might wish to consult. Barbara Elliott discusses specific and detailed physical requirements—such as major muscle groups, major/minor joints, muscle strength, speed, dexterity, respiration, cardiac output, vision—needed to play the standard instruments. The photographs show the playing positions required by many of the instruments. Clark and Chadwick provide a catalog of adaptations that can be used together with an assortment of instruments. All the adaptations are either photographed or illustrated, and the sources for the equipment identified. Each adaptation is described, and there is an explanation of how it is used. It is important, of course, that the choice of instrument, or use of an adaptation, be done in consultation with either a medical specialist, a music therapist, or both.

Adaptations may not be needed; selecting the right instrument may be the key. It may be a matter of choosing a lighter instrument, or one that can be played with minimum, or certain, movements. Electronic instruments, especially keyboards and drum machines, offer additional prospects because these instruments can usually be played with minimum physical strength. With the many choices of sounds and effects these instruments offer, there is the added advantage of having exposure to a wide variety of styles and instrument types.

Making movement easier

There are also practical ways to make many movements easier. For example, a drum surface could be enlarged, scarves or ribbons could be attached to guard against dropping equipment, and moving fingers along surfaces can be eased by using a little lotion to make the fingers more slippery. Scarves and ribbons also extend the scope of a gesture; a little movement of the wrist or finger can make a big effect and, moreover, an effect that is visible. On some instruments, such as Orff instruments, bars or bells can be removed. Having fewer bars or bells from which to choose would reduce the field of attention and would aid a child who has difficulty making precise movements by eliminating distraction.

For a child who uses orthopedic equipment such as braces or a wheelchair, it is important that an instrument be placed so that the child can play it comfortably and without jeopardizing her posture by trying to make inappropriate movements. In some cases, by using an adaptation like a standing or clamp-on frame, the child is able to play an instrument that it would not be possible for her to play otherwise.

Because a child with some physical limitation may have trouble sensing the bodily symmetrical feel that most of us take for granted—for example, the give-and-take involved in walking or swaying—he may be aided in a number of ways: by using songs that include movement or action, by "walking" his fingers, by being placed between cloth supports held by two people who gently swing him in time to the music or beat, or by wheelchair dancing. In some cases, moderate tempos and less complex rhythms are more successful than tempos that are either fast or slow or rhythmic patterns that use quickly repeated beats or notes. Each child, however, has ways of letting you know what works best for him, or what type of music he enjoys. It is also important to remember that a child with physical limitation needs adequate time for resting and relaxing between activities. Time-out periods may be aided by using calming music or recorded nature sounds.

Listening and singing

Listening to music and singing are further ways to involve a child with music and movement. Not only is a child stimulated by joining in singing, but also the lung capacity can be developed by using good breathing techniques. Many children with physical handicaps, especially those who use braces or wheelchairs, tend to slump, which reduces the space in the chest cavity. Singing, or at least making sound effects with the mouth, helps a child to use his lungs in addition to providing an outlet for his energy and expression.

Listening to music provides pleasure, relaxation, and distraction, just as it would for anyone. But for the child with special needs, music is also a link to an external world, one which he often feels is remote or threatening. A child with a physical handicap has less opportunity to interact with other children in ways that most children do when they play, explore, or even fight. Listening to music that is popular with other children, singing in a group, or playing an instrument as part of an ensemble has important overtones in the areas of social development and the building of a better self-image. This, more than anything else, may be the driving force behind getting your child involved with music.

Individual children are often drawn to different facets of musical-emotional experience, finding in the inherent qualities of certain songs something of an answer to their personal emotional needs.

—Paul Nordoff and Clive Robbins

The child with cognitive limitation

As with other disabilities, there are various degrees of cognitive limitation. Generally such a limitation is referred to as retardation, but the term is extremely broad and the means of defining degrees of retardation are sometimes disputed. Retardation refers to a slowing up of the developmental process, and usually this is reflected in a number of areas—social, physical, and behavioral—as well as mental. It is vital to keep in mind that a child with cognitive limitation develops, but at a slower pace.

Ordinarily, distinctions are made by identifying three levels of retardation—mild, moderate, and severe. A child with mild mental retardation has minimal difficulties (the condition may not be apparent until the first few years of school) and has a good chance of developing and reaching a comfortable degree of social conformity. A child with moderate mental retardation has less, but yet passable, motor and communication skills and, for this child, self-help training—especially that geared toward the development of daily living skills and training for supported employment—is often effective. Although the severely retarded child has significant problems, music can often reach and teach this child when nothing else can. It is a quality-of-life consideration.

> ***Do you know that a child with cognitive limitation***
> - enjoys music and the stimulation it offers?
> - could play almost any instrument?
> - does not need to read music in order to play?
> - can sing quite well if the music is in a lower range?
> - can develop attention skills by playing and singing?

Many things not immediately recognized as part of the thinking process—such as noting differences, following directions, coming to attention, and remembering—are nonetheless mental operations. A child with limitation in this area may find it difficult to concentrate, focus on one thing amid several stimuli, or deal with instructions that are wordy. For these as well as other reasons, the child may respond inconsistently or be highly distractible.

Music as a language

If your child is limited cognitively, making and listening to music can help him in a number of ways. Music is a way to communicate, and because it does not use words, it is possible for him to "converse" in this language without needing to deal with intellectual concepts. Attending to sound and making sound himself often enables your child to move toward a more natural and effective use of words. For example, a clapping game in which you and your child face each other and clap each other's hands (like giving "high fives") in time to music is a simple and direct way of getting his attention and encouraging him to cooperate in making rhythmic sounds. Nothing fancy is required. You can use recorded music or you can make up words to a well-known tune; for example, to the tune of "Twinkle, Twinkle Little Star" you can sing something like "Clapping hands, away we go, Clapping, clapping, ho, ho, ho." After repeated clapping sessions, both you and your child will find ways to vary your claps.

There is a lovely book by Elaine Streeter, written as a guide for parents, that is full of ideas for creating a home music time between you and your child. Each activity is explained simply and clearly, and most

Music really does bring people together. There is no reason why this should not be the case between parents and children, especially if other forms of communication are difficult.—Elaine Streeter

activities are accompanied by an action picture using children with assorted special needs. The activities are graded from very easy to more difficult, so you can go beyond beginnings and gain some sense of progress. Streeter uses simple instruments like tambourines, rattles, chime bars, horns, and bongo drums. This is a practical way for you to help your child yourself.

When actions such as clapping, tapping, beating, swaying, or shaking are done to music, these actions become easier because music itself is structured. In this way, a child can learn to anticipate repetitions of short patterns because the music has a beat and the beat keeps going. This does not mean that the results will be immediate or perfect. It is not necessary that your child learn a particular song or rhythm pattern. Songs and patterns are tools that encourage your child to act and to control her actions. They are a means to an end.

When interacting with your child, don't talk—*do*. Give as few directions and explanations as you can. A child who has language difficulties is frustrated by a supply of information. Get your child's attention, and begin by having him explore an instrument or hold a beater. Follow his lead by imitating his actions; take his tempo or pitch, for example. Imitation is itself a type of praise, and he will be more encouraged to act as he discovers that he has the power to initiate actions himself.

If you give directions, use demonstrations, pictures, or models rather than rely entirely on words. The more senses you involve, the more interesting it is for your child. His chances for success are multiplied. Music can be expressed in pitches, beats, movements, shapes, clicks, and rattles, just as in songs, dances, poems, drum patterns, chants, and stories. These are all ways to vary repetitions and experiences. Be sure not to combine multiple sensations since a child with cognitive limitation finds it difficult to pay attention to more than one stimulus.

Choosing instruments for the child with learning limitation

Your child may be able to play any instrument. The possibilities will vary with the degree of limitation and the physical shortcomings that may result from certain kinds of limitations, as well as the instrument that most attracts her. Unpitched percussion—drums, bells, and tambourines, for instance—are good starter instruments because they are small and easy to hold or control. Melodic percussion—such as a xylophone or a set of tone bars—are good follow-up instruments. These instruments are larger, require beaters or mallets, and are generally more expensive. Wind and brass instruments are also possible, although clarinets and saxophones will be easier to play than other instruments in these groups. Electronic keyboards offer a number of attractions. They do not require great effort to push down keys or buttons that control special sounds and effects, and it is the assortment of these sounds and effects that is both appealing and stimulating.

If your child is interested in singing, the first thing may be to establish the difference between talking (or shouting) and singing. This can be done by humming, by singing softly on "ooo," by making siren sounds up and down, by imitating the sound source, and by asking your child to "sing" silently in his mind as you sing out loud. It may also help to use a lower singing range in the beginning. Should he wish, or be able, to join a choral group, this would be as much a social as a music experience, and would pay dividends in fortifying his self-esteem.

No matter which instrument, including singing, is attractive to your child, keep in mind that her ability to *make* music does not depend on her capacity to learn to *read* music. Music-making can be taught by imitation, and this may be the chief, or only, means for your child to make progress. Many children with learning limitation, however, learn music basics and are able to do some independent work. In most cases, children who study music combine learning the skills of playing an instrument with learning to read, count, and deal with concepts relating to the way music is organized. Yet players and singers can derive pleasure and achieve considerable skill without knowing musical rules or definitions.

A child with cognitive limitation has the same need for stimulation, emotional outlets, and affection as any other child. Music may provide a means of arousal just as it may offer a mode of communication to a child who may have restricted opportunities to explore or respond.

The child with a hearing loss

The majority of children with hearing loss have residual hearing; they do not experience a total lack of sound. Responding to music, therefore, is possible and satisfying for them. Here, also, there are degrees of limitation and, once again, labels and types of hearing loss are defined in various ways. There is some agreement, however, that if the problem is located in the middle ear, there is a fairly uniform loss of hearing across all frequencies. When the inner ear is affected, the loss is principally of the upper frequencies. These distinctions are important because frequency—the number of vibrations occurring per second—determines how high or low a pitch is.

> ## Do you know that
>
> - there are signed songbooks—even signing choirs?
> - it is best to use records with male, or low female, voices?
> - headphones on electronic instruments help focus hearing?
> - it is best to place speakers face down on the floor so that the vibrations will be increased?
> - there are music recordings specially produced for the hard of hearing?

Developing residual hearing

It used to be thought that there were only two kinds of people—those who heard normally, and those who could hear nothing. The second group was called "deaf." Now we know that there are all kinds and degrees of hearing impairment.
    —Carol and Clive Robbins

One of the major issues in dealing with a child with a hearing loss is stimulating and guiding the child to make full use of residual hearing. Music may be a considerable aid in this process. First, music encourages relaxation. This is more important than it seems. A child with hearing impairment is cut off from many of the cues that warn of danger or intrusion, such as the sound of a car or someone entering the room. He is often on the alert as a means of self-protection, and this attentive state is apt to be reflected in bodily tension. Just exactly why music is soothing may be a matter of discussion, but it is likely that reliable steady beats inspire a feeling of security. While this is true for everyone, the benefits of such an aid are especially important to someone who may be anxious because of the need to remain "on guard."

Music also aids in the expansion of listening skills which, in turn, promotes development of your child's residual hearing. By using whistles, bells, or drums played out of sight, you can help your child discover where the sound is coming from and how far away it is. On a drum you can tap different kinds of beats at varied speeds and ask your child to walk, skip, sway, or march as the beat suggests. Using the same drum, you can have your child repeat short patterns that you tap, in echo fashion. This last game may be especially easy and useful since your child will be able to watch what you do.

Visual cues and aids play an important role in listening games and activities because a child with a hearing limitation relies heavily on these sensory inputs. There are many ways to help your child feel rhythm. Long and short sounds can be reinforced by showing objects that are longer or shorter (sticks, for example), or larger and smaller (such as cut-out circles). Depending on the age of your child, there is no reason why these cues should not also be pictures or models of notes. Action songs (such as "London Bridge") are another way of reinforcing rhythm which, in turn, stimulates listening. Signed songs are fun and useful for the same reasons. You can make up your own signs or refer to a collection like Warren and Shroyer's *Piggyback Songs to Sign*. Hold a drum "conversation" with your child. Sound and sight will once again be mutually reinforcing and will move you into the realm of using music as a way to communicate.

Music and hearing aids

If your child uses a hearing aid, remember that the hearing aid picks up all surrounding sounds. Try to eliminate extraneous sounds by using a room in which there are few competing noises such as air conditioners, barking dogs, or traffic sounds. Be careful not to play bells and drums too loudly since these sounds are rich in overtones (the reverberations you hear after hitting a gong, for example) and all this is amplified by the hearing aid. Any sound equipment that you use should be as good quality as you can afford. Pay special attention to whether the equipment can produce rich bass harmonics and sounds in the lower ranges. Vibrations are carried best by a wooden floor, and placing the speakers face down on it increases the ease with which your child may feel the vibrations. In recordings that use vocals, it will be easier for your child to distinguish male, or lower female, voices and songs that move at slower speeds. The Music for All to Hear company produces acoustically altered recordings, such as *Christmas for All to Hear*, for the hard of hearing.

Choosing instruments for the child with a hearing loss

When choosing an instrument for your child to play, one that transmits vibrations easily is apt to be the most successful. Drums or handheld percussion instruments fall into this category, as do single reeds such as the saxophone and clarinet. An electronic keyboard may also be a good choice because it can be used with headphones that will help your child focus on the musical sound and, to a large extent, cut out the background noise in the room. An electronic instrument, moreover, includes volume controls that can boost the sound if necessary. Any instrument on which the pitch is fixed (the player does not make or change the pitch in any way), such as a piano or marimba, will be easier for the child who is hard of hearing than one on which pitch results from the player's actions—for example, a string instrument.

A child with a hearing limitation should not be denied the excitements and satisfactions that making music can give. Residual hearing can expand, and your child's hearing will begin to develop when, and

Lip-synching performers not only mouth and sign words to pop hits, but also dance and act out a short narrative. This is the Quiet Zone Theatre, an amateur troupe catering to the deaf and hard of hearing.—Zan Dubin

to the extent, that it is stimulated. For your child who is hard of hearing, responding to music is not just a reward or an extra. It is a valuable resource that you should not overlook. It may, in fact, become a key means of communication and a special language.

The partially sighted or blind child

The idea that the partially sighted or blind are often musically talented is commonly accepted. Most people believe that those with visual loss hear more acutely, and are, therefore, less surprised when an unsighted person, rather than someone with a different disability, can play an instrument. Many blind musicians have achieved celebrity; Ray Charles and Stevie Wonder are two who are currently famous. It is also true that music training generally has been included in programs of study for the person who is partially sighted or blind, particularly if such education takes place in a special school.

This is not the place to confirm or dispute the claim that people with visual loss may be musically talented or inclined. Evidence could be gathered to support or question that position. It is likely, however, that developing a skill based on hearing is regarded as a natural for someone who must use aural cues as a main source of information.

There are degrees of sightedness, from partially sighted to legally blind. Other problems such as those associated with astigmatism or peripheral vision also affect how, and to what extent, someone can see. Just as with any other disability, the circumstances of each individual must be the basis on which activities are designed to aid that person's development. Some of the general recommendations that follow may need to be adapted.

> ### *Do you know that*
> - there is a form of braille called music braille?
> - large-print music scores exist for the partially sighted?
> - organizations make brailled and large-print scores available?
> - there are cassette courses of study for many instruments?
> - adjustable tilt racks can put the music score in better viewing positions?

If your child is visually challenged, you should know that music can benefit him even if it is not your, or his, desire that he learn to play an instrument. Because of the loss and the extent and nature of the disability, your child must gain a sense of space and distance if he is to move with a degree of security and freedom. Music and sound can help him develop better spatial orientation. You can begin with a simple activity, using a drum, bell, or whatever is handy. Guide your child across a room by playing the instrument, asking him to listen to the sound and move toward it, or to follow the sound in different directions. As you continue, you can vary the instrument, the speed, or create short rhythmic patterns to serve as cues for other movements. For example, a trill can signify "turn in a circle," or a short-short-long rhythm can designate "squat on your heels." Moving in this way is an alternative to touching and tapping, and helps to give your child a sense of balance and bodily well-being.

No matter what the degree of visual loss, your child must rely heavily on memorizing when learning concepts and skills. Rote training thus plays a large role in her education. Music can be of service here too. Singing is a memory aid. The alphabet song is a good example. Most of us learned the twenty-six letters in order by singing "A, B, C, D, E, F, G. . ." Setting lists or instructions to a tune helps to capture that information and provides a way to feed it back to yourself. Because the person with visual loss must rely on memory in order to make progress, any aid that music can offer to help store and retrieve data should be exploited. Use nursery, folk, pop, or holiday songs or make up your own. Encourage your child to do the same. You'll both be surprised at the difference this simple trick can make.

Choosing instruments for the partially sighted or blind child

If you wish to interest your child in playing an instrument and neither she nor you know just which one, give her the opportunity to try out several. In each case, make sure she hears the instrument first, perhaps repeatedly, and then give her plenty of time to feel, explore, and try out the instrument on her own. Do not begin by giving instructions or guiding her hands to do specific things. If she is interested, follow up on her curiosities by making suggestions.

You don't have to be a music teacher to take these first steps. Trust your own common sense and ingenuity to use whatever is at hand—bells, drums, or shakers, perhaps even a keyboard or saxophone. Percussion and keyboard instruments are useful because natural gestures quickly and easily produce sound. Doing gets immediate results, and often these results are pleasing and stimulate further exploration. These suggestions are not meant to imply that your child cannot try out a guitar or trombone if he wishes, just that it is more challenging to make the

When I taught a group of third- through fifth-graders in public school, I routinely led my class in a twelve-bar blues rendition of the multiplication tables on the guitar [we called it "The Time Tables Blues"].
—*Thomas Armstrong*

Parenting any child is hard, but special skills are particularly required to parent a disabled child. Just as is true with any other skill, these special skills must be learned.—*John Parrish*

"first sounds" on these instruments. Selecting an easier instrument may be more encouraging.

If and when your child begins to study music, some aspects of the instruction may take more time because everything will need to done by imitation. If your child is partially sighted, he will be able to use materials in large print and thereby help himself to some extent. This may make it necessary for you to provide him with a specially designed adjustable music stand and, while these are available, finding just the right distance and height may take experimenting.

If your child reads braille, she may be able to use music braille. This system uses the same configurations of raised dots as letters and numbers, but there are also many differences. Reading music braille is more complex and time-consuming than reading the usual form of braille, but it offers a means of independent reading. Even with music braille, however, the music must still be memorized. Information about music braille can be obtained by contacting the American Printing House for the Blind or the Association for Education of the Visually Handicapped.

Courses of instruction for many instruments are now available on cassette, as are lectures on musical topics. Electronic keyboards may come equipped with a device known as a sequencer, or a sequencer could be purchased separately and connected to the keyboard. This enables the user to record sounds on the keyboard that can be played back live or on headphones. It also makes it possible to record separate lines of music (tracks) and mix them together or in different combinations. This one-track-at-a-time technique is often the way someone who is visually impaired learns new music.

Perhaps the most important benefit that making music offers your child is social. Being able to sing or play an instrument establishes a special bond among those that do so together. Singing or playing as part of a group, even when the group members don't know one another well, creates a special human connection. Any experience that links a visually disabled person to others is valuable. Those who make music together do not need to see one another to feel that they are part of a shared reality.

The child with a learning disability

These days, learning disability gets the lion's share of attention. What was rarely discussed thirty years ago is now in the spotlight. The rush of information about learning disabilities is welcome, but also perplexing. We now know that this is a complex issue, and there are not yet many plain answers or useful solutions. As a government study observes, "the term 'learning disability' has appeal because it implies a specific neurological condition for which no one can be held particularly responsible. . . . It does not imply a lack of motivation on the part of the child. For . . . cosmetic reasons, it is a rather nice term to have around."

Learning disability is a term used to describe assorted behaviors. While the signs of learning disability—such as poor handwriting, left-right confusion, letter reversals, slow reading rate, and distractability—are apparent, what causes these behaviors is still a subject of dispute among specialists. To what extent these behaviors are neurologically based, and how a person with a learning disability may be aided, is hotly debated. One thing is clear. There is no single condition called "learning disability." Symptoms and conditions overlap and change markedly from person to person.

Trying to define learning disability opens the floodgates. Neurologists refer to dysfunctions of the central nervous system and point to the "hard" signs—tics, muscle atrophy, amnesia, seizures, and so on. Others, including parents, look for "soft" signs, such as right-left mix-ups, poor eye-hand coordination, hyperactivity, difficulty with memorizing, distractability, or inability to distinguish correctly among symbols or letters. Discussing learning disabilities in computer terms is simplistic, but not too far off the mark.

Margie, eleven years old, when asked what her father, a doctor, did, drew circles, which confused everyone. Finally she said, "He does rounds."
—*from* **Succeeding Against the Odds**

Because specialists cannot agree on who is learning disabled . . . [there is] no way of knowing the true dimensions of the problem.—Sally Smith

Your child may have difficulty with. . .

- **Keying in—Perception problems**
  Doesn't pick up sensory information accurately. Confuses letters, sounds, shapes, or directions.
- **Storing data—Organization problems**
  Can't put or keep things in sequence. Has difficulty distinguishing parts from the whole.
- **Finding the folder—Poor short- or long-term memory**
  Forgets spellings, names, directions, or instructions. Loses the train of thought.
- **Print out—Problems with reaction and movement**
  Can't "find the words." Might rather do than talk. Has trouble with handwriting or hitting balls.

Multiple intelligences

The idea of multiple intelligences advanced by Howard Gardner is helpful in this context. His position is that there are a number of equally valid ways to process information; each way has its own strengths and

**CHALLENGING
CHOICES**

*I argue that there is
persuasive evidence for the
existence of several relatively
autonomous human intellectual competences. These are
the "frames of mind."*
                —Howard Gardner

"language." What Gardner calls linguistic intelligence (language mastery) and logical-mathematical intelligence (problem solving) are what
is usually meant by "intelligence." In addition, there are other types:
spatial representation, using the body to solve problems and make
things work, understanding other individuals, understanding oneself,
and musical thinking. Gardner does not present these as ways to explain
learning disabilities; rather, his ideas support awareness of various
learning styles. The difficulties encountered by some learning-disabled
children are that they see, hear, and think in ways that society and the
educational system may not regard as "correct."

When noting signs of learning disabilities (the lists are long), it is difficult to distinguish between learning and behavioral disorders. The fact
that a child is aggressive, dreamy, anxious, or distractable cannot be
attributed to a single or specific disorder. Therefore, the following suggestions about how music may prove useful in influencing certain
behaviors make no attempt to separate causes and effects.

A good music program will offer the child opportunities to learn by
imitation, play or sing pieces, respond to aural cues, experiment, read
notation, create, and make music with others. These skills need not be
learned at once, nor does the learner need to succeed in each of them
to the same degree. The fact that music is able to incorporate so many
learning styles makes it a useful outlet for the child who may have difficulty with the verbal, logical, and mathematical slant of most school
curricula.

One key to dealing with the learning-disabled child is to determine
how he communicates and picks up information most successfully. He
does not have to read symbols, for example, to make music. Let him
experiment with an instrument; watch how he discovers and reacts.
Simple instruments, like a drum, tambourine, or xylophone work well
because sound can be produced easily, and the limits are clear. Sound is
also easily produced on a keyboard, but the scope of the instrument
may be distracting. Use whatever attracts your child. The secret is not in
the instrument, but in the connection between the instrument and your
child.

The active child

You may have an active child who enjoys moving and relating to space.
Use music to control the movement. Choose a recording that is highly
rhythmic, like a march or jig, and help your child find ways to parade
or hop that make sense to her. Using quiet music, such as a lullaby or
simple chant, may be an effective way to help her settle down or listen

more carefully. Action songs (such as "London Bridge") help set up a structure for moving, and repetitive variety songs (such as "Old Mac-Donald") give your child a chance to respond or be creative—perhaps "Old MacDonald" will get a boat, a bike, or a pool. All these contributions are clues to what she finds attractive. Go from there. Exploration, not logic or accuracy, is the point of this activity.

An active child will also find it useful to "do" a rhythm pattern first, perhaps by jumping or clapping. It could then be transferred to an instrument, expressed in pictures or colors, translated into nonsense or bebop syllables, or shown with traditional notation. Sound cues (a drum roll, chord, or a sung, "Come over to me") are often more powerful than words in getting your child's attention. Directions and requests that are simple and clear help a child who has difficulty in processing ideas in a series. For example, "Pick up the drum" is more effective than "Go over to the corner, get the drum and put it on the table."

If your child has tactile or visual strengths, ask him to respond to music by showing its shape, acting out its story, or drawing its mood. Use anything from "Old MacDonald" to the theme from *Star Wars*. For this child, seeing is believing. Don't plan what you *think* he should do, say, or draw; first *observe* what he does, and then encourage exploration or variety. Let him know that he is free to imagine, move, dance, pose, or act, and that there are no correct or expected responses.

Because there are so many ways to relate to music, there is a good chance that your child will be, and therefore feel, successful. This is not the same as saying that she will necessarily excel in playing some particular instrument or decide to take lessons. It means simply that music will exist as a connection to something outside herself that she can both comprehend and manage. Music may also help her to adjust socially. Games played with music usually have clear structures and controls. Taking turns, shifting places, or working with a new partner are built in and thus less threatening or forced. Playing in an ensemble, even a simple one, also creates an atmosphere in which cooperation is more likely to be tolerated because everything seems fair and the result is often applauded.

Adjustments and accommodations may be used effectively whenever the need for them is discovered and acknowledged. One piano student began study at nine years old, but it was only four years later that he was diagnosed as having Tourette syndrome. Throughout those four years, he had struggled with learning the complexities of keyboard study and practice. After learning of the diagnosis, his teacher suggested that he study percussion, electronic music composition, and improvisa-

Many kids labeled hyperactive and learning disabled are spatial and kinesthetic learners. They require innovative educational approaches that make use of art, music, movement and hands-on opportunities.
—Thomas Armstrong

tion. The change was effective. His discernible love of music developed, but the coordination and concentration needed for piano performance were eliminated, freeing him for more "active" response.

The good side

The most sensible and human way to deal with your learning-disabled child is to look on the good side. Whatever her challenges, it is also highly probable that she excels in other skills. As pointed out by Priscilla Vail in *Smart Kids with School Problems*, she is apt to be curious, creative, and energetic. In areas that interest her, she may be capable of intense concentration and grasp concepts rapidly. She may be quick to pick up on patterns and find unique solutions. Empathy for the problems of others is often the counterbalance to her own vulnerability. These are desirable and potent characteristics.

Beyond this chapter

There are certain areas not discussed in this chapter, such as autism, language disorders, and emotional disabilities. This is not to imply that music cannot reach children with such disabilities (in fact, it is a most important tool for just these very populations), nor does it relegate these disorders to positions of lesser concern. The entire area of special education is such a vast network of specialists, professionals, parents, and children that, within these pages, we can only make broad suggestions about how music may play an important and useful role in the context of a few situations.

Mainstreaming can work only when there are expert regular classroom teachers to implement it.—Jill Bloom

Another subject that goes unremarked is the matter of mainstreaming, placing the child in what the law refers to as the "least restrictive environment." Public Law 94-142, The Education for All Handicapped Children, in force for nearly two decades, has shifted emphasis away from providing an isolated education for children with special needs to making room for these children in the classroom. The idea, as Jill Bloom notes, "was to achieve a learning situation as near to normal as was constructively possible." To discuss mainstreaming in the light of music education with sufficient depth and scope to do justice to the idea and the reality would be to step beyond the boundaries of this chapter. For accurate and specific information about this, as well as the other omissions, we direct your attention to organizations and resources that are qualified and equipped to offer guidance.

As the parent of a child with special needs, you are aware that you will need to be active on behalf of your child to a much greater degree than you would for a child with no disability. As you consider options and possibilities, keep in mind that music may be an important resource to stimulate or encourage your child to socialize and communicate. Music, dance, and art can reach hidden places and shed inner light. Your special child deserves the chance to sing his own special song.

HIGHLIGHTS

☆ Music can play a useful role in the development of a child with special needs.

☆ In providing music for your child with special needs, it is wise to seek professional help.

    Music therapists are specially trained to use music therapeutically.

    Organizations dealing with specific disabilities offer guidance, information, and support.

☆ Labels are often imperfect and restricting.

☆ To help your child:

    Learn all you can about your child's condition.

    Be natural. Avoid overprotection.

    Avoid negativity. Positive comments help build a good self-image.

☆ When you work with your child:

    Establish routines and cues.

    Realize that much repetition will be necessary.

    Appeal to different senses, but not at the same time.

☆ Concerning physical limitation:

    There are many types and degrees of motor disabilities.

    Selecting the right instrument plays a big role in determing your child's success.

    Adaptations can be used, making the playing of many instruments possible.

    Make movements easier—use larger surfaces or fewer bells, for example.

    Choose music that uses moderate speeds and less complex rhythms.

    Singing helps to develop good breathing techniques and lung capacity.

☆ Concerning cognitive limitation:

    There are many degrees of mental retardation.

    Retardation is also reflected in social, physical, and behavioral areas.

    It is possible for your child to "converse" using musical language.

    Actions done to music become easier because music itself is structured.

    When interacting with your child, don't talk—do.

    It is not necessary for your child to read music in order to play an instrument.

☆ Concerning hearing loss:

Most children who are hard of hearing do not experience total lack of sound.

It is most important to stimulate your child's residual hearing.

Music helps to develop and expand your child's listening skills.

Visual cues and aids are important in communicating with a hearing-impaired child.

Signed songs are fun and useful.

Place speakers face down on the floor to help your child sense vibrations.

☆ Concerning visual disability:

There are degrees of sightedness and many conditions that affect vision.

Music and sound can be used to help your child develop better spatial orientation.

Songs can be good memory aids. Set lists, directions, and instructions to music.

First let your child explore an instrument. Don't begin by giving directions.

Reading music braille is more complex than using the usual form of braille.

Making music with others will benefit your child socially.

☆ Concerning learning disabilities:

There is no single condition called "learning disability."

Your child may have difficulty picking up, organizing, or remembering information.

There are various kinds of intelligence and many different learning styles.

The key is to determine how your child communicates most successfully.

A good music program offers many ways to pick up information and respond.

Look on the bright side. A child with a learning disability is often curious, creative, bright, and energetic.

CHAPTER RESOURCES

The resources listed below are appropriate for the types of children discussed in this chapter. Age recommendations are listed only if an item has more narrow appeal. Some items have wide appeal and are listed in the chapter resources of more than one chapter.

Take special note of Part IV, "General Resources," for a listing of books, recordings, movies, games, teaching aids, CD-ROMs, and catalogs.

A practical way to begin your search for books and materials is to order the catalog from MMB Music (see "General Resources"). Through MMB, you will be able to obtain most of the books listed as resources, as well as other books and materials. Ask for the *Creative Arts Therapy* catalog.

BOOKS FOR YOU

Batshaw, Mark. L., M. D. YOUR CHILD HAS A DISABILITY. Boston: Little, Brown, 1991.

Primarily a sourcebook for parents written by medical specialists, but expressed in layman's terms, and citing many case studies. It offers information as well as advice. The last sections, written by individual specialists, provide practical suggestions for managing behavior, working with physical and occupational therapists, and mainstreaming your child. There is no specific reference to music.

Birkenshaw-Fleming, Lois. MUSIC FOR ALL: TEACHING MUSIC TO PEOPLE WITH SPECIAL NEEDS. Toronto: Gordon V. Thompson, 1993.

Packed with ideas and activities some of which could be used by parents, even those with no, or limited, music background. After a section on general ideas, the chapters deal with specific disorders, such as mental disabilities, physical disabilities, and so on. Included is a chapter on seniors, and listings of useful addresses, books, records, and tapes.

Bloom, Jill. HELP ME TO HELP MY CHILD: A SOURCEBOOK FOR PARENTS OF LEARNING DISABLED CHILDREN. Boston: Little, Brown, 1990.

Bloom, a professional writer and the mother of a child with a learning disability, provides a vast amount of useful information about learning disabilities. She answers many "How do we find out" and "What can we do" questions, which enable the parent to take action. Bloom offers research data in an easy-to-read style. Listings of national and local resources, guides, and directories are extensive.

Clark, Cynthia and Donna Chadwick. CLINICALLY ADAPTED INSTRUMENTS FOR THE MULTIPLY HANDICAPPED. St. Louis, MO: MMB Music, 1980.

Brief, complete descriptions, photos, and illustrations of how standard instruments can be adapted for people with special needs. The quantity and ingenuity of the many adaptations is amazing and heartening. The extensive section on resources offers lists of companies and suppliers, bibliographies, and a glossary. For music therapists and teachers, but useful to parents.

Elliott, Barbara et al. GUIDE TO THE SELECTION OF INSTRUMENTS WITH RESPECT TO PHYSICAL ABILITY AND DISABILITY. St. Louis, MO: MMB Music, 1982.

Designed to aid the teacher and therapist in selecting an appropriate instrument for a student with physical handicaps. Elliott describes the physical abilities involved in the playing of each instrument, as well as the specific physical limitations that might affect the playing of a particular instrument. Full-body and close-up photographs (of adults) show playing positions on standard instruments. The book is dense with charts, lists, and text, but it offers unique information. A one-of-a-kind resource.

Farnan, Laurie and Faith Johnson. EVERYONE CAN MOVE: MUSIC AND ACTIVITIES THAT PROMOTE MOVEMENT AND MOTOR DEVELOPMENT. New Berlin, WI: Jenson, 1988.

A cassette containing all the music in the book is available from MMB Music. Original songs, for group participation, designed to be repetitive and specific. Each chapter begins with brief commentary on the types of movement involved. The music is in vocal/accompaniment style, and could be performed on a keyboard, guitar, autoharp, or similar instrument. The cassette provides music for those who can't play or read music. Could be used for family activities.

Farnan, Laurie and Faith Johnson. MUSIC IS FOR EVERYONE: A HANDBOOK FOR PROVIDING MUSIC TO PEOPLE WITH SPECIAL NEEDS. New Berlin, WI: Jenson, 1988.

A cassette containing all the music in the book is available from MMB Music. The original songs in this book are designed to stimulate movements such as looking up, breathing, picking up objects, and so on. A chart ranks the difficulties of using common rhythm instruments, from those that require minimum effort but produce maximum sound to those requiring maximum effort. Each song is preceded by a description of how and why to use it. The cassette provides music for those who can't play or read music. For teachers, but also a good resource for parents.

Gardner, Howard. FRAMES OF MIND. New York: Basic Books, 1985.

This book has already become a classic since Gardner's theory of multiple intelligences, introduced in this work, has attracted many followers. Musical intelligence is discussed more from the standpoint of the composer of music than the performer. Gardner speaks of how one perceives music in relation to the functions of the brain, and he also addresses unusual talents, such as that of the idiot savant. While the reading style is friendly, the general tone of the book is serious.

Levinson, Harold N., M.D. SMART BUT FEELING DUMB. New York: Warner Books, 1984.

Compassionately written in easy-to-understand, nonmedical language, with true case histories of countless adults and children, this book provides understanding of the entire dyslexic syndrome.

McDonald, Dorothy and Gene M. Simons. MUSICAL GROWTH AND DEVELOPMENT: BIRTH THROUGH SIX. New York: Schirmer Books, 1989.

This is a music education textbook, but it contains information that parents might find useful. It does a wonderful job of briefly explaining popular preschool programs, such as Dalcroze, Orff, Suzuki, and Kodály. Check your library for a copy. If you can read music, the "Materials for Instruction" information provides many songs and games you could use at home with your toddler or preschooler. There is also an extensive chapter, by Kate Gfeller, on working with the handicapped child.

Michel, Donald and Janet Jones. MUSIC FOR DEVELOPING SPEECH AND LANGUAGE SKILLS IN CHILDREN. St. Louis, MO: MMB Music, 1991.

This short book is written by music therapists as a guide for parents and therapists. It offers brief descriptions of how language and speech develop and how language and speech problems are diagnosed and assessed. There are many songs and activities for many specific speech and language problems. To use this book effectively, you need to be able to read simple, single-line music.

Smith, Sally L. SUCCEEDING AGAINST THE ODDS: HOW THE LEARNING DISABLED CAN REALIZE THEIR PROMISE. New York: Putnam, 1991.

This easy-to-read book discusses what learning disabilities are and how they affect the lives of those who exhibit these traits. Smith founded and directs a Washington, D.C., school for children with learning disabilities, a clinic, and a night school for adults with learning disabilities. Many celebrities have spoken as guests at the school, and the book is punctuated with personal anecdotes and direct quotes.

Streeter, Elaine. MAKING MUSIC WITH THE YOUNG CHILD WITH SPECIAL NEEDS: A GUIDE FOR PARENTS. London: Kingsley, 1993.

A practical book, full of ideas for creating a home music time for you and your child. Each activity is explained simply and clearly, and most activities are accompanied by action pictures that use children with special needs. Activities are graded from very easy to more difficult. Uses simple instruments like tambourines, rattles, chime bars, horns, and bongo drums.

Vail, Priscilla L. SMART KIDS WITH SCHOOL PROBLEMS. New York: Plume, 1987.

Vail's point of view is that the child with a learning disability is often gifted, especially in arts, athletic, or interpersonal skills. Through discussion and case histories, she offers suggestions about how this particular population can be stimulated and supported. The book is practical and accessible. There is an annotated list of resources and bibliography.

BOOKS FOR YOU WITH YOUR CHILD

Bennett, Jill. NOISY POEMS. New York: Oxford University Press, 1994.

This picture book of twelve solidly noisy poems by James Reeves, David McCord, Elisabeth Coatsworth, and Jack Prelutsky will surely provoke a robust response. Excellent material for inspiring movement and original music.

Cohn, Amy L. FROM SEA TO SHINING SEA: A TREASURY OF AMERICAN FOLKLORE AND FOLK SONGS. New York: Scholastic, 1993.

This treasury of folk songs and stories covers the entire history of America from the time before the early settlers to the present. There are generous color illustrations and easy piano scores for the songs. A family browser.

Dunn, Sonja. BUTTERSCOTCH DREAMS. Portsmouth, NH: Heinemann, 1987.

This collection of chants comes alive, given rhythmical reading. As texts for creating original songs, they are best presented to children at the four- to ten-year age level.

Feierabend, John. MUSIC FOR LITTLE PEOPLE. New York: Boosey & Hawkes, 1989.

Feierabend, John. MUSIC FOR VERY LITTLE PEOPLE. New York: Boosey & Hawkes, 1986.

Both of these delightful books have word games, music scored for voice only, accompanying cassette tapes, and charmingly illustrated text describing motions for finger plays and other activities. Two to seven years old.

Hausherr, Rosmarie. WHAT INSTRUMENT IS THIS? New York: Scholastic, 1992.

The great charm of this book is the photography (half in color, half in black-and-white). The color photographs are unique in showing small children of all races playing and reacting to instruments. Black-and-white photographs are shots from "real life" of varying instrumentalists, such as folk singers, country fiddlers, and concert and rock performers. There is minimal text, each instrument being introduced by a question (What instrument looks like a shiny boa constrictor with a wide-open mouth?). The answer and brief overview is on the next page. This is a book to savor for its beauty and quality rather than for its informational content. Read with younger children. Can be read alone by children eight and older.

Hughes, Langston. THE SWEET AND SOUR ANIMAL BOOK. New York: Oxford University Press, 1994.

The publication of a lost manuscript by Hughes is an important event in American literature. With fanciful three-dimensional animals built especially for the book by young students from the Harlem School of the Arts, an introduction by Ben Vereen, and an afterword for older children and adults by Hughes scholar George Cunningham, this has potential to become a classic. Three and older.

Mattox, Cheryl W. SHAKE IT TO THE ONE THAT YOU LOVE BEST. Book and cassette. El Sobrante: Warren-Mattox Productions. (3817 San Pablo Dam Road #336, El Sobrante, CA 94803. 415-223-7089).

Mattox has selected and adapted a wonderful collection of play songs, games, and lullabies from black musical traditions. The audio features performances by Taj Mahal and others.

Schenk, Beatrice de Regniers et al. SING A SONG OF POPCORN. New York: Scholastic, 1988.

This collection of poems vibrates with diversity in its wide range of moods and subjects—such as fun, spookiness, weather, animals, and people. These poems are perfect for inspiring musical responses. Nine of the world's best children's illustrators have each taken a chapter and brought it to life in vibrant color. An absolute treasure. All ages.

Turner, Jessica B. and Ronny S. Schiff. LET'S MAKE MUSIC: AN INTERACTIVE MUSICAL TRIP AROUND THE WORLD. Milwaukee, WI: Hal Leonard, 1995. Book and CD.

This book of multicultural songs and activities illustrates how to make simple ethnic instruments from recycled materials to accompany the music. One song uses American Sign Language (shown in photographs). For each song there is a vocal line, words, and guitar symbols. Occasional use of words and phrases from other languages extends the vocabulary.

Warren, Jean and Susan Shroyer. PIGGYBACK SONGS TO SIGN. Everett, WA: Warren Publishing, 1992. (PO Box 2250, Everett, WA 98203).

This book of signed songs, intended for use with deaf children, uses the American Sign Language and standard pop tunes ("Oh, What a Beautiful Morning," for example). Pictures of the signs, and directions about how to make them, are on the left-hand page; the song texts are on the right. There is no music in the book. For teachers, but also useful to parents.

Williams, Sarah. ROUND AND ROUND THE GARDEN. New York: Oxford University Press, 1994.

Williams, Sarah. PUDDING AND PIE. New York: Oxford University Press, 1994.

Two collections of knee-bouncing rhymes, clapping songs, lullabies, and nursery rhymes with colorful illustrations and accompanying cassettes.

BOOKS FOR YOUR CHILD

The nature and extent of your child's disability will determine which of the suggested books are appropriate. The annotations may help you determine which materials suit your child.

Blackwood, Alan. MUSICAL INSTRUMENTS. New York: The Bookwright Press, 1987.

This slight book gives a quick overview of many instruments, from alpenhorn to synthesizer. The large-size print and writing style is tailored to the young reader. There are many color photographs of various instruments and ethnic groups, from Peruvian panpipes to a pop concert. Six to eight years old.

Greves, Margaret. *THE MAGIC FLUTE*: THE STORY OF MOZART'S OPERA. New York: Henry Holt, 1989.

This picture-book account of Mozart's opera, stunningly illustrated by Francesca Crespi, is intended for the very young. The simple retelling of the story and the jewel-like illustrations bring this great work to life in book form. Four to eight years old.

Rachlin, Ann and Hellard, Susan. FAMOUS CHILDREN: BACH. HANDEL. HAYDN. MOZART. London: Victor Gollancz, 1992.

Delightful personal biographies of each of these composers relating incidents from their childhoods. Well illustrated. Your children will enjoy hearing the stories. At a comfortable reading level for elementary school children. Four to eight years old.

Storr, Catherine and Dianne Jackson. *HANSEL AND GRETEL. THE NUTCRACKER SUITE. PETER AND THE WOLF. SWAN LAKE.* London: Faber Music, 1991.

These beautifully illustrated books give a simple synopsis of each work. For parents who play the piano, there are short musical excerpts of major themes to help acquaint the child with the score. Even without the music, the books are an appealing introduction to these classic works. Four to ten years old.

Willard, Nancy. *THE SORCERER'S APPRENTICE*. New York: Scholastic, 1993.

This cautionary tale about a powerful sorcerer and the servant who misuses his master's magic was popularized in the late 1700s. Paul Dukas based an orchestral work on the tale. Walt Disney later used it in *Fantasia*. Poet Nancy Willard adds her own magic to the retelling, stunningly aided by the beautiful illustrations of Leo and Diane Dillon. An art book in every way. Four and older.

Willson, Robina B. MOZART'S STORY. London: A & C Black, 1991.

This short biography is written in a pleasant, intimate style. There are attractive color drawings and reproductions of paintings of the period, including portraits of Mozart. Six to ten years old.

RECORDINGS FOR SPECIAL NEEDS

MUSIC FOR ALL TO HEAR. RECORDINGS FOR THE HEARING IMPAIRED: BROADWAY FOR ALL TO HEAR; CHRISTMAS FOR ALL TO HEAR; CLASSICS FOR ALL TO HEAR; HEAR WE GO! St. Louis, MO: MMB Music.

Specially arranged and prepared recordings for the hard of hearing. Ranges from normal to profoundly hearing impaired. *Hear We Go!* contains songs for small children.

VIDEOS

AGAINST THE ODDS: LUDWIG VAN BEETHOVEN. Films for the Humanities. 800-257-5126.

The focus in this short biographical film is on Beethoven's ability to compose in spite of his increasing hearing loss. Extremely well produced. Though expensive, it gets its message across remarkably effectively. Eight and older.

DALCROZE EURHYTHMICS WITH ROBERT ABRAMSON. GIA Productions. 7404 South Mason Avenue, Chicago, IL 60638. 708-496-3800.

This is a vivid glimpse into the world of Dalcroze eurhythmics as taught to a group of adults by master teacher Robert Abramson. For parents and teachers.

REHABILITATION, MUSIC AND HUMAN WELL-BEING. MMB Music. 800-543-3771.

Highlights of ongoing music therapy sessions at Goldwater Memorial Hospital in New York City as well as scenes from the 1985 International Association of Music for the Handicapped Symposium.

SIGN SONGS. Aylmer Press. 800-541-9904.

This is an engaging music-storytelling video for both hearing and hard-of-hearing children. These upbeat songs offer creative, irresistible word play for expanding vocabularies in both spoken word and sign language. Humor is the primary ingredient.

ORGANIZATIONS

American Association for Music Therapy. P.O. Box 27177, Philadelphia, PA 19118.

The American Printing House for the Blind. 502-895-2405.

Has brailled music scores and large-print music available.

Association for Education and Rehabilitation of the Blind and Visually Impaired. 206 N. Washington Street, Suite 320, Alexandria, VA 22314. 703-548-1884.

Beach Center on Families and Disability. 913-864-7600 (Voice & TDD).

Has a newsletter and offers materials and tapes.

Council for Exceptional Children. 703-620-3660.

Learning Disabilities Association of America. 412-341-1515.

National Association for Music Therapy. 301-589-3300.

National Center for Learning Disabilities. 212-687-7211.

National Information Clearinghouse for Handicapped Children and Youths. 703-893-6061. 800-999-5599.

Office of Special Education and Rehabilitative Services, United States Department of Education. 202-245-9661.

Very Special Arts. 202-628-2800. 800-933-8721. [TDD] 202-737-0645.

An international organzation that provides programs in creative writing, dance, drama, literature, music, and the visual arts for individuals with physical and mental disabilities. Ask for the Fact Sheet that describes all the projects and programs.

Organization listings also found in the following books:

Birkenshaw-Fleming, Lois. MUSIC FOR ALL: TEACHING MUSIC TO PEOPLE WITH SPECIAL NEEDS.

Chapter Eleven provides useful addresses for several American and Canadian organizations, grouped according to disability. Also included is a short list of useful materials, books, and recordings.

Bloom, Jill. HELP ME TO HELP MY CHILD: A SOURCEBOOK FOR PARENTS OF LEARNING DISABLED CHILDREN.

Deals only with the area of learning disabilities. Appendix A is a very extensive list of addresses and phone numbers of special needs and advocacy organizations, parenting support and information agencies, plus regional and state-by-state organizations serving children with learning disabilities and their families.

Smith, Sally L. SUCCEEDING AGAINST THE ODDS: HOW THE LEARNING DISABLED CAN REALIZE THEIR PROMISE.

Appendix 1 offers an annotated list of organizations, periodicals, pamphlets, and newsletters related to the subject of learning disabilities.

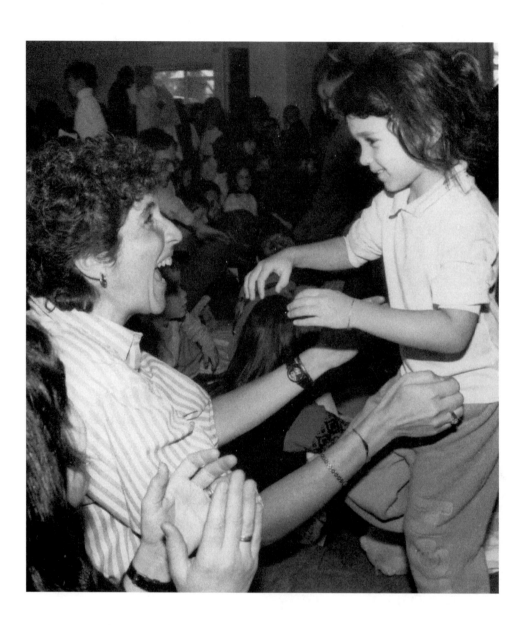

Making a Difference

*Music . . . should be a dynamic, evolving knowledge (and it)
should come from active participation that is shared.*
                                                    —Rena Upitis

*Y*OU ARE giving your child the gift of music—lessons, support, encouragement, enrichment. You are there to assist practice, pay the bills, applaud at recitals, and drive to rehearsals. You believe in what you do and celebrate your child's growth and development. You are enriching the world because you are preparing an informed and sensitive being to live in and react to it.

Stop a moment and consider that world. Imagine what it will be when your child is your age, parenting the *next* generation. By creating its own art, a generation identifies itself with civilizations past and to come. Ultimately, the art, music, dance, prose, poetry, and architecture of a generation are its most lasting and revealing symbols. Why is it, then, that arts education is the neglected aspect of the school curriculum? Why is it that painting, singing and playing, sculpting, dancing, and writing novels or poetry are considered extras—outside the limits of "real life"?

It is one thing to provide your child with arts experiences and lessons, and quite another to help ensure that your child, and all children, see art as a powerful and vital force, not merely as entertainment or decoration. That cannot happen until all children, in each school, learn art by experiencing it as an important part of daily life, just as important as numbers, letters, and facts. By giving children tools for their own pursuit of beauty, we give them not only a means for communicating their emotions, but we also nurture the young voices of our culture.

Exactly what can you do to promote art as part of daily life? We offer a few clues, more in order to show that fostering arts education can be practical and specific than to suggest that these are the best, or only, means to make something happen.

I feel I've been the recipient of a very rich musical education. It's changed my life. I want that for all students.
—Wynton Marsalis

Promote arts education. Join forces with those who speak out for arts education in the schools. Through your PTA, local arts council, or State Alliance for Arts Education, be vocal in expressing your views on the importance of music (and all arts) in the lives of the entire community.

Academic credit for music study. Inquire whether your community has a policy of music study for credit in public and private schools. If your school or school district doesn't grant credit, agitate to make this happen. When schools give credit for music study, they honor student effort and achievement in music as part of the mainstream of learning.

Early dismissal policy. Find out whether your school district allows early dismissal for music study, thereby recognizing that students who are heavily involved in such study need to have lessons and rehearsals during prime learning time, not in the leftover hours when they are tired. If this is not the case in your child's school, explore what can be done to change the situation. Check with school officials, other parents, and your local office holders and congressmen. Enlist their aid in beginning such a program.

Volunteer. Ask your school music teacher or supervisor what assistance you can volunteer to help the music program grow and thrive in your child's school. Perhaps it is a campaign for band funds, costumes for a musical, or CD-ROM equipment. Whatever the project, your school music faculty will appreciate your assistance and be encouraged by your interest.

Support local groups. Support your local performing and arts groups (such as orchestras, art galleries, dance organizations, and theater groups). This shows your child that you believe in the arts as more than a frill. You make the difference not only by your attendance at performances, but also by helping with fund raising and publicity, and by working to bring fine artists to the schools.

Music professionals themselves have formed a national coalition to "focus the nation's attention on the pressing need to include music and the other arts at the center of the school curriculum." The coalition has succeeded in convincing Congress to accept the idea of national standards in the arts, but that alone will not ensure the vitality of music education in *your child's* school. Local needs must be addressed and resolved by those closest to them.

A practical way for you to join that coalition is to send for materials and guidelines prepared by the Music Educators National Conference, the National Academy of Recording Arts and Sciences, and the National Association of Music Merchants. You can obtain from the Music Educators National Conference its "Action Kit for Music Education." It includes videotapes, the report of the National Commission on Music Education ("Growing Up Complete"), several brochures, and a practical guide called *Building Support for School Music* (see Chapter Six, "Resources"). The guide tells you how to organize, analyze your situation, plan strategy, communicate with decision makers, enlist allies, use the media, and evaluate progress. Although the guide is designed as a

A grounding in the arts will help our children to see, to bring a uniquely human perspective to science and technology. In short, it will help them as they grow smarter to also grow wiser.
—Robert E. Allen
Chairman and CEO, AT&T

tool for music educators, parents can profit equally from its suggestions and ideas.

By your "sound choice" in giving your child the gift of music, you have taken an important step in molding a part of the cultural future. Now go beyond that first step. Become an art-world sojourner. Your dedication to helping create a culturally rich community will resonate far beyond your own family circle.

PART FOUR

GENERAL
RESOURCES

BOOKS FOR YOU

Numbers in bold type indicate the chapters in which the books are reviewed. Please see "Chapter Resources" of cited chapter.

Alvino, James and the editors of Gifted Children Monthly. PARENTS' GUIDE TO RAISING A GIFTED CHILD: RECOGNIZING AND DEVELOPING YOUR CHILD'S POTENTIAL. Boston: Little, Brown, 1985. **8**

Andress, Barbara (ed.). PREKINDERGARTEN MUSIC EDUCATION. Reston, VA: Music Educators National Conference, 1989. **1**

Armstrong, Thomas. AWAKENING YOUR CHILD'S NATURAL GENIUS: ENHANCING CURIOSITY, CREATIVITY, AND LEARNING ABILITY. Los Angeles: Tarcher, 1991. **1, 2, 3, 6**

Batshaw, Mark. L., M. D. YOUR CHILD HAS A DISABILITY. Boston: Little, Brown, 1991. **9**

Bigler, Carole L. and Valerie Lloyd-Watts. MORE THAN MUSIC: A HANDBOOK FOR TEACHERS, PARENTS, AND STUDENTS. Athens, OH: Ability Development, 1979. **1, 2, 3**

Birkenshaw-Fleming, Lois. MUSIC FOR ALL: TEACHING MUSIC TO PEOPLE WITH SPECIAL NEEDS. Toronto: Gordon V. Thompson, 1993. **9**

Bloom, Benjamin S. (ed.). DEVELOPING TALENT IN YOUNG PEOPLE. New York: Ballantine, 1985. **8**

Bloom, Jill. HELP ME TO HELP MY CHILD: A SOURCEBOOK FOR PARENTS OF LEARNING DISABLED CHILDREN. Boston: Little, Brown, 1990. **9**

Canter, Lee and Lee Hausner. HOMEWORK WITHOUT TEARS. New York: Harper & Row, 1987. **2, 3**

Caviezel, Sandy et al. DIRECTORY OF SUMMER MUSIC PROGRAMS. 6716 Eastside Drive, NE, Tacoma, WA 98422. 206-927-3269. **4**

Chroninger, Ruby. TEACH YOUR KIDS ABOUT MUSIC. New York: Walker, 1994. **1, 2**

Clark, Cynthia and Donna Chadwick. CLINICALLY ADAPTED INSTRUMENTS FOR THE MULTIPLY HANDICAPPED. St. Louis: MMB Music, 1980. 800-445-0649 **9**

Csikszentmihalyi, Mihaly and Reed Larson. BEING ADOLESCENT: CONFLICT AND GROWTH IN THE TEENAGE YEARS. New York: Basic Books, 1984. **4**

Csikszentmihalyi, Mihaly, Kevin Rathunde, and Samuel Whalen. TALENTED TEENAGERS: THE ROOTS OF SUCCESS & FAILURE. New York: Cambridge University Press, 1993. **4, 8**

Elkind, David. Miseducation: PRESCHOOLERS AT RISK. New York: Knopf, 1993. **1, 6**

Elliott, Barbara et al. GUIDE TO THE SELECTION OF INSTRUMENTS WITH RESPECT TO PHYSICAL ABILITY AND DISABILITY. St. Louis: MMB Music, 1982. **5, 9**

Farnan, Laurie and Faith Johnson. **EVERYONE CAN MOVE: MUSIC AND ACTIVITIES THAT PROMOTE MOVEMENT AND MOTOR DEVELOPMENT.** New Berlin, WI: Jenson, 1988. A cassette containing all the music in the book is available from MMB Music, St. Louis. **1, 9**

Farnan, Laurie and Faith Johnson. **MUSIC IS FOR EVERYONE: A HANDBOOK FOR PROVIDING MUSIC TO PEOPLE WITH SPECIAL NEEDS.** New Berlin, WI: Jenson, 1988. A cassette containing all the music in the book is available from MMB Music, St.Louis. **9**

Feldman, David Henry with Lynn T. Goldsmith. **NATURE'S GAMBIT.** New York: Basic Books, 1986. **8**

Findlay, Elsa. **RHYTHM AND MOVEMENT APPLICATIONS OF DALCROZE EURHYTHMICS.** Evanston, IL: Summy-Birchard/Warner, 1971. **1**

Freeman, Joan (ed.). **THE PSYCHOLOGY OF GIFTED CHILDREN.** Chicester, England and New York: John Wiley & Sons, 1985. **8**

Gardner, Howard. **FRAMES OF MIND.** New York: Basic Books, 1985. **2, 3, 4, 8, 9**

Gardner, Howard. **THE UNSCHOOLED MIND: HOW CHILDREN THINK AND HOW SCHOOLS SHOULD TEACH.** New York: Basic Books, 1991. **1, 2, 3, 6**

Healy, Jane M. **ENDANGERED MINDS: WHY OUR CHILDREN DON'T THINK.** New York: Simon & Schuster, 1990. **1, 2, 6**

Levinson, Harold N., M.D. **SMART BUT FEELING DUMB.** New York: Warner Books, 1984. **9**

McDonald, Dorothy and Gene M. Simons. **MUSICAL GROWTH AND DEVELOPMENT: BIRTH THROUGH SIX.** New York: Schimer Books, 1989. **1, 9**

Michel, Donald and Janet Jones. **MUSIC FOR DEVELOPING SPEECH AND LANGUAGE SKILLS IN CHILDREN.** St. Louis: MMB Music, 1991. **9**

Miller, Alice. **THE DRAMA OF THE GIFTED CHILD.** New York: Basic Books, 1981. **8**

Satir, Virginia. **THE NEW PEOPLEMAKING.** Mountain View, CA: Science and Behavior Books, 1988. **2, 3, 4**

Saunders, Jacqulyn with Pamela Espeland. **BRINGING OUT THE BEST: A RESOURCE GUIDE FOR PARENTS OF YOUNG GIFTED CHILDREN.** Minneapolis: Free Spirit, 1991. **1, 8**

Shurkin, Joel N. **TERMAN'S KIDS.** Boston: Little, Brown, 1992. **8**

Smith, Sally L. **SUCCEEDING AGAINST THE ODDS: HOW THE LEARNING DISABLED CAN REALIZE THEIR PROMISE.** New York: Putnam, 1991. **9**

Streeter, Elaine. **MAKING MUSIC WITH THE YOUNG CHILD WITH SPECIAL NEEDS: A GUIDE FOR PARENTS.** London: Kingsley, 1993. **9**

Vail, Priscilla L. **SMART KIDS WITH SCHOOL PROBLEMS.** New York: Plume, 1987. **9**

Walker, Sally Y. **THE SURVIVAL GUIDE FOR PARENTS OF GIFTED KIDS.** Minneapolis: Free Spirit, 1991. **8**

Wlodkowski, Raymond J. and Judith Jaynes. EAGER TO LEARN: HELPING CHILDREN BECOME MOTIVATED AND LOVE LEARNING. San Francisco: Jossey-Bass, 1990. There are two videos, called "Motivation to Learn," associated with this book. (See Videos.) **2, 3, 4, 6**

BOOKS FOR YOU WITH YOUR CHILD

Many of these books have a short shelf life, but they are so valuable that it is worth the extra effort to locate them. If you cannot get them at a bookstore or from the publisher, check public and college libraries, or use a book-find service. For books more difficult to access, addresses have been provided.

Numbers in bold type indicate the chapters in which the books are reviewed. Please see "Chapter Resources" of cited chapter.

Aronoff, Frances Webber. MOVE WITH THE MUSIC. Pittsburgh: Music Innovations, 1982. **1**

Barlow, Amy. HAPPY LISTENING GUIDE. Secaucus, NJ: Summy-Birchard. **2, 3**

Bennett, Jill. NOISY POEMS. New York: Oxford University Press, 1994. **1, 2, 8, 9**

Campbell, Virginia. PUZZLING, PATTERNING, PRACTICING: A GUIDE TO MORE EFFECTIVE PIANO STUDY. Chapel Hill, NC: Hinshaw, 1985. **3, 4**

Chang, Nai Y. AN ILLUSTRATED TREASURY OF SONGS: NATIONAL GALLERY OF ART, WASHINGTON. New York: Rizzoli, 1994. **2, 8**

Cohn, Amy L. FROM SEA TO SHINING SEA: A TREASURY OF AMERICAN FOLKLORE AND FOLK SONGS. New York: Scholastic, 1993. **1, 2, 3, 9**

Danes, Emma. THE USBOURNE FIRST BOOK OF MUSIC. London: Usbourne, 1993. **1, 5**

Drew, Helen. MY FIRST MUSIC BOOK. New York: Dorling Kindersley, 1992. **1, 5**

Dunn, Sonja. BUTTERSCOTCH DREAMS. Portsmouth, NH: Heinemann, 1987. **1, 2, 8, 9**

Everett, Carole. THE PERFORMING ARTS MAJOR'S COLLEGE GUIDE. New York: Macmillan. 1994. **4, 6**

Feierabend, John. MUSIC FOR LITTLE PEOPLE. New York: Boosey & Hawkes, 1989. **1, 9**

Feierabend, John. MUSIC FOR VERY LITTLE PEOPLE. New York: Boosey & Hawkes, 1986. **1, 9**

Fellner, Betty et al. SOUND ALL AROUND. The Philadelphia Orchestra Association, 1420 Locust Street, Philadelphia, PA 19102. 215-893-1900, 1992. **1**

Fox, Dan and Claude Marks. GO IN AND OUT THE WINDOW. New York: Henry Holt, 1987. **1, 8**

Hausherr, Rosmarie. WHAT INSTRUMENT IS THIS? New York: Scholastic, 1992. **1, 2, 5, 9**

Hayes, Phyllis. MUSICAL INSTRUMENTS YOU CAN MAKE. New York: Franklin Watts, 1981. **1, 5**

Hughes, Langston. THE SWEET AND SOUR ANIMAL BOOK. New York: Oxford University Press, 1994. **1, 8, 9**

Kaplan, Burton. THE MUSICIAN'S PRACTICE LOG. New York: Perception Development Techniques, 1985. (Box 1068, Cathedral Station, New York, NY 10025). **4, 8**

Koch, Kenneth and Kate Farrell. TALKING TO THE SUN. New York: Henry Holt, 1985. **1, 2, 8**

Krull, Kathleen. GONNA SING MY HEAD OFF. New York: Knopf, 1992. **1, 2, 3**

Magadini, Peter. MUSIC WE CAN SEE AND HEAR. Oakville, Ontario, Canada: Frederick Harris, 1982. **1, 2**

Mattox, Cheryl Warren. SHAKE IT TO THE ONE THAT YOU LOVE BEST. El Sobrante: Warren-Mattox Productions. (3817 San Pablo Dam Road #336, El Sobrante, CA 94803. 415-223-7089). **9**

Parkinson, Marie G. MOMMY, CAN WE PRACTICE NOW? Athens, OH: Ability Development, 1981. **1**

Schenk, Beatrice de Regniers et al. SING A SONG OF POPCORN. New York: Scholastic, 1988. **1, 2, 9**

Turner, Jessica B. and Ronny S. Schiff. LET'S MAKE MUSIC: AN INTERACTIVE MUSICAL TRIP AROUND THE WORLD. Milwaukee, WI: Hal Leonard, 1995. Book and CD. **2, 9**

Uscher, Nancy. GUIDE TO SCHOOLS OF MUSIC AND CONSERVATORIES THROUGHOUT THE WORLD. New York: Schirmer Books, 1988. **6**

Warren, Jean and Susan Shroyer. PIGGYBACK SONGS TO SIGN. Everett: Warren Publishing, 1992. (P.O. Box 2250, Everett, WA 98203). **9**

Williams, Sarah. ROUND AND ROUND THE GARDEN. New York: Oxford University Press, 1994. **1, 9**

Williams, Sarah. PUDDING AND PIE. New York: Oxford University Press, 1994. **1, 9**

BOOKS FOR YOUR CHILD

There is much on the market in this category. We have opted for a selective, diverse, and high-quality list. You will find many more books in your local library, bookstores, and museum shops. Many of these books have a short shelf life, but they are so valuable that it is worth the extra effort to locate them. If you cannot get them at a bookstore or from the publisher, check public and college libraries, or use a book-find service. For books more difficult to access, addresses have been provided.

Numbers in bold type indicate the chapters in which the books are reviewed. Please see "Chapter Resources" of cited chapter.

Anderson, David. THE PIANO MAKERS. New York: Pantheon Books, 1982. **5**

Ardley, Neil. MUSIC. New York, Knopf, 1989. **3, 4, 5**

**GENERAL
RESOURCES**

Arnold, Caroline. **MUSIC LESSONS FOR ALEX.** New York: Clarion Books, 1985. **2, 5, 8**

Beránek, Vratislav. **THE ILLUSTRATED HISTORY OF MUSIC.** London, Sunburst Books, 1994. **4, 8**

Blackwood, Alan. **MUSICAL INSTRUMENTS.** New York: The Bookwright Press, 1987. **5, 9**

Blackwood, Alan. **THE ORCHESTRA.** Brookfield, CT: The Millbrook Press, 1993. **5, 8**

Bonis, Ferenc. **BÉLA BARTÓK: HIS LIFE IN PICTURES AND DOCUMENTS.** Budapest: Kossuth Printing House, 1972. **4**

Bosseur, Jean-Yves. **MUSIC: PASSION FOR AN ART.** New York: Skira/Rizzoli, 1991. **8**

Buettner, Stewart and Reinhard G. Pauly. **PORTRAITS: GREAT COMPOSERS— GREAT ARTISTS.** Portland, OR: Amadeus Press, 1992. **3, 4**

Donald, Dave. **BACH, BEETHOVEN, AND THE BOYS.** Toronto: Sound and Vision, 1986. (359 Riverdale Avenue, Toronto, Canada, M4J 1A4). **3, 4, 8**

Downing, Julie. **MOZART TONIGHT.** New York: Bradbury Press, 1991. **2**

Erlewine, Michael and Scott Bultman. **ALL MUSIC GUIDE.** Corte Madera: Miller Freeman c/o BMR Associates, 1984. (21 Tamal Vista Blvd., Suite 209, Corte Madera, CA 94925). **3, 4, 8**

Fowler, Charles. **MUSIC! ITS ROLE AND IMPORTANCE IN OUR LIVES.** New York: Macmillan/McGraw-Hill, 1994. **4, 8**

Galbraith, Judy. **THE GIFTED KIDS SURVIVAL GUIDE: FOR AGES 10 AND UNDER.** Minneapolis: Free Spirit, 1984. **8**

Galbraith, Judy and James Delisle. **THE GIFTED KIDS SURVIVAL GUIDE I AND II.** Minneapolis: Free Spirit, 1984, 1987. **8**

Gill, Dominic (ed.). **THE BOOK OF THE PIANO.** Ithaca, NY: Cornell University Press, 1981. **4, 5**

Goffstein, M.B. **A LITTLE SCHUBERT.** Boston: David R. Godine, 1984. **2, 4**

Greves, Margaret. **THE MAGIC FLUTE: THE STORY OF MOZART'S OPERA.** New York: Henry Holt, 1989. **1, 2, 9**

Hart, Mickey and Jay Stevens. **DRUMMING AT THE EDGE OF MAGIC: A JOUR-NEY INTO THE SPIRIT OF PERCUSSION.** San Francisco: Harper San Francisco, 1990. **4, 5**

Helpern, Mark. **SWAN LAKE.** Boston: Houghton Mifflin, 1989. **3, 4, 8**

Hoffman, E. T. A. **NUTCRACKER.** New York: Crown, 1984. **3**

Hughes, Langston. **JAZZ (Updated and Expanded by Sanford Brown).** New York: Franklin Watts, 1982. **3, 4, 8**

Kendall, Alan. **THE CHRONICLE OF CLASSICAL MUSIC: AN INTIMATE DIARY OF THE LIVES AND MUSIC OF THE GREAT COMPOSERS.** London: Thames & Hudson, 1994. **4, 8**

Koch, Karen. **MY OWN MUSIC HISTORY.** Trenton: The Music Studio. (442 N. Maple Street, Trenton, IL 62293). **3**

Krementz, Jill. **A VERY YOUNG MUSICIAN.** New York: Simon & Schuster, 1991. **5**

Krull, Kathleen. **LIVES OF THE MUSICIANS: GOOD TIMES, BAD TIMES (AND WHAT THE NEIGHBORS THOUGHT).** San Diego: Harcourt Brace Jovanovich, 1993. **3, 4, 8**

Kuskin, Karla. **THE PHILHARMONIC GETS DRESSED.** New York: Harper & Row, 1982. **1, 5**

Lewis, Richard. **MIRACLES.** New York: Simon & Schuster, 1966. **2**

Martin, Bill, Jr. **THE MAESTRO PLAYS.** New York: Henry Holt, 1994. **1, 5**

McLeish, Kenneth and Valerie McLeish. **THE OXFORD FIRST COMPANION TO MUSIC.** New York: Oxford University Press, 1982. **2, 3, 8**

Mundy, Simon. **THE USBOURNE STORY OF MUSIC.** London: Usbourne, 1980. **3, 4**

Nichols, Janet. **AMERICAN MUSIC MAKERS: AN INTRODUCTION TO AMERICAN COMPOSERS.** New York: Walker, 1990. **3, 4, 8**

Nichols, Janet. **WOMEN MUSIC MAKERS: AN INTRODUCTION TO WOMEN COMPOSERS.** New York: Walker, 1992. **3, 4, 8**

Nicholson, Stuart. Ella Fitzgerald: **A BIOGRAPHY OF THE FIRST LADY OF JAZZ.** New York: Charles Scribner, 1994. **4**

Onassis, Jacqueline (ed.). *THE FIREBIRD* **AND OTHER RUSSIAN FAIRY TALES.** New York: Viking, 1978. **1, 2, 8**

Price, Leontyne. *AÏDA:* **BASED ON THE OPERA BY GIUSEPPE VERDI.** San Diego: Harcourt Brace, 1990. **4, 8**

Rachlin, Ann and Susan Hellard. **FAMOUS CHILDREN: BACH. HANDEL. HAYDN. MOZART.** London: Victor Gollancz, 1992. **1, 2, 9**

Raeburn, Michael and Alan Kendall. **THE HERITAGE OF MUSIC.** New York: Oxford University Press, 1989. **4, 8**

Rosenberg, Jane. **SING ME A STORY.** New York: Thames & Hudson, 1989. **4**

Rubin, Mark and Alan Daniel. **THE ORCHESTRA.** Buffalo, NY: Firefly Books, 1992. **1, 5**

Sadie, Stanley and Alison Latham. **MUSIC GUIDE.** Englewoood Cliffs, NJ: Prentice-Hall, 1987. **4, 8**

Salmon, Paul G. and Robert G. Meyer. **NOTES FROM THE GREEN ROOM: COPING WITH STRESS AND ANXIETY IN MUSICAL PERFORMANCE.** New York: Macmillan, 1992. **4**

Schwartz, Elliott and Daniel Godfrey. **MUSIC SINCE 1945.** New York: Schirmer Books, 1993. **4**

Sharma, Elizabeth. **LIVE MUSIC! BRASS; KEYBOARDS; PERCUSSION; STRINGS; THE VOICE; WOODWINDS.** New York: Thomson Learning, 1992. **5**

Sommer, Elsey. **THE KIDS' WORLD ALMANAC OF MUSIC: FROM ROCK TO BACH.** New York: World Almanac, 1992. **3, 4**

Storr, Catherine and Dianne Jackson. **HANSEL AND GRETEL. THE NUTCRACKER. PETER AND THE WOLF. SWAN LAKE.** London: Faber Music, 1991. **1, 2, 9**

GENERAL RESOURCES

Tames, Richard. FREDERIC CHOPIN. New York: Franklin Watts, 1991. **3, 4**

Tatchell, Judy. UNDERSTANDING MUSIC. London: Usbourne, 1990. **3, 4, 5, 8**

Thompson, Wendy. COMPOSER'S WORLD SERIES: BIOGRAPHIES OF BEETHOVEN, HAYDN, MOZART, AND SCHUBERT. New York: Viking, 1991. **4, 8**

Van der Meer, Ron and Michael Berkeley. THE MUSIC PACK. New York: Knopf, 1994. **3, 4, 8**

Venturi, Piero. GREAT COMPOSERS. New York: Putnam, 1988. **4, 8**

Walther, Tom. MAKE MINE MUSIC! Boston: Little, Brown, 1981. **5**

Willard, Nancy. THE SORCERER'S APPRENTICE. New York: Scholastic, 1993. **1, 9**

Willoughby, David. THE WORLD OF MUSIC. Dubuque, IA: William C. Brown, 1993. **4, 8**

Willson, Robina B. MOZART'S STORY. London: A & C Black, 1991. **1, 2, 9**

Wolff, Virginia E. THE MOZART SEASON. New York: Henry Holt, 1991. **4, 8**

RECORDINGS

Building your own listening library is very personal. The best principle is to trust your own curiosity, taste, and preference. A mix-and-match library is healthy and stimulating.

The family listening starter collection indicates age levels. These can only be approximate. Your child's readiness for certain types of music may be different. Our aim in suggesting these composers, artists, and pieces is to provide a balanced collection as much as to remind you that music comes in even more flavors than Baskin-Robbins.

The list includes examples of classic, jazz, ethnic, and children's music. The worlds of rock, pop, soul, country and western, and the like are so varied and changing that listing examples of each type would result in a very long menu. Your interests will determine which of these styles and artists you include.

As you and your children listen to this music, keep in mind that listening does not require "sitting down" or "sitting still." Younger children should be encouraged to respond openly. This may mean humming, dancing, conducting, drawing to music, making up stories about what the music "says"(probably with your help), and certainly having music as an accompaniment to daily living.

There will, of course, also be times when you sit down with your child to enjoy the music, perhaps listening with eyes closed. At other times you and your child will talk about what you hear, the instruments, the time or country in which the composer lived, the performers, or anything else that strikes your fancy. When your child reaches the teen years, encourage him to keep a listening "journal" to record information about the music and personal impressions of it. This helps to focus listening. It takes all these ways to make listening to music important and vivid to your child.

FAMILY LISTENING STARTER COLLECTION

The collection is listed by composer or artist. Numbers in bold type indicate age category:
1 = under four years old, 2 = 4 to 8 years old, 3 = 8 to 12 years old, 4 = teens.

Chamber Music

Bartók, Béla. Contrasts for Clarinet, Violin, and Piano. **3, 4**

Bartók, Béla. String Quartets. **4**

Brahms, Johannes. Quintets for Clarinet and Strings, Op. 115. **4**

Eastern Brass Quintet. An American Collection. **3, 4**

Feldman, Morton. Quartet for Piano and Strings. **4**

Haydn, Franz J. String Quartet Number 67 (*Lark*). **3, 4**

Kraft, William. Chamber Music (percussion ensemble). **4**

Kronos Quartet. Music of Bill Evans. **3, 4**

Messaien, Olivier. Quartet for the End of Time. **4**

Mozart, Wolfgang A. String Quartet (*The Hunt*). **4**

Reich, Steve. Music for 18 Musicians. **3, 4**

Children's Music

Chapin, Tom. Family Tree. **1, 2, 3**

Chapin, Tom. ZagZig. **1, 2, 3**

Classical Kids. Beethoven Lives Upstairs. **2, 3**

Classical Kids. Mozart's Magic Fantasy (*The Magic Flute*). **2, 3**

Classical Kids. Tchaikovsky Discovers America. **2, 3**

Classical Kids. Vivaldi's Ring of Mystery. **2, 3**

Herdman, Priscilla. Star Dreamer (collection of night songs). **1, 2**

Ives, Burl. Burl Ives Sings Little White Duck. **1**

Manhattan Transfer. Manhattan Transfer Meets Tubby the Tuba. **1, 2**

McFerrin and Ma. Hush (unusual settings of classical works). **1, 2, 3, 4**

Palmer, Hap. Baby Songs (songs for toddlers). **1**

The Re-Bops. Funny 50s and Silly 60s (novelty oldies). **3, 4**

Schickele, Peter. Sneaky Pete and the Wolf (Prokofiev as a western). **1, 2, 3**

Tchaikovsky/Lewis. Lamb Chop's Nutcracker Suite. **1, 2**

Choral and Song

Augér, Arlene. Love Songs (by Copland, Britten, others). **4**

Bartoli, Cecilia. If You Love Me (Italian art songs). **3, 4**

Bernstein, Leonard. West Side Story. **3, 4**

Britten, Benjamin. A Ceremony of Carols (Christmas; original music). **3, 4**

Cash, Rosanne. Til Your Eyes Shine (famous mothers sing lullabies). **1**

Copland, Aaron. Old American Songs. **2, 3, 4**

Copland, Aaron. Folksongs from Barbados and Jamaica. **2, 3, 4**

Gilbert and Sullivan. H.M.S. Pinafore. **2, 3, 4**

Gilbert and Sullivan. The Pirates of Penzance. **3, 4**

Handel, George F. Messiah. **2, 3, 4**

Folk and Ethnic

Buck, Dennis and others. Children of the World (Brazil, Haiti, others). **1, 2**

Buck, Dennis and others. Multicultural Rhythm Sticks Fun. **1, 2**

Cliff, Jimmy. Reggae on the River. **1, 2, 3, 4**

Herdman, Priscilla. Daydreamer (folksongs). **1, 2**

Inajin, Tokeya. Keepers of the Dream (Lakota flute melodies). **1, 2, 3, 4**

Ladysmith Black Mambazo. Gift of the Tortoise (South African children's songs). **1, 2, 3, 4**

Seeger, Pete. Family Folk Festival. **1, 2, 3, 4**

Smithsonian. The Folkways Collection. **2, 3, 4**

Sweet Honey in the Rock. I Got Shoes (African American spirituals). **1, 2, 3, 4**

Sweet Honey in the Rock. Still on the Journey (African American songs). **1, 2, 3, 4**

Wiseman, Julie. Joining Hands with Other Lands. **1, 2, 3**

Various. The World Sings Goodnight (33 cultures, languages). **1, 2**

Instrumental

Brahms, Johannes. Hungarian Dances Numbers 1–21. **1, 2, 3, 4**

Canadian Brass. English Renaissance Music. **1, 2, 3, 4**

Chopin, Frédéric. Recital Collections (Artur Rubinstein). **3, 4**

Debussy, Claude. Sonata for Flute, Viola, and Harp. **3, 4**

Gottschalk, Louis. The American Romantic (Alan Feinberg). **3, 4**

Ma, Yo-Yo. Made in America (Ma plays Gershwin, Ives, others). **3, 4**

Mozart, Wolkfgang A. Sonatas for Violin and Piano. **3, 4**

Mussorgsky, Modeste. Pictures at an Exhibition (piano version). **3, 4**

Varese, Edgar. Ionisation. **3, 4**

Jazz

Armstrong, Louis. The Hot Fives, Volume 1. **4**

Armstrong, Louis. The Hot Fives and Hot Sevens, Volumes II, III. **4**

Davis, Miles. Kind of Blue. **3, 4**

Ellington, Duke. Black, Brown, and Beige. **4**

Evans, Bill. Sunday at the Village Vanguard. **3, 4**

Fitzgerald, Ella. The Best of Ella Fitzgerald, Volumes 1, 2. **4**

Franklin, Aretha. Amazing Grace. **3, 4**

Hubert Laws. The Best of Hubert Laws. **3, 4**

Redman, Joshua. MoodSwing. **3, 4**

Ritenour, Lee. Portrait. **3, 4**

Tatum, Art. Solos. **3, 4**

Orchestra

Bach, Johann S. Brandenburg Concertos Numbers 1–6. **1, 2, 3, 4**

Bach, Johann S. Double Concerto for Violin and Oboe. **1, 2, 3, 4**

Barber, Samuel. Adagio for Strings. **3, 4**

Bartók, Béla. Concerto for Orchestra. **2, 3, 4**

Bartók, Béla. Music for Strings, Percussion, and Celesta. **2, 3, 4**

Beethoven, Ludwig van. Symphony Number 3 in E-Flat Major (*Eroica*). **2, 3, 4**

Beethoven, Ludwig van. Symphony Number 5 in C Minor. **2, 3, 4**

Berlioz, Hector. Symphonie Fantastique. **3, 4**

Britten, Benjamin. Young Person's Guide to the Orchestra.. **2, 3, 4**

Chopin, Frédéric. Les Sylphides. **1, 2, 3, 4**

Chopin, Frédéric. Coppélia. **1, 2, 3, 4**

Copland, Aaron. Appalachian Spring. **2, 3, 4**

Copland, Aaron. Rodeo. **2, 3, 4**

Debussy, Claude. La Mer. **3, 4**

Debussy, Claude. Prélude a l'aprés-midi d'un faune. **3, 4**

Dukas, Paul. The Sorcerer's Apprentice. **1, 2, 3**

Dvořák, Antonin. Symphony from the New World. **3, 4**

Gershwin, George. An American in Paris. **3, 4**

Gershwin, George. Rhapsody in Blue. **3, 4**

Grieg, Edvard. Piano Concerto in A Minor. **3, 4**

Handel, George F. Music for the Royal Fireworks. **2, 3, 4**

Handel, George F. Water Music, Suites 1 and 2. **2, 3, 4**

Haydn, Franz J. Symphony Number 93 (Surprise). **1, 2, 3, 4**

Haydn, Franz J. Three Favorite Concertos (trumpet, violin, cello). **2, 3, 4**

Ives, Charles. Three Places in New England. **3, 4**

Kurtág, Gyorgy. Kafka Fragments, Op. 24. **4**

Machover, Tod. Flora. **4**

Mozart, Wolfgang A. Serenade in G Major (Eine Kleine Nachtmusik). **1, 2, 3, 4**

Mozart, Wolfgang A. Symphony Number 40 in G Minor. **3, 4**

Mozart, Wolfgang A. Symphony Number 41 in C Major (*Jupiter*). **3, 4**

Mussorgsky, Modeste. Pictures at an Exhibition (orchestral version). **3, 4**

Prokofiev, Serge. Peter and the Wolf. **1, 2, 3**

Prokofiev, Serge. Romeo and Juliet Ballet Suites Numbers 1, 2. **2, 3, 4**

Saint-Saëns, Camille. Carnival of the Animals. **1, 2, 3, 4**

Sousa, John Philip. Stars and Stripes Forever; other marches. **1, 2, 3, 4**

Strauss, Richard. Till Eulenspiegel. **3, 4**

Stravinsky, Igor. Firebird. **1, 2, 3, 4**

Stravinsky, Igor. Petrouchka. **2, 3, 4**

Takemitsu, Toru. River Run. **4**

Tchaikovsky, Peter. Nutcracker Suite. **1, 2, 3, 4**

Tchaikovsky, Peter. Piano Concerto in B-Flat Minor. **2, 3, 4**

Tchaikovsky, Peter. Swan Lake. **1, 2, 3, 4**

Villa-Lobos, Heitor. Bachianas Brasileiras. **3, 4**

Vivaldi, Antonio. Concertos for Oboe and Violin. **1, 2, 3, 4**

Vivaldi, Antonio. The Four Seasons. **2, 3, 4**

GUIDES TO CDs AND CASSETTES

Ballyk, Paul D. H & B RECORDINGS DIRECT. 800-222-6872.

A yearly catalog and newsletters that offer reviews of critic's choice classical music albums. Lists CDs by composer, collections, budget collections, laser discs, and VHS cassettes. All listings can be purchased from this source. An $8.00 membership allows you to take advantage of special member prices. Also available is a bimonthly jazz publication, *Jazz H & B Recording Direct* catalog.

DeCurtis, Anthony and James Henke (eds.). ROLLING STONE ALBUM GUIDE. New York: Random House, 1993.

Guide to rock, pop, rap, jazz, blues, country, soul, folk, and gospel. Concise, informed evaluations and one- to five-star ratings.

Erlwine, Michael and Scott Bultman (eds.). ALL MUSIC GUIDE. San Francisco: Miller Freeman, 1992.

Catalog of tapes, CDs, and albums, both in and out of print. All types of music including rock, pop, soul, vocal, rap, blues, Cajun zydeco, gospel, country and western, bluegrass, folk, contemporary instrumental, music videos, women's music, classical, twentieth century avant-garde, children's music, world music, reggae, and jazz.

Libbey, Ted. THE NPR GUIDE TO BUILDING A CLASSICAL CD COLLECTION. New York: Workman, 1994.

A personal evaluation of three hundred "essential" works of classical literature in the following categories: orchestral music, concertos, chamber music, solo keyboard works, sacred and choral music, and opera. There is an introduction, "On Listening to Music," by Mstislav Rostropovich.

March, Ivan, Edward Greenfield, and Robert Layton. THE PENGUIN GUIDE TO COMPACT DISCS AND CASSETTES. London: Penguin, 1992.

A comprehensive survey with critical, comparative commentary of classical music on CDs and cassettes in an updated edition. Includes best of old recordings as well as important new listings. There is a strong British/Continental viewpoint. Multiple critics.

Stevenson, Joseph. STEVENSON CLASSICAL COMPACT DISC GUIDE. P.O. Box 53286, Indianapolis, IN 46253.

This magazine is published quarterly and offers critical reviews (all by Stevenson) of selected albums, an honor roll of old and new listings, and main listings of collections, electronic music, film and show music, international music, and laser discs. There is also a yearly comprehensive guide.

Vroon, Donald R. (ed.). AMERICAN RECORD GUIDE. 513-941-1116.

A bimonthly magazine with articles, concert reviews from major U. S. cities, and substantial critical reviews of classical music recordings listed by composer and collections. Much shorter lists of classical music videos and classical Broadway. Multiple critics and reviewers.

VIDEOS

The videos listed below are available from your local library, from video dealers, educational materials retailers, catalogs listed in this section, or directly from the video producer. Films for the Humanities, GPN, and Teldec have more extensive listings of high-quality videos than is possible to list here. Check their catalogs for more complete offerings.

Numbers in bold type indicate the chapters in which the videos are reviewed. Please see "Chapter Resources" of cited chapters.

THE AFRICAN AMERICAN TALENT SHOW. GPN. 800-228-4630. **3, 4, 8**

AGAINST THE ODDS: LUDWIG VAN BEETHOVEN. Films for the Humanities. 800-257-5126. **2, 3, 4, 9**

ANDRÉS SEGOVIA: SONG OF THE GUITAR. Teldec Video. 212-399-7782. **3, 4**

ASHKENAZY OBSERVED: EPISODES FROM THE LIFE OF A WANDERING MUSICIAN. Teldec Video. 212-399-7782. **4**

BEETHOVEN LIVES UPSTAIRS. The Children's Group: Toronto. 800-456-2334. **2, 3**

CHICK COREA: ELECTRIC WORKSHOP. DCI Video. 800-628-1528. **4**

CHICK COREA: KEYBOARD WORKSHOP. DCI Video. 800-628-1528. **4**

THE COMPETITION. GPN. 800-228-4630. **3, 4, 8**

CONCERTO! SH Productions Inc. 800-336-1820. **4, 8**

CRITICAL STAGES. VideoPhases. 1250 Hanley Industrial Court, St. Louis, MO 63144. 314-963-8840. **4, 8**

DALCROZE EURHYTHMICS WITH ROBERT ABRAMSON. GIA Productions. 7404 S. Mason Avenue, Chicago, IL 60638. 708-496-3800. **1, 9**

DIGITAL MUSICAL INSTRUMENTS AND THE WORLD OF MIDI. Red Pohaku Productions, 1621 Dole Street, Honolulu, HI 96822. **4, 5, 8**

DOROTHY TAUBMAN: CHOREOGRAPHY OF THE HAND. The Taubman Institute. Medusa, NY 12120. 518-239-4284. **4**

EARLY MUSIC EDUCATION WITH SUZUKI. Films for the Humanities. 800-257-5126. **1, 2, 5**

AN EXCEPTIONAL CHILD: MUSICAL PRODIGY. Films for the Humanities. 800-257-5126. **8**

THE FIDDLE SHOW. GPN. 800-228-4630. **3, 4, 5, 8**

FOUR AMERICAN COMPOSERS: JOHN CAGE. Mystic Fire Video. 800-292-9001. **4, 8**

HOW YOUR GRAND PIANO WORKS. JMC Productions. Box 2415, W. Brattleboro, VT 05303. **4, 5**

IN CELEBRATION OF THE PIANO: AN ALL-STAR TRIBUTE TO THE STEIN-WAY. Music in Motion. 800-445-0649. **4**

JACQUELINE DU PRÉ: ELGAR CONCERTO. Teldec Video. 212-399-7782. **8**

LEONARD BERNSTEIN'S YOUNG PEOPLE'S CONCERTS SERIES WITH THE NEW YORK PHILHARMONIC. Music in Motion. 800-445-0649. **2, 3, 4, 5, 8**

MOTIVATION TO LEARN. HOW PARENTS AND TEACHERS CAN HELP. GUIDELINES FOR PARENT-TEACHER CONFERENCES. ASCD (Association for Supervision and Curriculum Development). 703-549-9110. **2, 3**

MUSIC ANIMATION MACHINE. Stephen Malinowski. 510-235-7478. **3, 4, 8**

NELITA TRUE AT EASTMAN: PORTRAIT OF A PIANIST-TEACHER. Alfred Publishing Company. 800-292-6122. **4, 8**

ORCHESTRA! INTRODUCTION TO THE ORCHESTRA. Films for the Humanities. 800-257-5126. **3, 5, 8**

THE PERFORMER PREPARES: 100% COMMITMENT. Pst . . . Inc. 214-991-7184. **4, 8**

THE PIANO SHOW. GPN. 800-228-4630. **3, 4, 5, 8**

PROKOFIEV: THE PRODIGAL SON. Films for the Humanities. 800-257-5126. **3, 4, 8**

REHABILITATION, MUSIC, AND HUMAN WELL-BEING. MMB Music. 800-543-3771. **9**

SIGN SONGS. Aylmer Press. 800-541-9904. **9**

THE SNOWMAN. Raymond Briggs. SVS: Snowman Enterprises. Available from educational retailers. **1, 2**

THE TROUT: AN HISTORIC COLLABORATION OF DANIEL BARENBOIM, ITZHAK PERLMAN, PINCHAS ZUCKERMAN, JACQUELINE DU PRÉ, AND ZUBIN MEHTA. Teldec Video. 212-399-7782. **4, 8**

TRYIN' TO GET HOME: A HISTORY OF AFRICAN AMERICAN SONG. Heebie Jeebie Music. 510-548-4613. **2, 3, 4**

TUBBY THE TUBA. Live Entertainment: Van Nuys, CA. Available from educational retailers. **1, 2, 5**

WE REINVENT THE CIRCUS. Nouvelle Experience. Saltimbanco. Cirque du Soleil. 800-727-2233. **2, 3, 4**

ABOUT MUSIC WITH TECHNOLOGY

If your child is studying with a teacher who is knowledgeable about technology, you probably do not need additional resources. If you do not have such a teacher, the following information may be of help until you find one.

SOFTWARE

The rate of software change is so rapid that we have opted to present software resources in a more general way than resources in other categories. The choice of a computer (hardware) is controlled chiefly by the availability of software to accomplish the task you have in mind. At this writing, software for MS-DOS, Windows, and Macintosh seems to dominate the field.

Software Applications

Software is available to fulfill a variety of functions. Some applications can be used independently by students. They are marked with an asterisk (*). Others require teacher guidance.

For Aural Instruction: Software that focuses on hearing
- Ear training*
- Tuning*
- Sight-singing*
- Creating
- Listening*

Music Information Training: Drill and practice software
- Music Fundamentals
- Music Theory
- Music History
- Instructional Gaming
- Practicing Techniques

Notation: Music printing and publishing
- Composing
- Arranging
- Copying parts
- Publishing

Performance:
- Composing
- Arranging
- Sequencing
- Recording
- Sound Design
- Morphing *(Gradual transition from one sound to another)*
- Accompanying

Software Companies

This is a selective list. You will find a more complete list of software suppliers in the Technology Directory of the *Association for Technology in Music Instruction* listed later in this section under "Music Technology Catalogs." When purchasing software, insist on a try-before-you-buy arrangement.

Alfred Publishing Company. 16380 Roscoe Blvd., Van Nuys, CA 91410. 818-891-5999.

Ars Nova. Box, 637, Kirkland, WA 98083. 206-889-0927.

Broderbund Software. 500 Redwood Drive, Novato, CA 94948. 415-382-4400.

Debut Music Systems. 422 Wards Corner Road, Loveland, OH 45140. 513-576-4676.

Digidesign. 1360 Willow Road, Menlo Park, CA 94025. 415-688-0600.

Dr. T's Music Software. 100 Crescent Road, Suite 306, Needham, MA 02194. 617-455-1454.

Electronic Courseware Systems. 800-832-4965.

Fisher-Price Learning Software. 800-432-5437.

Maestro Music, Inc. 2403 San Mateo NE, Albuquerque, NM 87110. 505-881-9181.

Mark of the Unicorn. 1280 Massachusetts Ave, Cambridge, MA 02138. 617-576-2760.

Mibac. Box 468, Northfield, MN, 55057. 507-645-5851.

Microsoft. 800-426-9400.

Notable Software. Box 1166-MC, Philadelphia, PA 19105. 215-736-8355.

OpCode Systems. 3950 Fabian Way, Suite 100, Palo Alto, CA. 94303. 415-856-3333.

Passport Designs, Inc. 100 Stone Pine Road, Half Moon Bay, CA, 94019. 415-726-0280.

Piano Partners, Inc. 521 East 72nd Street, Suite 3 A, New York, NY 10021. 212-628-3912.

Pygraphics. 800-222-7536.

Roland Corp US. 7200 Dominion Circle, Los Angeles, CA 90040. 213-685-5141

Temporal Acuity Products. 800-426-2673.

Twelve Tone Systems. 800-234-1171.

Voyager Co. 1351 Pacific Coast Highway, Santa Monica, CA 90401. 310-451-1383.

Voyetra Technologies. 5 Odell Plaza, Yonkers, NY, 10701. 914-966-0600.

Yamaha Music Corp. 6600 Orangethorpe Avenue, Buena Park, CA 90602. 213-355-4901.

How to Evaluate Software

When acquiring software consider the following:
- Is the program easy to use?
- Are directions clear?
- Are the menu sections easy to follow?
- Is the instruction manual helpful?
- Is there a concise list of all program features for quick reference?
- Does the program fill your needs?
- Did you enjoy using the program?
- Are graphics attractive and appropriate?
- Is the sound quality and intonation good?

- Does the program flow smoothly from one step to another?
- Can you escape the program at any point?
- Are there clear exit instructions?
- Does the program recover from mistakes (including pressing reset key)?
- Is the program "crashproof"?
- Does the publisher provide easy access to at least one backup copy?
- Does the publisher provide good support and assistance in answering your questions?
- Is there a try-before-you-buy arrangement?

BOOKS ABOUT MUSIC, MULTIMEDIA, AND TECHNOLOGY

Apple Computer. MULTIMEDIA DEMYSTIFIED. New York: Random House, 1994.
Comprehensive guide to every aspect of multimedia technology and production, with many interviews and examples. Up-to-date resource guide to other publications and software at end of volume.

ATMI, Barbara Murphy (ed.). TECHNOLOGY DIRECTORY. Association for Technology in Music Instruction, Michigan State University School of Music, East Lansing, MI 48824. Electronic mail: 21798BAM@MSU.EDU
A comprehensive directory published annually that includes information on audio-visual products, books, bulletin boards, CAI (computer-assisted instruction), catalogs, conferences, music-related products, organizations, publisher addresses, and detailed index. Submission forms are available for those who wish to list music technology-related information for possible inclusion. A read-only disk for IBM or Macintosh may be purchased at minimal cost.

Bowen, Jeff. BECOMING A COMPUTER MUSICIAN: THE INTERACTIVE APPROACH TO USING COMPUTERS WITH MUSIC. Indianapolis, IN: Macmillan Computer Publishing, 1994.
A paperback book and CD-ROM for Windows, Macintosh, and DOS. Includes complete music scores by the author and video clips. The reader is guided through learning to compose using a computer and setting up a recording studio.

Higgins, William R. A RESOURCE GUIDE TO COMPUTER APPLICATIONS IN MUSIC EDUCATION. Champaign, IL: Electronic Courseware Systems, 1991.
A guide to music software with alphabetical listings as well as listings by computer, publisher, and application with brief descriptions of each entry. For teachers, but useful to students seeking applications for particular hardware.

Holland, Sam. TEACHING TOWARD TOMORROW. Van Nuys, CA: Alfred, 1995.
This is a primer for using electronic keyboards, computers, and MIDI equipment. Although written for teachers, there are a number of assignments that self-directed teens would enjoy. Directions are clear and the work is attractively printed. There is a helpful encyclopedia of technical terms.

Holsinger, Erik. HOW MUSIC AND COMPUTERS WORK. Emeryville, CA: Ziff-Davis Press, 1994.

An illustrated introduction to music and technology. Comes with audio CD of interviews, musical examples, and technology demonstrations.

Lehrman, Paul and Tim Tully. MIDI FOR THE PROFESSIONAL. New York: Amsco, 1993.

Although this volume is very useful for professionals, it is also a lucid introduction to every aspect of MIDI music-making for student and parents. Easy to read and use, this book starts with the basics. It also has a valuable chapter on music education with MIDI.

Music Teachers National Association. THE MTNA GUIDE TO MUSIC INSTRUCTION SOFTWARE. Cincinnati, OH, 1994.

Detailed evaluations of music instruction programs listed by subject matter and skill.

Muro, Don. THE ART OF SEQUENCING. Miami: CPP Belwin, 1993.

A plain-language guide that demonstrates MIDI sequencers, tells how to create simple and multitrack sequences, and shows various editing techniques. Soon to be issued in VHS format.

Negroponte, Nicholas. BEING DIGITAL. New York: Knopf, 1995.

A visionary look at the future of digital technology and how it will affect our lives, by the founding director of the MIT Media Laboratory. Written for nonprofessionals, this book gives a fascinating look at how "being digital" will change the arts and entertainment, learning, teaching, and virtually every aspect of the world around us.

Rothstein, Edward. EMBLEMS OF THE MIND: THE INNER LIFE OF MUSIC AND MATHEMATICS. New York: Random House, 1995.

An elegantly written exploration of the concept of the beauty and symmetry of both math and music. Especially meaningful to the teen with ability and interest in both subjects.

Rowe, Robert. INTERACTIVE MUSIC SYSTEMS. Cambridge, MA: MIT Press, 1993.

This book is designed for computer music professionals, but gives a valuable overview of how computers can be used to participate "intelligently" in music teaching, performing, and composing. Very useful for serious high school students. Accompanied by a CD-ROM containing musical examples as well as software that can be tried on Macintosh computers.

MUSIC TECHNOLOGY CATALOGS

ABOUT MUSIC: A CATALOG. 203-453-9794.

A catalog of audio and video cassettes covering ethnic music, the history and theory of music, music education, and composers.

ART, MUSIC, ARCHITECTURE ON VIDEO. 212-721-6316.

A catalog of videos on various topics including music history, music appreciation, world music, voice, choral, opera, gospel, blues and jazz, 20th- century music, history of art and music, aesthetics, and creativity.

CD-ROM DIRECT CATALOG. 800-950-3513.

Listing of full range of CD-ROMs and equipment.

CD-ROM WAREHOUSE CATALOG. 800-237-6623.

Listing of full range of CD-ROMs and equipment.

CHILDREN'S SOFTWARE REVIEW. 313-480-0040.

A monthly newsletter with descriptions and evaluations of children's software, all of which is child tested before review. Occasional reviews of music software.

COMPUTERS AND MUSIC REPORT. 800-767-6161.

Catalog of computer hardware and software from various publishers for Atari, IBM, and Macintosh.

EDUCATIONAL RESOURCES CATALOG. 800-624-2926.

A catalog of software programs for younger students.

EDUCATIONAL SOFTWARE GUIDE. 800-672-6002.

A collection of software available on disk and CD-ROM.

EISI MASTER RESOURCE GUIDE. 800-955-5570.

A 616-page guide with 6,300 titles from 350 publishers, all grouped by subject area. There is a condensed version as well.

LISTEN! THE BEST IN FAMILY ENTERTAINMENT. 800-668-0242.

A catalog of recordings for children of all ages. Features cassettes, CDs, and videos.

MACWAREHOUSE. 800-255-6227.

A comprehensive general catalog for Macintosh with some music listings included.

MIX BOOK SHELF. 800-233-9604.

A listing of books about technology.

MUSIC ON VIDEO CATALOG. 800-257-5126.

A listing of videos produced by Films for the Humanities on such topics as music biography, early musical instruments, music in performance, science and music, and music from around the world. Although expensive, these are quality videos.

MUSIC TECHNOLOGY RESOURCE GUIDE FOR EDUCATORS: ADVANCED TECHNOLOGIES. 800-348-5003.

Clear descriptions in many categories: software for scoring, sequencing, composing, multimedia, and courseware instruction; hardware for MIDI interfaces; computer/printer accessories; multimedia; MIDI instruments; other equipment. This concise catalog includes informative articles on notation software, computer-based instruction, and MIDI. Very well done. For the computer-literate or music student learning about technology.

MUSICOMP: MUSIC TEACHING SOFTWARE. 214-323-0520.

Lists music teaching software by application and by hardware suitability. The descriptions are commercial, but very clear. Concise and well printed.

PC-CONNECTION. 800-755-4619.

A comprehensive general catalog for PC (IBM) with some music listings included.

TIGERSOFTWARE. 800-666-2562. (MAC) 800-888-4437 (PC).

A catalog of products for Macintosh and IBM PC computers including software, hardware, and CD-ROMs.

THE VOYAGER GUIDE TO INTERACTIVE MEDIA. 800-446-2001.

Reviews of CD-ROMs and general software. Included are several "expanded books"—books that are published on floppy disks.

MUSIC TECHNOLOGY MAGAZINES

COMPUTER MUSIC JOURNAL. 617-253-2889. Electronic mail: journals-orders@mit.edu.

A serious quarterly. Articles report on latest research in computer music. Reviews, events, publications, new products, and recordings.

ELECTRONIC MUSICIAN. 800-843-4086.

Devoted exclusively to the use of electronic musical instruments and personal computers.

FAMILY PC. 800-413-9749.

A user-friendly technology magazine for the whole family. Articles on family-tested software in a wide number of subject (including music-related) areas. Discussion of the Internet. Reviews of hardware and software. For PC and MAC.

INTERACTIVITY. 415-358-9500. FAX: 415-358-9527.

This how-to interactive multimedia magazine focuses on the creative applications of new technology, and includes in-depth case studies on CD-ROM titles, Web sites, and other music technology topics.

KEYBOARD. 415-358-9500. FAX: 415-358-9527

Magazine for keyboard players containing extensive MIDI information and hardware and software reviews.

MUSIC AND COMPUTERS. 415-358-9500. FAX: 415-358-9527.

This is a user-friendly music technology magazine by the publishers of *Keyboard*. Its language is more direct since it is aimed at entry-level users. An excellent choice for the novice.

CD-ROMs

With interactive music CD-ROMs, people not only can play music created by favorite composers, but can play *with* the music in ways never before available. A huge amount of both music and computer data is stored on the same CD, making it possible for the user to browse and manipulate information at will. The combination of aural, visual, and verbal data makes this a powerful medium. The field is in its infancy and the number of choices is somewhat limited, but the potential is great.

It should be noted that the computer game industry is surpassing the music industry in sophisticated use of technology. Although there are not many computer-type games devoted specifically to music, many state-of-the-art games (like "Myst," "Myst II," "Mister Bones," and "Ecco the Dolpin") are interesting for their use of music in new, interactive ways to support the games.

The following is only a sampling of the increasing variety of offerings in this new medium. Most CD-ROMs are under $100. Call each company to ask for a catalog. Check system requirements before ordering. Ask for a try-before-you-buy arrangement.

ALL MY HUMMINGBIRDS HAVE ALIBIS. The Voyager Company. 800-446-2001. **4, 8**

CD TIME SKETCH: COMPOSER SERIES. Electronic Courseware Systems. 800-832-4965. **4, 8**

A GERMAN REQUIEM: THE GREATEST CHORAL WORK OF THE ROMANTIC ERA. Time Warner New Media. 800-482-3766. **4, 8**

MULTIMEDIA BEETHOVEN: NINTH SYMPHONY. Microsoft. 800-426-9400. **4, 8**

MULTIMEDIA MOZART: THE DISSONANT QUARTET. Microsoft. 800-426-9400. **4, 8**

MULTIMEDIA STRAUSS: THREE TONE POEMS. Microsoft. 800-426-9400. **4, 8**

MULTIMEDIA STRAVINSKY: THE RITE OF SPRING. Microsoft. 800-426-9400. **4, 8**

MUSICAL INSTRUMENTS. Microsoft. 800-426-9400. **1, 2, 3, 4, 5**

THE MUSICAL WORLD OF PROFESSOR PICCOLO: THE FUN WAY TO LEARN ALL ABOUT MUSIC. OpCode Systems. 415-856-3333. **1, 2, 3**

MYST. Broderbund Software. 415-382-4400. **4, 8**

THE ORCHESTRA: THE INSTRUMENTS REVEALED. Time Warner New Media. 800-482-3766. **3, 4, 5, 8**

PUPPET MOTEL: LAURIE ANDERSON WITH HSIN-CHIEN HUANG. The Voyager Company. 800-446-2001. **4, 8**

ROCK, RAP, AND ROLL. Paramount Interactive. 415-812-8200. **3, 4, 8**

A SILLY NOISY HOUSE. The Voyager Company. 800-446-2001. **1**

SO I'VE HEARD. The Voyager Company. 800-446-2001. **3, 4, 8**

ORGANIZATIONS

ASSOCIATION FOR TECHNOLOGY IN MUSIC INSTRUCTION (ATMI). Timothy Kloth, ATMI Treasurer, 2336 Donnington Lane, Cincinnati, OH 45244. Electronic mail: kloth@xavier.xuedu.

ATMI was formed in 1975 to help the development of technological aids for music education, facilitate an active exchange of ideas among developers, and serve as a source of information for users of technolgy-based systems in music instruction. ATMI conducts a yearly meeting in conjunction with the College Music Society and publishes a quarterly newsletter and an invaluable Technology Directory.

INTERNATIONAL MIDI ASSOCIATION. Woodland Hills, CA. 818-598-0088.

As a public information network, the IMA provides a source for information relating to MIDI and computer music. Membership includes a subscription to the IMA newsletter.

THE INFORMATION HIGHWAY

The national information highway is a major and fast-growing source of information about music. Listings of books, CDs, CD-ROMs, catalogs, other pertinent information, and even music, can be gotten quickly from a wide variety of sources. Whether on America Online, Internet, Prodigy, World Wide Web, more specialized on-line services like Artswire, or other commercial on-line services, the information is easy to access and is frequently updated Over the next five years, more and more companies will put catalogs on network, more specialized bulletin boards will be established, and the rate of information exchange will grow dramatically.

MOVIES

This list of movies was selected because in most of them the music plays a prominent part; young people figure importantly in others. They vary in cinematic quality. We tried to be sensitive to subject matter and appropriateness. There are some annotations. Otherwise the title should suffice. Available from any complete video store.

AMADEUS. Fictional biography of Mozart.

AN AMERICAN IN PARIS. Music of George Gershwin.

THE BUDDY HOLLY STORY.

CAMELOT.

CINDERELLA. Music of Prokofiev with Berlin Comic Opera Ballet.

THE COMPETITION. Two classical pianists fall in love while competing for top honors in a competition.

EUBIE. About jazz pioneer Eubie Blake.

FAME. Focus is on the aspirations, struggles, and personal lives of talented and ambitious students at New York City's High School for the Performing Arts.

FANTASIA. This movie masterpiece features Leopold Stokowski and the Philadelphia

Orchestra. Disney animation accompanies the music, including Tchaikowsky (*Nut-cracker Suite*), Dukas (*The Sorcerer's Apprentice*), and Stravinsky (*The Rite of Spring*). A CD of the soundtrack is available separately.

FIDDLER ON THE ROOF.

HANS CHRISTIAN ANDERSON. Nominated for six academy awards, this story of the famous writer of fairy tales stars the incredible Danny Kaye. Hans entrances the children of Copenhagen with his songs, stories, and dancing. The ballet sequence adds a special dimension.

A HARD DAY'S NIGHT. The Beatles.

LITTLE MAN TATE. About Fred, a young genius born to a single mother. The dilemma is what's best for Fred—education in a special institute or knocking about with the neighborhood kids. Fred's experiences with other children are all too real and poignant.

MADAME SOUSATZKA. An eccentric piano teacher and the gifted prodigy who comes to her for lessons.

THE MAGIC FLUTE. The Ingmar Bergman version of this Mozart opera makes this a double work of art.

MARY POPPINS.

MEET ME IN ST. LOUIS. About the 1903 World's Fair, with Judy Garland.

MIKADO. D'Oyly Carte Opera performs a Gilbert and Sullivan work.

THE MUSIC MAN.

OKLAHOMA.

OLIVER. Musical based on Charles Dickens's Oliver Twist.

ONE HUNDRED MEN AND A GIRL. About an ambitious singer and a conductor. With Leopold Stokowski and Deanna Durbin.

OTELLO. Franco Zeffirelli's masterpiece of filmed opera, with Placido Domingo.

PETER PAN. Live TV adaptation of the Broadway play. Mary Martin is the boy who didn't want to grow up.

THE PIRATES OF PENZANCE. Gilbert and Sullivan.

RHAPSODY IN BLUE. A fictionalized biography of George Gershwin.

SEARCHING FOR BOBBY FISHER. About a chess prodigy.

SINGIN' IN THE RAIN.

SONG OF NORWAY. Fictional biography of Edvard Grieg. The music is better than the story.

A SONG TO REMEMBER. Fictional biography of Chopin with superb music.

SOUND OF MUSIC.

STORMY WEATHER. A kaleidoscope of musical numbers with Lena Horne and jazz great Fats Waller.

SUNDAY IN THE PARK WITH GEORGE. Pulitzer prize-winning musical by Stephen Sondheim about the life of artist Georges Seurat.

SWEET DREAMS. About country and western singer Patsy Cline.

TALES OF HOFFMAN. A blend of opera, ballet, and cinematic effects with Offenbach's score as a backdrop.

WEST SIDE STORY. The great Leonard Bernstein musical.

THE WIZARD OF OZ.

YANKEE DOODLE DANDY. The story of dancing vaudevillian George M. Cohan, with James Cagney.

GAMES AND TEACHING AIDS

See the Catalog heading for a more extensive listing of music games and teaching aids.

CONCENTRATION, TANGLE, AND BASS CLEF BOOGIE. Bevstuff, 992 Kenmore Lane, Santa Rosa, CA 95407.

Teaches music literacy to elementary students. Reinforces information children receive in music lessons. Included are instructions, playing pieces, a list of symbols, and what the symbols are called.

FUN FOR FOUR DRUMS. MMB Music. 800-543-3771.

A learning game (for voices, piano, and drums) to develop rhythmic perception and confidence.

MUSIC GAMES 'N THINGS: FORWARD MARCH. TIME OUT. CIRCLE OF KEYS. KEYNOTE WRITER. Karen Harrington. 800-866-6468.

"Forward March" is a board game that reviews music theory; each playing card has questions on three advancing levels. "Time Out" is a rhythm dictation game using flash cards. "Circle of Keys" and "Keynote Writer" use erasable boards.

MUSIC MIND GAMES. Michiko Yurko. 800-628-1528 x 214 or 215.

Six to eight games are available at each of three levels. These include card and board games dealing with reading, rhythm, symbols, tempos, scales, keys, and chords. There are three additional games: "Grand Staff Notes," "Incredible!" (full of practicing ideas and directions), and "Musopoly." Games can be used at home, in the music studio or classroom, and at music camps. Some games may be used with preschoolers. *Music Mind Games* may also be purchased as a book that contains over two hundred creative game ideas and directions.

RECREATION EXPERIENCES FOR THE SEVERELY IMPAIRED OR NON-AMBULATORY CHILD. MMB Music. 800-543-3771.

Provides many ideas to stimulate movement activities, arts and crafts, music and listening activities, tactile and sensory activities, and finger games to use with children who have multiple impairments. Interviews with eight families provide insight and ideas for therapeutic activities.

SOUNDTRACKS. Music for Little People. 800-727-2233.

Audio lotto games give the young child practice in concentration and listening. There are recorded sounds from all over the world—waves on a beach, footsteps in snow, traffic in a city. There are picture boards and a cassette to match a photo card to the sound. Three to six years old.

MAGAZINES

ACOUSTIC GUITAR. 415-485-6946.
A diverse coverage of the acoustic guitar world.
THE BRASS PLAYER. 212-581-1480.
A quarterly magazine dealing with all brass instruments.
BBC MUSIC. 800-284-0200.
This British classical music magazine comes with a high-quality CD each month. There are articles, reviews of new recordings, and suggestions for building a listening library.
CLASSICAL CD. 908-531-4990.
This American magazine-plus-CD has articles and reviews, as well as a section on building a listening collection. Both this and BBC Music have an international point of view.
CLAVIER. 708-446-8550.
Written for the music teacher, this magazine has listings of competitions for young students and lists summer camps and workshops in the March issue.
CLAVIER'S PIANO EXPLORER. 708-446-8550.
This magazine for upper elementary school students has articles, biographies of musicians, puzzles, games, and music to play.
DOUBLE REED. 318-343-5715.
For oboe and bassoon players.
DOWNBEAT. 708-941-2030.
A comprehensive magazine about jazz.
FLUTE TALK. 708-446-8550.
Focused on the needs and interests of serious flute players.
HARP JOURNAL. 201-836-8909.
The official publication of the American Harp Society, with much detailed information about the harp.
THE INSTRUMENTALIST. 708-446-5600.
Of interest to all orchestral players.
KEYBOARD COMPANION. 800-824-5087.
The focus is on early-level piano study. Presents student, parent, and teacher points of view.
OPERA NEWS. 212-582-7500.
Interviews and articles about the world of opera.

PIANO AND KEYBOARD. 415-458-8672.

Addresses the interests of those who play the acoustic piano as well as those who are involved with digital keyboards and synthesizers.

STRINGS. 415-485-6946.

Addresses the needs and interests of string players, classical as well as folk. Styles itself as the magazine for players and makers of bowed instruments.

WINDPLAYER. 310-456-5813.

For the full range of windplayers, from classical to jazz.

CATALOGS, DIRECTORIES, AND GUIDES

Note: catalogs about music technology are found under the heading "About Music and Technology."

ANYONE CAN WHISTLE. 800-435-8863.

Unusual, quality musical instruments from around the world, CDs, audiocassettes, and unique musical gifts.

THE BEST TOYS, BOOKS, AND VIDEOS FOR KIDS. Joanne Oppenheim. New York: Harper Perennial.

The 1994 guide to kid-tested classic and new products for childred from birth to ten years old includes special mention of musical toys, instruments, and recordings as well as toys for kids with special needs.

BOOKS, VIDEOS, AND RECORDINGS GIFT CATALOG. Smithsonian Institution Press. 800-927-7377.

Outstanding recordings of folk music, jazz, and other music of historical value.

CHILDREN'S BOOK AND MUSIC CENTER. 800-443-1856.

This catalog lists books, videos, musical instruments, tapes, and records for infants and children through nine years old.

CHILDREN'S RECORDINGS. Box 1343, Eugene, OR 97440. 503-485-1634.

This catalog includes stories and music.

COLLECTOR'S CHOICE MUSIC CATALOG. 800-923-1122.

A concise CD catalog listing a wide range of genres: classical, country, blues, rock, folk, jazz, pop, and blues.

COLLEGE MUSIC SOCIETY DIRECTORY OF MUSIC FACULTIES IN COLLEGES AND UNIVERSITIES IN U.S. AND CANADA. College Music Society Publications. Box 8208, Missoula, MT 59807. 406-721-9616

Includes over twenty-nine thousand music faculty listings in more than seventeen hundred institutions. A resource for finding the institution in which a particular teacher is a faculty member.

DIRECTORY OF SUMMER MUSIC PROGRAMS. Music Resources. 6716 Eastside Dr. NE, Tacoma, WA 98422. 206-927-3269.

An annual description of over four hundred national and international summer music programs, organized geographically. There is infomation on tuition, camp size, age range, deadlines, and focus.

EDUCATIONAL RECORD CENTER, INC. 800-438-1637.

Offers films, videos, cassettes, and records of children's music and movie favorites.

EDUCATIONAL RESOURCES. 800- 624-2926.

A listing of educational hardware, software, CD-ROMs, and multimedia, indexed alphabetically and by subject. There is no indexed category for music, but there are a number of excellent items that include music.

FILMS FOR THE HUMANITIES. 800-257-5126.

The quality of the music videos is superior. Selected videos are described in the video category of this "General Resource" section. Many of these videos are expensive, produced with schools rather than individuals in mind. The catalog includes music biographies, music in performance, a survey of classical western music, a survey of early musical instruments, and a series on man and music.

FRIENDSHIP HOUSE. 800-791-9876.

Musical games, gifts, books, videos, cassettes, and sundry accessories.

GPN. 800-228-4630.

GPN is the production company for *Musical Encounters,* a collection of thirty-six or more short videos produced by the University of Nebraska. Each is 30 minutes long, and reasonable in price. Subjects include almost every instrument and musical style. This is a listing worth having.

LITTLE EARS. Box 56168, Tucson, AZ 85703. 602-888-2830.

Music and story recordings for children at 10 to 20 percent less than retail.

MASTER CATALOG. 800-348-5003.

A complete listing of musical instruments and accessories. Separate catalogs available: *The Woodwind; The Brasswind; Rock 'n Rhythm; Music Technology Resource Guide for Educators; General Music Store* (Orff instruments, recorders, classroom supplies); *Discount String Center.*

MMB MUSIC INC. 800-543-3771.

Diverse materials in music, movement, dance, art, drama, play, poetry, healing, and creative arts therapy. Ask for specific catalogs in any of these areas.

MUSIC FOR LITTLE PEOPLE. 800-727-2233.

An attractive catolog of quality family entertainment. Well-selected CDs, audio- and videocassettes, and musical instruments. Age range given for each item.

MUSIC IN MOTION. 800-445-0649.

A diverse and helpful catalog of music-related books, games, recordings, gifts, and videos for students, parents, and teachers.

MUSIC TOGETHER. 800-728-2692.

Catalog of superior tapes, musical instruments, and songbooks for infants and children to six or seven years old.

SYLVIA WOODS HARP CENTER CATALOG. 800-272-4277.

Here is everything you wanted to know about the harp. Lists nearly sixty different harps; recordings of Celtic, Irish, Paraguayan, Welsh, medieval, classical, fusion, and jazz harp music; harp music; accessories; and gifts.

COMPETITONS

Neither of these guides is complete, especially for younger students, but they provide a useful start for securing information about competitions.

CONCERT ARTIST GUILD GUIDE TO COMPETITIONS. 850 Seventh Ave., Suite 1205, New York, NY 10019-5230. 212-333-5200.

INTERNATIONAL PIANO COMPETITIONS. Volume 1 : Gathering Results; Volume 2: 15,000 Pianists. Volume 3: The Results. Gustav Alink, P. O. Box 85657, NL-2508 AR, den Haag, The Netherlands.

Index